Lecture Notes in Computer Science 9148

Commenced Publication in 1973
Founding and Former Series Editors:
Gerhard Goos, Juris Hartmanis, and Jan van Leeuwen

More information about this series at http://www.springer.com/series/7410

Magnus Almgren · Vincenzo Gulisano
Federico Maggi (Eds.)

Detection of Intrusions and Malware, and Vulnerability Assessment

12th International Conference, DIMVA 2015
Milan, Italy, July 9–10, 2015
Proceedings

 Springer

Editors
Magnus Almgren
Chalmers University of Technology
Gothenburg
Sweden

Vincenzo Gulisano
Chalmers University of Technology
Gothenburg
Sweden

Federico Maggi
Politecnico di Milano
Milan
Italy

ISSN 0302-9743 ISSN 1611-3349 (electronic)
Lecture Notes in Computer Science
ISBN 978-3-319-20549-6 ISBN 978-3-319-20550-2 (eBook)
DOI 10.1007/978-3-319-20550-2

Library of Congress Control Number: 2015941495

LNCS Sublibrary: SL4 – Security and Cryptology

Springer Cham Heidelberg New York Dordrecht London

Printed on acid-free paper

Springer International Publishing AG Switzerland is part of Springer Science+Business Media
(www.springer.com)

Preface

It is my pleasure, on behalf of the Program Committee, to present the proceedings of the 12th International Conference on Detection of Intrusions and Malware and Vulnerability Assessment (DIMVA 2015). The conference was hosted by Politecnico di Milano, Italy, during July 9–10, 2015. DIMVA is an international conference advancing the state of the art in intrusion detection, malware detection, and vulnerability assessment. It brings together delegates from academic, industrial, and governmental institutions to discuss novel ideas as well as mature research results.

This year, DIMVA received 75 submissions from 23 countries. These submissions were carefully reviewed by the Program Committee, where each valid submission had at least three independent reviews. In the end 17 papers were chosen to be presented at the conference and included in the final proceedings. Several of these papers presented large-scale or long-term studies of attacks, documenting important findings that will allow the community to better understand the threats from such attacks. As was the case in previous years, results regarding system hardening, attack detection, Web security, and mobile security were also presented. Owing to the increased threats against critical infrastructures and industrial control systems, we encouraged submissions in these areas, including work that considers the cross-area obstacles (e.g., privacy, societal and legal aspects) that arise when deploying protection measures in the real world. One paper in particular described attacks and countermeasures in a special environment, the air traffic management system, while another paper considered controlled data sharing of alerts in a privacy-preserving way.

I would like to thank the Program Committee and external reviewers for their timely reviews and active discussion phase. I would like to acknowledge the work of the publication chair, Vincenzo Gulisano, for his help in organizing the program and proceedings. I am also grateful to the general chair, Federico Maggi, and to all local volunteers. Through the excellent work of Federico, my job as a PC chair was made much easier.

It is my pleasure to thank the invited speakers at the conference Vicente Diaz (Kaspersky Labs Global Research and Analysis Team) and Morgan Marquis-Boire (University of Toronto and First Look Media). I am also grateful for the support provided by Maglan Europe, HP Labs Bristol, Reply Communication Valley, Kaspersky Lab, Trend Micro, Micron Foundation, the FACE Project, the CINI Cyber Security National Lab, and the Tech and Law Center. We appreciate their help and financial support to the security community.

Having a successful and interesting conference depends on the contributions of the authors and the visiting delegates to DIMVA. I hope you enjoyed this year's conference and I look forward to your next contribution to DIMVA.

April 2015   Magnus Almgren

Organization

DIMVA is organized by the special interest group Security Intrusion Detection and Response (SIDAR) of the German Informatics Society (GI).

Organizing Committee

General Chair
Federico Maggi   Politecnico di Milano, Italy

Program Chair
Magnus Almgren   Chalmers University of Technology, Gothenburg, Sweden

Publication Chair
Vincenzo Gulisano   Chalmers University of Technology, Gothenburg, Sweden

Program Committee

Gianluca Stringhini	University College London, UK
Hervé Debar	Télécom SudParis, France
Nick Nikiforakis	Stony Brook University, USA
Cristiano Giuffrida	Vrije Universiteit Amsterdam, The Netherlands
Marco Balduzzi	Trend Micro Research, Italy
Lorenzo Cavallaro	Royal Holloway, University of London, UK
Mauro Conti	University of Padua, Italy
Konrad Rieck	University of Göttingen, Germany
Andreas Schaad	SAP AG, Germany
Ulrich Flegel	Infineon Technologies AG, Germany
Simin Nadjm-Tehrani	Linköping University, Sweden
Corrado Leita	Lastline Inc., UK
Michael Meier	University of Bonn and Fraunhofer FKIE, Germany
Christian Rossow	Saarland University, Germany
Davide Balzarotti	Eurecom, France
James Riordan	MIT Lincoln Laboratory, USA
Sven Dietrich	City University of New York - John Jay College of Criminal Justice, USA
Hanno Langweg	HTWG Konstanz, Germany
Federico Maggi	Politecnico di Milano, Italy
Andrea Lanzi	Università degli studi di Milano, Italy
Leyla Bilge	Symantec Research Labs, France
Dina Hadziosmanovic	Delft University of Technology, The Netherlands

Mashael Al-Sabah   Qatar Computing Research Institute (QCRI) and Qatar
                            University (QU), Qatar
Vincenzo Gulisano   Chalmers University of Technology, Sweden
Sotiris Ioannidis   FORTH, Greece
Matthias Neugschwandtner   IBM Research, Switzerland
Urko Zurutuza   Mondragon University, Spain
Manuel Egele   Boston University, USA
Thorsten Holz   Ruhr-Universität Bochum, Germany
Felix Freiling   Friedrich-Alexander Universität, Erlangen, Germany
Jason Polakis   Columbia University, USA
Aziz Mohaisen   Verisign Labs, USA

Additional Reviewers

Andrea Continella   Magnus Almgren
Andreas Dewald   Marco Savi
Andreas Kurtz   Matthias Wübbeling
Benjamin Stritter   Mauro Baluda
Christoph Pohl   Milen Hringov
Daniel Simionato   Ronald Heinrich
Dimitris Mitropoulos   Santanu Kumar Dash
Earlence Fernandes   Sebastian Eschweiler
Eugenio Massa   Srdan Moraca
Fabian Yamaguchi   Steffen Wendzel
Giacomo Verticale   Suphannee Sivakorn
Hossien Fereidooni   Thanasis Petsas
Hugo Gascon   Tilo Müller
Jernej Tonejc   Tobias Wahl
Justin Paupore   Valentin Tudor
Lazaros Koromilas   Zinaida Benenson

Steering Committee (Chairs)

Ulrich Flegel   Infineon Technologies, Germany
Michael Meier   University of Bonn, Germany

Steering Committee (Members)

Herbert Bos   Vrije Universiteit Amsterdam, The Netherlands
Danilo M. Bruschi   Università degli Studi di Milano, Italy
Roland Bueschkes   RWE AG, Germany
Lorenzo Cavallaro   Royal Holloway, University of London, UK
Herve Debar   Telecom SudParis, France

Sven Dietrich	City University of New York, USA
Bernhard Haemmerli	Acris GmbH, HSLU Lucerne, Switzerland
Marc Heuse	Baseline Security Consulting, Germany
Thorsten Holz	Ruhr-Universität Bochum, Germany
Marko Jahnke	Federal Office for Information Security, Germany
Klaus Julisch	Deloitte, Switzerland
Christian Kreibich	ICSI, USA
Christopher Kruegel	UC Santa Barbara, USA
Pavel Laskov	University of Tübingen, Germany
Konrad Rieck	University of Göttingen, Germany
Robin Sommer	ICSI/LBNL, USA
Diego Zamboni	CFEngine AS, Norway

Sponsoring Institutions (Gold)

Sponsoring Institutions (Silver)

Sponsoring Institutions (Academic)

Contents

Attacks

Cutting the Gordian Knot: A Look Under the Hood of Ransomware Attacks

Amin Kharraz[1]([✉]), William Robertson[1], Davide Balzarotti[3], Leyla Bilge[4], and Engin Kirda[1,2]

[1] Northeastern University, Boston, USA
mkharraz@ccs.neu.edu
[2] Lastline Labs, Santa Barbara, CA, USA
[3] Institut Eurecom, Sophia Antipolis, France
[4] Symantec Research Labs, Sophia Antipolis, France

Abstract. In this paper, we present the results of a long-term study of ransomware attacks that have been observed in the wild between 2006 and 2014. We also provide a holistic view on how ransomware attacks have evolved during this period by analyzing 1,359 samples that belong to 15 different ransomware families. Our results show that, despite a continuous improvement in the encryption, deletion, and communication techniques in the main ransomware families, the number of families with sophisticated destructive capabilities remains quite small. In fact, our analysis reveals that in a large number of samples, the malware simply locks the victim's computer desktop or attempts to encrypt or delete the victim's files using only superficial techniques. Our analysis also suggests that stopping advanced ransomware attacks is not as complex as it has been previously reported. For example, we show that by monitoring abnormal file system activity, it is possible to design a practical defense system that could stop a large number of ransomware attacks, even those using sophisticated encryption capabilities. A close examination on the file system activities of multiple ransomware samples suggests that by looking at I/O requests and protecting Master File Table (MFT) in the NTFS file system, it is possible to detect and prevent a significant number of zero-day ransomware attacks.

Keywords: Malware · Ransomware · Malicious activities · Underground economy · Bitcoin

1 Introduction

Over the past few years, a class of malware known as scareware has become popular among cybercriminals. This malware takes advantage of people's fear of revealing their private information, losing their critical data, or facing irreversible hardware damage. In particular, this paper focuses on ransomware, a particular class of scareware that locks the victims' computers until they make a payment to re-gain access to their data.

M. Almgren et al. (Eds.): DIMVA 2015, LNCS 9148, pp. 3–24, 2015.
DOI: 10.1007/978-3-319-20550-2_1

Although the first version of ransomware appeared in the wild almost 10 years ago, the volume of ransomware incidents was not significant until a couple of years ago. As number of ransomware attacks increased over 500 % on 2013 compared to the previous years, the ransomware threat made the headlines as the most notable malware trend after targeted attacks in 2013 [37]. For example, the Cryptolocker ransomware alone managed to infect approximately 250 thousand computers around the world, including an entire police department that needed to pay a ransom to decrypt their documents [15, 30].

Given the significant growth of ransomware attacks [37], it is very important to develop a protection technique against this type of malware. However, designing effective defense mechanisms is not practically possible without having an insightful understanding of these attacks. Currently, many of the recent security reports about ransomware [12, 15] rely on ad-hoc procedures rather than a scientific assessment. Moreover, these reports mainly focus on the advancements in ransomware attacks and their levels of sophistication, rather than providing some insights about effective defense techniques that should be adopted against this threat. In this paper, we investigate the key functionalities of ransomware samples such that we can propose effective detection mechanisms leveraging our findings.

We created a collection of ransomware samples that were categorized in 15 different families. Our data set covers the majority of the existing ransomware families that have been observed in the wild between 2006 and 2014. The data set is created using multiple sources including manual and automatic crawling of public malware repositories, and the ransomware samples submitted to Anubis [7] since 2011. The results of our analysis confirm the folk wisdom that such attacks have a continuous increase in the number of families and distinct samples per year [25, 37] and also the advances in certain aspects of the specific functionalities of few ransomware families. However, our results also reveal that in a significant number of samples, the core parts of ransomware samples lack the technical complexity to perform successful attacks. While a small fraction of the samples can really prevent the victims from accessing the resources and cause severe problems, a significant number of samples fail to seriously take the victims' resources as hostage. More specifically, we show that more than 94 % of ransomware samples in our data set simply try to lock the victims' computer desktop and request ransom, or use very similar and superficial approaches to target the victims' resources.

We also performed an analysis of the charging methods adopted by different ransomware families and also traced the transactions of 1,872 Bitcoin addresses that were used during the Cryptolocker attack. The analysis of the transactions shows that cybercriminals started to adopt evasive techniques (e.g., using new addresses for each infection to keep the balances low) in order to better conceal the criminal activity of the Bitcoin accounts. Our analysis also confirms that the Bitcoin addresses used for malicious intents share similar transaction records (e.g., short activity period, small Bitcoin amounts, small number of transactions). However, determining malicious addresses in the Bitcoin network based on the transaction history is significantly difficult, in particular when cybercriminals use multiple independent addresses with small amount of Bitcoins.

In addition to our long-term study, we also evaluate the feasibility of implementing defense mechanisms against destructive ransomware attacks. We provide an analysis of the file system activity of ransomware samples that target users' files. Our analysis shows that different classes of ransomware attacks with multiple levels of sophistication share very similar characteristics from a file system perspective, due to the nature of these attacks. Our analysis suggests that when an infected system is under attack, one can notice a significant change in the file system activity since the malicious process generates a large number of similar file system access requests. Consequently, if we effectively monitor the file system activity (e.g., the changes in Master File Table (MFT) and the types of I/O Request Packets (IRP) to the file system), it is possible to detect multiple different types of destructive ransomware attacks that target users' files. This contradicts recent discussions in the security community about the impossibility of detecting or stopping these types of attacks due to the use of sophisticated destructive techniques [5,25,34,37]. Based on our analysis, we conclude that detecting and stopping a large number of destructive ransomware attacks is not as complex as it has been reported and deploying practical defense mechanisms against these attacks is possible due to the engineering of NTFS file system.

In summary, the contributions of our paper are as follows:

- We analyzed 1,359 ransomware samples, describing previously undocumented aspects of ransomware attacks with the focus on distinctive and common behaviors among different families.
- We explain how the core parts of ransomware samples are engineered and how these findings can potentially be used to detect these attacks. Our analysis shows that the abnormal file system activity can be accurately monitored in destructive ransomware attacks with different levels of sophistication.
- We perform an analysis of charging methods adopted among ransomware families and also investigate how cybercriminals used cryptocurrency in recent ransomware attacks. Our analysis of illicitly-gained Bitcoins suggests that cybercriminals adopted multiple evasive techniques to protect their privacy in Bitcoin network, making the tracing procedure significantly more difficult.
- We suggest avenues that can be used to defend against a large number of destructive zero-day ransomware attacks. We propose a general methodology to detect these attacks without making any assumptions on how they attack the users' files.

The rest of the paper is structured as follows. In Sect. 2, we present our data set and ransomware families we categorized. In Sect. 3, we present experiments we conducted and discuss our findings. In Sect. 4, we discuss the financial incentives and payment methods. In Sect. 5, we briefly present related work. Finally, we conclude the paper in Sect. 6.

2   Ransomware Data Set

Since collecting the malware data set was a critical part of our research, in this section, we provide some details about our ransomware sample selection procedure. To achieve a comprehensive ransomware data set, we collected malware samples from multiple sources. While we obtained 37.9 % of our samples from Anubis, 48.38 % were collected by automatically crawling public malware repositories [1,2,4]. We captured the remainder 13.8 % by manually browsing through security forums [3,23].

We collected 3,921 ransomware samples from all those sources. However, after removing the samples that did not execute properly in our environment and those for which we were not able to find a release date, our data set contained a total of 1,359 active ransomware samples. To obtain accurate labels for these samples, we cross-checked the malware samples by automatically submitting the list of MD5 hashes to VirusTotal. To be conservative on our ransomware malware selection, we consider a malware to be ransomware if at least three AV engines recognized it as belonging to this category.

To obtain the family names, we parsed the naming schemes of the AV vendors that are commonly used to assign malware labels. In 77 % of samples, AV engines followed the same labeling scheme and our naming policy was mainly based on the popularity of the family name in the community (e.g., Gpcode, Reveton). The remaining 23 % of the samples were labeled in an inconsistent way among the different antivirus software, and in this case we simply selected the most common label among the list of the top 39 AV engines. For example, some samples were labeled both as Pornoasset and as Tobfy by top AV engines, but we labeled these samples as Tobfy due to the perceived popularity of the label.

To the best of our knowledge, our analysis covers the majority of the existing ransomware families observed between 2006 to 2014. However, as our data collection module relies on external sources, we are aware of the possibility of missing some types of ransomware attacks. Furthermore, in order to conduct balanced experiments over the ransomware families, and also to avoid biased results due to polymorphic techniques, we performed our analysis not only based on individual samples, but also based on the families and distinct variants per family. Table 1 shows the total number of distinct samples per family as well as distinct variants in each family. It also shows the first time they appeared in the wild and the most recent sample in our data set.

As it can be clearly seen from Table 1, there is a rapid emergence of new families between 2012 and 2014, as well as a significant growth on the number of new samples in each family. This may be due to a bias on the data set toward more recent samples, or to the multiplication of samples due to polymorphism in newer families. (e.g., Winlock, Urausy, and Reveton). The Table also shows the types of ransomware attacks we observed among each family in our data set (in addition to locking the user desktop). In particular, we observed that 61.22 % of the samples (57 variants) only targeted the desktop of compromised computers, without touching the documents in the file system. More details on the locking procedure are discussed in Subsect. 3.1. Encrypting the victim files in addition to locking the desktop was observed in 5.37 % of samples in four families (Cryptolocker, CryptoWall, Filecoder, and Gpcode). We also observed the emergence of other malicious activities, such as changing the browser setting or performing multiple infections to install other malware, in 3.23 % of the

Table 1. The list of malware families used in our experiments. Some families such as Reveton, Winlock, and Urausy aggressively employed polymorphic techniques.

Family	Family Description				Types of Attacks			
	Samples	Variants	First Seen	Most Recent	Encypting Files	Changing MBR	Deleting Files	Stealing Info
Reveton	244(17.95 %)	14	2012	2014			✓	✓
Cryptolocker	32 (2.35 %)	4	2013	2014	✓			✓
CryptoWall	11(0.8)	2	2014	2014	✓			
Tobfy	122 (8.97 %)	12	2010	2014			✓	
Seftad	23 (1.69 %)	4	2006	2010		✓		
Winlock	308(22.66 %)	27	2008	2013			✓	
Loktrom	4 (0.29 %)	2	2012	2013				
Calelk	9 (0.663 %)	2	2009	2010				
Urausy	523 (38.48 %)	16	2009	2014			✓	✓
Krotten	17 (1.25 %)	3	2008	2009				
BlueScreen	4 (0.29 %)	1	2008	2009				
Kovter	8 (0.58 %)	2	2013	2013				✓
Filecoder	9 (0.66 %)	3	2012	2014	✓	✓		
GPcode	21 (1.54 %)	4	2004	2008	✓			
Weelsof	24 (1.76 %)	3	2012	2013				
No. of Samples	1,359	-	-	-	73(5.37 %)	23(1.69 %)	484(35.61 %)	44(3.23 %)
No. of Variants	-	99	-	-	13(13.13 %)	4(4.04 %)	29(21.33 %)	6(6.06 %)

samples. Despite the fact that the number of samples performing additional malicious activities (e.g., stealing private information) is not alarmingly high, this phenomenon is now increasing. For example, our analysis shows that information stealing was first seen in `Reveton` in early 2012, but other families such as `Kevtor`, `Urausy`, and `Cryptolocker` started to add stealing information capabilities to their samples after that date [16,21]. We provide more details on the malicious behaviors among ransomware families in Sect. 3.

2.1   Experimental Setup

We performed all malware execution experiments according to common scientific guidelines [33] inside a Cuckoo Sandbox [14] running Windows XP SP3 32bit, with a controlled access to the Internet via NAT. Network traffic (e.g., IRC, DNS and HTTP) were allowed to enable commands and controls (C&C) communication. In order to control harmful traffic (e.g., spam) during the execution of the experiments, we redirected this traffic to a local honeypot. The network bandwidth was also reduced to mitigate potential DoS attacks.

The environment installed inside the malware analysis system includes typical data in an user session such as saved credentials, browser history, and other customizations. We also emulated some basic user activity by running an script in each malware run (e.g., opening a window, moving the mouse, opening a website). We then executed each sample in the analysis environment for 45 min to capture the execution traces of the sample. Since current ransomware samples typically start attacking the user's files right after the malicious program is executed by the user, we believe that the 45 min threshold is sufficient for most ransomware samples to exhibit their malicious behavior. After each execution, the entire system is rolled back to a clean state to prevent any interference across executions.

3   Characterization and Evolution

In this section, we describe our findings based on the types of malicious activities detected in ransomware samples during our experiments. We partition the malicious activities into multiple categories and discuss our findings in each of them.

3.1   File System Activity

One of our first goals was to describe how a malicious process interacts with the file system when a compromised computer is under a ransomware attack. To answer this question, we investigate the common characteristics of ransomware attacks from a file system perspective regardless of the technical differences that these attacks might have (such as the infection and the key generation techniques). In order to monitor the file system activity, multiple approaches could be used. One classic approach is to hook the SSDT table [19,22] to monitor interesting function calls. In our analysis, we developed a minifilter driver [26] to capture all I/O requests that the I/O manager generates on behalf of user-mode processes to access the file system.

To monitor the I/O requests the minifilter driver registers callback routines to the filter manager. In our analysis, we defined pre-operation and post-operation callback routines for all IRP functions in order to precisely record any I/O and transaction activity on the files. For each file system request, we collected the process name, the process ID, the parent process ID, the pre-operation and post-operation callback time, the IRP type, the arguments and the result of the operation. Each record is a tuple:

```
<PName,PID,PPID,PreOpTime,PostOpTime,IRPFlag,Args,Result>
```

The minifilter with different callback routines allows us to capture all the the read, write, and attribute change requests to the file system at the closest possible level to the file system driver. Our minifilter driver is deployed in a privileged kernel mode that has access to nearly all objects of the operating system. Furthermore, since we captured the file system activity directly from the I/O manager in the kernel, there was a low chance that cybercriminals could bypass our monitor. When looking at the execution traces of the malware program in the analysis environment, we observed that the way malicious processes generate requests to access file system was significantly different from benign processes. By performing a close examination of the file system activity of multiple ransomware samples, we were able to distinguish multiple attack strategies that ransomware families used while the system was under the attack. We discuss our findings in the following sections.

Encryption Mechanisms. As presented in Table 1, 5.37 % of the samples among four families employed some encryption mechanisms during the experiments. Our analysis shows that existing ransomware samples use both customized and standard cryptosystems during the attacks. The customized cryptosystems are not necessarily more reliable or complicated than the standard cryptosystems that Windows platforms provide (e.g., `CryptoAPI`). Cybercriminals develop their own cryptosystems for multiple reasons. One reason is probably to decrease the chance of being easily detected by common malware analysis techniques (e.g., PE header checking, Hooking standard API functions). One of the key features crypto-style ransomware samples should have is to reliably minimize the chance of recovering the original data after generating the encrypted files. Some of the modern crypto-style ransomware families such as `cryptolocker` and `CryptoWall` make use of standard Windows functions to perform their file encryption. They simply call `CryptEncrypt` with an handle to the encryption key and a pointer to a buffer that contains the plaintext to be encrypted. In these families, the plaintext in the buffer is directly overwritten with the encrypted data created by this function. As depicted in Table 2, the I/O manager generates `IRP_MJ_CREATE` on behalf of the malicious process to open the user's file. The file content is read via `IRP_MJ_READ` for encryption and is overwritten with the ciphertext buffer using the `IRP_MJ_WRITE` function each time a file encryption occurs.

We also observed that even if the samples do not use standard cryptosystems, it is still possible to recognize how they attack users' files. For instance, a member of the `Filecoder` family uses a simple customized approach to encrypt files. Unlike `Cryptolocker` and `CryptoWall`, the sample first generates an encrypted version of a file using an AES-256 encryption key and then overwrites the original file's data with the encrypted file. Table 3 shows how the malicious process interacts with the file system to encrypt an arbitrary file when the system is under the attack. The types of IRPs generated when the malicious process operates show how a ransomware sample targets the victim's files. For example, the sequence of IRPs shows that the ransomware sample first queries the given location to find the user's file and creates handles to the original and encrypted files. The file's data is read via a `IRP_MJ_READ` IRP and the encrypted data buffer is written to the destination file via a `IRP_MJ_WRITE` IRP. Consequently, `IRP_MJ_SET_INFORMATION` is used to delete the original file after the file is closed and also to overwrite the original file with the encrypted file. The sequence of IRPs shown in Table 3 is repeated for every file on the infected system.

Another sample from `Filecoder` makes use of the `Defragmentation API` to get raw access to each file's data based on the volume sector and the cluster size. The sample overwrites the files with custom data patterns based on how

Table 2. The IRP requests generated on behalf of the malicious process during Cryptowall attack. Similar file system activity traces were also observed in Cryptolocker attack due to the use of Windows standard cryptosystem. The table does not show all the captured information for each I/O operation.

Process Name	Operation	Path	Result
mal.exe	IRP_MJ_CREATE	E:\MySubmissions	SUCCESS
mal.exe	IRP_MJ_DIRECTORY_CONTROL	E:\MySubmissions\dimva2015-submission.tex	SUCCESS
mal.exe	IRP_MJ_CLEANUP	E:\MySubmissions\	SUCCESS
mal.exe	IRP_MJ_CLOSE	E:\MySubmissions\	SUCCESS
mal.exe	IRP_MJ_CREATE	E:\MySubmissions\dimva2015-submission.tex	SUCCESS
mal.exe	IRP_MJ_READ	E:\MySubmissions\dimva2015-submission.tex	SUCCESS
mal.exe	IRP_MJ_WRITE	E:\MySubmissions\dimva2015-submission.tex	SUCCESS
mal.exe	IRP_MJ_READ	E:\MySubmissions\dimva2015-submission.tex	SUCCESS
mal.exe	IRP_MJ_WRITE	E:\MySubmissions\dimva2015-submission.tex	SUCCESS
.			
.			
.			
mal.exe	IRP_MJ_CREATE	E:\MySubmissions\dimva2015-submission.tex	SUCCESS
mal.exe	IRP_MJ_SET_INFORMATION	E:\MySubmissions\dimva2015-submission.tex	SUCCESS
mal.exe	IRP_MJ_CLOSE	E:\MySubmissions\dimva2015-submission.tex	SUCCESS

the files are kept on the disk. For example, if the file mapping check shows that the file has multiple extents, the physical disk offsets of each extent should be retrieved to be overwritten with the custom data pattern. If the file does not have any extents, it means that the file is small and is kept as a MFT entry in the MFT table. The malware uses the `DeviceIoControl` from `kernel32.dll` to get the file map on the physical disk. Figure 1 shows how a malicious process finds the file's data and overwrites the data after the encryption. When NTFS finds the file record for the MFT, it obtains the VCN-to-LCN mapping information in the file records data attribute. Consequently, the malicious process can easily retrieve the information and locate the file's data on the disk.

Encryption techniques (e.g., key generation and key management) in cryptostyle ransomware families have also evolved significantly. For example, a `Gpcode` variant generates a static key during the attack. This key is also used to encrypt all the non-system files. Finding the encryption key in this variant is fairly simple and we were able to retrieve the key by comparing the encrypted file and the original one. The most recent `Gpcode` variant in our data set encrypts the files using a unique AES-256 encryption key. The encryption key is then encrypted using a 1024-bit RSA public key. Another change we observed over time is the place where an asymmetric key pair is generated. For example, in a sample (md5:ffcf2bb69f23c7c234d2f2ee380cdaa4) created in 2012, the master key is generated locally in the compromised computer and can be extracted by looking into the memory. The use of RSA keys with different key length in `Cryptolocker` was previously reported [30], but at the time of writing, we observed only samples with 1024-bit RSA public key in our data sets. The RSA public key is generated remotely on the C&C server once the

Table 3. The types of IRPs requested by a malicious process to encrypt and overwrite the victim's files during a ransomware attack. The attack strategy can be detected by analyzing the I/O requests sent to the file system.

Process Name	Operation	Path	Result
mal.exe	IRP_MJ_CREATE	E:\MySubmissions	SUCCESS
mal.exe	IRP_MJ_DIRECTORY_CONTROL	E:\MySubmissions\dimva2015-submission.tex	SUCCESS
mal.exe	IRP_MJ_CLEANUP	E:\MySubmissions\	SUCCESS
mal.exe	IRP_MJ_CLOSE	E:\MySubmissions\	SUCCESS
mal.exe	IRP_MJ_CREATE	E:\MySubmissions\dimva2015-submission.tex	SUCCESS
mal.exe	IRP_MJ_CREATE	E:\MySubmissions\dimva2015-submission.tex.crypt	SUCCESS
mal.exe	IRP_MJ_READ	E:\MySubmissions\dimva2015-submission.tex	SUCCESS
mal.exe	IRP_MJ_READ	E:\MySubmissions\dimva2015-submission.tex	SUCCESS
.			
.			
.			
mal.exe	IRP_MJ_WRITE	E:\MySubmissions\dimva2015-submission.tex.crypt	SUCCESS
.			
.			
mal.exe	IRP_MJ_CLEANUP	E:\MySubmissions\dimva2015-submission.tex.crypt	SUCCESS
mal.exe	IRP_MJ_CLEANUP	E:\MySubmissions\dimva2015-submission.tex	SUCCESS
.			
.			
mal.exe	IRP_MJ_CREATE	E:\MySubmissions\dimva2015-submission.tex	SUCCESS
mal.exe	IRP_MJ_SET_INFORMATION	E:\MySubmissions\dimva2015-submission.tex	SUCCESS
mal.exe	IRP_MJ_CLEANUP	E:\MySubmissions\dimva2015-submission.tex	SUCCESS
mal.exe	IRP_MJ_CLOSE	E:\MySubmissions\dimva2015-submission.tex	SUCCESS
.			
.			
mal.exe	IRP_MJ_CREATE	E:\MySubmissions\dimva2015-submission.tex.crypt	SUCCESS
mal.exe	IRP_MJ_SET_INFORMATION	E:\MySubmissions\dimva2015-submission.tex.crypt	SUCCESS
mal.exe	IRP_MJ_CLOSE	E:\MySubmissions\dimva2015-submission.tex.crypt	SUCCESS

compromised computer successfully sends a POST request to C&C servers. If the sample cannot connect to C&C servers, the malicious behavior is not triggered. The sample md5:04fb36199787f2e3e2135611a38321eb only encrypted users' files in logical drives introduced in the system. An evolution in this family is the encryption of connected drives. The sample (md5:f1e2de2a9135138ef5b15093612dd813) encrypts all non-system files including network shares to minimize the possibility of recovering files without paying the ransom. These ransomware samples simply employ GetLogicalDrives, GetDriveType or similar functions to find network drives.

Deletion Mechanisms. In this part, we specifically discuss file deletion mechanisms that are unique to ransomware attacks. 35.6 % of samples among five common ransomware families do not perform any encryption mechanisms. Instead, they delete the user's files if the user does not pay the ransom. On the other hand, we observed that certain samples in Gpcode and Filecoder families

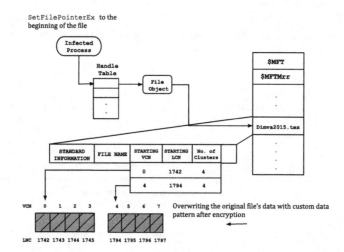

Fig. 1. The malicious process attempts to get the file map on the physical disk in order to overwrite the file's data after the encryption.

deleted the original unencrypted file's data after the encryption occurred. Consequently, deletion operation is a common task among multiple ransomware families in our data set. Table 4 shows a sequence of IRPs collected while running a sample from the Filecoder family. The malicious process uses the IRP_MJ_DIRECTORY_CONTROL function to list the files and then requests to open the file via a Win32 CreateFile. Any create requests are performed by IRP_MJ_CREATE function which returns a handle to the file objects. Finally, the file is deleted by IRP_MJ_SET_INFORMATION when the file is closed. We observed very similar approaches in other families such as Gpcode, Reveton and Urausy in spite of differences in other aspects of the attacks.

In the NTFS file system, each file has an entry in the Master File Table (MFT) that reflects the changes of the corresponding file or folder [10]. The core file's attributes in each MFT entry can be found in the $STANDARD_INFORMATION attribute, and the $DATA attribute that contains the content of the corresponding file. The content of the $DATA attribute could be resident or non-resident in the MFT entry depending on the size of a file. Figure 2 shows the disk layout for files with different sizes in the NTFS file system. The status of a file is determined by both a flag and a $BITMAP in an MFT entry. $BITMAP manages the information about allocation status of clusters within the disk.

When a ransomware attack occurs, the malware lists the non-system files and initiates a delete operation for each of them. The MFT entry for each file is updated by changing the status flag value of the file from 0x01 to 0x00. Furthermore, the $BITMAP attribute in MFT file is set to zero for the corresponding file. For large files, since multiple clusters might be allocated, the location of fragmented data is saved in the runlist in the header of MFT entry. When the file is deleted, the clusters that are used to keep the file's data are set to unallocated in $BITMAP attribute in the MFT file. Consequently, when a file is deleted in a

Table 4. A set of IRP requests generated on behalf of a malicious process to delete files during an attack. The process simply searches the directory, creates a handle to files and deletes them via IRP_MJ_SET_INFORMATION.

Process Name	Operation	Path	Result
mal.exe	IRP_MJ_DIRECTORY_CONTROL	E:*	SUCCESS
mal.exe	IRP_MJ_CLEANUP	E:\	SUCCESS
mal.exe	IRP_MJ_CLOSE	E:\	SUCCESS
mal.exe	IRP_MJ_CREATE	E:\	SUCCESS
mal.exe	IRP_MJ_DIRECTORY_CONTROL	E:\MySubmissions*	SUCCESS
mal.exe	IRP_MJ_CLEANUP	E:\MySubmissions\	SUCCESS
mal.exe	IRP_MJ_CLOSE	E:\MySubmissions\	SUCCESS
mal.exe	IRP_MJ_CREATE	E:\MySubmissions\dimva2015-submission.tex	SUCCESS
mal.exe	IRP_MJ_DIRECTORY_CONTROL	E:\MySubmissions\dimva2015-submission.tex	SUCCESS
mal.exe	IRP_MJ_SET_INFORMATION	E:\MySubmissions\dimva2015-submission.tex	SUCCESS
mal.exe	IRP_MJ_CLEANUP	E:\MySubmissions\dimva2015-submission.tex	SUCCESS
mal.exe	IRP_MJ_CLOSE	E:\MySubmissions\dimva2015-submission.tex	SUCCESS

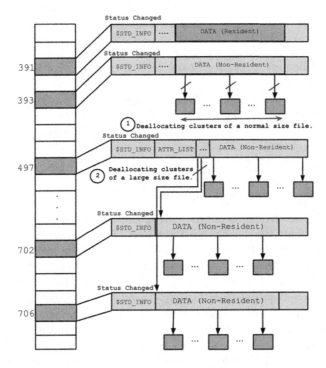

Fig. 2. Disk layout for files with different sizes in NTFS file system. The content of large files is defined as non-resident $DATA and is managed by a runlist attribute in each MFT entry. During a ransomware attack, the clusters are deallocated and the status of the file is changed.

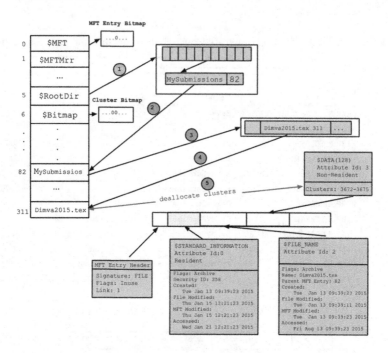

Fig. 3. A ransomware attack(Gpcode) with a simple delete operation. The clusters used to keep the file $data are deallocated in an MFT entry.

typical ransomware attack, the MFT entry is updated, but the content of the file is not deleted immediately. Therefore, our analysis suggests that we can detect ransomware attacks that target users' files based on the changes in the MFT table and also recover the content associated with the deleted files due to the engineering of the NTFS file system. Finally, Fig. 3 shows the delete operation from a different perspective- when the malicious process tries to delete a large file that is fragmented among multiple clusters.

Changing Master Boot Records. One of the ransomware families (Seftad) was developed to attack the Master Boot Records (MBR) which contains the executable boot code and the partition table. The MBR is located on the first sector of a hard disk, and it is loaded into memory at boot time when the system transfer control to the code stored in the MBR. Samples that target the MBR prevent the infected system from loading the boot code in the active partition by simply replacing it with a bogus MBR that displays a message asking for a ransom. Defeating this type of ransomware attack is quite simple. For example, in early samples, the unlock code was hard-coded into the binary and could be acquired by reverse engineering. Following this procedure, we discovered the unlock code in 18 Seftad samples in our data set.

Locking Procedure. An important step in a successful ransomware attack is to lock the desktop of the computer under attack. This is typically done by creating a new desktop and making it persistent. Ransomware samples simply use `CreateDesktop` to create a fresh desktop environment and eliminate unnecessary processes. The new desktop is created via a `DESKTOP_SWITCHDESKTOP` access mode that enables the `SwitchDesktop` function to activate the new desktop and receive input from the victim. The desktop is assigned to a thread using the `SetThreadDesktop` function. A significant number of samples in our data set (61.22 %) use very similar approaches to establish a persistent desktop lock.

A small number of samples (8 variants) in families like `Urausy`, `Reveton`, and `Winlock` employed another approach to lock the desktop. In these families, the lock banner is simply downloaded as a HTML page with corresponding images based on the victim's geographical location and it is then displayed in full screen in a `IE` window with hidden controls. The banner plays a local law enforcement warning in the language used in the victim's geographical location. The warning typically says that the operating system is locked due to infringement against certain laws (e.g., distributing copyrighted materials or visiting child pornography sites) in that location.

Disabling certain keyboard shortcuts such as toggling (e.g., Windows key + `Tab`) is automatically done once a new desktop is created because no other applications are open to toggle through. However, disabling special keys is another part of the locking procedure. This is done by installing hook procedures that monitor keyboard input events. The number of disabled keys was different in different ransomware families. For example, 18 variants in `Reveton` and `Urausy` disabled Windows keys to prevent the victims from entering the start menu and 72 variants among 15 families attempted to disable the Esc Key to prevent the victims from using keyboard shortcuts (e.g., starting Windows Task Manager) during the attack.

3.2   Mitigation Strategies

API Call Monitoring. As discussed in Subsect. 3.1, a significant number of ransomware samples use Windows API functions to lock the victim's desktop. Those API calls can be used to model the application behavior and train a classifier to detect suspicious sequence of Windows API calls. This approach is not necessarily novel, but it would allow us to stop a large number of ransomware attacks that are produced with little technical efforts. For example, a sequence of `GetThreadDesktop`, `CreateDesktopW` and `SwitchDesktop` functions can be converted to a sequence of API calls. Of course, cybercriminals might be able to evade detection using different techniques. For example, they may use native APIs to directly lock the system under the attack. However, the implementation of such ransomware samples requires significant work since the native APIs are not properly documented and may change among different versions, which can limit the portability of the attack.

Monitoring File System Activity. Our analysis also suggests that it is possible to detect ransomware attacks – even the ones using deletion and encryption capabilities – based on our findings in Subsect. 3.1. Our analysis shows that significant changes occur in the file system activities (e.g., a large number of similar encryption, deletion requests) when the system is under a ransomware attacks. By closely monitor the MFT table, one can detect the creation, encryption or deletion of files. For example, when the system is under a ransomware attack, a significant number of status changes occur in a very short period of time in MFT entries of the deleted files. For encrypted files, we notice a large number of MFT entries with encrypted content in the $DATA attribute of files that do not share the same path (e.g., files within a directory). In our definition, a malicious MFT entry is a MFT entry that is generated or modified in a system under a ransomware attack. A classifier can be trained on benign and malicious MFT entries to detect abnormal file system activities when the system is under an attack.

In order to distinguish between benign and malicious file system activity, another possible approach consists of monitoring all the file system requests that user-mode processes generate. A system with protection capabilities can intercept all the requests and discard the suspicious requests before they reach the file system driver.

Recovering the deleted files from the ransomware attacks would also be possible. If the $DATA attribute is resident in the MFT entry, the content of the file can be simply copied to another location. For non-resident $DATA attributes, we need to parse the RunList in the MFT entry and copy the raw data to another location and perform the recovery. In any case, early detection of the attack is critical in order to successfully recover the content of deleted files, since the deallocated clusters can be allocated to new files and the content of the deleted file will be overwritten. This approach can be applied to most of the ransomware samples with either customized or standard cryptosystems since the file level activity is a common characteristic of ransomware samples that target users' files.

Using Decoy Resources. The attack strategies adopted to encrypt or delete the user files are very similar among ransomware families. For example, the malicious process aggressively attacks all files (in different paths, and with different extensions) and tries to encrypt and/or delete them in a very short period of time. Therefore, defining a file system activity model that reflects the normal interaction with the file system is possible. However, cybercriminals could try to evade detection by launching attacks while mimicking a normal user behavior. For example, a cybercriminal may avoid aggressively encrypting all files and starts by encrypting files with recent access or modification time. Approaches like this might not be detected by approaches that monitor the behavior of the system. However, one technique to detect these attacks could be to install decoy files in multiple locations of the disk that are constantly monitored. The use of decoy resources to detect security breaches and insider attacks was first proposed in [9,40]. Decoy resources have also been recently used to improve the security of hashed passwords [20] and to detect illegally obtained data from file hosting services [28].

In our definition, monitoring decoy files can be an additional layer of defense on the top of file system activity monitoring to detect ransomware attacks. The decoy files should be indexed at multiple places in the user environment and should be generated in a way that is computationally difficult for an adversary to discern them. This approach can increase the chance of detecting the malicious process in early stages of the attacks regardless of the fact that the ransomware sample uses novel strategies or customized/standard cryptosystems.

4 Financial Incentives

Since the ultimate goal of ransomware attacks is to get money from victims, the payment method is an important aspect of the attacks. Cybercriminals continuously strive to find more reliable charging methods by improving two important properties: (1) the difficulty of tracing the recipient of the payments, and (2) the ease of exchanging payments into a preferred currency. Table 5 provides a breakdown of the charging methods used by ransomware families over the past

Table 5. Summary of types of charges in 15 ransomware families.

Families	Type of Charge			
	Premium Number	Untraceable Payments	Online Shopping	Bitcoin Transactions
Reveton		✓	✓	
Cryptolocker		✓		✓
CryptoWall				✓
Tobfy		✓		
Seftad	✓			
Winlock				
Loktrom	✓			
Calelk	✓			
Urausy		✓	✓	
Krotten		✓		
BlueScreen		✓		
kovter		✓	✓	
Filecoder		✓		
GPcode		✓		
Weelsof		✓		
Number of Samples	132 (9.71 %)	1,199 (88.22 %)	14(1.03 %)	28 (2.86 %)
Number of Variants	18 (19.35 %)	75 (80.64 %)	4 (4.30 %)	4 (4.3 %)

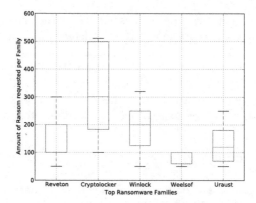

Fig. 4. The amount of ransom money among common ransomware families. Around 89.2 % of Cryptolocker victims paid more than 100 dollars. One reason is the significant increase in the value of Bitcoin between mid-September and mid-November. We observed more changes in the amount of requested ransom in Cryptolocker probably due to low stability in Bitcoin exchange rates.

years. Our analysis suggests that sending SMS to premium numbers is not necessarily used in old types of ransomware attacks. For example, the charging method in `Calelk` is still based on using premium numbers. The premium rate numbers were hard-coded in the ransomware sample or were downloaded from the C&C servers in each infection. This class of ransomware attacks requires the least amount of technical background and when propagated in a large scale the revenue could be significant.

A large fraction of ransomware samples (88.22 %) used prepaid online payment systems such as Moneypak, Paysafecard, and Ukash cards, since they provide limited possibilities to trace the money. These services are not tied to any banking authority and the owner of the money is anonymous. The ransomware business model takes advantage of these systems since there are no records of the vouchers to trace cybercriminals. In a typical scenario, once a ransomware criminal receives the vouchers, in order to monetize them, he can sell vouchers in underground voucher exchange forums, ICQ, or other untraceable communication channels for a lower price than the nominal value of the vouchers. We also found some unconventional methods used for charging victims. We found two variants of `Kevtor` family that forced users to buy a software package which unlocked the compromised computer. Figure 4 represents the amount charged per family based on our data set. The amount of money required by ransomware owners to unlock the computer changes based on variants and families. For examples, 48.43 % of samples among top six families demanded between 150 to 250 dollars.

4.1   Bitcoin as a Charging Method

Bitcoin provides some unique technical and privacy advantages for miscreants behind ransomware attacks. Bitcoin transactions are cryptographically signed messages that embody a fund transfer from one public key to another and only the corresponding private key can be used to authorize the fund transfer. Furthermore, Bitcoin keys are not explicitly tied to real users, although all transactions are public. Consequently, ransomware owners can protect their anonymity and avoid revealing any information that might be used for tracing them.

We performed an analysis of the use of Bitcoins in recent ransomware attacks where victims had to buy Bitcoins in order to access their resources. We acquired the Bitcoin addresses by searching the web as well as public forums [31] that conducted discussions on `Cryptolocker` attacks. Victims typically participated in the discussions by posting information about their infection and the Bitcoin addresses to which they were required to send the ransom. We collected 1,872 Bitcoin addresses during the experiments. We automatically queried the transactions from publicly accessible Bitcoin block explorer websites [8] and parsed the results into a database.

The number of Bitcoins collected by cybercriminals during `Cryptolocker` attack is previously reported [35]. Our main focus in this part is to provide insights into how cybercriminals employed Bitcoin to collect the ransom fee based on the transactions history. One of the questions we wanted to answer was whether it is possible to detect illicitly-gained Bitcoins based on the transaction history of a Bitcoin address. Our analysis suggests that identifying these Bitcoins is getting significantly difficult since cybercriminals have started to use evasive approaches to protect their privacy (e.g., multiple independent Bitcoin addresses, small Bitcoin amounts, short activity period, small transaction records) after receiving large volumes of Bitcoins from victims. One reason to use multiple independent addresses with small Bitcoin amounts could be that concealing the source of thousands of illicitly-obtained Bitcoins is a critical task if cybercriminals want to transfer the Bitcoins via recognized exchanges without being noticed. In fact, this is the main evolution in employing Bitcoin in ransomware attacks to make the potential tracing procedures more difficult in the Bitcoin network.

Our analysis on Bitcoin transactions shows that 84.46 % of Bitcoin addresses had no more than six transactions. Furthermore, a significant fraction of these Bitcoin addresses (68.93 %) were active for at most 10 days. These addresses were directly used to receive Bitcoins from victims. Another type of addresses had more transactions and were active for a longer period of time (e.g., more than 10 days). These addresses were used to aggregate the collected ransom fees. Figure 5(a) shows the CDF of number of Bitcoin per Bitcoin address. In 48.9 % of Bitcoin addresses that we analyzed, a Bitcoin address received at most two Bitcoins. These transactions have occurred in early steps of the attacks when two Bitcoins were worth roughly 200 dollars equal to the ransom fee required by cybercriminals to send the decryption key.

As shown in Fig. 5(b), approximately 72.9 % of Bitcoin transactions belong to Bitcoin addresses with two transactions. The incoming transaction was made by victims to pay the ransom and, the outgoing transaction was performed by cybercriminals. The collected Bitcoins were transferred through tens of temporary intermediate accounts or split into many small amounts in order to be recombined in a new account later to decrease possibilities of tracing the money.

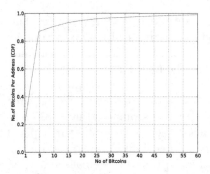
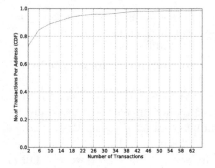

(a) The number of Bitcoins per address.   (b) The total number of transactions per Bitcoin address

Fig. 5. 20.1 % of Bitcoin addresses received no more than one Bitcoin probably because victims were charged less due to a dramatic increase of Bitcoin value in late November 2013. Furthermore, approximately 73 % of Bitcoin addresses had only two transactions. The incoming transaction is made by victims to pay the ransom and the outgoing transaction is performed by the ransomware owner to send the Bitcoin to another addresses in order to make tracing infeasible.

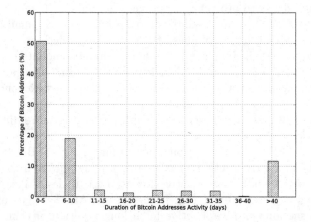

Fig. 6. The duration of activity for Bitcoin addresses. Approximately 50 % of Bitcoin addresses have zero to five days of active life.

As provided in Fig. 6, our observation also suggests that Bitcoin addresses that were used to collect Bitcoins from victims have a relatively short duration of activity. This is due to the fact that the accumulated Bitcoins had to be transferred to other accounts within a few hours or a few days probably to use mix services and conceal the source of the money.

5   Related Work

Ransomware and Underground Economy. Various security vendors have reported the threat potential of ransomware attacks based on the number of infections that they observed [6, 29, 37]. The use of cryptography to mount extortion based attacks was first introduced in [38]. Employing Microsoft Cryptographic API (MS CAPI) calls to design cryptovirus samples was presented by Young [39]. Young demonstrated how to use MS CAPI to generate keys and encrypt the user's data.

The first step to analyze specific ransomware families was made by Gazet by analyzing three primitive ransomware families [18]. He concluded that while these early families were designed for massive propagation, they did not fulfill the basic requirements (e.g., sufficiently long encryption keys) for mass extortion.

The presence of scareware as rogue security software has been also studied over the past few years. Stone-Gross et al. performed an analysis of underground economy of fake antivirus software. They built an economic model that showed how cybercriminals performed refunds and chargebacks in order to conceal their criminal nature for a longer period of time [36]. Cova et al. provided an analysis of fake antivirus structure and measured the number of victims and the profits gained based on the web servers used by several fake antivirus groups [13].

Bitcoin Privacy. Bitcoin has also recently received considerable interest regarding the security and anonymity in security research. Meiklejohn et al. developed a clustering heuristic that was used to cluster Bitcoin addresses belonging to a particular user [24]. They discussed the potential anonymity in the Bitcoin protocol and the actual anonymity achieved by users. Reid et al. constructed two graphs based on publicly available transaction history [17]. They used the properties of these graphs to illustrate how information leakage can be used to de-anonymize the system's users. Using this technique, they described the flow of stolen money from MyBitcoin. Recently, Ron et al. performed an analysis over the user graph and provided an in-depth analysis of the largest transactions in Bitcoin history [32]. In another work, Möser performed an analysis of the anonymity and transaction graph of three Bitcoin mix services. He found that all the three Bitcoin mix services had a distinct transaction graph pattern, but some of them were more successful than others [27]. In order to characterize the popularity of illicit goods, Christin performed an analysis by extracting data from Silk Road marketplace [11]. Although the work does not examine the Bitcoin block chain, it provides an estimation of the market value of such transactions.

A closer and concurrent work to our interest was performed by Spagnuolo et al. that parsed the blockchain and clustered the Bitcoin addresses that were likely to belong to certain users or groups [35]. They labeled the users based on the information that was scraped from openly available resources. They were able to label Bitcoin addresses on real-world cases such as Silk Road and Cryptolocker ransomware. We also used public repositories to extract Bitcoin addresses that belong to cybercriminals behind ransomware attacks. However, unlike

Stagnuolo et al. work [35], our goal is to characterize the Bitcoin addresses used for malicious intents based on the transaction history rather than de-anonymizing the Bitcoin users.

6 Conclusion

In this paper, we performed a long-term analysis of ransomware families with a special focus on their destructive functionality. The characterization of ransomware attacks was based on 1,359 ransomware samples among 15 families that have emerged over the last few years. Our results show that a significant number of ransomware families share very similar characteristics in the core part of the attacks, but still lack reliable destructive functions to successfully target victims' files.

We also describe how a malicious process interacts with the file system when a compromised computer is under a ransomware attack. We observed that suspicious file system activity of multiple types of destructive ransomware families can be reliably monitored. When looking at the execution traces of the malware programs, we observed that the way malicious processes generate requests to access file system was significantly different from benign processes. We also observed that different classes of ransomware attacks with multiple levels of sophistication share very similar characteristics from file system perspective due to the nature of these attacks. Unlike recent discussions in security community about ransomware attacks, our analysis suggests that implementing practical defense mechanisms is still possible, if we effectively monitor the file system activity for example the changes in Master File Table (MFT) or the types of I/O Request Packets (IRP) generated on behalf of processes to access the file system. We propose a general methodology that allow us to detect a significant number of ransomware attacks without making any assumptions on how samples attack users' files.

Acknowledgements. This work is supported by the National Science Foundation (NSF) under grant CNS-1116777, and Secure Business Austria.

References

1. Minotaur Analysis - Malware Repository. http://minotauranalysis.com
2. VX Vault - Online Repository of Malware Samples. http://vxvault.siri-urz.net
3. Malware Tips - Your Security Advisor. http://malwaretips.com/forums/virus-exchange.104/
4. MalwareBlackList - Online Repository of Malicious URLs. http://www.malwareblacklist.com
5. Police ransomware threat assessment. Europol Public Information (2014)
6. Ajjan, A.: Ransomware: Next-Generation Fake Antivirus (2013). http://www.sophos.com/en-us/medialibrary/PDFs/technicalpapers/SophosRansomwareFakeAntivirus.pdf

7. Bayer, U., Kruegel, C., Kirda, E.: TTAnalyze: a tool for analyzing malware. In: Proceedings of the European Institute for Computer Antivirus Research Annual Conference, April 2006
8. Blockchain.info. Bitcoin Block Explorer. https://blockchain.info
9. Bowen, B.M., Hershkop, S., Keromytis, A.D., Stolfo, S.J.: Baiting inside attackers using decoy documents. Springer (2009)
10. Carrier, B.: File System Forensic Analysis. Addison-Wesley Professional (2005)
11. Christin, N.: Traveling the silk road: a measurement analysis of a large anonymous online marketplace. In: Proceedings of WWW 2013, May 2013
12. Cisco, Inc., Ransomware on Steroids: Cryptowall 2.0. (2015). http://blogs.cisco.com/security/talos/cryptowall-2
13. Cova, M., Leita, C., Thonnard, O., Keromytis, A.D., Dacier, M.: An analysis of rogue AV campaigns. In: Jha, S., Sommer, R., Kreibich, C. (eds.) RAID 2010. LNCS, vol. 6307, pp. 442–463. Springer, Heidelberg (2010)
14. Cuckoo Foundation. Cuckoo Sandbox: Automated Malware Analysis (2014). http://www.cuckoosandbox.org
15. Dell SecureWorks. Cryptolocker Ransomware (2014). http://www.secureworks.com/cyber-threat-intelligence/threats/cryptolocker-ransomware/
16. Donohue, B.: Reveton Ransomware Adds Password Purloining Function (2013). http://threatpost.com/reveton-ransomeware-adds-password-purloining-function/100712
17. Reid, F., Harrigan, M.: An analysis of anonymity in the bitcoin system. In: Altshuler, Y., Elovici, Y., Cremers, A.B., Aharony, N., Pentland, A. (eds.) Security and Privacy in Social Networks, pp. 197–223. Springer, New York (2012)
18. Gazet, A.: Comparative analysis of various ransomware virii. J. Comput. Virol. 6(1), 77–90 (2010)
19. Hoglund, G., Butler, J.: Rootkits: Subverting the Windows Kernel. Addison-Wesley Professional (2005)
20. Juels, A., Rivest, R.L.: Honeywords: Making password-cracking detectable. In: Proceedings of the 2013 ACM SIGSAC Conference on Computer & Communications Security, pp. 145–160. ACM (2013)
21. Krebs, B.: Inside a Reveton Ransomware Operation (2012). http://krebsonsecurity.com/2012/08/inside-a-reveton-ransomware-operation/
22. Lanzi, A., Balzarotti, D., Kruegel, C., Christodorescu, M., Kirda, E.: Accessminer: using system-centric models for malware protection. In: Proceedings of the 17th ACM Conference on Computer and Communications Security, CCS 2010, pp. 399–412. ACM (2010)
23. Malware Don't Need Coffee. Guess who's back again? Cryptowall 3.0. (2015). http://malware.dontneedcoffee.com/2015/01/guess-whos-back-again-cryptowall-30.html
24. Meiklejohn, S., Pomarole, M., Jordan, G., Levchenko, K., McCoy, D., Voelker, G. M., Savage, S.: A fistful of bitcoins: characterizing payments among men with no names. In: Proceedings of the 2013 Conference on Internet Measurement Conference, IMC 2013, pp. 127–140 (2013)
25. Microsoft, Inc. Microsoft Security Intelegence Report, vol. 16 (2013). http://www.microsoft.com/security/sir/default.aspx
26. Microsoft, Inc. File System Minifilter Drivers (2014). https://msdn.microsoft.com/en-us/library/windows/hardware/ff540402
27. Möser, M.: Anonymity of bitcoin transactions: an analysis of mixing services. In: Proceedings of Monster Bitcoin Conference (2013)

28. Nikiforakis, N., Balduzzi, M., Acker, S.V., Joosen, W., Balzarotti, D.: Exposing the lack of privacy in file hosting services. In: Proceedings of the 4th USENIX Conference on Large-Scale Exploits and Emergent Threats, LEET 2011 (2011)
29. O'Gorman, G., McDonald, G.: Ransomware: A Growing Menance (2012). http://www.symantec.com/connect/blogs/ransomware-growing-menace
30. Prince, B.: CryptoLocker Could Herald Rise of More Sophisticated Ransomware (2013). http://www.darkreading.com/attacks-breaches/cryptolocker-could-herald-rise-of-more-sophisticated-ransomware
31. QuickBT. Disturbing Bitcoin Virus, October 2013. http://www.reddit.com/r/Bitcoin/comments/1o53hl/
32. Ron, D., Shamir, A.: Quantitative analysis of the full bitcoin transaction graph. In: Sadeghi, A.-R. (ed.) FC 2013. LNCS, vol. 7859, pp. 6–24. Springer, Heidelberg (2013)
33. Rossow, C., Dietrich, C.J., Grier, C., Kreibich, C., Paxson, V., Pohlmann, N., Bos, H., Van Steen, M.: Prudent practices for designing malware experiments: status quo and outlook. In: 2012 IEEE Symposium on Security and Privacy (SP), pp. 65–79. IEEE (2012)
34. Sophos, Inc. Security Threat Report 2014, Smarter, Shadier, Stealthier Malware (2014). http://www.sophos.com/en-us/medialibrary/PDFs/other/sophos-security-threat-report-2014.pdf
35. Spagnuolo, M., Maggi, F., Zanero, S.: BitIodine: extracting intelligence from the bitcoin network. In: Christin, N., Safavi-Naini, R. (eds.) FC 2014. LNCS, vol. 8437, pp. 452–463. Springer, Heidelberg (2014)
36. Stone-Gross, B., Abman, R., Kemmerer, R.A., Kruegel, C., Steigerwald, D.G., Vigna, G.: The underground economy of fake antivirus software. In: Schneier, B. (ed.) Economics of Information Security and Privacy III, pp. 55–78. Springer, New York (2013)
37. Symantec, Inc. Internet Security Threat Report (2014). http://www.symantec.com/security_response/publications/threatreport.jsp
38. Young, A., Yung, M.: Cryptovirology: extortion-based security threats and countermeasures. In: Proceedings of the 1996 IEEE Symposium on Security and Privacy, 1996, pp. 129–140. IEEE (1996)
39. Young, A.L.: Building a cryptovirus using microsoft's cryptographic API. In: Zhou, J., López, J., Deng, R.H., Bao, F. (eds.) ISC 2005. LNCS, vol. 3650, pp. 389–401. Springer, Heidelberg (2005)
40. Yuill, J., Zappe, M., Denning, D., Feer, F.: Honeyfiles: deceptive files for intrusion detection. In: Proceedings from the Fifth Annual IEEE SMC Information Assurance Workshop, pp. 116–122. IEEE (2004)

"Nice Boots!" - A Large-Scale Analysis of Bootkits and New Ways to Stop Them

Bernhard Grill[1][(✉)], Andrei Bacs[2], Christian Platzer[3], and Herbert Bos[2]

[1] SBA Research, Vienna, Austria
bgrill@sba-research.org
[2] VU University Amsterdam, Amsterdam, The Netherlands
{a.bacs,h.j.bos}@vu.nl
[3] Secure Systems Lab, Vienna University of Technology, Vienna, Austria
cplatzer@iseclab.org

Abstract. Bootkits are among the most advanced and persistent technologies used in modern malware. For a deeper insight into their behavior, we conducted the first large-scale analysis of bootkit technology, covering 2,424 bootkit samples on Windows 7 and XP over the past 8 years. From the analysis, we derive a core set of fundamental properties that hold for all bootkits on these systems and result in abnormalities during the system's boot process. Based on those abnormalities we developed heuristics allowing us to detect bootkit infections. Moreover, by judiciously blocking the bootkit's infection and persistence vector, we can prevent bootkit infections in the first place. Furthermore, we present a survey on their evolution and describe how bootkits can evolve in the future.

Keywords: Bootkits · Large-scale malware analysis · Bootkit detection · Bootkit infection prevention · Bootkit evolution

1 Introduction

Bootkits are a class of malware specifically designed to interfere with the operating system's (OS) boot process. They were hugely popular in the 1980s/1990s [37], then faded into oblivion in the years after, to return with a vengeance from 2006 onward. Some of the most advanced and persistent malware today builds on bootkit technology. Their renewed popularity is caused by modern security mechanisms in Windows, which forced malware authors to look for alternative ways to "own" the OS. In particular, most of the attacks utilize bootkit technology to circumvent common measures like the Windows driver signing policy [26], kernel patch protection [25], but also regular AV software. Moreover, even governmental and commercial *"Remote Surveillance and Forensic Solutions"*, as offered by FinFisher and Hacking Team, apply bootkit technology in their tools [4].

© Springer International Publishing Switzerland 2015
M. Almgren et al. (Eds.): DIMVA 2015, LNCS 9148, pp. 25–45, 2015.
DOI: 10.1007/978-3-319-20550-2_2

Virtually all protection strategies today have a weakness in common: they rely on the integrity of the underlying operating system, either because they use its services (e.g., AV solutions), or because they reside in the OS itself. Consequently, malware subverting the system's initialization steps remains undetected. A bootkit executes early during the boot process, long before the OS protection mechanisms kick in, allowing the bootkit to retain control throughout the infected system's boot phase. Combined with the fact that startup code is rarely modified on a typical system, bootkits often survive and stay undetected for a long time after the initial infection.

To this end, we developed *Bootcamp*, a bootkit detection, analysis and prevention framework. We performed a dynamic analysis for 25,513 malware samples from 29 different bootkit relevant families, spanning almost a decade of time (our first sample is from 2006 and our last from 2014) and analyzed their infection and runtime behavior, whereof 2,424 samples revealed bootkit behavior. To our knowledge, this makes it the single largest bootkit study ever conducted. From our study, we extract key properties to detect and prevent bootkit infections in common computer systems. Finally, we present an overview of bootkit technology evolution and describe how it may evolve.

Contributions. Our paper makes the following contributions:

1. We conduct the first large-scale study of 8 years worth of bootkit technology.
2. Based on the study, we propose new techniques to stop bootkit attacks.
3. We present *Bootcamp*, a platform to detect, analyze and prevent bootkits.

To our knowledge, the detection method we present cannot be evaded by any known MBR, VBR, or bootloader based bootkit. Thus, it significantly raises the bar for developers of malicious software who now have to target other components, such as the BIOS. The focus of our study is on systems that boot from a device's master boot record. As there are virtually no UEFI bootkits that are not research proof-of-concepts, we left them out of scope for our study.

2   How Bootkits Interfere with the Boot Process

Booting. Figure 1 sketches the boot process for BIOS based systems. The CPU boots in *real mode* and executes the BIOS, which locates and passes control to the Master Boot Record (MBR). The MBR is located within the first 512 bytes of the system's hard disk. The MBR code parses the partition table (PT) to determine the "bootable" partition (containing the OS) and hands over control to the Volume Boot Record (VBR). The VBR resides within the bootable partition's first 512 bytes and contains further information necessary for booting such as the filesystem parameters and the bootloader's disk location. The VBR code then loads the bootloader's (BL) first stage into memory and passes control to it. Finally, the BL loads further code from the disk, switches to *protected mode*, and loads and executes the kernel.

Dark Regions. We define a *dark region* (DR) as a contiguous physical disk region which is not part of a filesystem. Since it is not part of a filesystem,

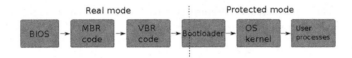

Fig. 1. Boot sequence for BIOS based systems

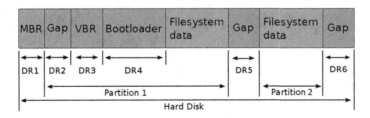

Fig. 2. Typical *dark region* (DR) layout - *dark regions* in gray, filesystem areas in green (Color figure online)

it is also not accessible and invisible to the user during normal system operation. Examples include the MBR, the sectors between the MBR and VBR, the bootloader, the inter-partition gaps, and the space *beyond the last partition* and the *end of the physical disk* (these gaps have up to several MB size on most systems). Figure 2 shows a typical disk layout and corresponding *dark regions* (*dark regions* are colored in gray). Some of these regions (e.g., the MBR, VBR, and bootloader) are used during system startup, while others (like inter-partition gaps) are never used at all. What makes dark regions interesting for attackers is that only very rare events (like major OS updates) ever modify them and current protection mechanisms typically do not cover them, as they operate at the filesystem level.

Bootkit Infection Techniques. Bootkits interfere with the startup process by replacing any boot stage prior to the kernel's execution (e.g., the MBR, VBR or bootloader) with the initial infection vector. They execute malicious code before the OS employs protection techniques and subvert the kernel to keep control throughout the infected system's runtime. Typically the initial infection vector initializes the bootkit (e.g.,. by hooking certain interrupts, see below), loads further malicious code from the disk and redirects execution there. After executing the malicious code, the bootkit returns to the original bootstrap code continuing the intended (but now infected) boot process.

Due to the limited disk space for startup code, bootkits typically utilize further disk areas (e.g. *dark regions* with sufficient space) to store configuration settings and additional code, which is finally executed or injected into the kernel's memory (e.g. a kernel driver). Modern bootkits often encrypt those hidden storage areas [24]. Bootkits have several hard requirements. (1) They must execute at least once before the kernel takes control and activates defensive measures. (2) Bootkits need to survive system restarts. (3) They must be space efficient as the available space for the initial infection vector is highly limited. (4) The code has to run in *real* and *protected mode* and survive mode switches. (5) They should not delay OS startup significantly.

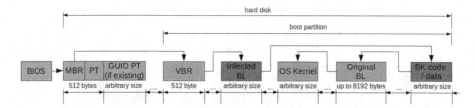

Fig. 3. An example execution flow exploiting the bootloader as initial infection vector - infected areas in red, benign in green [14] (Color figure online)

As an example, Fig. 3 shows the execution flow for a bootkit utilizing an infected bootloader. The BIOS passes control to the MBR code which in turn loads and executes the VBR. The VBR code loads the infected bootloader (BL) which executes further malicious code from the system's disk (e.g. the *dark region* at the drive's end). The latter code performs additional malicious activity—like interrupt hooking. Later, the bootkit executes the original bootloader in order to load the kernel into memory. When this is done, the bootkit regains control by means of a hooked interrupt and infects the kernel in memory. Finally, it proceeds initializing and executing the (now infected) system.

Strictly speaking, there are more possible bootkit types. Besides the ones targeting the MBR or VBR (like TDSS, Sinowal, and Pihar [3]) and the ones aiming for the bootloader (like Cidox/Carberp [21]), bootkits could target the BIOS and other technology also. For instance, the research PoC IceLord bootkit [2], writes its code directly into the BIOS FLASH/ROM. At the other extreme, bootkits may in principle target Windows specific components like `boot.ini` or hive [23]. As MBR, VBR, and bootloader bootkits are by far the most popular (and the others are hardly seen in practice), we will focus on these.

Interrupt Hooking. Bootkits need to regain control *after* the kernel is loaded in memory by the bootloader, but *before* it executes, so they can infect it before it runs. For this purpose, a bootkit hooks the system's interrupts. Specifically, the CPU holds a data structure known as the Interrupt Vector Table (IVT) in the lower 1 K of memory in *real mode*. The IVT contains 256 entries, each representing one interrupt and containing a pointer to the corresponding Interrupt Service Routine (ISR). Whenever an interrupt occurs, the CPU consults the IVT and executes the corresponding ISR. After processing the interrupt, the ISR returns control to the instruction executed at the time the CPU was interrupted. Bootkits typically install interrupt hooks by overwriting the original ISR's address with a malicious one (e.g., interrupt `0x13` which provides low-level disk services). This allows them to regain control after executing benign code such as the original bootloader. After executing the malicious routine they redirect control to the original so that it may continue its intended function.

3   A Large Scale Analysis of Bootkit Technology

We conducted a large scale analysis of bootkit technology using a dataset of
25,513 malware samples to get a deeper insight into bootkit behavior. This
section presents the results of the analysis, as well as the evolution of bootkit
technology for a timespan of 8 years. We start by presenting the bootkit dataset,
experimental setup and containment measures. Striving for sound experimenta-
tion, Table 1 shows the checklist advocated by Rossow et al. for malware experiments [34], and to what extent we apply the suggested guidelines.

Table 1. Rossow's checklist for malware experiments [34]

Criterion	Satisfied	Criterion	Satisfied	Criterion	Satisfied
Removed goodware	Y	Interpreted FPs	Y	Removed moot samples	N
Avoided overlays	Y	Interpreted FNs	N	Real-world FP exp	NA
Balanced families	Y	Interpreted TPs	N	Real-world TP exp	NA
Separated dataset	NA	Listed malware families	Y	Used many families	Y
Mitigated artifacts/biases	NA	Identified environment	Y	Allowed Internet	Y
Higher privileges	Y	Mentioned OS	Y	Added user interaction	Part
		Described naming	Y	Used multiple OSes	Y
		Described sampling	Y		
		Listed malware	Y		
		Described NAT	Y		
		Mentioned trace duration	Y		

Bootkit Dataset for Evaluation. Altogether, we utilized 25,513 malware
samples from 29 different families for our experiments. The malware samples
were chosen based on their likelihood to install a bootkit [35]. The samples
were selected by an AV vendor's malware label, matching one of 29 predefined
families. Table 2 outlines the annual distribution on the bootkit dataset over a
timespan of 8 years, while Table 5 shows more details of the families and sample
set. Additionally, we analyzed 100 benign binaries to examine the behavior for
non-malicious executables.

Experimental Setup. We monitored the boot process in a virtualized environment running Windows XP SP3 and Windows 7 (both 32 bit) and extracted

Table 2. Annual distribution of malware sample set

First appeared	Sample count	Share per year
2006	30	0.1 %
2007	26	0.1 %
2008	575	2.3 %
2009	1,737	6.8 %
2010	2,902	11.4 %
2011	6,431	25.2 %
2012	7,771	30.5 %
2013	2,647	10.4 %
2014	3,394	13.3 %
	25,513	100.0 %

defining features for bootkits. We describe in detail the virtualized analysis environment in a Sect. 5. Following the guidelines from Rossow [34] we deactivated the Windows firewall on both systems and disabled the UAC on Windows 7, as the weaker security measures allow us to observe more malware behavior. The evaluation was performed between September 2014 and February 2015. We provided a dedicated CPU core and a main memory size of 1024 MB for XP and 2048 MB for Win7 for each analysis environment. Each sample had about 90 seconds to perform the infection. After infection, the systems were rebooted. They were allowed to use up to 2 min for the boot phase, which is more than sufficient for fully booting the OS. If the OS took longer to boot, the system was killed and marked as broken by the malware. The Win7 environment used a disk layout (and hence *dark region* layout) with MBR partitioning and a single system partition, identical to Fig. 2 (*Partition 2* in the figure is equivalent to the hidden system partition Windows 7 is typically generating). The Windows XP environment used a similar layout but with a single partition.

Containment. We performed initial experiments allowing internet access for the samples but performed the main evaluation without. When we allowed internet access we state it next to the experiment. In general, we did not allow internet access, as it would distort the results on the historic evolution of bootkit technology: a dropper with internet access may fetch a new bootkit version instead of installing the embedded, historic one. Furthermore, there is hardly any difference allowing or denying internet for our sample set, as shown in Sect. 3.1. When allowing internet, the system was behind a NAT and rate limited.

3.1 Large-Scale Bootkit Analysis Results

We define the terms "***bootkit like behavior***" as samples writing to any *dark region*, "***bootkit detected***" as samples writing either the MBR, VBR or bootloader during the bootkit infection (so *bootkit detected* implies *bootkit like* *behavior* but not necessarily the other way round), **"working infections"** as samples satisfying *bootkit detected* definition and the system reboots successfully after infection and **"successful infection rate"** as the rate (in %) between the number of samples with *bootkit like behavior* and *working infections*. Table 3 compares the results for Windows XP allowing or denying internet access to samples. Allowing internet access increased the number of samples with *bootkit like behavior* by 16.7 % on Windows XP. Interestingly the number of *detected bootkits* and *working infections* increased only by 1.4 % respectively 1.1 %. Hence, there is little difference between allowing or prohibiting internet access for *working infections*. This was the only experiment we performed with internet access. The other tests denied internet access, for the reasons discussed earlier.

Table 3. Comparing analysis' outcome with and without internet access on XP

	XP without internet	XP with internet	Difference
BK like behavior	2,405	2,888	16.7 %
Bootkit detected	2,042	2,073	1.4 %
Working infections	1,143	1,156	1.1 %
Succ. infection rate	47.5 %	40.0 %	7.5 %

Table 4 outlines the analysis results separated by OS. The category *XP and Win7* defines the number of samples working on both OSes, whereas *XP or Win7* specifies the amount of executables working on at least one of both systems. Though, we detected slightly more bootkits or XP, we observed more *working bootkit infections* on Win7. Only 43.8 % of the samples operate on both OSes. 258 samples work exclusively on XP, whereas 15 samples operate on Windows 7 only. Hence, nearly all samples working on Win7 are functional on XP too. This observation does not hold for the other direction. Altogether, 2,424 samples out of 25,513 revealed *bootkit like behavior* on at least one OS.

Table 4. Experimental sample set's operability on different operating systems

	XP	Win7	XP and Win7	XP or Win7
BK like behavior	2,405	2,147	2,128	2,424
Bootkit detected	2,042	1,799	1,784	2,057
Working infections	1,143	1,647	931	1,859
System boot fails	1,262	500	1,197	565
Succ. infection rate	47.5 %	76.7 %	43.8 %	76.7 %

Table 5 highlights details and outlines evaluation results for each malware family contained in our bootkit dataset. The *successful infection rate* strongly varies between families and OS. Some families target only XP e.g. Finfish and Lapka, while others like Pihar and TDSS exclusively focus on Win7, but in general most target both OSes, as Cidox, Sinowal and Smitnyl do. Especially most recent samples have relatively high *successful infection rates* as Pihar, Sinowal, Smitnyl and TDSS have for Windows 7 and Niwa, Sinowal, Smitnyl have for XP. Tough some families hold a high *sample count* they feature a very low *successful infection rates*. This might have multiple explanations. For example they might target only particular systems (e.g. a specific language), perform anti-VM / anti-analysis techniques (as discussed in Sect. 7) or fail to install a properly working bootkit for our analysis system.

Table 5. Overview on evaluation results per malware family contained in sample set

Malware family	First appeared	Last appeared	Sample count	XP Working infections	XP Succ. infection rate	Win7 Working infections	Win7 Succ. infection rate
Yurn	2006-05	2013-06	43	1	2.3 %	1	2.3 %
SST	2006-05	2012-10	61	0	0.0 %	0	0.0 %
Sinowal	2006-05	2014-06	2,938	678	23.1 %	582	19.8 %
Plite	2006-10	2014-06	3,908	1	0.0 %	1	0.0 %
Infinaeon	2007-10	2007-10	1	0	0.0 %	0	0.0 %
Trup	2007-12	2014-06	1,862	72	3.9 %	50	2.7 %
TDSS	2008-07	2014-06	2,945	0	0.0 %	495	16.8 %
Zhaba	2008-10	2010-05	5	0	0.0 %	0	0.0 %
Qvod	2009-03	2014-06	2,831	0	0.0 %	0	0.0 %
Stoned	2009-07	2014-02	23	4	17.4 %	2	8.7 %
Smitnyl	2009-08	2014-03	297	56	18.6 %	65	21.9 %
Xpaj	2009-10	2014-06	547	16	2.9 %	17	3.1 %
Niwa	2009-10	2014-06	38	8	21.1 %	1	2.6 %
Phanta	2010-03	2014-05	954	80	8.4 %	27	2.8 %
Wistler	2010-05	2014-06	814	1	0.1 %	0	0.0 %
Nimnul	2010-07	2014-06	2,499	0	0.0 %	2	0.1 %
Finfish	2010-10	2014-06	29	1	3.4 %	0	0.0 %
Fisp	2011-03	2014-04	246	0	0.0 %	0	0.0 %
ZAccess	2011-05	2014-07	1,948	0	0.0 %	0	0.0 %
Lapka	2011-06	2014-06	94	15	16.0 %	0	0.0 %
Cidox	2011-07	2014-06	2,858	193	6.8 %	193	6.8 %
Mybios	2011-07	2014-03	47	13	27.7 %	0	0.0 %
Pihar	2011-08	2013-03	447	0	0.0 %	209	46.8 %
GoodKit	2011-11	2011-11	1	0	0.0 %	0	0.0 %
CPD	2012-05	2014-06	38	3	7.9 %	1	2.6 %
Geth	2012-06	2012-10	6	0	0.0 %	0	0.0 %
Korablin	2012-08	2014-06	27	0	0.0 %	0	0.0 %
Backboot	2013-03	2013-03	1	1	100.0 %	1	100.0 %
Careto	2014-02	2014-02	5	0	0.0 %	0	0.0 %
			25,513	1,143	4.8 %	1,647	6.9 %

Recall, bootkits have to acquire additional disk space as the initial infection vector is typically too small for their complete code and data (requirement 3 in

Sect. 2). Hence, they have to store their data somewhere else. Table 6 outlines which dark regions (DR) were exploited as data storage by the bootkits. *End of disk* indicates exploitation of the space beyond the last partition (*DR6* in Fig. 2), whereas *between partitions* includes any space between the partitions, including the gap between MBR and VBR (*DR5* and *DR2* for Win7 and *DR2* for XP). Sometimes bootkits use both locations to store data, indicated by *both*. On average 81.1 % store their data at the *end of the disk*, 18.2 % on average utilize the space *between partitions*, while only a few samples split the data storage and exploit both locations. In general, we observe a trend toward utilizing the space *between partitions*. All samples wrote to *dark region* 2 or 5 on XP respectively 2, 5 or 6 on Win7 (see Fig. 2). Later, we use this property in our detection and prevention system.

Table 6. Exploited *dark regions* as data storage locations from successful infections

Data storage location	XP		Win7		
	Count	Share	Count	Share	Avg on both
End of disk	957	83.7 %	1,306	79.3 %	81.1 %
Between partitions	170	14.9 %	337	20.5 %	18.2 %
Both	16	1.4 %	4	0.2 %	0.7 %
Writes to DR	**1,143**	**100.0 %**	**1,647**	**100.0 %**	**100.0 %**
	1,143	100.0%	1,647	100.0%	100.0%

Table 7 outlines the exploited initial infection vectors to gain control during the boot process. The MBR is by far the dominant infection vector utilized by 86.1 % on average, followed by the bootloader exploited by 13.8 % samples on average. The VBR is used by hardly any sample. There is a noticeable trend from exploiting the MBR toward utilizing the bootloader (and perhaps VBR, in an incipient phase). We describe this shift in more detail in Sect. 3.2.

Table 7. Initial infection vectors from successful infections

Infection vector	XP		Win7		
	Count	Share	Count	Share	Avg on both
MBR	948	82.9 %	1,453	88.2 %	86.1 %
VBR	2	0.2 %	1	0.1 %	0.1 %
BL	193	16.9 %	193	11.7 %	13.8 %
	1,143	100.0 %	1,647	100.0 %	100.0 %

The hooked interrupts are shown in Table 8. As some samples hook multiple interrupts the sum increased to 1,172 / 1,660 (XP / Win7). The most exploited interrupt are 0x13 (85.1 %), and 0x15 (14.1 %). Interrupt 0x13 is normally used to load disk content into memory and is therefore convenient to verify whether the kernel is loaded into memory. The obvious drawback of interrupt 0x13 is the huge number of calls, as it is called a few thousand times during startup. On the other hand interrupt 0x15 is typically called once during the boot phase—to gain the system's memory map and executed before passing control to the kernel. Hence, it's an excellent interrupt hooking target for bootkits. The hooks for interrupt 0x83 and 0x85 were exploited by 8 *Niwa* samples on XP and one on Win7 between 2009 and 2012. 13 *Mybios* samples on XP and 1 *Plite* on both OSes do not hook any interrupt as those families feature a slightly different attack model. Instead of patching the kernel directly in memory, those samples replace explorer.exe with a malicious one on the disk, but therefore leave traces on the filesystem [1]. We discuss these techniques in more detail in Sect. 3.2.

Table 8. Exploited interrupt hooks from successful infections

Hooked interrupt	XP		Win7		
	Count	Share	Count	Share	Avg on both
0x13	947	80.8 %	1,464	88.2 %	85.1 %
0x15	203	17.3 %	194	14.0 %	14.1 %
0x83 & 0x85	8	0.7 %	1	0.1 %	0.3 %
None	14	1.2 %	1	0.1 %	0.5 %
	1,172	100.0 %	1,660	100.0 %	100.0 %

3.2   Historic Perspective on the Evolution of Bootkit Technology

This subsection discusses the historic evolution of bootkits. Table 9 highlights the historic perspective on successful infections rates. We observe a high *successful infection rate* for the samples dating from 2008 and 2009, followed by intense decline hitting the low-point in 2011. Starting with 2012 the *successful infection rate* raised again to peak in 2014. We did not observe any working bootkit for Win7 before 2009, since Win7 was released in the end of that year. From 2010 to 2012 the *successful infection rate* for XP was relatively low. This might indicate a focus on Win7 and Win8 (which we did not evaluate in this paper) prior to maintain operability on the older XP. But in general the trend indicates an improvement and professionalisation in the underground malware industry for bootkits. The historic development on used infection vectors is outlined in Fig. 4. Until 2011 the MBR was the only initial infection vector exploited. In 2012 and 2013 a few samples used the VBR as initial infection vector, while the bootloader (BL) became more popular starting with 2013. In 2014, the BL was the most exploited infection vector. The tremendous increase in BL infections is very likely related to the *Carberp* botnet's source code leak from 2013 [21]. It contained the source code of the *Cidox* bootkit which was applied by *Carberp* [35]. Likely *Cidox* will become the new de facto standard template for bootkits

Table 9. Overview on the historic evolution on successful infection rates

Year	XP			Win7		
	BK like behavior	Working infections	Succ. infections	BK like behavior	Working infections	Succ. infections
2006	0	0	-	0	0	-
2007	0	0	-	0	0	-
2008	7	7	100.0 %	0	0	-
2009	464	450	97.0 %	453	380	83.9 %
2010	422	189	44.8 %	379	216	57.0 %
2011	907	128	14.1 %	793	577	72.8 %
2012	318	127	39.9 %	275	240	87.3 %
2013	48	37	77.1 %	37	27	73.0 %
2014	239	205	85.8 %	210	207	98.6 %
	2,405	1,143		2,147	1,647	

as *Zeus* did for banking trojans after its infamous leak in 2011 [10]. Regrettably the *Zeus* leak also lead to a dramatic amount of mutations and peaked in various highly sophisticated banking trojans like Citadel [5], SpyEye [36] or Zeus P2P variants like ZeroAccess and Kelihos [32]. Figure 5 shows the evolution of the *dark region* usage by bootkits. In 2008 the space *between partitions* and at the *end of the disk* were both utilized by bootkits to store their code and / or data. This behavior changed dramatically in the next years, as samples almost exclusively exploited the space beyond the last partition. In 2010 the preferred data storage location started shifting again, resulting in equal exploitation of space at the *end of the disk* and *between partitions* in 2014. The evolution of interrupt hooking is outlined in Fig. 6. In 2008 we observed the first samples hooking interrupt 0x13. The *Niwa* family started hooking interrupt 0x13, 0x15, 0x83 and 0x85 in 2009. They exploited 0x83 and 0x85 to call the original ISR for interrupt 0x13 and 0x15. *Niwa* is the only family we observed hooking the interrupts 0x83 and 0x85, but we did not monitor any *Niwa* sample after 2012 anymore. There is a clear shift of exploiting interrupt 0x13 to utilizing 0x15 throughout the years. This shift might be explained by the *Carberp* leakage [21] again, as it also exploits interrupt 0x15. Therefore interrupt 0x15 will remain the dominant hook in the future. *Mybios* introduced an interesting technique in 2011. They avoided interrupt hooking and in memory kernel patching techniques, by replacing the original *explorer.exe* with a malicious one on disk during the boot process. Though this is a highly interesting technique and simplifying bootkit development, it did not establish itself in the scene, likely because it relies on changing files within the filesystem leaving potential suspicious traces there. This technique was later adopted by *Plite* in 2014.

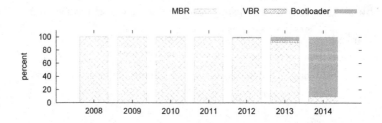

Fig. 4. Overview on initial infection vector evolution

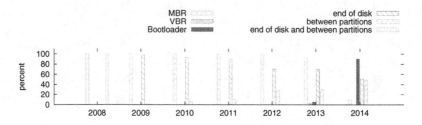

Fig. 5. Overview on *dark region* utilization evolution

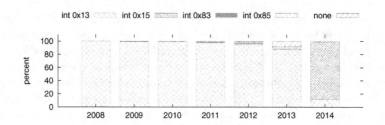

Fig. 6. Overview on interrupt hooking evolution

4   Detecting and Preventing Bootkit Infections

4.1   Detecting Bootkit Attacks

Bootkits are installed either (1) by a malware dropper during system operation
(which is the common case), or (2) when the physical disk is modified directly
while the target system is off. Given the characteristics of the previous section, we
propose heuristics to detect bootkit infections either during installation but also
after the system is already infected (except dark region modification heuristic).

(1) *Dark Region* Modification Heuristic. As discussed, bootkits have to
modify the target system's bootstrap code located in *dark regions* (MBR, VBR,
bootloader) to infect the system and survive system restarts (first and second
requirements in Sect. 2). Furthermore, they store additional code and data in
other *dark regions*, as this space is typically not used under normal operation

and hence, is not in danger of being accidentally overwritten by the OS or detected by filesystem based protection solutions (see requirement three). Thus, *dark region* modifications (i.e. disk writes to any *dark region*) are indicators for suspicious behavior. Figure 2 outlines a typical disk and *dark region* layout (with two partitions). For example in an infected system the MBR (*DR1*), the gap between the MBR and the VBR (*DR2*), and the space beyond the last partition (*DR6*) could be utilized by the bootkit.

(2) Dark Region Read Heuristic. While booting an infected system its malicious code may need to load additional content from its hidden storage (requirement three), e.g. at the disk's end. Therefore a read operation from a *dark region* normally not involved in the boot process is another indicator for compromise.

(3) Interrupt Hooking Heuristic. Bootkits must execute at least once, but typically multiple times at different stages during the boot process. As mentioned earlier, a good and proven solution to do so is by means of hooking. Interrupt hooking is not performed in *real mode* on a clean system. Therefore, an interrupt hook during system bootstrap is a good indicator for bootkit activity.

(4) Reuse Existing Code Heuristic. In a clean system the BIOS loads the MBR code at address 0000h:7C00h and starts executing it. The MBR code loads the VBR code from the boot partition again at 0000h:7C00h, and executes the address again. Hence, during a clean system's startup process the number of jumps to this fixed address is exactly two. Bootkits exploiting the MBR or VBR as initial infection vector typically backup the original code on the disk to reuse it. As the malicious and the benign code is both loaded to 0000h:7C00h the number of jumps to this fixed address for infected systems is greater than two. This heuristic was also utilized by Haukli to detect system startup anomalies [15].

Misdetection and Evading the Heuristics. We now look at the strength of our heuristics. *(1) Dark region modification heuristic*: False positives may occur in case of legitimate *dark region* updates, e.g., during a major system upgrade, partitioning or a complete reinstallation of the system, but malware cannot evade detection since it has to write to boot process relevant disk sectors. Some bootkits may mark disk sectors as bad but still use them. This evasion would fail because this heuristic checks the location of changed sectors and not their quality. *(2) Dark region read heuristic*: The bootkit may store its data in unsuspicious disk sectors inside a filesystem. This technique would induce more risk for the bootkit to get accidentally overwritten by the OS, as it is unaware of the disk sectors utilized by the bootkit. Furthermore, it may be detected by filesystem based protection solutions. *(3) Interrupt hook heuristic*: Samples may not exploit interrupt hooking as discussed in Subsection 3.2. Those samples lack the ability to regain control after executing legitimate boot code and hence rely on a different attacker model. They change files directly within the filesystem instead of patching / injecting code in memory, but replacing files on the disk leaves suspicious traces within the filesystem. *(4) Reuse existing code heuristic*: As discussed in Sect. 6.1 bootkits infecting the bootloader can circumvent this heuristic. Those samples do not execute a malicious MBR / VBR, followed by the benign one and therefore execute the address 0000h:7C00h just twice. Moreover an attacker might patch the original MBR / VBR to be loaded and executed to a different memory address or refrain from reusing existing code.

False-Positives. False positives may be induced by major OS upgrades which change the way bootstrapping is done until now or exotic / self written boot-loaders exploiting bootkit-like techniques but for benign purposes. Such intended but suspicious behavior could be whitelisted for a specific system without affecting detection performance, as the heuristics seek for boot process anomalies and hence, such whitelists would redefine permitted boot behavior. For example one could allow the bootloader to read (even write) from (to) certain additional dark regions during the boot process. Interrupt hooks may be allowed during certain boot stages, for particular interrupt numbers, to specific ISR target addresses executing predefined (e.g. verified via cryptographic secure hashing) ISR code. The *reuse existing code* heuristic may be adapted for deviating boot behavior by adjusting the number of at most allowed jumps to a certain address, as reusing code still increases this count beyond the allowed maximum.

Application Scenarios. Our detection heuristics can be divided into two types: (1) heuristics for bootkit attacks at installation time on a running system and (2) heuristics for existing infections while booting a system, after a potential infection. Although the heuristics are implemented in a virtual machine, detecting bootkits is not restricted to VMs. The VM with heuristics can take any disk as input, e.g. another VM's disk or a physical hard disk. This use case is interesting in post-infection scenarios, forensics or in settings where one is not sure whether a system is infected or not. The *dark region modification* heuristic detects bootkits at installation time. The other three detect bootkit activity during an infected system's boot phase. The three heuristics can be used to detect an infected disk even **after** infections.

4.2   Preventing Bootkit Infections

In this subsection we discuss a bootkit prevention technique for virtualized environments. Full system emulators such as QEMU, Bochs, VMware or VirtualBox are capable of implementing our proposed preventive measures directly inside the emulated hardware. Based on the information provided in Sect. 2, restricting *dark region* modifications (e.g. MBR, VBR, bootloader, inter-partition space) defeats the bootkit's persistence requirement (see requirements 2 and 3 in Sect. 2). This prevention measure blocks the initial infection vector and further data persistence within the system's *dark regions*. We can prevent write operations to the *dark regions* or redirect them to another specially created shadow area, as some malware droppers may verify whether *dark region* modifications succeeded by rereading the corresponding disk sectors. Another more conservative measure is to kill the virtual environment upon detecting a bootkit infection attempt. AV solutions often use emulators to provide a contained environment for each scan of a suspicious file. The described detection and prevention techniques can thus be integrated with existing solutions. Altough the detection system can also detect infections on physical machines (non VMs), the prevention system can only be implemented in VMs.

5   Bootcamp

This section presents *Bootcamp*, a detection, analysis and prevention framework implementing the detection heuristics, as well as the prevention measure proposed in Sect. 4 and already used in production. *Bootcamp* is fully automated, hence no user interaction is required during malware analysis.

Dynamic Bootkit Analysis. Armed with the heuristics described in Sect. 4 we distinguish two phases for dynamic bootkit analysis: a *bootkit infection phase* and an *bootkit execution phase*. During the *infection phase* the malware dropper executes and potentially installs a bootkit. In this phase, the *dark region modification* heuristic precisely describes the changes and locations within the *dark regions* by the bootkit attack, i.e., the modifications for the initial infection vector and its additional code and data. Preventive measures apply during the *infection phase* to stop bootkit attacks. After a certain time, we automatically restart the infected system to enter the *bootkit execution phase*. In this phase, we monitor the bootkit's behavior during the system's boot process. Therefore, we apply all previously described heuristics to detect, describe and analyze bootkit activity during the bootstrap process.

Architecture. Figure 7 outlines *Bootcamp*'s components. Malicious samples enter a central database via the *submission* module. The *Bootcamp server* distributes the malicious files to *Bootcamp workers* which in turn start virtual machines (VM) to analyze the samples dynamically. Each *worker* starts a different virtual analysis environment per sample and reports the analysis' results into the database. The *worker* performs the *bootkit infection phase* for each sample while recording the sample's infection behavior. After restart, the infected virtual environment enters the *bootkit execution phase* applying the bootkit detection heuristics to detect and analyze the potentially installed bootkit. In case prevention measures are applied, the *infection phase* also implements the prevention component. The analysis does not rely on any knowledge from the OS running inside the VM and all monitoring takes place in the emulated hardware.

6   Bootcamp Evaluation

To evaluate *Bootcamp* we utilized 32 bit Windows XP and Win7, with their standard bootloaders *NTLDR* and *bootmgr*, respectively, and used the same experimental setup and dataset as described in Sect. 3.

6.1   Bootkit Detection Results

Table 10 shows the results for our proposed bootkit detection heuristics. The *dark region read* heuristic caught all bootkit infections on both OSes. This behavior

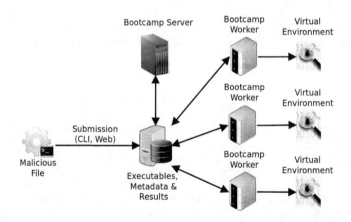

Fig. 7. Bootcamp's architecture

also correlates with our observation highlighted in Table 6 as every bootkit wrote to at least one *dark regions* not responsible for the boot process (MBR, VBR, BL). The *interrupt hook* heuristic also performed extremely well as it triggered for 98.8 % samples on XP and 99.9 % on Win7. This heuristic missed infections not employing interrupt hooking as described in Subsect 3.2. The *reuse existing code* heuristic caught 86.2 % of infections on average. This heuristic missed samples infecting the bootloader stage as those do not execute a malicious MBR / VBR, followed by the benign MBR / VBR and therefore they execute the address 0000h:7C00h just twice. Furthermore, we analyzed 100 benign samples utilizing our detection system and monitored the results during one hour of typical office usage (web browsing, text processing). To see the impact on the detection heuristics of a different bootloader, we ran Linux with *GRUB*. We did not encounter any false positives for these scenarios as writes outside partitions are very unlikely for benign samples respectively during normal system operation. There are very few executables potentially writing outside partitions (tools to repartition a system or correct errors in the MBR/VBR/BL) like *gparted* or *fixmbr.exe*. Thus *Bootcamp*'s heuristics work with setups that use 3 major bootloaders: *NTLDR*, *bootmgr* and *GRUB*.

Table 10. Performance of proposed detection heuristics

Detection heuristic	XP	XP (%)	Win7	Win7 (%)	Avg
Dark region reads	1,143	**100.0 %**	1,647	**100.0 %**	**100.0 %**
Interrupt hooks	1,129	**98.8 %**	1,646	**99.9 %**	**99.5 %**
Reuse existing code	951	83.2 %	1,455	88.4 %	86.2 %
Dark region writes (during bootkit infection phase)	1,143	**100.0 %**	1,647	**100.0 %**	**100.0 %**

6.2 Bootkit Prevention Results

Finally we evaluated the dataset applying the prevention technique described in Sect. 4.2. The experiment was performed for all 2,424 samples with *BK like behavior* on XP or Win7. During *bootkit infection phase* the system prevented the samples from writing outside of partitions and therefore hindering the bootkit's infection. After restarting the system and entering the *bootkit execution phase* we monitored the system's boot behavior. Applying the detection heuristics we determined whether an infection occurred in spite of the prevention system being in place. The system did not boot successfully after executing the malware in 2.9% of the cases on Windows XP and 7.3% on Win7. This was caused by the malicious modifications to essential OS components located inside the filesystem. After applying the detection heuristics on successful booting systems, we did not detect any infections during the boot phase anymore i.e. for all successful booting systems on both operating systems none of the detection heuristics triggered in any case. Applying our detection heuristics, the prevention system prohibited all 2,424 bootkit infection attempts on both OSes.

7 Discussion and Limitations

General Limitations. *Bootcamp* works for UEFI systems for the *bootkit infection phase* utilizing the heuristic for dark region tracking. The bootkit execution phase heuristics may not be effective in this case and we did not evaluate this scenario, as there are virtually no UEFI bootkits being not research proof-of-concepts. Hence, we evaluated our approach with MBR/VBR and BL-based bootkits which are the most popular bootkit types in the wild. Our heuristics are still relevant in a UEFI world for legacy systems that cannot be migrated. Bootkits may evade our system by directly attacking the BIOS, trying to flash a malicious one into the system and refraining from writing to boot process sectors. The malware can refrain attacking the boot process and stay inside the filesystem, e.g., by replacing system components directly on the filesystem like classic viruses do. However, this technique leaves suspicious tracks on the filesystem.

Evasion Techniques. There are several problems inherent to all dynamic analysis systems. Malware samples can employ techniques to detect a system emulator [29] and decline malicious behavior. Malware could fingerprint our analysis environment e.g. by MAC / IP addresses, Windows serial keys, deployed hard-/software combinations. For now we do not perform any cloaking of our system. Additionally the sample might wait some time before performing the infection. Though Kolbitsch et al. proposed a stalling code detection and mitigation [20] it can not deal with all kinds of this awkward behavior. It is extraordinarily difficult to circumvent such behavior within limited time and resource constraints. Therefore, we are not able to monitor malware utilizing such techniques. Evasive techniques for the heuristics are already discussed in Sect. 4.1.

Future Bootkit Evolution. We estimate the following future bootkit evolution trends: (1) Based on our results in Sect. 3, we expect the majority of bootkits exploiting the **bootloader** as the initial infection vector in the future as it is stealthier and offers slightly more space compared to the MBR and VBR infections. (2) Figure 5 shows a **diversification of dark region utilization** with time and we expect this to expand to sections within the filesystem (e.g., metadata, alternate data streams, file slack space). But such techniques introduce more complexity and risk for the bootkit. For example it could be accidentally overwritten by the OS, as it is not aware of the disk sectors used by the bootkit. Furthermore, the bootkit would have to be aware of the filesystem's implementation, know the location of every single utilized file and its slack space and monitor move, copy, update and delete operations on all utilized files to keep the data consistent. (3) **BIOS/UEFI based bootkits** might be another future trend. In 2011 the first BIOS based bootkit was detected in the wild [13], but hardly spotted since then because they are highly complex to implement and have to consider BIOS vendor and version specific details for their attack to succeed. Though a few UEFI PoC bootkits exist, to the best of our knowledge none has been spotted in the wild ever. Still they might be a future trend. (4) We expect bootkits to increase their capabilities by using recent CPU features, e.g. advanced virtualization instructions. This would enable **VM based bootkits** applying ideas from SubVirt [18]. Already new bootkits sometimes inject kernel drivers in order to hide bootkit data in DRs from detection systems inside the infected host (e.g., AV software). Utilizing VM based bootkits could shift the whole infected system into a VM leveraging the concealment to a new level, as such systems could get along without injecting any code or data into the infected system, but completely control the whole machine via the malicious VM.

8   Related Work

Dynamic Malware Analysis. Researchers have proposed and developed many approaches for dynamic malware analysis. Most rely on sandboxing and execute malware in virtual environments, e.g. Anubis [9], Argos [28] or CWSandbox [38]. Most approaches focus on capturing Windows API calls in user mode as Anubis [9] or CWSandbox [38] do, while others target kernel level infections like K-Tracer [22], dAnubis [27]. Some target network traffic produced by malware like Sandnet [33], whereas others focus on analysis-based evasive malware detection [19]. None target bootkits or analyze them in detail. Large-scale malware studies were performed by many papers for various goals. Most focus on scanning and in depth analysis of malware samples, e.g. [7,28,38]. Other target the problem of scaling for large malware datasets like [8,16] do. However, none of those papers focus on the subset of malware that contains bootkit technology.

Bootkits. Li et al. [23] and Gao et al. [12] present a survey on bootkit attacking approaches like BIOS-, MBR-, NTLDR- or other technology based bootkit infection vectors. Rodionov and Matrosov [11] outline a bootkit classification based on their infection vector (MBR / VBR / BL) and present a bootkit threat evolution overview. This evolution survey is not built on certain bootkit technology characteristics as our historic evolution overview is, but highlights the first occurrence of certain technologies. Haukli [15] uses the number of jumps to address 0000h:7C00h during the system's boot process as a heuristic to detect suspicious behavior but does not perform an evaluation of this approach. In 2007 IceLord, the first BIOS based bootkit PoC, was published which tries to inject a malicious BIOS and gains control even before the MBR is executed. Research in this area was done by Schlaikjer [31] and Wojtczuk and Tereshkin [39] in 2009 and 2013. None of them presented a historic, large-scale and detailed bootkit analysis as we do. Kaspersky Labs [17] studied GrayFish, an advanced malware created by the Equation group. GrayFish has a bootkit component that modifies the VBR and hijacks the loading of the first kernel driver. More components are loaded afterwards from the registry. Our detection heuristics would detect GrayFish's VBR component and the prevention component would stop the infection.

Preventing Infections. [14] proposed a bootkit prevention system based on an AV solution and relies on components inside of the system. Hence, an attacker can disable the system before performing the infection. This drawback does not apply to our proposed bootkit infection prevention approach. Bacs et al. [6] used low level disk monitoring to recover from infections, including bootkit attacks, and prevent persistent malicious storage inside as well as outside of the filesystem. NICKLE [30], a lightweight VMM, attempts to prevent unauthorized kernel code execution by using shadow memory. This technique may prevent bootkit kernel level code execution but not necessarily the infection. Compared to other defensive measures like the sometimes controversial trusted computing/boot or TPM approaches our solution does not require UEFI or additional hardware.

9   Conclusion

We presented a large-scale bootkit analysis and proposed detection and prevention mechanisms. We showed the results of a large scale bootkit analysis for a malware dataset composed of 25,513 samples collected over the last 8 years, whereof 2,424 samples revealed *bootkit like behavior*. The results give insights into specific bootkit behavior and show the evolution of bootkit technology from 2006 until now. We detected a major shift from exploiting the MBR as infection vector to utilizing the bootloader instead. The same applies for interrupt hooking where we detected a movement from using interrupt 0x13 to 0x15 as preferred hooking target throughout the years. Additionally recent bootkits try to hide their presence by exploiting the space between partitions instead of occupying the space at the very end of the disk. Furthermore, we detected that every bootkit in our dataset stores its data in *dark regions* outside partitions. We evaluated our proposed detection heuristics with our complete dataset which detected all bootkit infections. We did not observe any false-positives during our evaluation with benign samples and boot processes, though false-positives may occur as discussed in Sect. 4. Moreover, we showed that the proposed prevention approach has successfully stopped all bootkit infections from our dataset.

Acknowledgements. The research was partly funded by the COMET K1 program by the Austrian Research Funding Agency (FFG). Sponsored by the ERC StG "Rosetta" and NWO VICI "Dowsing" projects.

References

1. Plite bootkit. http://labs.bitdefender.com/2012/05/plite-rootkit-spies-on-gamers/
2. BIOS Rootkit: Welcome home, my Lord! (2007). http://blog.csdn.net/icelord/article/details/1604884
3. Backdoor.pihar, (2011). http://www.symantec.com/security_response/writeup.jsp?docid=2011-120817-1417-99&tabid=2
4. Finfisher malware dropper analysis, (2014). https://www.codeandsec.com/FinFisher-Malware-Dropper-Analysis
5. Aditya, S., Rohit, B.: Prosecting the citadel botnet revealing the dominance of the zeus descendent. In: VB (2014)
6. Bacs, A., Vermeulen, R., Slowinska, A., Bos, H.: System-level support for intrusion recovery. In: Flegel, U., Markatos, E., Robertson, W. (eds.) DIMVA 2012. LNCS, vol. 7591, pp. 144–163. Springer, Heidelberg (2013)
7. Bayer, U., Habibi, I., Balzarotti, D., Kirda, E., Kruegel, C.: A view on current malware behaviors. In: USENIX LEET (2009)
8. Bayer, U., Kirda, E., Kruegel, C.: Improving the efficiency of dynamic malware analysis. In: ACM SAC (2010)
9. Bayer, U., Kruegel, C., Kirda, E.: Ttanalyze: A tool for analyzing malware. In: EICAR 2006 (2006)
10. Dela Paz, R.: ZeuS Source Code Leaked, Now What? (2013). http://blog.trendmicro.com/trendlabs-security-intelligence/the-zeus-source-code-leaked-now-what/
11. Eugene Rodionov, D.H., Matrosov, A.: Bootkits: Past, Present and Future. In: VB Conference (2014)
12. Gao, H., Li, Q., Zhu, Y., Wang, W., Zhou, L.: Research on the working mechanism of bootkit. In: ICIDT (2012)
13. Giuliani, M.: Mebromi: the first bios rootkit in the wild, (2011). http://www.webroot.com/blog/2011/09/13/mebromi-the-first-bios-rootkit-in-the-wild/
14. Grill, B., Platzer, C., Eckel, J.: A practical approach for generic bootkit detection and prevention. In: EUROSEC (2014)
15. Haukli, L.: Exposing bootkits with bios emulation. Black Hat US (2014)
16. Hu, X., Chiueh, T.-C., Shin, K.G.: Large-scale malware indexing using function-call graphs. In: ACM CCS (2009)
17. Kaspersky Lab. Equation group: Questions and answers, (2015). https://securelist.com/files/2015/02/Equation_group_questions_and_answers.pdf
18. King, S.T., Chen, P.M., Wang, Y.-M., Verbowski, C., Wang, H.J., Lorch, J.R.: Subvirt: Implementing malware with virtual machines. In: IEEE S&P (2006)
19. Kirat, D., Vigna, G., Kruegel, C.: Barecloud: bare-metal analysis-based evasive malware detection. In: USENIX Security (2014)
20. Kolbitsch, C., Kirda, E., Kruegel, C.: The power of procrastination: detection and mitigation of execution-stalling malicious code. In: ACM CCS (2011)
21. Krebs, B.: Carberp source code leak, (2013). https://krebsonsecurity.com/tag/carberp-source-code-leak/
22. Lanzi, A., Sharif, M.I., Lee, W.: K-tracer: A system for extracting kernel malware behavior. In: NDSS (2009)

23. Li, X., Wen, Y., Huang, M., Liu, Q.: An overview of bootkit attacking approaches. In: MSN (2011)
24. Matrosov, A.: ESET - Rovnix bootkit framework updated, (2012). http://www.welivesecurity.com/2012/07/13/rovnix-bootkit-framework-updated
25. Microsoft. Kernel Patch Protection. http://msdn.microsoft.com/en-us/library/windows/hardware/Dn613955
26. MSDN. Driver Signing. http://msdn.microsoft.com/en-us/library/windows/hardware/ff544865(v=vs.85).aspx
27. Neugschwandtner, M., Platzer, C., Comparetti, M., Bayer, U.: Danubis-dynamic device driver analysis based on virtual machine introspection. In: DIMVA (2010)
28. Portokalidis, G., Slowinska, A., Bos, H.: Argos: an emulator for fingerprinting zero-day attacks. In: EuroSys (2006)
29. Raffetseder, T., Kruegel, C., Kirda, E.: Detecting system emulators. In: Garay, J.A., Lenstra, A.K., Mambo, M., Peralta, R. (eds.) ISC 2007. LNCS, vol. 4779, pp. 1–18. Springer, Heidelberg (2007)
30. Riley, R., Jiang, X., Xu, D.: Guest-transparent prevention of kernel rootkits with VMM-based memory shadowing. In: Lippmann, R., Kirda, E., Trachtenberg, A. (eds.) RAID 2008. LNCS, vol. 5230, pp. 1–20. Springer, Heidelberg (2008)
31. Ross, S.: Overview of bios rootkits, (2013). https://tuftsdev.github.io/DefenseOfTheDarkArts/students_works/final_project/rschlaikjer.pdf
32. Rossow, C., Andriesse, D., Werner, T., Stone-Gross, B., Plohmann, D., Dietrich, C.J., Bos, H.: Sok: P2pwned-modeling and evaluating the resilience of peer-to-peer botnets. In: IEEE S&P (2013)
33. Rossow, C., Dietrich, C.J., Bos, H., Cavallaro, L., Van Steen, M., Freiling, F.C. , Pohlmann, N.: Sandnet: Network traffic analysis of malicious software. In: BADGERS (2011)
34. Rossow, C., Dietrich, C.J., Kreibich, C., Grier, C., Paxson, V., Pohlmann, N., Bos, H., van Steen, M.: Prudent Practices for Designing Malware Experiments: Status Quo and Outlook. In: IEEE S&P (2012)
35. Rusakov, V., Golovanov, S.: Attacks before startup, (2014). http://securelist.com/blog/research/63725/attacks-before-system-startup/
36. Sean, B.: First zeus, now spyeye. https://www.damballa.com/first-zeus-now-spyeye-look-the-source-code-now/
37. White, S.R., Kephart, J.O., Chess, D.M.: Computer viruses: A global perspective. In: Virus Bulletin International Conference (1995)
38. Willems, C., Holz, T., Freiling, F.: Toward automated dynamic malware analysis using cwsandbox. In: IEEE S&P (2007)
39. Wojtczuk, R., Tereshkin, A.: Attacking intel bios. In: BlackHat US (2009)

C5: Cross-Cores Cache Covert Channel

Clémentine Maurice[1]([⊠]), Christoph Neumann[1], Olivier Heen[1],
and Aurélien Francillon[2]

[1] Technicolor, Rennes, France
{clementine.maurice,christoph.neumann,olivier.heen}@technicolor.com
[2] Eurecom, Sophia-Antipolis, France
aurelien.francillon@eurecom.fr

Abstract. Cloud computing relies on hypervisors to isolate virtual machines running on shared hardware. Since perfect isolation is difficult to achieve, sharing hardware induces threats. Covert channels were demonstrated to violate isolation and, typically, allow data exfiltration. Several covert channels have been proposed that rely on the processor's cache. However, these covert channels are either slow or impractical due to the *addressing uncertainty*. This uncertainty exists in particular in virtualized environments and with recent L3 caches which are using complex addressing. Using shared memory would elude addressing uncertainty, but shared memory is not available in most practical setups.

We build C5, a covert channel that tackles addressing uncertainty without requiring any shared memory, making the covert channel fast and practical. We are able to transfer messages on modern hardware across any cores of the same processor. The covert channel targets the last level cache that is shared across all cores. It exploits the inclusive feature of caches, allowing a core to evict lines in the private first level cache of another core. We experimentally evaluate the covert channel in native and virtualized environments. In particular, we successfully establish a covert channel between virtual machines running on different cores. We measure a bitrate of 1291 bps for a native setup, and 751 bps for a virtualized setup. This is one order of magnitude above previous cache-based covert channels in the same setup.

Keywords: Covert channel · Cache · Cross-VM · Virtualization · Cloud computing

1 Introduction

Cloud computing leverages shared hardware to reduce infrastructure costs. The hypervisor, at the virtualization layer, provides isolation between the virtual machines. However, the last years have shown a great number of information leakage attacks across virtual machines, namely covert and side channels [13,14, 23,26–28,30]. These attacks evidently violate the isolation.

Covert channels involve the cooperation of two attackers' processes to actively exchange information. Side channels imply passive observation of a victim's

© Springer International Publishing Switzerland 2015
M. Almgren et al. (Eds.): DIMVA 2015, LNCS 9148, pp. 46–64, 2015.
DOI: 10.1007/978-3-319-20550-2_3

process by an attacker's process. Covert and side channels have been built in a native environment between two processes, and in a virtualized environment between two virtual machines. These attacks leverage elements of the microarchitecture that are accessible remotely by an attacker, such as the memory bus [26], the data cache [4,21,23,28], the instruction cache [1,30] or the branch target buffer [2].

In this article, we focus on covert channels. They are used to exfiltrate sensitive information, and can also be used as a co-residency test [29]. There are many challenges for covert channels across virtual machines. Core migration drastically reduces the bitrate of channels that are not cross-core [27]. Simultaneous execution of the virtual machines over several cores prevents a strict round-robin scheduling between the sender and the receiver [26]. Functions of address translation, and functions that map an address to a cache set are not exposed to processes, and thus induce uncertainty over the location of a particular data in the cache. This *addressing uncertainty* (term coined in [26]) prevents the sender and the receiver to agree on a particular location to work on.

Covert channels that don't tackle the *addressing uncertainty* are limited to use private first level caches, thus to be on the same core for modern processors [26]. This dramatically reduces the bitrate in virtualized environment or in the cloud, with modern processors that have several cores with a shared and physically indexed last level cache. Ristenpart et al. [23] target the private cache of a core and obtain a bitrate of 0.2 bps, with the limitation that the sender and receiver must be on the same core. Xu et al. [27] quantify the achievable bitrate of this covert channel: from 215 bps in lab condition, they reach 3 bps in the cloud. This drop is due to the scheduling of the virtual machines across cores. Yarom and Falkner [28] circumvent the issue of physical addressing by relying on deduplication offered by the hypervisor or the OS. With deduplication, common pages use the same caches lines. However, deduplication can be deactivated for all or some specific security relevant pages, e.g., OpenSSL pages, making the previous attacks impractical. Wu et al. [26] avoid the shortcomings of caches by building a covert channel across cores that is based on the memory bus, using the lock instruction. We refer the reader to Sect. 6 for more details on state of the art techniques.

We differentiate our covert channel by tackling the issue of the *addressing uncertainty* without relying on any shared memory. Our covert channel works between two virtual machines that run across any cores of the same processor. We revisit the method of Ristenpart et al. [23], and take advantage of the shared and inclusive feature of the Last Level Cache in modern processors. We obtain a high bitrate, arguing that the covert channel is practical.

Contributions

In this paper, we demonstrate the information leakage due to a new covert channel that uses the last level cache.

1. We build the C5 covert channel across virtual machines, on modern hardware. In particular, we tackle the *addressing uncertainty* that severely limits the previous covert channels.
2. We analyze the interferences that are the root causes that enable this covert channel, *i.e.*, microarchitectural features such as the shared last level cache, and the inclusive feature of the cache hierarchy.
3. We evaluate the C5 covert channel in a native environment and achieve a bitrate of 1291 bps (error rate: 3.1 %). We evaluate the C5 covert channel in a virtualized environment and achieve a bitrate of 751 bps (error rate: 5.7 %). We explore the relation between the bitrate and the error rate.

The remainder of this paper is organized as follows. Section 2 covers background on the cache internals needed for the remainder of the article. Section 3 details our technique to build a cache-based covert channel. Section 4 exposes our experiments in lab-controlled native and virtualized setups. Section 5 discusses the factors that impact performance, as well as mitigations. Section 6 presents the related work and the differences with our work. Section 7 summarizes our results and their implications.

2   Background

In this section, we provide background notions on cache internals. We then review techniques that exploit cache interferences for the communication between two processes. Finally, we discuss the effect of virtualization and complex addressing on the cache addressing, and its impact on cache-based covert channels.

2.1   Cache Fundamentals

The cache is faster than main memory and stores recently-used data. Intel processors[1] use a cache hierarchy similar to the one depicted in Fig. 1 since the Nehalem microarchitecture (2008) and until the most recent Haswell microarchitecture [12]. There are usually three cache levels, called L1, L2 and L3. The levels L1 and L2 are private to each core, and store several kilobytes. The L3 cache is also called Last Level Cache (LLC in the rest of this paper). The LLC is divided into slices that are connected to the cores through a ring interconnect. The LLC is shared between the cores, *i.e.*, each core can address the entire cache. It is also the largest, usually several megabytes.

To read or write data in main memory, the CPU first checks the memory location in the L1 cache. If the address is found, it is a *cache hit* and the CPU immediately reads or writes data in the cache line. Otherwise, it is a *cache miss* and the CPU searches for the address in the next level, and so on, until reaching the main memory. A cache hit is significantly faster than a cache miss.

---

[1] In this article, we focus on Intel processors. Still, most of this discussion on caches applies also to other x86 processors.

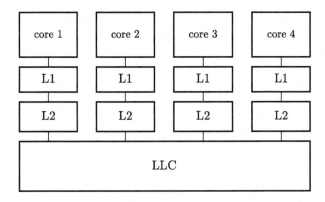

Fig. 1. Cache hierarchy of a quad-core Intel processor (since Nehalem microarchitecture). The LLC is inclusive, which means it is a superset of the L1 and L2 caches.

Data is transfered between the cache and the memory in 64 bytes blocks called *lines*. The location of a particular line depends on the cache structure. Today's caches are *n-way associative*, which means that a cache contains sets of n lines. A line is loaded in a specific set depending on its address, and occupies any of the n lines.

With caches that implement a *direct addressing* scheme, memory addresses can be decomposed in three parts: the tag, the set and the offset in the line. The lowest o bits determine the offset in the line, with: $o = \log_2(\text{line size})$. The next s bits determine the set, with: $s = \log_2(\text{number of sets})$. And the remaining t bits form the tag. A 48 bit address can be represented as follows:

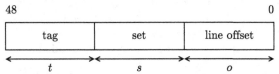

In contrast to direct addressing, some caches implement a *complex addressing* scheme, where potentially all address bits are used to index the cache. The function that maps an address to a set is not documented. This has important implications for covert channels.

The address used to compute the cache location can be either a physical or a virtual address. A *Virtually Indexed, Virtually Tagged* (VIVT) cache only uses virtual addresses to locate the data in the cache. Modern processors involve physical addressing, either *Virtually Indexed Physically Tagged* (VIPT), or *Physically Indexed Physically Tagged* (PIPT). The physical address is not known by the processes, *i.e.*, a process cannot know the location of a specific line for physically addressed caches. This too has important implications for covert channels.

When a cache set is full, a cache line needs to be evicted before storing a new cache line. When a line is evicted from L1 it is stored back to L2, which can lead to the eviction of a new line to LLC, etc. The replacement policy decides the victim line to be evicted. Good replacement policies choose the line that is the least likely to be reused. Such policies include Least Recently Used (LRU), Least Frequently Used, Pseudo Random, and Adaptive.

Depending on the cache design, data stored on one level may also be stored on other levels. A level is *inclusive* if it is a superset of the lower levels. To guarantee the inclusion property, when a line is evicted from the LLC, the line is also removed (invalidated) in the lower caches L1 and L2. A level is *exclusive* if a data is present at most once between this level and the lower levels. Intel CPUs from Nehalem to Haswell microarchitecture have exclusive L2 caches, and an inclusive LLC.

2.2 Playing with Caches for Fun and Profit

Isolation prevents processes from directly reading or writing in the cache memory of another process. Cache-based covert and side channels use indirect means and side effects to transfer information from one process to another. One side effect is the variation of cache access delays.

Cache hits are faster than cache misses. This property allows monitoring access patterns, and subsequently leaking information. In *access-driven attacks*, a process monitors the time taken by its own activity to determine the cache sets accessed by other processes.

Two general strategies exist: *prime+probe* [18,19,21,24] and *flush+reload* [8,28]. With *prime+probe*, a receiver process fills the cache, then waits for a sender process to evict some cache sets. The receiver process reads data again and determines which sets were evicted. The access to those sets will be slower for the receiver because they need to be reloaded in the cache. With *flush+reload*, a receiver process flushes the cache, then waits for a sender process to reload some cache sets. The receiver process reads data again and determines which sets were reloaded. The access to those sets will be faster for the receiver because they don't need to be reloaded in the cache. The *flush+reload* attack assumes shared lines of cache between the sender and the receiver – and thus shared memory – otherwise the sets reloaded by the sender will not be faster to reload by the receiver than the evicted ones. Indeed, the receiver cannot access sets reloaded by the sender if they don't share memory.

2.3 The Problem of *Addressing Uncertainty*

The previous attacks rely on the fact that it is possible to target a specific set. However, two conditions individually create uncertainty on the addressing, making it difficult to target a specific set: virtualization and complex addressing.

Processors implement virtual memory using a Memory Management Unit (MMU) that maps virtual addresses to physical addresses. With virtual machines, hypervisors introduce an additional layer of translation, known as Extended Page Tables on Intel processors. The guest virtual pages are translated to the guest physical pages, and further to the actual machine pages. The hypervisor is responsible for mapping the guest physical memory to the actual machine memory. A process knowing a virtual address in its virtual machine has no way of learning the corresponding physical address of the guest, nor the actual machine address. In a native environment, the layer of translation from virtual to physical addresses does not create uncertainty on the set if both processes allocate large portions of aligned and contiguous memory[2]. In a virtualized environment, the additional layer of translation does create uncertainty, as the alignment is not guaranteed.

In addition to this, the complex addressing scheme maps an address to a set with a function that potentially uses all address bits. As the function is undocumented, a process cannot determine the set in which it is reading or writing. Even aligned memory does not guarantee that two processes will target the same set.

This has implications for the design of covert channels. Indeed, with the *addressing uncertainty*, two processes without any shared memory cannot directly agree on a set to work on.

3   C5 Covert Channel

Our covert channel relies on the fact that the LLC is shared and inclusive. Those two characteristics are present in all CPUs from Nehalem to Haswell microarchitectures, *i.e.*, all modern Intel CPUs, including most CPUs that are found in, e.g., Amazon EC2 (Table 1).

The sender process sends bits to the receiver by varying the access delays that the receiver observes when accessing a set in the cache. At a high level view, the covert channel encodes a '0' as a fast access for the receiver and a '1' as a slow access. In this sense, our covert channel strategy is close to *prime+probe*.

Figure 2 illustrates our covert channel. The receiver process repeatedly probes one set. If the sender is idle (a '0' is being transmitted), the access is fast because the data stays in the private L1 cache of the receiver, see Fig. 2-1. The data is also present in the LLC because of its *inclusive* property.

To send a '1', the sender process writes data to occupy the whole LLC, see Fig. 2-2; in particular this evicts the set of the receiver from the LLC. Because of the *inclusive* property, the data also gets evicted from the private L1 cache

Table 1. Characteristics of the CPUs found on Amazon EC2 [3,7,20].

Model	Microarch	Year	Cores	LLC	Potential for C5
Opteron 270	K8	2005	2	private L2 exclusive	not cross-core
Opteron 2218 HE	K8	2007	2	private L2 exclusive	not cross-core
Xeon E5430	Core	2007	4	2×6MB L2 non-inclusive	not cross-core
Xeon E5507	Nehalem	2010	4	**shared 4MB L3 inclusive**	✓
Xeon E5645	Nehalem	2011	6	**shared 12MB L3 inclusive**	✓
Xeon E5-2670	Sandy Bridge	2012	8	**shared 20MB L3 inclusive**	✓
Xeon E5-2670 v2	Ivy Bridge	2013	10	**shared 25MB L3 inclusive**	✓
Xeon E5-2666 v3	Haswell	2014	9	**shared 25MB L3 inclusive**	✓

---

[2] It cannot be guaranteed using `malloc` on 4 kB pages, but it is possible to use huge pages of 2 MB or 1 GB if the CPU supports it.

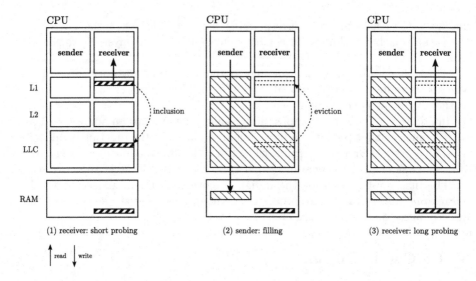

Fig. 2. Cross-core covert channel illustration of sender and receiver behavior. Step (1): the receiver probes one set repeatedly; the access is fast because the data is in its L1 (and LLC by inclusive feature). Step (2): the sender fills the LLC, thus evicting the set of the receiver from LLC and its private L1 cache. Step (3): the receiver probes the same set; the access is slow because the data must be retrieved from RAM.

of the receiver. The receiver now observes that the access to its set is slow; the data must be retrieved from RAM, see Fig. 2-3.

We now provide a detailed description of the sender and the receiver.

3.1 Sender

The sender needs a way to interfere with the private cache of the other cores. In our covert channel, the sender leverages the inclusive feature of the LLC (see Sect. 2.1). As the LLC is shared amongst the cores of the same processor, the sender may evict lines that are owned by other processes, and in particular processes running on other cores.

A straightforward idea is that the sender writes in a set, and the receiver probes the same set. However, due to virtualization and complex addressing, the sender and the receiver cannot agree on the cache set they are working on (see Sect. 2.3). Our technique consists of a scheme where the sender flushes the whole LLC, and the receiver probes a single set. That way, the sender is guaranteed to affect the set that the receiver reads, thus resolving the *addressing uncertainty*.

In order to flush the whole LLC, the sender must evict cache lines and therefore writes data into a buffer. In fact, either writing or reading data would provoke a cache miss. We choose to write because a read miss following a write induces a higher penalty for the receiver than a read miss following a read. This leads to a stronger signal. We further discuss the influence of this choice in Sect. 5.

We leverage the replacement policy within a set to evict lines from the LLC. The replacement policy and the associativity influence the buffer size b of the

---

Algorithm 1. Sender: $f(n, o, s, c, w)$

---

message $\leftarrow \{0,1\}^*$
$n \leftarrow$ LLC associativity
$o \leftarrow \log_2(\text{line size})$
$s \leftarrow \log_2(\text{number of sets in LLC})$
$b \leftarrow n \times 2^{o+s} \times c$
buffer[b]
for each bit in message **do**
   wait(w)
   if bit $== 1$ **then**
     for $i = 0$ to number of sets **do**
       for $j = 0$ to $n \times c$ **do**
         buffer$[2° i + 2^{o+s} j] = $ constant
       end for
     end for
   end if
end for

---

sender. Considering a pure LRU policy, writing n lines in each set is enough to flush all the lines of the LLC, n being the associativity. The replacement policies on modern CPUs drastically affect the performance of caches; therefore they are well guarded secrets. Pseudo-LRU policies are known to be inefficient for memory intensive workloads of working sets greater than the cache size. Adaptive policies [22] are more likely to be used in actual processors. Since the actual replacement policy is unknown, we determine experimentally the size b of the buffer to which the sender needs to write.

The order of writes into the buffer is highly dependent on the cache microarchitecture. Ideally, to iterate over the buffer we would take into account the function that maps an address to a set. However this function is undocumented, thus we assume a direct addressing; other types of iterations are possible. The sender writes with the following memory pattern $2^o i + 2^{o+s} j$ as described in Algorithm 1. 2^s is the number of sets of the LLC and 2° the line size; j and i are line and set indices respectively.

Algorithm 1 summarizes the steps performed by the sender. The parameters are the LLC associativity n, the number of sets 2^s, the line size 2°, and a constant c to adapt the buffer size. To send a '1', the sender flushes the entire LLC by writing in each line j ($n \times c$ times) of each set i, with the described memory pattern. To send a '0', the sender does nothing. The sender waits for a determined time w before sending a bit to allow the receiver to distinguish between two consecutive bits.

3.2   Receiver

The receiver repeatedly probes all the lines of the same cache set in its L1 cache. Algorithm 2 summarizes the steps performed by the receiver. The iteration is dependent on the cache microarchitecture. To access each line i (n times) of

---

Algorithm 2. Receiver: $f(n, o, s)$

$n \leftarrow$ L1 associativity
$o \leftarrow \log_2(\text{line size})$
$s \leftarrow \log_2(\text{number of sets in L1})$
buffer$[n \times 2^{o+s}]$
loop
   read $\leftarrow 0$
   begin measurement
   for $i = 0$ to n **do**
      read $+ =$ buffer$[2^{o+s}i]$
   end for
   end measurement, record $(localTime, accessDelay)$
end loop

---

the same set, the receiver reads a buffer – and measures the time taken – with the following memory pattern: $2^{o+s}i$. The cumulative variable `read` prevents optimizations from the compiler, by introducing a dependency between the consecutive loads so that they happen in sequence and not in parallel. In the actual code, we also unroll the inner `for` loop to reduce unnecessary branches and memory accesses.

The receiver is able to probe a set in its L1 cache because the L1 is virtually indexed, and does not use complex addressing. We do not seek to probe the L2 or L3, because all read and write accesses reach the L1 first and they might evict each other, creating differences in timing that are not caused by the sender.

The receiver probes a single set when the sender writes to the entire cache, thus one iteration of the receiver is faster than one iteration of the sender. The receiver runs continuously and concurrently with the sender, while the sender only sends one bit every w microseconds. As a consequence, the receiver performs several measurements for each bit transmitted by the sender.

One measurement of the receiver has the form $(localTime, accessDelay)$, where $localTime$ is the time of the end of one measurement according to the local clock of the receiver and $accessDelay$ is the time taken for the receiver to read the set. Figure 3 illustrates the measurements performed by the receiver.

Having these measurements, the receiver decodes the transmitted bit-sequence. First, the receiver extracts all the '1's. The receiver removes all points that have an $accessDelay$ below (or equal to) typical L2 access time. Then the receiver only keeps the $localTime$ information and applies a clustering algorithm to separate the bits. We choose DBSCAN [6], a density-based clustering algorithm, over the popular k-means algorithm. A drawback of the k-means algorithm is that it takes the number k of clusters as an input parameter. In our case, it would mean knowing in advance the number of '1's, which is not realistic. The DBSCAN algorithm takes two input parameters, $minPts$ and ϵ:

1. $minPts$: the minimum number of points in each cluster. If $minPts$ is too low, we could observe false positives, reading a '1' when there is none; if $minPts$

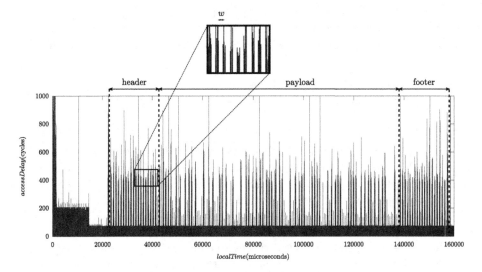

Fig. 3. Reception of a 128-bit transmission. *Laptop* setup in native environment, with $w = 500\mu s$, $b = 3\,MB$.

is too high, we could observe false negatives, not reading a '1' when there is one. In practice, we use $minPts$ between 5 and 20.

2. ϵ: if a point belongs to a cluster, every point in its ϵ-neighborhood is also part of the cluster. In practice, we choose ϵ below w.

Once all the '1's of the transmitted bit-sequence have been extracted, the receiver reconstructs the remaining '0's. This step is straightforward as the receiver knows the time taken to transmit a '0' which is w.

4 Experiments

In this section, we evaluate the C5 covert channel on native and virtualized setups. We then illustrate the effect of the complex addressing regarding *addressing uncertainty*.

4.1 Testbed

Table 2 summarizes the characteristics of the *laptop* and *workstation* setups. Some parameters of the architecture are constant for the considered processors. The line size in all cache hierarchy is 64 bytes, and the L1 is 8-associative and has 64 sets. We conduct our experiments in lab-controlled native and virtualized environments.

We adjust two parameters: the size b of the buffer that evicts the LLC, and the delay w between the transmission of two consecutive bits. The size b and the delay w impact the bitrate and the error rate of the clustering algorithm, as

Table 2. Experimental setups, LLC characteristics.

Name	Model	Microarch	Cores	Size	Sets	Asso.	Complex addressing
Laptop	i5-3340M	Ivy Bridge	2	3 MB	4096	12	yes
Workstation	Xeon E5-2609v2	Ivy Bridge	4	10 MB	8192	20	yes

depicted in Figs. 4 and 5. The precision of the clustering algorithm increases with the size b, however the bitrate is proportionally reduced. The size b is controlled by the multiplicative parameter c and must be at least the size of the LLC. The bitrate increases with lower values of w, but the precision of the clustering algorithm decreases.

To evaluate the covert channel, the sender transmits a random 4096-bit message to the receiver. We transmit series of 20 consecutive '1's as a header and a footer framing the payload to be able to extract it automatically. The receiver then reconstructs the message from its measurements. We run 10 experiments for each set of parameters, and calculate the bitrate and the error rate. We derive the error rate from the Levenshtein distance between the sent payload and the received payload. The Levenshtein distance is the minimum number of characters edits and accounts for insertions, deletions and bit flips. We provide the evaluation results for each environment: native in Sect. 4.2 and virtualized in Sect. 4.3.

Establishing cache-based channels demands fine grained measurements. Processors provide a timestamp counter for the number of cycles since reset. This counter can be accessed by the `rdtsc` and `rdtscp` instructions. However, reading the counter is not sufficient as modern processors use out-of-order execution. The actual execution may not respect the sequence order of instructions as written in the executable. In particular, a reordering of the `rdtsc` instruction can lead to the measurement of more, or less, than the wanted sequence. We prevent reordering by using serializing instructions, such as `cpuid`. We follow Intel recommendations for fine-grained timing analysis in [11].

4.2 Native Environment

We evaluate C5 in the *laptop* and *workstation* setups, in a native (non-virtualized) environment. We run the sender and the receiver as unprivileged processes, in Ubuntu 14.04. To demonstrate the cross-core property of our covert channel, we pin the sender and the receiver to different cores[3]. Figure 3 illustrates a transmission of 128 bits in the *laptop* setup, for $w = 500\mu s$ and $b = 3$ MB.

Figure 4 presents the results in the *laptop* setup, for two values of b, and three values for waiting time w. For $b = 3$ MB (the size of the LLC), varying w we obtain a bitrate between 232 bps and 1291 bps. The error rate is comprised between 0.3 % (with a standard deviation $\sigma = 3.0 \times 10^{-3}$) and 3.1 % ($\sigma = 0.013$).

---

[3] Using the `sched_setaffinity(2)` Linux system call.

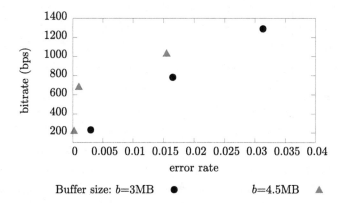

Fig. 4. Bitrate as a function of the error rate, for two sizes of buffer *b*. *Laptop* setup (3MB LLC) in native environment.

When we increase b to 4.5 MB, the bitrate slightly decreases but stays in the same order of magnitude, between 223 bps and 1033 bps. The error rate decreases between 0.02 % ($\sigma = 8.5 \times 10^{-5}$) and 1.6 % ($\sigma = 1.1 \times 10^{-4}$). The standard deviation of the error rate also decreases, leading to more reliable transmission. We conclude that it is sufficient to write n lines per set, but that the transmission is more reliable if we write more than n lines. This is a tradeoff between the bitrate and the error rate.

In the *workstation* setup, we obtain a bitrate of 163 bps for $b = 15$ MB ($1.5 \times$ LLC), for an error rate of 1.9 % ($\sigma = 7.2 \times 10^{-3}$). As expected, we observe that when the size of the LLC increases the bitrate decreases, since it takes longer to send a '1'. Compared to the *laptop* setup, the error rate and the standard deviation have also increased. There are two factors that can explain these results. First, the ratio of the associativity over the number of cores is smaller in the *workstation* setup, which means that lines have a greater probability of being evicted by processes running in other cores, leading to a higher error rate. Second, the LLC is bigger in the *workstation* setup, which means that the allocation of a buffer might not cover all the sets of the LLC, leading to a difference in the error rate between runs, and thus a higher standard deviation.

4.3   Virtualized Environment

We evaluate C5 in the *laptop* setup, using Xen 4.4 as hypervisor. We run the sender as an unprivileged process in a guest virtual machine, and the receiver as an unprivileged process in another guest virtual machine. The guests and dom0 run Ubuntu 14.04. Each guest has one vCPU, and dom0 uses the default algorithm to schedule guest virtual machines.

Figure 5 presents the results for two values of b ($b = 3$ MB and $b = 4.5$ MB), and two waiting time w ($w = 4000\mu$s and $w = 1000\mu$s). For $b = 3$ MB (the size of the LLC), varying w we obtain a bitrate between 229 bps and 751 bps. When we increase b to 4.5 MB, the bitrate goes from 219 bps to 661 bps. There is a

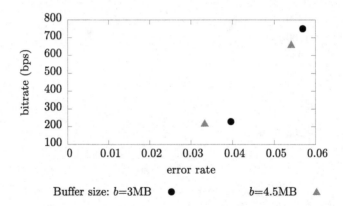

Fig. 5. Bitrate as a function of the error rate, for two sizes of buffer *b*. *Laptop* setup (3MB LLC) in virtualized environment.

performance degradation compared to the native setup, but the bitrate stays in the same order of magnitude. The error rate is slightly higher than in the native setup, between 3.3 % ($\sigma = 0.019$) and 5.7 % ($\sigma = 8.8 \times 10^{-3}$), and is comparable for the two values of b. The standard deviation of the error rate is also higher than in the native setup, and is higher for a low value of b.

4.4   Complex Addressing Matters

We illustrate the impact of complex addressing on the cache-based covert channel proposed in the first part of [26]. The sender accesses a sequence of lines that map the memory pattern $M + X \cdot 256$k. The pattern is crafted such as to change the bits that correspond to the tag of the memory address. All accesses following this pattern target the same set. The receiver measures the access latency of another sequence of lines that follow the same pattern. The receiver then accesses the same set than the sender, and observes a longer access when the sender has flushed the lines. The authors of [26] evaluate the covert channel with a Core 2 Q8400 processor, which does not use a complex addressing scheme.

We reproduce this covert channel in the *laptop* setup in a native environment. The microarchitecture of the *laptop* CPU is more recent than the Q8400 processor, and the LLC uses complex addressing. We align the memory allocated by the sender and the receiver, and access the same memory pattern. As expected, we observe that the receiver is unable to retrieve the message. This is due to the complex addressing, causing the sender and the receiver to access different sets, removing the interference needed to establish a covert channel.

5   Discussion

In this section we expose the factors that impact – positively or negatively – the performances of the C5 covert channel. We also discuss the effects of a number of existing mitigation methods.

5.1   Performance

Evicting cache lines by reading or writing memory modifies the quality of the signal. A read is generally less costly than a write, so the sender could prefer to perform reads instead of writes in our covert channel. However, reads do not have the same impact in terms of timing for the receiver. When the receiver loads a new cache line, there are two cases. In the first case, the line had previously only been read by the sender, and not modified. The receiver thus requires a single memory access to load the line. In the second case, the line had previously been modified by the sender. At the time of eviction, it needs to be written back in memory. This requires an additional memory access, and thus takes longer. We choose to evict caches lines using memory writes because of the higher latency, which improves the signal quality.

Whenever the sender and the receiver run on the same core, the C5 covert channel may benefit from optimizations. In this case, there is no need to flush the entire LLC: flushing the L1 cache that is 32 kB is sufficient and faster. However, the sender and the receiver are scheduled by the OS or the hypervisor, and frequently run on different cores [27]. We would need a method to detect when both run on the same core, and adapt the sender algorithm accordingly. Our method is simpler as it is agnostic to the scheduler.

The detection algorithm of the receiver impacts the overall bitrate. We put the priority on having a good detector at the receiver end, to minimize the error rate. In our implementation, the sender is waiting between the transmission of consecutive bits. The receiver uses a density-based clustering algorithm to separate the bits. Further work can be dedicated to reduce or eliminate the waiting time on the sender side, by using a different detection algorithm on the receiver side.

The C5 channel depends on the cache design. In particular, it depends on the shared and inclusive LLC. We believe this is a reasonable assumption, as this is the case since several generations of microarchitectures at Intel. The caches of AMD processors have historically been exclusive, and our covert channel is likely not to work with these processors. However, inclusive caches seem to be a recent trend at AMD. Indeed, they were recently introduced in the new low-power microarchitecture named Jaguar. As Wu et al. [26] note, cache-based covert channels also need to be on the same processor. On a machine with two processors, two virtual machines are on average half the time on the same processor. Such a setting would introduce transmission errors. These errors may be handled by implementing error correcting codes or some synchronization between the receiver and the sender. In any case the bitrate of our covert channel would be reduced.

In a public cloud setup such as on Amazon EC2, several factors may impact the performance and applicability of the C5 covert channel. First, the sender and receiver must be co-resident, *i.e.*, run on the same hardware and hypervisor despite the virtual machine placement policy of the cloud provider. Ristenpart et al. [23] showed that it is possible to achieve co-residency on Amazon EC2. A test is also required to determine co-residency; the assigned IP addresses, the round-trip times [23] and clock-skews [16,17] help establish if two machines are co-resident or not. Second, the hypervisor, and in particular the associated vCPU scheduler, may have an impact on performances. Amazon EC2 relies on a customized version of Xen. The exact scheduler used is unknown. As a consequence, the results obtained in our lab experiments using Xen cannot be translated as is to a cloud setting. We expect the performance to be degraded in a cloud environment.

Similarly, we expect the error rate to increase in presence of a high non-participating workload, as it is the case with other cache covert channels [27]. The resulting error rate depends on the memory footprint of the workload, the core on which it executes, and on its granularity of execution compared to the transmission delay of the message.

5.2   Mitigation

Several papers focus on mitigating cache-based side channels, at the software and hardware levels. We review some of these solutions to determine if they also apply to the mitigation of covert channels.

Domnister et al. [5] propose to modify the replacement policy in the cache controller. Their cache design prevents a thread from evicting lines that belong to other threads. Although they state that L2/L3 attacks and defense are out of the scope of their paper, if the policy is applied to the LLC, the sender cannot evict all lines of the receiver, so it may partially mitigate our covert channel too. However, the performance degradation of the method on L1 cache is about 1 % on average, up to 5 % on some benchmarks. The mitigation might impact even more the performances if done also on the LLC. Wang and Lee [25] propose two new cache architectures. The Partition Locked Cache avoid cache interference by locking cache lines, and preventing processes from evicting cache lines of sensitive programs. Changes to the system are necessary to manage which lines should be locked, and would target specific programs, so it may not mitigate our covert channel. The Random Permutation Cache randomizes the interferences such that information about cache timings is useless to the attacker. It is done by creating permutations tables so that the memory-to-cache-sets mapping are not the same for sensitive programs as for others. However, our covert channel is agnostic to this mapping since we target the whole cache, so this solution may not mitigate our covert channel. These hardware-based solutions are currently not implemented.

Zhang et al. [31] designed a countermeasure for side channels in the cloud. The guest VM itself repeatedly cleans the L1 cache. This introduces noise on the timing measurements of the attacker, thus rendering them useless. As the mitigation is only performed on the L1 cache, it may not mitigate our covert channel that exploits the LLC. Furthermore, applying this countermeasure to the whole cache hierarchy would lead to an important performance penalty, as this would nullify the purpose of the cache.

The above mitigations do not take into account the specificities of the C5 covert channel. Exclusive caches, generally used by AMD processors, mitigate our covert channel as it prevents the LLC from invalidating sets of private L1 caches. Other mitigations might be implemented in the context of virtualization. Similar to Kim et al. [15], the hypervisor can partition the LLC such that each virtual machine works on dedicated sets within the LLC. This way the sender cannot evict the lines of the receiver that is running in a different virtual machine. Of course these mitigations might degrade the overall performance of the system. These mitigations are subject of future work.

6 Related Work

Covert channels using caches have been known for a long time. Hu [9] in 1992 is the first to consider the use of cache to perform cross-process leakage via covert channels. Covert channels in the cloud were introduced by Ristenpart et al. [23] in 2009, and were thus performed on older generations of processors. In particular, it was not possible to perform a cross core channel using the cache. Ristenpart et al. built a covert channel for Amazon EC2, based on L2 cache contention that uses a variant of *prime+probe* [19,21]. Despite its low bitrate of 0.2bps, this covert channel shows deficiencies in the isolation of virtual machines in Amazon EC2. However, this covert channel has some limitations: the sender and receiver must synchronize and share the same core. Xu et al. [27] quantify the achievable bit rate of such a covert channel: they reach 215bps in lab condition, but only 3bps in the cloud. The dramatic drop is due to the fact that the covert channel does not work across cores, and thus the channel design has to take into account core migration. In contrast with these works, we leverage the properties of modern hardware to build a covert channel that works across cores.

To make cache-based covert channels across cores in a virtual environment, the protocol has to resolve or bypass the issues brought by *addressing uncertainty*. Wu et al. [26] observe that the data transmission scheme has to be purely time-based. This contrasts with the covert channel designed by Percival [21] for a native environment that used cache regions to encode information. To illustrate the time-based transmission scheme, Wu et al. propose a cache-based covert channel for which the sender and receiver are not scheduled in a round-robin fashion, but simultaneously. However, the sender and receiver have to agree on a set to work on, which ignores the addressing issue. Their experiment has been tested on a non-virtualized environment, and on a CPU with an older microarchitecture that does not feature complex addressing. They further assume that cache-based covert channels are impractical due to the need of a shared cache. However, modern processors – including those used by Amazon – have all the right properties that make cache-based covert channels practical, and thus this assumption needs to be revisited. Moreover, complex addressing on the LLC is now a common feature. The main contribution of Wu et al. is a new covert channel that is based on the memory bus, using the lock instructions, that works across processors. Their experiment performed in the cloud obtains a bitrate of over 100 bps.

To bypass the *addressing uncertainty*, Yarom and Falkner [28] rely on deduplication offered by the hypervisor. With deduplication, common pages use the same cache lines. They build a side channel on the GnuPG implementation of RSA and extract more than 90 % of the key in a cross-VM attack. They use the clflush instruction that flushes a line from the whole cache hierarchy, and also exploit the inclusive feature of LLC caches. This attack has also been used to target AES in a cross-VM setting [14]. However, using deduplication imposes constraints on the platform where the attack can be performed. For instance, to the best of our knowledge, the Xen version used in Amazon EC2 does not allow deduplication. Thus the attacks [14,28] do not work on Amazon EC2. In contrast with these papers, we tackle the *addressing uncertainty* without any shared memory. Hund et al. [10] resolve the addressing uncertainty by reverse engineering the function that maps a physical address to a slice in order to circumvent the kernel space ASLR. While this is a first step to resolve the addressing uncertainty brought by complex addressing on modern processors, the authors only reversed the function for a given Sandy Bridge processor. It is unknown if the function differs for processors of the same micro-architecture, or for processors of different micro-architecture. Our covert channel is agnostic to this function, hence it applies to a large range of modern processors.

Most covert channels are used in offensive scenarios. Zhang et al. [29] propose to use cache covert channels in a defensive scenario. The goal is to detect the co-residency of foe virtual machines on a physical machine that is supposed to be exclusively owned by a user. The user coordinates its VMs to silence them, avoiding using portions of the cache.

7   Conclusion

Virtualized setups are becoming ubiquitous with the adoption of cloud computing. Moreover, modern hardware tends to increase the number of cores per processor. The cross-core and cross virtual machines properties become mandatory for covert channels. In this paper, we built the C5 covert channel that transfers messages across different cores of the same processor. Our covert channel tackles *addressing uncertainty* that is in particular introduced by hypervisors and complex addressing. In contrast to previous work, our covert channel does not require any shared memory. All these properties make our covert channel fast and practical.

We analyzed the root causes that enable this covert channel, *i.e.*, microarchitectural features such as the shared last level cache, and the inclusive feature of the cache hierarchy. We experimentally evaluated the covert channel in native and virtualized environments. We successfully established a covert channel between virtual machines despite the CPU scheduler of the hypervisor. We measured a bitrate one order of magnitude above previous cache based covert channels in the same setup.

Future work will investigate specific countermeasures against the C5 covert channel. Countermeasures should be investigated at different levels, ranging from the microarchitectural features of processors to the memory management of the hypervisor.

References

1. Acıçmez, O.: Yet another microarchitectural attack: exploiting i-cache. In: Proceedings of the 1st ACM Computer Security Architecture Workshop (CSAW 2007) (2007)
2. Acıçmez, O., Koç, Ç.K., Seifert, J.-P.: Predicting secret keys via branch prediction. In: Abe, M. (ed.) CT-RSA 2007. LNCS, vol. 4377, pp. 225–242. Springer, Heidelberg (2006)
3. Amazon Web Services. Amazon EC2 Instances. https://aws.amazon.com/ec2/instance-types/. Accessed 21 April 2015
4. Bernstein, D.J.: Cache-timing attacks on AES. Statistics, and Computer Science, Technical report, Department of Mathematics, University of Illinois at Chicago (2005)
5. Domnitser, L., Jaleel, A., Loew, J., Abu-Ghazaleh, N., Ponomarev, D.: Non-monopolizable caches: low-complexity mitigation of cache side channel attacks. ACM Trans. Archit. Code Optim. (TACO) **8**(4) (2011)
6. Ester, M., Kriegel, H.-P., Sander, J., Xu, X.: A density-based algorithm for discovering clusters in large spatial databases with noise. In: Proceedings of 2nd International Conference on Knowledge Discovery and Data Mining (KDD 1996) (1996)
7. Farley, B., Varadarajan, V., Bowers, K.D., Juels, A., Ristenpart, T., Swift, M.M.: More for your money: exploiting performance heterogeneity in public clouds. In: Proceedings of the 3rd ACM Symposium on Cloud Computing (SOCC 2012) (2012)
8. Gullasch, D., Bangerter, E., Krenn, S.: Cache games - bringing access-based cache attacks on AES to practice. In: S&P 2011 (2011)
9. Hu, W.-M.: Lattice scheduling and covert channels. In: Proceedings of the IEEE Symposium on Security and Privacy, pp. 52–61 (1992)
10. Hund, R., Willems, C., Holz, T.: Practical timing side channel attacks against kernel space ASLR. In: 2013 IEEE Symposium on Security and Privacy, pp. 191–205 (2013)
11. Intel. How to Benchmark Code Execution Times on Intel IA-32 and IA-64 Instruction Set Architectures White Paper (2010)
12. Intel. Intel 64 and IA-32 Architectures Optimization Reference Manual (2014)
13. Apecechea, G.I., Inci, M.S., Eisenbarth, T., Sunar, B.: Fine grain Cross-VM Attacks on Xen and VMware are possible! Cryptology ePrint Archive, Report 2014/248 (2014)
14. Irazoqui, G., Inci, M.S., Eisenbarth, T., Sunar, B.: Wait a minute! a fast, cross-VM attack on AES. In: Stavrou, A., Bos, H., Portokalidis, G. (eds.) RAID 2014. LNCS, vol. 8688, pp. 299–319. Springer, Heidelberg (2014)
15. Kim, T., Peinado, M., Mainar-Ruiz, G.: StealthMem: system-level protection against cache-based side channel attacks in the cloud. In: Proceedings of the 21st USENIX Security Symposium (2012)
16. Kohno, T., Broido, A., Claffy, K.: Remote physical device fingerprinting. IEEE Trans. Dependable Secure Comput. **2**, 93–108 (2005)
17. Murdoch, S.J.: Hot or not: revealing hidden services by their clock skew. In: CCS 2006 (2006)
18. Neve, M., Seifert, J.-P.: Advances on access-driven cache attacks on AES. In: Biham, E., Youssef, A.M. (eds.) SAC 2006. LNCS, vol. 4356, pp. 147–162. Springer, Heidelberg (2007)
19. Osvik, D.A., Shamir, A., Tromer, E.: Cache attacks and countermeasures: the case of AES. In: Pointcheval, D. (ed.) CT-RSA 2006. LNCS, vol. 3860, pp. 1–20. Springer, Heidelberg (2006)

20. Ou, Z., Zhuang, H., Nurminen, J.K., Ylä-Jääski, A., Hui, P.: Exploiting hardware heterogeneity within the same instance type of amazon EC2. In: HotCloud 2012 (2012)
21. Percival, C.: Cache missing for fun and profit. In: Proceedings of BSDCan (2005)
22. Qureshi, M.K., Jaleel, A., Patt, Y.N., Steely, S.C., Emer, J.: Adaptive insertion policies for high performance caching. ACM SIGARCH Comput. Archit. News **35**(2), 381 (2007)
23. Ristenpart, T., Tromer, E., Shacham, H., Savage, S.: Hey, you, get off of my cloud: exploring information leakage in third-party compute clouds. In: CCS 2009 (2009)
24. Tromer, E., Osvik, D.A., Shamir, A.: Efficient cache attacks on AES, and counter-measures. J. Cryptol. **23**(1), 37–71 (2010)
25. Wang, Z., Lee, R.B.: New cache designs for thwarting software cache-based side channel attacks. ACM SIGARCH Comput. Archit. News **35**(2), 494 (2007)
26. Wu, Z., Xu, Z., Wang, H.: Whispers in the hyper-space: high-speed covert channel attacks in the cloud. In: USENIX Security Symposium (2012)
27. Xu, Y., Bailey, M., Jahanian, F., Joshi, K., Hiltunen, M., Schlichting, R.: An exploration of L2 cache covert channels in virtualized environments. In: Proceedings of the 3rd ACM Cloud Computing Security Workshop (CCSW 2011) (2011)
28. Yarom, Y., Falkner, K.: Flush+reload: a high resolution, low noise, L3 cache side-channel attack. In: USENIX Security Symposium (2014)
29. Zhang, Y., Juels, A., Oprea, A., Reiter, M.K.: Homealone: co-residency detection in the cloud via side-channel analysis. In: S&P 2011 (2011)
30. Zhang, Y., Juels, A., Reiter, M.K., Ristenpart, T.: Cross-VM side channels and their use to extract private keys. In: CCS 2012 (2012)
31. Zhang, Y., Reiter, M.: Düppel: retrofitting commodity operating systems to mitigate cache side channels in the cloud. In: CCS 2013 (2013)

Attack Detection

Intrusion Detection for Airborne Communication Using PHY-Layer Information

Martin Strohmeier[1]([✉]), Vincent Lenders[2], and Ivan Martinovic[1]

[1] University of Oxford, Oxford, UK
martin.strohmeier@cs.ox.ac.uk
[2] Armasuisse, Thun, Switzerland

Abstract. With passenger and cargo traffic growing rapidly worldwide, and unmanned aerial vehicles (UAV) poised to enter commercial airspaces, a secure next generation of air traffic management systems is required. Recent articles in the academic and hacker community highlight crucial security challenges faced by integral parts of these next generation protocols, with the most dangerous attacks based on classic message injection. In this article, we analyze the possibility and effectiveness of detecting such attacks on critical air traffic infrastructures with a single receiver based on physical layer information. Using hypothesis testing and anomaly detection schemes, we develop an intrusion detection system (IDS) that can accurately detect attackers within 40 s.

1 Introduction

The air traffic load has experienced tremendous growth over the last decade. The reported average number of registered flight movements over Europe is around 26,000 per day. Large European airports may spike to more than 1,500 daily takeoffs and landings. This tendency is still increasing and forecasts assume that movements will nearly double between 2009 and 2030. With growing adoption of unmanned aerial vehicle technology for civil applications, we may even expect an additional boost in overall air traffic over the coming years.

The Automatic Dependent Surveillance-Broadcast (ADS-B) protocol is a crucial part of the procedural improvements of the next generation of air traffic management. In less dense airspaces above large unpopulated areas such as in Canada, Australia, or the Atlantic Ocean, ADS-B is already the only means of air traffic surveillance today. With single sensors providing a coverage radius of up to 400 km, the system offers not only high accuracy but is also very cost-efficient. Both of these features are strong drivers of a quick adoption and the use of ADS-B will be mandatory by 2017 in Europe and 2020 in the US. However, the protocol is also widely considered to be insecure by hacker and academic communities and by practitioners because of its lack of authentication. Consequently, recent high-profile cases of aircraft incidents such as the disappearance of Malaysian aircraft MH370 or hijacked emergency signals created a lot of speculation about insecure air traffic control (ATC) protocols [3,8].

© Springer International Publishing Switzerland 2015
M. Almgren et al. (Eds.): DIMVA 2015, LNCS 9148, pp. 67–77, 2015.
DOI: 10.1007/978-3-319-20550-2_4

Due to decade-long roll out and planning times for new protocols and related prohibitive costs, there is currently no upgrade on the horizon which could address the security flaws of ADS-B in the foreseeable future. Taking the former into account, there is an urgent need for separate, transparent countermeasures that do not require modifications to the current ADS-B systems but can significantly improve the real-world security of the protocol.

In this paper, we make the following contributions:

- We develop an IDS based on physical layer measurements to detect false-data injection attacks into ATC networks in less than 40 s without additional cooperation by the aircraft or infrastructure overhead.
- We analyse different features based on statistical tests and combine them into a unified approach using one-class anomaly detection.
- We validate our system against real-world data from our OpenSky sensor network and simulated attackers conducting message injection attacks.

Related Work. There are several works that use statistical testing of received signal strength (RSS) patterns to detect attackers in wireless networks but to the best of our knowledge, this work is the first to apply such techniques in the unique aircraft domain. The works most similar to ours are [2] and [12]. In [2], the authors consider attacks on RSS-based wireless localization systems in WiFi and ZigBee. Their models use statistical hypothesis testing to detect significant deviations from the expected RSS readings of the landmarks used for localization. While we also utilize statistical tests in our IDS, the aircraft location problem is different since an attacker does not use signal strength to change the outcome of the localization but directly injects messages with false data. In [12], the authors use RSS patterns to detect the spoofing of a MAC address, which shares some similarities to spoofing identities with ADS-B. They analyze antenna diversity and use it to improve on the examined detection algorithms.

In contrast to LANs, in our work we exploit the location data encoded in ADS-B, and the large velocities and distances found in air traffic. While RSS is a difficult property in settings without line-of-sight (LOS) that are affected by multi-path, the LOS propagation of air traffic communication provides sound conditions for physical layer schemes. Furthermore, we go beyond statistical tests and apply an anomaly detection approach that can integrate arbitrary features.

2   Overview of ADS-B Security Concerns

In this section, we give a short overview of the ADS-B protocol, its known security flaws and non-technical considerations about potential solutions.

The ADS-B Protocol. Currently rolled out into all major airspaces, and mandatory by 2017 (Europe) / 2020 (USA), ADS-B is a satellite-based replacement of traditional primary and secondary surveillance radar systems. Aircraft use onboard satellite navigation (e.g., GPS) to fetch their own position and velocity; these and other relevant data are periodically transmitted by the *ADS-B Out* subsystem. The broadcasted messages are processed by ATC ground stations, and in the future also by other aircraft close by, if equipped with *ADS-B In* (see Fig. 1 for an illustration).

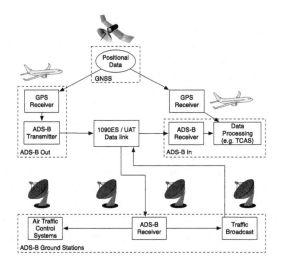

Fig. 1. ATC system architecture. [14] The position provided by the global navigation satellite system (GNSS) is processed by the aircraft and broadcasted through the ADS-B Out system alongside other situational information. ATC ground stations and other aircraft (via ADS-B In) receive these messages over the two possible data links, 1090 Extended Squitter (1090 ES) or Universal Access Transceiver (UAT).

Security Overview. In recent years, ADS-B's susceptibility to radio frequency attacks has generated a lot of attention in hacker circles [4,6], the mainstream media [15], and among academic researchers [7,10]. It has been shown that an attacker can easily record and analyze the unencrypted ADS-B messages. Worse, an adversary actively interfering with ATC communication poses a severe threat to aviation safety. As adversarial action on the ADS-B data link can also impact the traffic collision avoidance system (TCAS), it is crucial to deploy countermeasures promptly to facilitate widespread deployment of the protocol.

When the ADS-B protocol was designed in the early 1990 s, precise manipulation of radio frequency communication was possible only for powerful military adversaries. The required cost and engineering knowledge were considered too prohibitive to add security mechanisms to the protocol. With the recent advent of cheap, accessible software-defined radios and specialized hardware for the reception of ATC communication, the threat model has shifted considerably. Today, typical wireless attacks such as eavesdropping, jamming and modification, insertion and deletion of messages are feasible for anyone with widely available off-the-shelf hard- and software (see, e.g., [4,7,10]). For a full overview of such attacks and their potential impact, and also possible ways to address these vulnerabilities, see [13]. Here, we focus on the insertion of fake data into radar systems as detailed in the next section. Crucially, all proposed countermeasures require either upgrades to the protocol or a large number of sensors to facilitate physical layer defenses such as passive localization. These characteristics make them unsuitable in many scenarios due to some non-technical considerations:

Legacy Requirements. A viable security design for ADS-B must not require changes to the existing protocol, or additional cooperation from the aircraft. This legacy requirement is common to slow-changing industries such as aviation. ADS-B, for example, has been in development since the early 1990 s and is only now being deployed, more than two decades later. Hence, countermeasures against ADS-B attacks need to work alongside the current system without disrupting it.

Cost Effectiveness. Cost is considered a main driver for the adoption of new ATC protocols. Conventional radar technologies are both more expensive to deploy and experience much higher maintenance cost compared to ADS-B. The International Civil Aviation Organization (ICAO) specifies the technological cost of operating traditional radar techniques to monitor an en-route airspace at $6–14 million, while ADS-B surveillance comes in significantly cheaper at $380,000 [5]. The ability to rely solely on ADS-B data would be very cost effective. This is a crucial argument, especially considering the massive investments already made during the development of ADS-B. Countermeasures requiring a large number of stations also negate this cost advantage and ignore the reality of ATC deployments in Canada, Australia or over oceans, where single sensors cover a radius up to the radio horizon of about 400 km.

The Case for Intrusion Detection. As argued in [13] and [14], we believe that given the current state of the ADS-B roll out, there is a strong need for transparent countermeasures as cryptographic means are not a feasible option in the medium term due to the requirements discussed above. Air traffic management as a critical infrastructure system has many characteristics of supervisory control and data acquisition (SCADA) systems. Cardenas et al. [1] note that threats on these systems need to be dealt with by defense-in-depth mechanisms and anomaly detection schemes. They argue an adversary may hide the *specific* exploits but cannot conceal their ulterior goals and intentions. Indeed, there must be a noticeable adverse effect to the *physical* system (i.e., the management of air traffic), otherwise the attack may even be ignored, e.g., when somebody is simply relaying live ADS-B data.

As such physical effects are achieved through injection of malicious data which does not match the expected behaviour, an anomaly detection system can help with the discovery of the attacker and provide the base for defense-in-depth mechanisms. A high rate of attack detection is at the heart of any such system where non-detection might cause disastrous consequences. However, in the real world low false positive rates are just as crucial. While they can normally be sorted out by using voice communication with the aircraft, constant nagging and false alarms can potentially have an adverse effect on overall system safety.

3   Modeling False-Data Injection Attackers

In the following, we describe the model that an attacker uses to inject false data into an ADS-B target receiver. The injection of false data provides the basis of most of the attacks on the ADS-B system as discussed in the literature [7]. Executed correctly, they are subtle but have devastating effects on the system.

We assume that the attacker injects a ghost aircraft, either collected at an earlier time and replayed, or created from scratch. In both cases, we assume a non-naive attacker who has sufficient knowledge to inject valid-looking messages that are well-formed with reasonable content, withstanding a superficial check.

This means the attacker creates correctly formatted ADS-B messages, covering the expected types (position, velocity, identification) in valid sequential orders and spacings according to the standard specification [9]. We also assume the attacker uses a legitimate ICAO address and reasonable flight parameters (e.g., believable altitude and speed) to create a valid-looking aircraft that cannot be distinguished from a real one using standard ATC procedures.

Signal Strength. We model the attacker's use of different RSS patterns using a single antenna. We assume all attackers are more or less stationary on the ground attacking specific sensors in transmission distance, i.e., we do not consider UAVs. Weather effects on RSS have proven negligible for our use case [14].

- **Attacker 1:** This attacker uses a straight-forward constant sending strength, resulting in a Gaussian distribution due to the noisy nature of the channel. Without loss of generality, we assume the standard settings of a typical software-defined radio with a 100 mW power output and a distance of 500 m to the sensor under attack. This creates a signal with a RSS of about -65 dBm at the receiver; the standard deviation of the random noise is 3.5 dB.
- **Attacker 2:** The RSS is a random variable X, within the limits of the hardware. To simulate a random stationary non-adjusting attacker, we assume the RSS received at the attacked sensor to be fully random within the typical values of legitimate aircraft (in our case, the 5 %/95 % percentiles are -75.60 dBm and -63.54 dBm, respectively).
- **Attacker 3:** This attacker adjusts the sending strength in an attempt to be in line with the position the injected messages are representing to the attacked sensors. More concretely, the attacker knows the position of the receiver with a maximum error of 1 km (mean: 500 m) on which he bases the calculation of the distance to the claimed flight positions.

Our goal is to get an accurate read of legitimate aircraft behavior, enabling us to detect all but the most knowledgeable, powerful and carefully carried out attacks by entities who have perfect knowledge of the IDS and its sensor locations.

4   Intrusion Detection

In this section, we describe the physical layer features that we select for our IDS and how we combine them in a unified detection approach. When receiving ADS-B messages from an aircraft, the ground station can measure and store the RSS. Due to the attacker's positioning on the ground, the measurements of injected ADS-B messages are highly unlikely to match the RSS of legitimate samples. Furthermore, they should be comparably constant over time compared to aircraft covering distances of hundreds of miles in relation to the receiver. Using standard hypothesis testing, an IDS can judge the probability whether a collected RSS sample stems from a legitimate aircraft or not.

Pearson Correlation Coefficient. In physical space, we calculate the Pearson correlation coefficient ρ between the distance (derived from the position claim in the ADS-B messages) and the RSS. Path loss suggests a strong negative relationship in legitimate flights, while an injection attacker who does not adjust the sending strength in line with the claimed distance should show no correlation. Formally, we test the null hypothesis $\mathcal{H}_0$ stating that there is no association between the two variables in the population against the alternative hypothesis $\mathcal{H}_A$, stating that there is a negative association between the two variables in the population:

$$\mathcal{H}_{0:}\ \rho = 0 \tag{1}$$
$$\mathcal{H}_A : \rho < 0 \tag{2}$$

We consider a sample where $\mathcal{H}_0$ is rejected at the 99 % significance level a legitimate flight sample and an attack if the hypothesis is accepted.

Autocorrelation Coefficient. In signal space, we use the autocorrelation coefficient (ACF) to identify attackers that are stationary and/or do not adapt their sending strength. Autocorrelation is the cross-correlation of a signal with itself. It can be used to show that a time series is not random, but instead exhibits significant correlations between the original observations and the same observations shifted backwards by a lag τ. The ACF helps to find repeated patterns such as periodic signals in a noisy channel. Formally, we test the null hypothesis $\mathcal{H}_0$ which states that there is no autocorrelation $R(\tau)$ in the population against the alternative hypothesis $\mathcal{H}_A$, saying that there is a positive autocorrelation:

$$\mathcal{H}_{0:}\ R(\tau) = 0 \tag{3}$$
$$\mathcal{H}_A : R(\tau) > 0 \tag{4}$$

We run these tests for lags 1 to 8 and take their mean to create a single measure for finding autocorrelation significant at the 1 % level. We again consider a sample where $\mathcal{H}_0$ is rejected at the 99 % significance level a legitimate flight sample and an attack if the hypothesis is accepted.

Detection of Multiple Antennas. Legitimate ADS-B-equipped flights send alternatingly using two separate antennas, one on top of the aircraft and one on the bottom, as specified in [9]. This setup creates a behavior that a sophisticated attacker needs to mimic. Figure 2 shows an example of the distinctive RSS patterns. To exploit this feature, we divide the full RSS time series into their two antenna subparts according to their time slots and compare various features that show only on the newly created time series. For example, with 300 samples per flight, we found a difference of around 1.8 dBm ($\sigma = 1.4$) in the means of the two antennas in our sample data. A single-antenna attacker, who does not adapt his sending power to mimic two antennas, is expected to exhibit no significant difference between the RSS of messages in alternating time slots. Based solely on RSS time series, we can identify other differences between a single-antenna user (i.e., an anomaly that would most likely be caused by an attacker) and messages sent out by commercial aircraft:

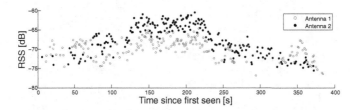

Fig. 2. RSS samples of a flight's two separate antennas.

- The ACF of the divided antenna time series falls much faster than the one by a single-antenna attacker.
- Even lags (2, 4, 6, 8) of the combined ACF are greater than odd lags.
- Similarly, the ACF for a lag of 1 is typically higher for the separated antennas, while for an attacker divided and combined ACF are similar.

Furthermore, we found that separating the antennas first vastly improves the results of the correlation features discussed in this section.

Combined Anomaly Detection. We combine our features in a one-class classification problem. One-class classifiers try to separate one class of data, the target data, from the rest of the feature space. Our target class is a well-sampled class of aircraft behavior based on collected RSS data. The outlier class is unknown and online target samples are used at the time of learning. The process creates an n-dimensional classifier, where n is the number of features. For new samples, this classifier decides if they fit into the expected space or if they are rejected (i.e., classified as an anomaly worth investigating).

5   Experimental Design

First, we analyze the effectiveness of our selected features on their own, using standard hypothesis testing before we combine them with a machine learning approach to create a more robust IDS. We employ the MATLAB toolkits Dd_Tools and PRTools[1] to create data descriptions of our air traffic data. We define one-class datasets based on legitimate data collected with an ADS-B sensor and use various one-class classifiers to create descriptions which include the data.

Fig. 3. Visualization of the 7,159 flight trajectories used for our anomaly analysis.

Data. We used a data sample consisting of 7,159 flights, each flight with 200 or more received messages, collected over 24 hours and visualized in Fig. 3. The data collection was conducted with an OpenSky sensor installed at the top of our lab building. OpenSky is a participatory sensor network that collects raw ADS-B message data and stores them in a database for further research [11].

For our anomaly detection approach, we test several different classifiers with 5-fold cross validation and the fraction of outliers in training set to zero (i.e., all training samples are accepted as legitimate). While the training sets are drawn from our collected sample of legitimate flights only, the separate test sets for each attacker have an added 2 % of falsely-injected data (amounting to 143 flights) to be detected by the classifier. To verify our models and test our IDS, the RSS patterns of the attackers are simulated as described in Sect. 3.

---

[1] See http://prlab.tudelft.nl/david-tax/dd_tools.html and http://prtools.org.

6   Results

Table 1 shows the results of the examined detection approaches. The hypothesis tests each detect attackers 1 and 2 with more than 99 % probability. Especially the autocorrelation feature proves to be accurate, with few legitimate flights misclassified as false positives (0.1 %). As expected, both tests fail to detect the more sophisticated attacker 3. To counter this, we analyze the distinct antenna characteristics, which detects over 90 % of all three attackers with a false positive rate of 3.9 %. On its own, the antenna method requires 300 messages to become reliable enough, as aircraft may move in ways that can obfuscate their antenna features in the short run.

Table 1. Effectiveness of the examined detection approaches. We used 7,159 legitimate flights and 143 simulated attackers for every class, with 200+ messages per flight. The percentages show the average detection rates over 5-fold cross validation.

Detection rate [%]	Attacker 1	Attacker 2	Attacker 3	Legit flights (FPs)
Pearson	99.8	99.9	0.2	18.6
Autocorrelation	99.6	99.4	0.3	0.1
Antenna detection	92.6	94.0	95.5	3.9
Combined detection	100	100	98.8	<0.01

With the combined classifier, we can accurately detect all attackers 1 and 2 without false negatives and one single false positive (less than 0.01 %), using a small RSS sample of 200 messages. At the standard rate of 5.4 ADS-B messages per second, this allows detection in under 40 s, assuming no message loss. Even with a typical loss of 30 % [14], this can be achieved in less than one minute.

As illustrated in Fig. 4(a), attacker 3 who easily deceives the individual hypothesis tests, can be *too* good. He would need to introduce additional randomness and patterns similar to the spoofed airplanes to fall within the expected data range. This demonstrates the strength of the anomaly detection approach where the precise type of anomaly need not be known in advance. The results may see further improvement through the collection of more samples. This naturally increases the confidence of the system and improves detection results at the cost of slower reaction times.

Figure 4(b) shows the results of the comparison between various tested classifiers, depending on the number of samples. The Parzen classifier performs best, having the lowest number of misclassified attackers. It is followed by K-Means, but the Minimax, Minimum Spanning Tree and k-Nearest Neighbors classifiers also achieve a near-zero false negative rate as 200 samples are collected, still significantly improving on pure hypothesis testing.

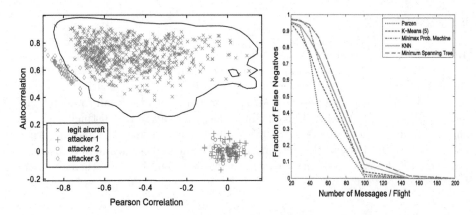

Fig. 4. (a) 2D-Parzen classifier example with 200 collected samples. Red crosses are legitimate flight samples. Attacker 1 and 2 are entirely classified as anomaly here, while attacker 3 creates few false positives. (b) Complete classifier comparison with 5-fold cross validation. Joint false negative rates for attackers 1 + 2.

7 Conclusion and Future Work

In this article, we proposed an IDS for false-data injection attacks on the ADS-B protocol used in air traffic control. We provided a threat model for such injection attacks on ADS-B and developed an IDS based on RSS measurements. We validated our system against real-world data from our OpenSky sensor network and found that the Parzen classifier performed best in our sample. In future work, we plan to analyze more sophisticated attackers, additional features to deal with them such as the angle of arrival, and the long-term stability of our system.

References

1. Cardenas, A.A., Amin, S., Lin, Z.S., Huang, Y.L., Huang, C.Y., Sastry, S.: Attacks against process control systems: risk assessment, detection, and response. In: Proceedings of the 6th ACM Symposium on Information, Computer and Communications Security, pp. 355–366. ACM (2011)
2. Chen, Y., Xu, W., Trappe, W., Zhang, Y.: Attack detection in wireless localization. In: Chen, Y., Xu, W., Trappe, W., Zhang, Y. (eds.) Securing Emerging Wireless Systems, pp. 1–22. Springer, USA (2009)
3. Clayton, M.: Malaysia airlines flight MH370: are planes vulnerable to cyber-attack? Christian Science Monitor, March 2014
4. Costin, A., Francillon, A.: Ghost in the air (Traffic): on insecurity of ADS-B protocol and practical attacks on ADS-B devices. In: Black Hat. USA (2012)
5. ICAO: Guidance Material on Comparison of Surveillance Technologies (GMST). Technical report, September 2007
6. Kunkel, R.: Air traffic control insecurity 2.0. In: DefCon 18 (2010)
7. McCallie, D., Butts, J., Mills, R.: Security analysis of the ADS-B implementation in the next generation air transportation system. Int. J. Crit. Infrastruct. Prot. **4**(2), 78–87 (2011)

8. Moran, N., De Vynck, G.: Westjet hijack signal called false alarm. Bloomberg, January 2015
9. RTCA Inc.: Minimum Operational Performance Standards for 1090 MHz Extended Squitter Automatic Dependent Surveillance - Broadcast (ADS-B) and Traffic Information Services - Broadcast (TIS-B). DO-260B with Corrig. 1 (2011)
10. Schäfer, M., Lenders, V., Martinovic, I.: Experimental analysis of attacks on next generation air traffic communication. In: Jacobson, M., Locasto, M., Mohassel, P., Safavi-Naini, R. (eds.) ACNS 2013. LNCS, vol. 7954, pp. 253–271. Springer, Heidelberg (2013)
11. Schäfer, M., Strohmeier, M., Lenders, V., Martinovic, I., Wilhelm, M.: Bringing up opensky: a large-scale ADS-B sensor network for research. In: ACM/IEEE International Conference on Information Processing in Sensor Networks (2014)
12. Sheng, Y., Tan, K., Chen, G., Kotz, D., Campbell, A.: Detecting 802.11 MAC layer spoofing using received signal strength. In: The 27th Conference on Computer Communications. INFOCOM 2008. IEEE (2008)
13. Strohmeier, M., Lenders, V., Martinovic, I.: On the security of the automatic dependent surveillance-broadcast protocol. Communications Surveys Tutorials PP(99). IEEE (2014)
14. Strohmeier, M., Schäfer, M., Lenders, V., Martinovic, I.: Realities and challenges of nextgen air traffic management: the case of ADS-B. Commun. Mag. **52**(5), 111–118 (2014)
15. Zetter, K.: Air traffic controllers pick the wrong week to quit using radar. In: Wired, July 2012

That Ain't You: Blocking Spearphishing Through Behavioral Modelling

Gianluca Stringhini[1]([✉]) and Olivier Thonnard[2]

[1] University College London, London, UK
g.stringhini@ucl.ac.uk
[2] Amadeus, Sophia Antipolis, France
olivier.thonnard@amadeus.com

Abstract. One of the ways in which attackers steal sensitive information from corporations is by sending *spearphishing* emails. A typical spearphishing email appears to be sent by one of the victim's coworkers or business partners, but has instead been crafted by the attacker. A particularly insidious type of spearphishing emails are the ones that do not only claim to be written by a certain person, but are also sent by that person's email account, which has been compromised. Spearphishing emails are very dangerous for companies, because they can be the starting point to a more sophisticated attack or cause intellectual property theft, and lead to high financial losses. Currently, there are no effective systems to protect users against such threats. Existing systems leverage adaptations of anti-spam techniques. However, these techniques are often inadequate to detect spearphishing attacks. The reason is that spearphishing has very different characteristics from spam and even traditional phishing. To fight the spearphishing threat, we propose a change of focus in the techniques that we use for detecting malicious emails: instead of looking for features that are indicative of attack emails, we look for emails that claim to have been written by a certain person within a company, but were actually authored by an attacker. We do this by modelling the email-sending behavior of users over time, and comparing any subsequent email sent by their accounts against this model. Our approach can block advanced email attacks that traditional protection systems are unable to detect, and is an important step towards detecting advanced spearphishing attacks.

1 Introduction

Spearphishing has become one of the most common ways used by attackers to infiltrate the network of a company, gain access to additional machines in it, or acquire sensitive information. For this type of attack, an email is crafted and sent to a specific person within a company, with the goal of infecting her machine with malware, luring her to hand out access credentials or to provide sensitive information. Recent research showed that spearphishing is a real threat, and that large companies are constantly targeted by this type of attack [37].

In a typical case, spearphishing emails appear to be coming from accounts within the same company or coming from a trusted party, to avoid raising suspicion by the victim [39]. This can be done in a trivial way, by forging the `From:`

© Springer International Publishing Switzerland 2015
M. Almgren et al. (Eds.): DIMVA 2015, LNCS 9148, pp. 78–97, 2015.
DOI: 10.1007/978-3-319-20550-2_5

field in the attack email. In more sophisticated attacks, however, the malicious emails are sent from an actual employee's email account whose machine has been compromised, or whose account credentials have been stolen. For the attacker, this modus operandi has the advantage that it leverages a user's social connections: previous research showed that users are more likely to fall for scams if the offending message is sent by somebody they trust [16]. Spearphishing attacks are particularly insidious for companies, because they can lead to large-scale compromises in their networks and to high financial losses, due to the sensitive information that might get stolen as a consequence of them [1,2].

Spearphishing is not Spam. The techniques that are currently used to detect spearphishing attacks are totally inadequate to counter them. Nowadays, the systems used to detect spearphishing attacks leverage traditional anti-spam techniques. However, these techniques were designed with a different threat model in mind: blocking unwanted bulk email. Adaptations of anti-spam techniques are not effective in fighting the spearphishing threat mainly for three reasons.

The first reason is that many anti-spam techniques are designed to fight bulk email, typically sent by botnets, and therefore leverage *similarity*. Techniques that leverage the similarities in the email templates or fingerprint the email lists to which bots send emails [24,32,43] work well in detecting spam and bot-infected machines, but fall short in detecting one-of-a-kind targeted email attacks, in which an attacker crafts an email tailored to the victim, and sends it only once. Even systems that look for changes of behavior in email accounts leverage the fact that accounts compromised by the same cybercriminals will show a similar behavior [10,29,30].

The second reason is that the *origin* of spearphishing emails is often times the correct one: there are numerous techniques that can detect emails sent by senders with a low reputation, and block them [14,20,41,42]. However, if the attack email is coming from a reputable user's mailbox, whose machine has been compromised, these techniques will fail in detecting that email as malicious.

The third reason is that the words used in advanced targeted attack emails are the ones that are typically used in regular business emails. Therefore, techniques that analyze the email content, looking for words that are indicative of spam [9,22,27], are ineffective too. Moreover, even if malicious code is used in the email attachment, these binaries will not be off-the-shelf malware samples, and will therefore be unknown to traditional anti-virus and signature-based systems.

A New Paradigm in Fighting Attack Emails. Given how different spearphishing emails are compared to traditional spam and phishing emails, we propose a new detection paradigm to fight this threat. Instead of looking for signs of maliciousness in emails (such as offending words or suspicious origin) we want to determine if an email was actually written by the author that it claims to come from. Our approach is based on a simple, yet effective observation: users develop habits when sending emails. These habits include frequent interactions with certain people, sending emails at specific hours of the day, and using certain greetings and modal words in their emails. The core of our approach consists in building a profile for the email-sending behavior of a user. When the user's account gets compromised, the attack emails that are sent are likely to show differences from this behavioral profile. We implemented our approach in a system, called IDENTITYMAILER.

Anomalies can be more or less evident. An example of a "noisy" attack is a worm that sends an email to the entire address book of a user [38], which is a behavior that typical users do not show. In other cases, attackers might be more careful, and try to mimic the typical behavior of the person that they are impersonating in their emails. What they could do is sending emails only at hours in which the user is typically sending them, and only to those people she frequently interacts with, or even imitate the user's writing style.

To make it more difficult for attackers to successfully evade IDENTITY-MAILER, we build the email-sending behavior for a user by leveraging both the emails that the user sent in the past and a set of emails that the other users in the organization authored. In a nutshell, IDENTITYMAILER compares the emails written by the user to the ones written by everybody else, and extracts those characteristics that are the most representative of the user's behavior. For example, certain functional words only used by a given user (and rarely by others) would model her behavior very well. When an attacker tries to learn a victim's sending behavior to mimic it in his attack emails, he only has access to that user's emails (since he compromised her account, or her machine), but not to the ones authored by the other users in the company. Therefore, what he can do is learning the most common habits of the user (such as the email address that is more frequently contacted, and at what time the user generally sends emails), but he has no guarantee that those traits are actually representative of the user's behavior. For example, most people send many emails on Monday morning, after they come back to the office from the weekend. Our system would give a low importance to this fact, since many users show the same behavior. On the other hand, there might be some times at which the user is the only one sending emails. Even if they are not that common, those emails are more representative of the user's behavior. However, an attacker has no way of knowing this, and might replicate the most common behavior in his attack emails.

IDENTITYMAILER performs the analysis when emails are sent, before they are forwarded to the outgoing SMTP server. More specifically, IDENTITYMAILER builds a behavioral profile based on the emails that a user sent in the past (and a set of emails authored by the other people in the organization). Then, every time an email is sent by that account, IDENTITYMAILER checks this email against the profile learned for the account's owner. If the email does not match the learned profile, we consider it anomalous. The account might have been compromised, and the email might actually be an attempted attack. However, the anomaly might also be a false positive. Perhaps the user is working on a deadline, and is sending emails late at night, or is sending a personal email, and using a colloquial language, while the account is primarily used to send work-related emails. False positives are a big problem in traditional anti-spam systems, because they annoy users in the best case, and they prevent them from receiving important information in the worst case.

Luckily, the fact that IDENTITYMAILER operates on the sending side of the email process comes to our aid. Any time an email is flagged as anomalous, we can start a process to verify the identity of a user. This process might be asking the user to answer a security question or some more sophisticated mechanism, such as a two-factor authentication scheme [6]. If the user correctly confirms her identity, we consider the anomaly as a false positive, and we send the email. In addition, we update the user's behavioral profile to include this email, to avoid similar false positives in the future. However, if the user does not solve the challenge, we consider the email as an attack, and we discard it. Of course, having to go through an identity-verification process is annoying for users. However, we think that having users confirm their identity once in a while is a fair price to pay to protect a company against advanced email attacks, as long as the verifications are rare enough (for example, one in every 30 emails).

In summary, this paper makes the following contributions:

- We present IDENTITYMAILER, a novel approach to detect spearphishing emails: instead of looking for signs of maliciousness, we introduce a set of features that are representative of the email-sending behavior of a user, and propose a method to check emails against the learned sending behavior.
- We propose to leverage an identity-verification mechanism to mitigate false positives by IDENTITYMAILER. We argue that such verification process, if reasonably rare, is acceptable for users.
- We tested IDENTITYMAILER on a large dataset of publicly-available emails, as well as on multiple datasets of attack emails. We show that IDENTITYMAILER works well in detecting attack emails.

2 Behavioral Profiles

It is important to accurately learn and model the email-sending behavior of a user, because this allows to perform a better detection of anomalous emails. However, it is not trivial to define user-specific traits that best distinguish a user's sending behavior. To determine these traits, IDENTITYMAILER requires two datasets: a set $\mathbf{M}_u$ of emails written by a user U and a set $\mathbf{M}_o$ of legitimate emails written by other people. By comparing the emails in $\mathbf{M}_u$ to the ones in $\mathbf{M}_o$, we can extract the distinguishing characteristics of the email-sending behavior of U.

$\mathbf{M}_o$ should be composed of both emails sent by people working in the same organization as U, as well as of emails written by people who are completely unrelated to U. As we will explain later, the privacy concerns of our approach are minimal, because we do not save the full email, but only a feature vector associated to it. On one side, having $\mathbf{M}_o$ built from the emails sent by the users working in the same organization as U helps in giving less importance to those characteristics that are common for the people who work in that company. For example, if no user in the organization ever sends emails on a Sunday, it is less peculiar if the user also does not. On the other hand, having emails sent by users who are completely unrelated to U in $\mathbf{M}_o$ helps giving to the model examples of which behavioral characteristics are uncommon in the organization, but common outside of it. We provide a more detailed description on how we build $\mathbf{M}_o$ in Sect. 2.2. By using only legitimate emails to build our behavioral profiles, we do not need to have ever observed any attack email to perform detection, similarly to what happens with traditional anomaly-detection systems. This is important, since the number of targeted attack emails is not high compared to legitimate emails [37]. In addition, this makes our approach independent from specific attack schemes.

To build the email-sending behavioral profile for a user, IDENTITYMAILER proceeds in two steps. First, we extract a number of features for each email in $\mathbf{M}_u$ and $\mathbf{M}_o$. As a second step, we leverage the learned feature vectors to build a classification model, which represents the actual behavioral profile. This profile allows us to check any email that the user will send in the future, and determine whether it was likely written by the user, or if it might have been written by somebody else (i.e., a malicious party).

2.1 Features Characterizing an Email

For each email, we define three types of features: *writing habits*, *composition habits*, and *interaction habits*. Previous research showed that authorship identification is possible by just looking at stylometry features (which are a subset of what we call writing habits) [8]. However, these approaches rely on texts of a certain length [12]. Unfortunately, as we show in Sect. 4, many emails are short. If IDENTITYMAILER relied only on the writing habits of a user, it would fail in flagging attack emails that are short as anomalous. Therefore, we need additional information for emails that are short in content. In the following, we describe the features that our approach uses to characterize an email.

Writing Habits. People have their own style when writing. For example, some people use certain functional words (such as "although") more often than others, or write dates in a certain way. Analyzing a user's style has been used in the past to determine authorship of texts and emails [4,8,23]. Similarly, we consider a user's writing style a strong indicator that a certain email was indeed written by that user. An attacker could, in principle, learn the characteristics of his victim's style, and replicate them in the attack emails that she sends. However, previous research showed that imitation of another person's writing style is usually detectable [5].

In the following, we define a number of feature types that help defining a user's writing style. The complete list of writing-habit features can be found in our technical report [33].

(1) Character Occurrence. These features represent how often a character, or a set of characters, appear in the email text. Given a set of characters $\mathbf{C}$ and an email text M, we define the character occurrence of $\mathbf{C}$ in M o_c as the number of times that any of the characters in $\mathbf{C}$ occur in M, divided by the length of M. Examples of character occurrence features include the frequency of alphabetical

letters (such as "a"), the frequency of certain punctuation signs (such as ";"), and the frequency of sets of characters (such as capital letters or cardinal numbers).

(2) Functional Word Occurrence. These features represent how often the person uses specific functional words. We define as functional words those words that do not serve to express content, but instead are used to express grammatical relationships with other words within a sentence. These include adverbs (such as "when"), auxiliary verbs (such as "is"), and prepositions (such as "for"). Some of these features are useful to determine whether a user uses certain functional words in their extended or shortened form, and to what extent (for example, whether she usually uses "don't" instead of "do not"). Given a word FW and a set of words $\mathbf{W}_m$ in an email, we calculate the word occurrence o_{fw} in $\mathbf{W}_m$ as the number of times FW occurs in the email, divided by the size of $\mathbf{W}_m$.

(3) Special Word Occurrence. These features represent how often a user uses certain "special" words in her emails. Special words include full names, dates, and acronyms. Given a regular expression R_{sw} representing the special word, an email M, and a set $\mathbf{W}_m$ containing the words in M, we calculate the special word occurrence o_{sw} of R_{sw} as the number of matches in M for R_{sw}, divided by the size of $\mathbf{W}_m$.

(4) Generic Style Characteristics. These features represent generic characteristics of the style of a user. Examples include the type of bullets that the user uses in lists ("1-", "1.", or others), whether she uses a comma as a separator for large digits or not, and whether she uses a space after punctuation. Given a set of regular expressions $\mathbf{R}_{sc}$ representing a style characteristic, an email M, and a set $\mathbf{W}_m$ containing the words in M, we define the style characteristic s_c as the number of matches of the regular expressions in $\mathbf{R}_{sc}$ in the email M, divided by the size of $\mathbf{W}_m$.

(5) Style Metrics. These features capture information about the style of entire emails. Some features are rather simple, such as the number of paragraphs in the email. Others are more advanced, and depict the expressiveness of the language used in the email. Examples are the *Sichel measure* or the *Yule metric*, which describe how complex the vocabulary used by an author is. These metrics have been already used in previous work [40, 44].

Composition and Sending Habits. Other habits that users develop regarding their email-sending behavior do not have to do with their writing style, but rather with their way of composing emails. In the following, we describe this type of features.

(1) Message Characteristics. These features capture specific habits that the user has in the emails that she writes. Examples of such habits are including the original email at the end of a reply, including quotes to the original email interleaved with the text, or adding a signature at the end of the email. Message-characteristic features are boolean, meaning that they are set to 1 if a certain behavior is present in an email, and to 0 otherwise.

(2) Time Characteristics. Users tend to send emails at specific times of the day, and only during specific days. For example, most people working in an office will send emails between 9 am and 5 pm, from Monday to Friday. Given this observation, an email sent at midnight on a Saturday would be very suspicious. These features keep information about when an email has been sent. In particular, they look at the day of the week and at the hour at which the email was composed. Similarly to other composition-habit features, time-characteristic features are boolean. We define seven features for the days of the week, and 24 features for the hours of the day.

(3) URL Characteristics. Some users include URLs in their emails. Users include links to pages that are needed for their job, or to websites that they consider interesting or entertaining. Over time, the domains of the URLs that a user includes in her emails tend to belong to a limited set (as previous research already noted [10]). On the other hand, if the user sent an email with a URL pointing to a domain that she has never included before, this might be suspicious.

To instantiate URL-characteristic features, we need a set of domains L_u that the user, as well as the other people in her organization, referenced in the past. This helps identifying those resources that are "internal" to the organization (which should be referenced often in the company's emails), and those that are not. We also include an *"other"* feature to take into account those domains that were never referenced by anybody in the organization. Similarly to the other composition-habit features, URL-characteristic features are boolean, and are set to 1 if that domain is referenced in the email, and 0 otherwise.

Interaction Habits. The last type of features involve the social network of a user. Typical users will send most emails to a handful of contacts, who are coworkers or close friends. Having an email sent to an address that was never contacted before might be suspicious, especially if that user does not usually interact with many users.

To characterize the social network of a user, we look, for each email, at the email addresses that the email is addressed to (the To: field), as well as at the addresses that the email is sent to in carbon copy (the CC: field). We define four types of interaction-habit features, representing the addresses and the domains that a user sends emails to. The *recipient address list* features take into account the email addresses that an email is addressed to, while the *recipient domain list* ones look for the domains that those email addresses belong to. The idea behind this distinction is that if a user sends an email to an address that she has never referenced before, but that belongs to an organization that she often interacts with, this is less suspicious than an email addressed to a completely unknown domain. The *carbon copy address list* and the *carbon copy domain list* features work in the same way, but take into account the addresses in the CC: field of the email, rather than the ones in the To: field.

To instantiate the interaction-habit features, we need a list L_a of email addresses that the user, as well as the other people in the same organization, contacted in the past. It is important to look at the email addresses that the user has never contacted, but some of her coworkers have. This is because having a user sending an email to an executive she has never contacted before is very suspicious, and might be a sign of spearphishing. In addition, to account for those addresses and domains with which nobody in the organization has interacted before we add, for each of the four feature types, an *"other"* feature. Similarly, we leverage a list $\mathbf{L}_d$ of domains to which the users in the organization have written emails in the past.

Interaction-habit features are boolean: they are set to 1 if an email is addressed to the address (or domain) represented by a given feature, and to 0 otherwise. If, for any of the four feature types, all features of that type have a value of 0, the *"other"* feature is set to 1.

2.2   Building Behavioral Profiles

To learn the distinguishing characteristics of the email-sending behavior for a user U, IDENTITYMAILER compares the feature vectors built from the emails sent by the user ($\mathbf{M}_u$) to the feature vectors built from a set of legitimate emails sent by other people ($\mathbf{M}_o$). The challenge in picking $\mathbf{M}_o$ is to select a set of emails that is representative enough to make the most characteristic features of the behavior of the user stand out.

Given a user U who wrote a set of emails $\mathbf{M}_u$, we pick the set of emails $\mathbf{M}_o$ as follows. First, for each user U_i in the organization (other than U), we keep a set of emails that U_i has sent in the past. We call this set $\mathbf{M}_{ui}$. In addition, we consider a "special" user U_x. The set of emails $\mathbf{M}_{ux}$ corresponding to the user U_x consists of emails that were not written by the users in the organization. This set of emails could be a subset of the emails that were received by the company's mail server, or a set of publicly-available legitimate emails. Second, for each email in $\mathbf{M}_u$, we pick a random email written by another user U_i and add it to $\mathbf{M}_o$. We change the user U_i for each email in $\mathbf{M}_u$, in a round-robin fashion. By doing this, we ensure that the distribution of emails written by different users in $\mathbf{M}_o$ is uniform.

After having collected $\mathbf{M}_u$ and $\mathbf{M}_o$, we train a classifier to learn the email-sending behavioral profile of user U. To this end, we leverage Support Vector Machines (SVMs) trained with Sequential Minimal Optimization (SMO) [25]. The SMO algorithm is an iterative algorithm used to efficiently solve the optimization problem required for training SVMs. In Sect. 4.2 we analyze the classifier in detail.

Since the email-sending behavior of a user is likely to slightly change over time (for example, as the user makes new social connections), in IDENTITYMAILER we keep updating the behavioral profile, by adding the new emails that the user sends. The identity-verification mechanism that we describe in Sect. 3 allows us to be sure that the emails that we add to the behavioral profile have been genuinely written by the user. Having a behavioral profile that is not static is important also because the behavioral profile for a user gets more accurate as the number of emails sent by the user increases. However, the strength of the model also depends on how consistent a user is in her email-sending habits. As we will discuss in Sect. 4.2, the features that we defined all contribute in defining the email-sending behavior of a user. The weight of the different features actually depends on each user's specific habits, and cannot be generalized.

3   Detecting Anomalous Emails

After having built the email-sending behavioral profile for a user, IDENTITY-MAILER checks any email that the user tries to send against it. To do this, we go through the following algorithm:

Step 1: For each email M that the user U sends, we extract a feature vector $\mathbf{V}_m$.

Step 2: We compare $\mathbf{V}_m$ against the behavioral profile for U, which we call $\mathbf{BP}_u$. If $\mathbf{V}_m$ complies with $\mathbf{BP}_u$, we declare the email as being written by U, and go to step 4. Otherwise, we consider M as anomalous, and go to step 3.

Step 3: To make sure that the email has not been written by the user, we perform an identity-verification process for U. If the user correctly confirms her identity, M is considered as a false positive. We go to step 4. If, on the other hand, the user fails in confirming her identity (or decides not to, because she recognizes an attack), the email is considered as malicious, and discarded. In the next section, we describe how we envision the identity-verification process to happen.

Step 4: We add $\mathbf{V}_m$ to the set of feature vectors that are used to calculate $\mathbf{BP}_u$. This information will be used the next time that the behavioral profile is updated.

It is not necessary to update the behavioral profile for a user for every email that she sends. The reason is that, although the email-sending habits of a user change over time, they do not change that fast. In addition, as we will discuss in Sect. 4.4, updating the behavioral profile for all users may require a certain amount of time and resources. For these reasons, we envision the behavioral profile update as a batch process that could be performed daily or weekly.

Verifying a User's Identity. One of the main challenges that anti-spam systems have to face are false positives. Flagging a legitimate email as spam has a high impact on the user, because it might prevent that user from seeing that email at all. This happens because traditional anti-spam techniques operate on the receiving side of the email process, and often times it is impossible to verify that the sender of an email is who he actually claims to be. Operating on the sending side, on the other hand, has the advantage that we can ask the user whether she intended to send a certain email that looks suspicious, before the emails is actually sent.

In IDENTITYMAILER, we propose to start an identity-verification process when an account tries to send an email that looks anomalous. This verification process might be answering a security question or a more advanced method, such as a text message sent to the user's mobile phone as part of a two-factor authentication process [6]. Each method has advantages and disadvantages. However, analyzing the single identity-verification methods that one could implement goes beyond the scope of this paper. For our purposes, we just assume that, by going through the identity-verification process, the user can prove her identity with a high confidence.

Of course, we are aware that having to go through such a process might annoy users. However, we think that if the number of identity-verification processes that a user has to go through is reasonably low, this is a fair price to pay to significantly increase the security of a company. In Sect. 4.2 we perform an analysis of how often a user would have to go through an identity-verification process, on average, and show that this number is reasonably low.

4   Evaluation

In this section, we evaluate the effectiveness of IDENTITYMAILER. First, we describe the evaluation datasets that we used in our experiments. Then, we perform an analysis of the classifier used to build the email-sending behavioral profiles, and we show how the behavioral profiles built by IDENTITYMAILER are useful to detect attack emails sent by compromised accounts.

4.1   Evaluation Datasets

To test IDENTITYMAILER we leveraged a number of email datasets. First, we leveraged the *Enron corpus* [19] as a large-scale dataset of legitimate emails. This publicly-available dataset contains the emails sent by the executives of a large company, over the time of multiple years. In total, there are 148 users who sent emails in the dataset, for a total of 126,075 emails. The Enron dataset is representative of the type of emails sent in a large corporation (sending times, language, interactions), and this makes it suitable for our testing purposes. In the remainder of the paper, we call this dataset D_1. As a second dataset of legitimate emails we used a set of emails that were donated to a large security company by their customers, for research purposes. This dataset is composed of 1,776 emails. The emails in this dataset are useful to complement D_1 and give diversity. In particular, they are useful to populate M_{ux}, as we explained in Sect. 2.2. We call this dataset D_2. We use the datasets D_1 and D_2 for training purposes. In particular, for each user in D_1, we build an email-sending behavioral profile, by leveraging both the emails in D_1 and in D_2.

For testing purposes, we needed a number of emails sent by compromised accounts, and preferably that were part of a targeted attack. The problem here is that, unlike regular spam, it is not easy to collect a large dataset of such emails. To overcome this problem, we manually selected three datasets of malicious emails. These emails come from a set of malicious messages that were not blocked by the anti-spam software of a large security company, and that were submitted by their customers for checking. The first dataset, that we call S_1, is composed of generic spam emails. Such emails typically advertise goods or services, such as stock trading, pharmaceuticals, and dating sites. The main difference between the emails in

$\mathbf{S}_1$ and common spam is that a state-of-the-art system failed in detecting them as malicious, and therefore we can consider them as "hard" to detect; we test IDENTITYMAILER on this dataset to show that, although the system has not been designed to fight traditional spam, it performs well in detecting it, in case it was sent by compromised email accounts. $\mathbf{S}_1$ is composed of 43,274 emails. The second dataset, that we call $\mathbf{S}_2$, is composed of malicious emails (mostly phishing scams) that were sent by email accounts that had been compromised. We selected these emails by looking at emails in the dataset that were malicious, but that had valid DKIM and/or SPF records [20,42]. In particular, these emails were sent by compromised accounts in the same domain as the customer who submitted them. In total, $\mathbf{S}_2$ contains 17,473 emails. The third dataset, which we call $\mathbf{S}_3$, is a dataset of sophisticated spearphishing emails. Such emails try to lure the user into handing out corporate-specific sensitive information (such as access credentials) to a malicious party, usually via social engineering. As we said, spearphishing emails are particular insidious to companies, because it can lead to high financial losses. $\mathbf{S}_3$ contains 546 emails. The emails in $\mathbf{S}_2$ and $\mathbf{S}_3$ closely resemble the threat model that we are trying to counter with IDENTITYMAILER. In the next sections, we leverage these datasets to evaluate the effectiveness of IDENTITYMAILER.

4.2   Analysis of the Classifier

In this section, we first describe how we selected the features used by IDENTITY-MAILER. Then, we investigate how well these behavioral profiles can determine if an email has been actually written by a user. As a third step, we show that the writing habits are usually not enough to detect whether an email is forged or not.

Instantiation of the Features. As we explained in Sect. 2.1, some of the features used by our approach are specific to the organization in which the system is run. In particular, we need to know which email addresses and domains have been contacted by the users in the organization in the past, as well as the domains that have been referenced in the body of the emails, as part of URLs. We leveraged the dataset $\mathbf{D}_1$ to calculate the sets $\mathbf{L}_u$, $\mathbf{L}_a$, and $\mathbf{L}_d$. In particular, $\mathbf{L}_u$ was composed of 595 domains, $\mathbf{L}_a$ of 22,849 email addresses, and $\mathbf{L}_d$ of 3,000 domains. Note that, in a production environment, the size of $\mathbf{L}_u$, $\mathbf{L}_a$, and $\mathbf{L}_d$ would increase over time, since the users in the company would post more URLs, and contact new people. This means that the number of features used by IDENTITYMAILER increases over time as well. However, this is not a problem, since the auxiliary lists are stored in a centralized location.

Accuracy of the Classifier. To evaluate to what extent the behavioral profiles built by IDENTITYMAILER are representative of the sending behavior of users, we proceeded as follows. First, for each user U in $\mathbf{D}_1$, we extracted the sets $\mathbf{M}_u$ and $\mathbf{M}_o$ for that user, following the algorithm described in Sect. 2.2. As we said, we use the emails sent by U as positive examples, and a mix of emails from $\mathbf{D}_1$ and $\mathbf{D}_2$ as negative examples.

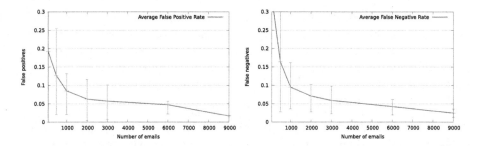

Fig. 1. Analysis of false positives (left) and false negatives (right) on the ten-fold cross validation. The X axis shows the number of emails that a user has sent in the past. As it can be seen, both false positives and false negatives decrease as the user sends more emails.

After having a training set for each user, we performed a 10-fold cross validation on them, to investigate the accuracy of the behavioral profiles generated from them. The 10-fold cross validation gives us an idea of how the system would behave in the wild, while encountering previously-unseen emails. In particular, it gives us an estimate of how many emails written by the user would be flagged as malicious because of a change in behavior by the user, as well as how many attack emails would actually be missed by IDENTITYMAILER. In this experiment, a false positive would indicate an email that was authored by the user, but that IDENTITYMAILER considered as anomalous. In this case, IDENTITYMAILER would have started an identity-verification process for the user, who would have correctly confirmed her identity, and have the email sent. We want the number of false positives to be low, because having to confirm her identity too often would annoy the user. Conversely, a false negative would indicate an email that had been written by somebody else, but that IDENTITYMAILER mistakenly attributed to the user. We want false negatives to be as low as possible, because, in a real scenario, each of them would correspond to an attack that went undetected.

Intuitively, there are two factors that influence the robustness of the behavioral profile for a user. The first factor is the number of emails that a user has sent in the past. Having a larger number of examples of a user's sending style and habits makes the model more representative and less prone to false positives and false negatives. The second factor is how consistent is the sending behavior of a user. A user who always sends emails in the morning, and only to a small fraction of recipients, will be a lot more recognizable than a user who uses her account for both professional and personal use, and quite frequently sends emails at night.

The number of emails sent by the users in D_1 varies substantially. On average, each user in D_1 sent 840 emails, with a standard deviation of 1,345. The largest number of emails sent by a user in D_1 is 8,926. As Fig. 1 shows, the accuracy of the email-sending behavioral profile built by IDENTITYMAILER increases as the user sends more emails. The error bars in the figure show that the accuracy of a behavioral profile does not only depend on the number of emails, but also on the user style and habits. For users who have consistent habits, IDENTITYMAILER can reach almost no false positives and false negatives. On the other hand, certain users who have more variable habits end up having higher false positives and false negatives than average. However, this variability gets lower as the number of emails sent by the user increases.

Figure 1 (left) shows the average number of false positives generated during the 10-fold cross validation, broken down by the number of emails sent in the past by each user. As we explained, a false positive in this context would result in the user being required to solve an identity-verification mechanism. As it can be seen, a user who sent 1,000 emails in the past would have to confirm her identity every 12 emails that she sends, on average. Increasing the history of sent emails, a user who sent 8,000 emails would have to confirm her identity on average once every 58 emails that she sends. Given the number of emails that an average corporate user sends nowadays — 33 per day, according to a recent report [36], reaching this amount of interaction history does not take long. As we mentioned, these are average numbers. Users with a more stable email-sending behavior already reach 2 % false positives after having sent 1,000 emails. This means that, on average, they would only have to go through the identity-verification process once every 50 emails they send. We think that these numbers are reasonable in a corporate environment, where the hassle of confirming a user's identity is repaid by having the users protected from identity theft.

Similarly, Fig. 1 (right) shows the number of false negatives for the 10-fold cross validation. As it can be seen, having sent 1,000 emails in the past allows IDENTITYMAILER to build a model that can block 90 % of the emails that have not been written by the user. Recall gets better as the number of sent emails increases. The behavioral profile of a user who sent more than 8,000 emails has an average recall of 96 %. The accuracy of IDENTITYMAILER is lower than the one of state-of-the-art anti-spam systems. However, as we said, the purpose of our system is very different than the one of anti-spam techniques. We are trying to ensure that no email is sent on behalf of a user, if she did not compose it. As we have already discussed, current anti-spam techniques are not appropriate to deal with such attacks.

Analysis of the Features. Previous research showed that it is possible to identify the author of an email just by looking at stylometry features (what we call *writing habits* in this paper) [8]. However, Forsyth et al. showed that such approaches are only reliable in presence of a consistent amount of text [12]. In particular, they identified the amount of text after which stylometry-based author identification becomes reliable to 250 words. Unfortunately, 78 % of the emails in $\mathbf{D}_1$ are shorter than that. In particular, 50 % of the emails in that set are shorter than 100 words.

Given the short length of emails, we use two other types of features in IDENTI-TYMAILER: *composition habits* and *interaction habits*. We wanted to investigate how much these features help in making correct detections and whether it is true that writing-habit features are not enough. To show this, we performed the same

10-fold cross validation that we ran to evaluate the classifier, but this time we only used writing-habit features. The results show that writing-habit features are indeed not enough to perform an accurate detection. For a user who sent 1,000 emails in the past, the average number of false positives is 22 %, almost three times higher than with the full classifier. The lowest rate of false positives reached in this case is for users who have sent at least 8,000 emails, but it is still around 9.8 %, almost six times higher than what we obtained with the full classifier. Clearly, if stylometry-based methods might be useful in forensic cases, they are not enough to determine whether an email has been sent by an attacker or not.

4.3   Detecting Attack Emails

We evaluated IDENTITYMAILER on the attack datasets $\mathbf{S}_1$, $\mathbf{S}_2$, and $\mathbf{S}_3$. First, we created the email-sending behavioral profiles for each user U in $\mathbf{D}_1$, as explained in Sect. 2.2. Then, for each email in $\mathbf{S}_1$, $\mathbf{S}_2$, and $\mathbf{S}_3$, and each user U, we edited the From: field in the email to look like it was sent by U, and ran IDENTITYMAILER on it, to see whether the email would have been flagged as anomalous or not, in case user U sent it. Since IDENTITYMAILER does not take into account header fields such as the X-Mailer one, but only the set of recipients of the email, and the hour and day that the email was written at, no additional editing is required.

As it happened for the validation of the classifier, the performance of IDEN-TITYMAILER depends on how many emails each user has sent in the past, as well as on how consistent the behavior of a user is while sending emails. In general, an email history of 200 messages is enough to reach a true positive rate of 80 %, while histories of 1,000 emails or more lead to 90 % detection rate. As a peak, IDENTITYMAILER reaches 98 % true positives for certain users. This number is still lower than what traditional anti-spam techniques can detect. However, as we mentioned, state-of-the-art systems are inadequate to detect this kind of threats, and fail in detecting them as malicious most of the time. Therefore, IDENTITYMAILER fills this gap well, detecting most of these advanced attack emails as malicious.

4.4   Performance of IDENTITYMAILER

A critical part of evaluating anti-spam techniques, and systems that deal with email in general, is understanding how much delay would be introduced by the technique in the delivery process. IDENTITYMAILER has to undergo two main operations to detect malicious emails: building a behavioral profile for a user and checking each sent email against this behavioral profile. Building the behavioral profile for a user is not time-critical, because we expect the behavior of a user to be constant, or change slowly. For these reasons, the server can update the behavioral profile of users in batch, for example once a day, and during periods in which the email activity is minimal. According to our experiments, building the behavioral model for a user in $\mathbf{D}_1$ takes, on average, 34 s, and can take up to 141 s for certain users.

On the other hand, checking emails for maliciousness is more time-critical, because it actively delays emails as they get sent. On average, IDENTITYMAILER requires 0.22 s to extract the feature vector for an email and compare it to the behavioral profile for that user. This time is comparable to state-of-the-art content-based anti-spam systems — SpamAssassin requires 0.5 s on average to process an email [3]. We consider this performance acceptable, also because the number of emails that a typical organization sends is four times lower than the number of emails that it receives, and therefore IDENTITYMAILER would have to process less emails than the ones that anti-spam systems have to [36].

5   Discussion and Limitations

Our results show that IDENTITYMAILER is successful in detecting and blocking attack emails that appear to have been written by a user, but have actually been authored by an attacker. However, as most detection systems, IDENTITYMAILER has some limitations, as well as some caveats that an organization should keep in mind while operating it.

The main limitation is that, to be effective, IDENTITYMAILER requires an email history of 1,000 emails or more. This makes it hard to protect, for example, the new hires of a company. We argue that email is such a pervasive communication medium that it should not take too long to collect a large number of emails from a new employee. In addition, a new employee is probably not going to be a good target for an attacker, who would favor more influential people in the company. Those people, however, will have a long email-sending history, and IDENTITYMAILER will protect them well. Another possible limitation in a corporate setting is that high-ranked executives might delegate their assistants to write some emails on their behalf. This practice might generate false positives, because IDENTITYMAILER would detect that those emails were not written by the owner of the account. A possible mitigation here is to learn multiple email-sending behaviors, one for each of the people using an account, and not generating an alert if the email results to be written by any of those users.

Another limitation of IDENTITYMAILER is that writing-habit features are specific to the English language. If our approach had to protect the employees of a company whose main language is different than English, we would have to develop another set of language-specific features. Previous research showed that this is feasible even for Asian languages, that have completely different characteristics than English [47].

Another problem that we have to consider is the privacy of users. The email sending behavior is built not only by leveraging a user's personal emails, but also by leveraging the ones sent by her coworkers too. However, for how we designed IDENTITYMAILER, the feature vectors built from the emails are kept within the server, and are never seen by the users. Also, the server has to only keep the feature vector relative to an email, and not the email itself. Therefore, we believe that the privacy concerns revolving around IDENTITYMAILER should be minimal.

Another concern is that some domains, such as large webmail services, have a very diverse set of users, and it might be challenging to model their behavior well. For IDENTITYMAILER, we focus on corporate users, assuming that their behavior is more consistent than the one of general-purpose email providers. In addition, large webmail services have access to additional signals that are not included in our threat model (such as login patterns and IP addresses), which can also be leveraged to build a behavioral profile.

Another limitation is that an attacker could try is imitating the email-sending behavior learning phase of our system. To this end, he might leverage the emails that other users sent to the victim in the past as M_o. The attacker can find these emails, for example, in the *Inbox* of the victim's mailer program. In principle, this technique could help in making the attack more successful, and evade IDENTITYMAILER. However, the information that an attacker can learn from the emails received by a user in the past is rather limited. For example, it does not give any information on what the social network of the other users in the company looks like, and it only shows the behavior that third party showed when interacting with that specific user. An attacker might get additional knowledge of the company's emails by compromising additional employee email accounts. If he obtained access to enough accounts, he might be able to replicate the learning process of IDENTITYMAILER and evade our system. However, an attack of such breadth is hard to set up, and once an attacker gets such a pervasive presence is the company's network, there is not much that our approach can do. In our technical report we show that IDENTITYMAILER is in general difficult to evade by an attacker, unless he achieved a complete view on the email that have been sent by the company in the last months [33].

6   Related Work

Our approach protects the identity of users against attackers sending emails on their behalf. To this end, we borrow some ideas from anti-spam techniques, as well as from the field of forged text detection and authorship identification. In the following, we discuss how our approach is related to previous work, and elaborate on the novelty of our method.

Spam Filtering: Existing work on spam filtering can be distinguished in two main categories: *origin-analysis* and *content-analysis* techniques. Origin-analysis techniques try to determine whether emails are good or bad by looking at their origin. Examples of characteristics that are indicative of a malicious emails can be the IP address or autonomous system that the email is sent from, or the geographical distance between the sender and the recipient [14, 26, 32, 41]. Other origin-based techniques include *Sender Policy Framework* (SPF) and *DomainKeys Identified Mail* (DKIM) [20, 42]. These techniques try to determine whether an email is actually coming from the address it claims to come from, by looking at the sender IP, or at a signature in the email headers. Origin-based techniques are widely deployed, because they allow servers to discard spam emails as soon as the malicious end connects to the mail server, saving resources and time. In addition, they reach good coverage, because most spam is sent by hosts that are part of a botnet, and therefore have a low reputation [34]. However, in the scenario in which IDENTITYMAILER works, origin-based techniques are useless, because the only thing they can do is confirming that an email has been sent by a certain account, regardless if it is a compromised one or not.

Content-analysis techniques look at the words in the message itself to determine if it is spam or not. Proposed methods include Naïve Bayes, Support Vector Machines, or other machine learning algorithms [9,22,27,28]. Other systems detect spam by looking at malicious URLs in the email [17,45]. Content-analysis techniques work well in detecting spam, however are too computationally intensive to be applied to every email that a busy mail server receives [35]. In IDENTITYMAILER, we solve this problem by analyzing emails as they get sent. We claim that this analysis is feasible, because the number of emails that a mail server sends is lower than the number of emails that it receives. Another problem of traditional content-analysis techniques is that they look for words that are indicative of spam. In the presence of a targeted attack, there might be no such words, since an attack email will use a language that is similar to the one used in everyday business emails. This is why in IDENTITYMAILER we learn the typical sending behavior of a user, and match it against the emails she sends, to detect attacks.

A number of systems have been proposed to counter specific types of spam, such as phishing. Such systems either look at features in the attack emails that are indicative of phishing [11], or at characteristics of the web page that the links in the email point to [46]. IDENTITYMAILER is more general, since it can detect any type of attack emails that is sent by compromised accounts. In addition, existing phishing techniques fail in detecting those emails that rely on advanced social engineering tactics, instead of redirecting the user to a phony login page.

Another category of spam detection techniques looks at the way in which spammers use the TCP or SMTP protocol [18,31]. These techniques work well in practice against most spam, but are focused on detecting hosts that belong to a botnet, and are therefore useless in detecting the type of attacks that IDENTITYMAILER is designed to prevent.

Forged Message Detection: A large corpus of research has been performed on determining the author of an email. These techniques typically leverage stylometry and machine learning and return the most probable author among a set of candidates [4,7,8,13,15]. From our point of view, these approaches suffer of two major problems: the first one is that they typically need a set of possible authors, which in our case we do not have. The second problem is that email texts are often times very short, and this does not allow to determine an author by just looking at stylometry [12]. Lin et al. proposed a system that looks at the writing style of an email, and is able to tell whether that email was written by an author or not [21]. This approach solves the first problem, but does not solve the second one, in which we have emails that are too short to make a meaningful decision. To mitigate this problem, in IDENTITYMAILER we leverage information other than stylometry, such as the typical times in which a user sends emails, or her social network.

Stolfo et al. presented Email Mining Toolkit (EMT) [29,30]. This tool mines email logs to find cliques of users who frequently contact each other. After learning the cliques, the system flags as anomalous emails that are addressed to people outside them. Although EMT leverages an idea similar to IDENTITYMAILER's interaction features, it is tailored at detecting large-scale threats, such as worms spreading through email. The fact that IDENTITYMAILER leverages other types of features allow our system to detect subtle, one-of-a-kind attack emails.

Egele et al. proposed a system that learns the behavior of users on Online Social Networks and flags anomalous messages as possible compromises [10]. Because of the high number of false positives, their system can only detect large-scale malicious campaigns, by aggregating similar anomalous messages. As we have shown, IDENTITYMAILER is able to detect attacks that are composed of a single email, and that have not been seen before.

7 Conclusions

We presented IDENTITYMAILER, a system that protects the identity of corporate users, by checking if an email has been written by the owner of an email account. This work is the first step towards the protection of individuals and companies against advanced email attacks, such as spearphishing. IDENTITYMAILER does this by learning the typical sending behavior of the account's owner and checking any email that the account sends against this profile. We showed that IDENTITYMAILER is able to detect attacks that state-of-the-art systems are unable to detect.

Acknowledgments. This work was supported by a Symantec Research Labs Graduate Fellowship for the year 2012. We would like to thank the anonymous reviewers for their useful comments. We would also like to thank the people at Symantec, in particular Marc Dacier, David T. Lin, Dermot Harnett, Joe Krug, David Cawley, and Nick Johnston for their support and comments. We would also like to thank Adam Doupè and Ali Zand for reviewing an early version of this paper. Your feedback was very helpful.

References

1. Hacking attack at RSA targeted Flash flaw. http://www.ft.com/cms/s/2/96518afc-5cb1-11e0-ab7c-00144feab49a.html
2. Shamoon was an external attack on Saudi oil production. http://www.infosecurity-magazine.com/view/29750/shamoon-was-an-external-attack-on-saudi-oil-production/
3. SpamAssassin: performance. http://wiki.apache.org/spamassassin/UsingNetwork Tests
4. Abbasi, A., Chen, H., Nunamaker, J.F.: Stylometric identification in electronic markets: scalability and robustness. J. Manage. Inform. Syst. **25**, 49–78 (2008)
5. Afroz, S., Brennan, M., Greenstadt, R.: Detecting hoaxes, frauds, and deception in writing style online. In: IEEE Symposium on Security and Privacy (2012)

6. Aloul, F., Zahidi, S., El-Hajj, W.: Two factor authentication using mobile phones. In: IEEE/ACS International Conference on Computer Systems and Applications (2009)
7. Calix, K., Connors, M., Levy, D., Manzar, H., MCabe, G., Westcott, S.: Stylometry for e-mail author identification and authentication. In: Proceedings of CSIS Research Day, Pace University (2008)
8. Corney, M.W.: Analysing E-mail Text Authorship for Forensic Purposes
9. Drucker, H., Wu, D., Vapnik, V.N.: Support vector machines for spam categorization. IEEE Trans. Neural Networks **10**, 1048–1054 (1999)
10. Egele, M., Stringhini, G., Kruegel, C., Vigna, G.: COMPA: detecting compromised social network accounts. In: Symposium on Network and Distributed System Security (NDSS) (2013)
11. Fette, I., Sadeh, N., Tomasic, A.: Learning to Detect Phishing Emails
12. Forsyth, R., Holmes, D.: Feature finding for text classification. Literary Linguist. Comput. **11**, 163–174 (1996)
13. Frantzeskou, G., Stamatatos, E., Gritzalis, S., Chaski, C.E., Howald, B.S.: Identifying authorship by byte-level n-grams: the source code author profile (scap) method. Int. J. Digit. Evid. (2007)
14. Hao, S., Syed, N.A., Feamster, N., Gray, A.G., Krasser, S.: Detecting spammers with SNARE: spatio-temporal network-level automatic reputation engine. In: USENIX Security Symposium (2009)
15. Iqbal, F., Hadjidj, R., Fung, B., Debbabi, M.: A novel approach of mining writeprints for authorship attribution in e-mail forensics. Digit. Invest. **5**, S42–S51 (2008)
16. Jagatic, T.N., Johnson, N.A., Jakobsson, M., Menczer, F.: Social phishing. Commun. ACM **50**, 94–100 (2007)
17. John, J.P., Moshchuk, A., Gribble, S.D., Krishnamurthy, A.: Studying spamming botnets using botlab. In: USENIX Symposium on Networked Systems Design and Implementation (NSDI) (2009)
18. Kakavelakis, G., Beverly, R., Young, J.: Auto-learning of SMTP TCP transport-layer features for spam and abusive message detection. In: USENIX Large Installation System Administration Conference (2011)
19. Klimt, B., Yang, Y.: Introducing the enron corpus. In: CEAS (2004)
20. Leiba, B.: DomainKeys Identified Mail (DKIM): Using digital signatures for domain verification. In: CEAS (2007)
21. Lin, E., Aycock, J., Mannan, M.: Lightweight client-side methods for detecting email forgery. In: Lee, D.H., Yung, M. (eds.) WISA 2012. LNCS, vol. 7690, pp. 254–269. Springer, Heidelberg (2012)
22. Meyer, T., Whateley, B.: SpamBayes: effective open-source, Bayesian based, email classification system. In: CEAS (2004)
23. Narayanan, A., Paskov, H., Gong, N.Z., Bethencourt, J., Stefanov, E., Shin, E.C.R., Song, D.: On the feasibility of internet-scale author identification. In: IEEE Symposium on Security and Privacy (2012)
24. Pitsillidis, A., Levchenko, K., Kreibich, C., Kanich, C., Voelker, G.M., Paxson, V., Weaver, N., Savage, S.: Botnet Judo: fighting spam with itself. In: Symposium on Network and Distributed System Security (NDSS) (2010)
25. Platt, J., et al.: Sequential minimal optimization: a fast algorithm for training support vector machines
26. Ramachandran, A., Feamster, N., Vempala, S.: Filtering spam with behavioral blacklisting. In: ACM Conference on Computer and Communications Security (CCS) (2007)

27. Sahami, M., Dumais, S., Heckermann, D., Horvitz, E.: A Bayesian approach to filtering junk e-mail. In: Learning for Text Categorization (1998)
28. Sculley, D., Wachman, G.M.: Relaxed online SVMs for spam filtering. In: ACM SIGIR Conference on Research and Development in Information Retrieval (2007)
29. Stolfo, S.J., Hershkop, S., Hu, C.-W., Li, W.-J., Nimeskern, O., Wang, K.: Behavior-based modeling and its application to email analysis. ACM Trans. Internet Technol. (TOIT) **6**, 187–221 (2006)
30. Stolfo, S.J., Hershkop, S., Wang, K., Nimeskern, O., Hu, C.-W.: Behavior profiling of email. In: Chen, H., Miranda, R., Zeng, D.D., Demchak, C.C., Schroeder, J., Madhusudan, T. (eds.) ISI 2003. LNCS, vol. 2665, pp. 74–90. Springer, Heidelberg (2003)
31. Stringhini, G., Egele, M., Zarras, A., Holz, T., Kruegel, C., Vigna, G.: B@BEL: leveraging email delivery for spam mitigation. In: USENIX Security Symposium (2012)
32. Stringhini, G., Holz, T., Stone-Gross, B., Kruegel, C., Vigna, G.: BotMagnifier: locating spambots on the internet. In: USENIX Security Symposium (2011)
33. Stringhini, G., Thonnard, O.: That ain't you: detecting spearphishing emails before they are sent. arXiv preprint arXiv:1410.6629 (2014)
34. Symantec Corp. Symantec intelligence report (2013). http://www.symanteccloud.com/mlireport/SYMCINT_2013_01_January.pdf
35. Taylor, B.: Sender reputation in a large webmail service. In: CEAS (2006)
36. The Radicati Group. Email Statistics Report. http://www.radicati.com/wp/wp-content/uploads/2011/05/Email-Statistics-Report-2011-2015-Executive-Summary.pdf
37. Thonnard, O., Bilge, L., O'Gorman, G., Kiernan, S., Lee, M.: Industrial espionage and targeted attacks: understanding the characteristics of an escalating threat. In: Balzarotti, D., Stolfo, S.J., Cova, M. (eds.) RAID 2012. LNCS, vol. 7462, pp. 64–85. Springer, Heidelberg (2012)
38. Threatpost. New Email Worm Turns Back the Clock on Virus Attacks (2010). http://threatpost.com/en_us/blogs/new-email-worm-turns-back-clock-virus-attacks-090910
39. Trend Micro Inc., Spear-Phishing Email: Most Favored APT Attack Bait (2012)
40. Tweedie, F., Baayern, R.: How variable may a constant be? Measures of lexical richness in perspective. Comput. Humanit. **32**, 323–352 (1998)
41. Venkataraman, S., Sen, S., Spatscheck, O., Haffner, P., Song, D.: Exploiting network structure for proactive spam mitigation. In: USENIX Security Symposium (2007)
42. Wong, M., Schlitt, W.: RFC 4408: Sender Policy Framework (SPF) for Authorizing Use of Domains in E-Mail, Version 1 (2006). http://tools.ietf.org/html/rfc4408
43. Xie, Y., Yu, F., Achan, K., Panigrahy, R., Hulten, G., Osipkov, I.: Spamming botnets: signatures and characteristics. SIGCOMM Comput. Commun. Rev. **38**, 171–182 (2008)
44. Yule, G.: The Statistical Study of Literary Vocabulary. Cambridge University Press, Cambridge (1944)
45. Zalewski, M.: p0f v3 (2012). http://lcamtuf.coredump.cx/p0f3/
46. Zhang, Y., Hong, J.I., Cranor, L.F.: Cantina: A Content-based Approach to Detecting Phishing Web Sites
47. Zheng, R., Li, J., Chen, H., Huang, Z.: A framework for authorship identification of online messages: writing-style features and classification techniques. J. Am. Soc. Inform. Sci. Technol. **57**, 378–393 (2005)

Robust and Effective Malware Detection Through Quantitative Data Flow Graph Metrics

Tobias Wüchner[✉], Martín Ochoa, and Alexander Pretschner

Technische Universität München, Munich, Germany
wuechner@in.tum.de

Abstract. We present a novel malware detection approach based on metrics over quantitative data flow graphs. Quantitative data flow graphs (QDFGs) model process behavior by interpreting issued system calls as aggregations of quantifiable data flows. Due to the high abstraction level we consider QDFG metric based detection more robust against typical behavior obfuscation like bogus call injection or call reordering than other common behavioral models that base on raw system calls. We support this claim with experiments on obfuscated malware logs and demonstrate the superior obfuscation robustness in comparison to detection using n-grams. Our evaluations on a large and diverse data set consisting of about 7000 malware and 500 goodware samples show an average detection rate of 98.01 % and a false positive rate of 0.48 %. Moreover, we show that our approach is able to detect new malware (i.e. samples from malware families not included in the training set) and that the consideration of quantities in itself significantly improves detection precision.

1 Introduction

Despite the increasing availability and deployment of intrusion detection systems and anti-virus engines, malicious software (malware) remains a severe threat. One reason is the steadily increasing sophistication of modern malware. Most new malware families found in the wild employ some kind of functionality to avoid or harden detection by traditional security measures. Examples range from rather simplistic attempts to disable known security software upon infection; over polymorphism and metamorphism techniques to alter and obfuscate the executable binaries of malware in order to harden detection by signature-based approaches; up to more sophisticated behavioral obfuscation techniques, such as mimicry attacks, that aim at altering the runtime behavior to trick behavior-based detection approaches [35].

One challenge of malware detection research is thus the new threat of stealthy and obfuscated malware; and how to counteract their attempts to avoid detection and remain "below the radar". We contribute towards this goal with a novel behavior-based malware detection methodology which we show to be less prone to circumvention by obfuscation mechanisms. The idea is to discriminate malicious from benign processes by analyzing their behavior *in terms of induced quantitative data flows between system resources*. We interpret the execution of

© Springer International Publishing Switzerland 2015
M. Almgren et al. (Eds.): DIMVA 2015, LNCS 9148, pp. 98–118, 2015.
DOI: 10.1007/978-3-319-20550-2_6

system calls, e.g. a process calling the Windows API *ReadFile* function to read data from a file, as causing a quantifiable flow of data from one system entity, in this example a file, to another entity, in this example a process.

We aggregate the set of data flow events in a system within a specific time interval into so-called quantitative data flow graphs (QDFGs). These represent the interaction between all system entities within this time frame. QDFGs are abstractions of a system's behavior in terms of data flows, and thus can be used for behavior-based malware detection. On the basis of this model our approach aims at identifying QDFG nodes that refer to potentially malicious processes. To do so, we use metrics inspired by research done in the area of social network analysis, to profile typical data flow behavior of benign and malicious processes, and then use these profiles to train a machine learning classifier.

In contrast to related work on graph-based malware detection [9,12,13,32], we do not rely on fixed detection patterns and expensive subgraph isomorphism checks. Instead, we perform approximate similarity comparison of unknown process behavior with a more flexible metric-based quantitative data flow model. By this, in contrast to isomorphism-based approaches that are challenged if malware does not exactly match defined patterns or models, we are able to detect unknown or obfuscated malware. In contrast to recently published metric-based approaches [16,22] we incorporate quantitative data flow aspects into our model which we show to provide better detection precision and superior obfuscation resilience, as well as novel features (which we call *local*).

Contributions: (a) To the best of our knowledge, we are the first to combine *quantitative* data flow tracking with machine learning for checking for behavioral similarity of processes in the context of malware detection. (b) Our experiments demonstrate the utility of *quantitative* data flow aspects for detection precision. (c) In particular we show that the consideration of quantities in data flow graphs can effectively halve false positive and false negative rates. (d) Our evaluations indicate that our approach is more robust against common types of behavioral obfuscation than approaches that build on raw system calls such as n-gram based approaches and (e) We show that we are able to detect samples from unknown malware families with good accuracy.

Organization: We recap an abstract QDFG model from the literature in Sect. 2. We present graph metrics and their semantic relevance in terms of malware detection in Sect. 3.1; describe the training phase in Sect. 3.2; and discuss the detection procedure in Sect. 3.3. We evaluate effectiveness, obfuscation robustness, and efficiency in Sect. 4. We put our approach in context in Sect. 5. We conclude with a discussion of capabilities, limitations, and future work in Sect. 6.

2 Preliminaries

We first recap some preliminaries. For the subsequent sections we assume a basic understanding of the Windows NT operating system architecture.

2.1 Quantitative Data Flow Model

We study the identification of potentially malicious processes in a system by analyzing quantitative data flow graphs (QDFGs) that represent a system's data flow activities within a certain period of time. To this end, we use a slightly simplified generic quantitative data flow graph model from the literature [32]. This model uses QDFGs to capture all aggregated and quantified data flows between interesting entities in a system, such as processes, files, or sockets. These are represented by nodes $(\overline{N})$. Labeled directed edges $(\overline{E})$ between two nodes intuitively reflect that there has been a transfer of a certain amount of data.

A QDFG is a graph in the set $\mathcal{G} = \overline{N} \times \overline{E} \times \overline{A} \times ((\overline{N} \cup \overline{E}) \times \overline{A} \to Value^{\overline{A}})$, where $\overline{N}$ denotes the set of all possible nodes, $\overline{E} \subseteq \overline{N} \times \overline{N}$ the set of possible edges between two nodes, and a set of labeling functions $((\overline{N} \cup \overline{E}) \times \overline{A}) \to Value^{\overline{A}}$ assign defined values from the set $Value^{\overline{A}}$ to an attribute $a \in \overline{A}$ of a node or an edge. These labeling functions are needed to annotate nodes and edges with additional information such as amount of transferred data $(size \in \mathbb{N})$ or corresponding set of time stamps $(time \in 2^{\mathbb{N}})$.

QDFGs are incrementally built on the basis of data flow relevant system events, e.g. functions to read data from a file or to write data to a socket. These events are modeled as a set $\mathcal{E}$. In an actual system, they are intercepted by runtime monitors which interpret the data flow semantics and perform corresponding graph updates such as the creation or modification of nodes or edges. One QDFG $G = (N, E, A, \lambda) \in \mathcal{G}$ describes all data flow activities of a system that happened during a certain time interval. The labeling function λ maps attributes of an edge or a node to their assigned values.

Events $(src, dst, size, t, \lambda) \in \mathcal{E}$ represent transfers of $size \in \mathbb{N}$ units of data from a node $src \in \overline{N}$ to a node $dst \in \overline{N}$ with a timestamp $t \in \mathbb{N}$ and a labeling function λ for additional information on the corresponding data flow. To ease presentation, we will not always cleanly distinguish between an event and its corresponding edge. We are not interested in exactly which event causes which amount of data flow between two system entities. We thus simplify our model by aggregating semantically related data flows between pairs of nodes through summation of the $size$ attribute of the respective edges rather than creating one distinct edge per event.

Before formally defining the corresponding graph update function, triggered by the execution of a data flow related event, we first need to introduce some auxiliary notations and syntactic sugar: For $(x, a) \in (N \cup E) \times \overline{A}$, we define

$$\lambda[(x, a) \leftarrow v] = \lambda' \text{ with } \lambda'(y) = \begin{cases} v & \text{if } y \in dom(\lambda) \\ \lambda(y) & otherwise \end{cases}.$$

We furthermore introduce some syntactic sugar for updating labeling functions: $\lambda[(x_1, a_1) \leftarrow v_1; \ldots; (x_k, a_k) \leftarrow v_k] = (\ldots (\lambda[(x_1, a_1) \leftarrow v_1]) \ldots)[(x_k, a_k) \leftarrow v_n]$.

Correspondingly we denote the composition of two labeling functions by:

$$\lambda_1 \circ \lambda_2 = \lambda_1[(x_1, a_1) \leftarrow v_1; \ldots; (x_k, a_k) \leftarrow v_n]$$

where $v_i = \lambda_2(x_i, a_i)$ and $(x_i, a_i) \in dom(\lambda_2)$. Finally, the QDFG update function $update : \mathcal{G} \times \mathcal{E} \to \mathcal{G}$ is formally defined in Fig. 1.

$$update(G, (src, dst, s, t, \lambda')) =$$

$$\begin{cases} \begin{pmatrix} N, \\ E, \\ A \cup \mathsf{dom}(\lambda'), \\ \lambda \begin{bmatrix} (e, size) \leftarrow \lambda(e, size) + s; \\ (e, time) \leftarrow (\lambda(e, time) \cup \{t\}) \end{bmatrix} \circ \lambda' \end{pmatrix} & \text{if } e \in E \\[2em] \begin{pmatrix} N \cup \{src, dst\}, \\ E \cup \{e\}, \\ A \cup \mathsf{dom}(\lambda'), \\ \lambda \begin{bmatrix} (e, size) \leftarrow s; \\ (e, time) \leftarrow \{t\} \end{bmatrix} \circ \lambda' \end{pmatrix} & \text{otherwise} \end{cases}$$

where $e = (src, dst)$ and $G = (N, E, A, \lambda)$

Fig. 1. Graph update function

For later definitions of node features, we need to introduce auxiliary functions. Function $pre : \overline{N} \times \mathcal{G} \rightarrow 2^{\overline{N}}$ computes all immediate predecessor nodes of a node of the graph. Functions $in, out : \overline{N} \times \mathcal{G} \rightarrow 2^{\overline{E}}$ compute the set of incoming and outgoing edges of a node.

2.2   Windows Instantiation

To instantiate the abstract QDFG model for real-world malware detection, we need to map it to resources and events in actual execution environments. In this paper, the execution environment is that of typical Windows operating systems.

We identified a set of system resources that are relevant for malware data flow behavior: *Processes* interact with all other relevant system entities in a way that they are either sources or sinks of flows from or to other *Registry*, *Socket* or *Process* nodes. To type these nodes we introduce a special *type* $\in \overline{A}$ attribute: Process nodes have *type* P, File nodes F, Socket nodes S, URL nodes U, and Registry nodes R.

In addition to *entities*, we also need to map all data flow relevant *events*. These are all Windows API functions that lead to a flow of data between the above system entities. This includes functions to interact with resources from the file system like *ReadFile* or *WriteFile* to functions to send or receive data to or from a socket like the Winsock *recv* and *send* functions. To give an intuition how the data flow semantics is formally modeled, we present two sample function definitions, a more comprehensive list can be found for instance in [32]:

– **ReadFile.** Using this function a process reads a specified amount of bytes from a file to its memory. *Relevant Parameters*: Calling Process (P_C), Source File (F_S), ToReadBytes (S_R). *Mapping*: $(F_S, P_C, S_R, t, \lambda(F_S, size) := \lambda(F_S, size) + S_R)) \in \mathcal{E}$.

- **WriteFile.** Using this function a process can write a specific number of bytes to a file. *Relevant Parameters*: Calling Process (P_C), Destination File (F_D), ToWriteBytes (S_W). *Mapping*: $(P_C, F_D, S_W, t, \lambda(F_D, size) := \lambda(F_D, size) + S_W)) \in \mathcal{E}$.

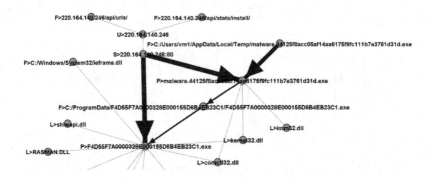

Fig. 2. Excerpt of QDFG for a system infected with Cleaman.

To motivate the utility of this model for malware detection, Fig. 2 exemplarily visualizes a typical malware QDFG, built by applying the previously mentioned model on the intercepted activities of an executed Cleaman trojan. The size of the edges in the graph visualization represents the relative amount of transferred data with respect to all other edges of that graph. The type of the nodes is denoted by the first letter of the node label. By focusing on the part of the graph with the highest amount of transferred data one can easily spot the core malign activities of the analyzed malware, i.e. self-replication, or download and execution of additional malicious payload from a remote server.

3   Approach

Our core idea is to learn statistical profiles for benign and malicious nodes in QDFGs that represent known infected and non-infected systems. We later use these profiles for matching feature sets of unknown processes against them.

The overall architecture is depicted in Fig. 3. Dashed lines mark components and interactions that are only used in the training phase. Dotted lines refer to the ones only relevant for detection.

3.1   Features

Like others [16, 22] we see a strong analogy between social networks and (Q)DFGs and hence use graph characteristics inspired from social network analysis [5, 25]. Nodes in a social network typically represent communicating entities, and the edges between them their interaction in form of exchanged messages or friendship

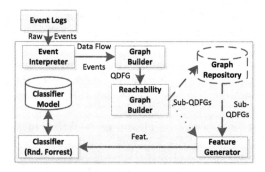

Fig. 3. Architecture

relations. Analogously, nodes in our graphs represent system entities and the edges between them their interaction in form of data flows.

The following features were selected using both an inductive and a deductive approach. The inductive selection was done based on a preliminary analysis of graphs of a small set of malware-infected systems where we applied several standard metrics from statistics and graph theory and tried to correlate malware activities with the applied metrics. The deductive selection was performed through an analysis of standard graph metrics. For each analyzed feature we tried to correlate its intuition with typical malware behavior or properties. For instance, malware that tries to infect other processes or files results in a high connectivity of the corresponding node to certain types of other nodes.

Features are functions $\phi \in \Phi$ that map a QDFG node to a real number: $\phi : \overline{N} \times \mathcal{G} \to \mathbb{R}$. We enrich the QDFG model to store the value of features as attributes of nodes n in graph G, so $\lambda(n, \phi) = \phi(n, G)$. Additionally, we distinguish between two basic types of graph features, *local features* (Φ_l) and *global features* (Φ_g). Local features have a single-hop scope. This means that they only capture the relationship of a node with its direct neighbors. Global features in contrast have a multi-hop scope and represent relationships of one node with all other nodes of a graph.

As opposed to recently published metric-based approaches [16,22], that also exploit graph-theoretical properties to derive discriminating features, we take into account quantitative data flow aspects by exploiting the additional information given by the weighted edges of QDFGs.

Local Features (Φ_l) To define the features, we need some auxiliary notation. Function $d_\psi : (\overline{N} \times \overline{N} \times \mathcal{G}) \to \mathbb{R}$ with ψ returns the shortest path between two nodes in a graph, where $\psi : \overline{E} \to \mathbb{R}$ with $\psi(e) = \lambda(e, size)$ defines the edge distance, or cost, i.e. the amount of data transferred via this edge.

1. **Entropy** $\phi^1 \in \Phi_l$ computes the normalized entropy of the distribution of edge feature values such as size, event count, or sensitivity of all outgoing edges of a process node $n \in N$. The entropy captures the uniformity of the distribution of percental flows, number of contributing events, or relative sensitivity of all outgoing edges of a node n.

Rationale: Viruses like Parite infect other executable binaries or processes by injecting or appending their own binary image. The respective subgraphs tend to have a comparably uniform distribution of specific features of outgoing edges, because the majority of triggered events by that malware are targeted at the infection with roughly the same size of the events as consequence of them relating to reading or writing the same binary image.

Computation: Let $\vec{s} = (s_1, \ldots, s_k)$ and $e_i \in out(n)$ in $s_i = \frac{\psi(e_i)}{\sum\limits_{e' \in out(n)} \psi(e')}$.

Then we define: $\phi^1(n, G) := NE(\vec{s})$ where $NE(\vec{s}) := \frac{- \sum\limits_{i=1}^{k} s_i * \log(s_i)}{\log(k)}$.

2. **Variance** $\phi^2 \in \Phi_l$ expresses the statistical population variance of the distribution of a certain edge feature for all outgoing edges of a node $n \in N$. A low statistical variance indicates that most of the elements of the distribution elements are close to the statistical mean, whereas a high variance indicates a spread of elements. Due to its similar focus on uniformity of underlying input distributions, the variance feature is closely correlated with the entropy feature. First evaluations indicated, however, that the entropy metric performed comparably badly if a node has only a few outgoing edges, but better for larger sets of outgoing edges. The variance metric seemed to exhibit exactly the inverse characteristics.

Rationale: The motivation is similar to that for entropy: malware often exhibits outgoing edge distribution characteristics different from benign ones.

Computation:

$$\phi^2(n, G) := \frac{\sum_{e \in out(n)} \left(\psi(e) - \frac{1}{|out(n)|} \sum_{e' \in out(n)} \psi(e') \right)}{|out(n)|}$$

3. **Flow Proportion** $\phi_t^3 \in \Phi_l$ captures the proportion of a certain type of outgoing data flows of a node $n \in N$ w.r.t. all outgoing flows of that node. The type of a flow is determined by the target node's type of the outgoing edge. We define different variants of the proportion feature that consider different edge attributes.

Rationale: Malware processes often exhibit different flow proportion characteristics than goodware. Examples include ransomware or virus processes that have an irregularly high percentage of outgoing edges that point to file nodes, as they either encrypt several sensitive files, or infect all executable binary files on the hard disk.

Computation: Let $t \in \{Process, Registry, File, Socket\}$.

$$\phi_t^3(n, G) := \frac{\sum\limits_{e=(src,dst) \in out(n), \lambda(dst,type)=t} \psi(e)}{\sum\limits_{e \in out(n)} \psi(e)}$$

Global Features (Φ_g). Global features represent the relation between one node and—possibly all—other nodes of a graph. In contrast to local features, capture the importance of one node within the overall graph. Note that a crucial feature of global features is the fact that the weight of edges (given by the size of data flows between them) is considered when computing the shortest path between nodes (given by the function $\psi(e)$).

1. **Closeness Centrality** $\phi^4 \in \Phi_g$ for a node $n \in N$ represents the inverse of that node's average distance to all other nodes of the same graph. A high closeness centrality indicates that the respective node is closely connected to all other graph nodes [25].

   Rationale: High connectivity with other nodes indicates a node manipulating or infecting other system resources like processes or executable binaries. Such behavior is typical for viruses like Parite that replicate by infecting other processes and binaries. This leads to a close connectivity of the corresponding malware process node with other process and binary file nodes.

   Computation:
   $$\phi^4(n, G) := \frac{|N| - 1}{\sum\limits_{n' \in N \setminus \{n\}} d_\psi(n, n', G)}$$

2. **Betweenness Centrality** $\phi^5 \in \Phi_g$ of a node $n \in N$ represents the relative portion of all shortest paths between all possible pairs of nodes of a graph that pass through that specific node n. A high betweenness centrality means that one specific node is part of a multitude of "communications" between nodes [25].

   Rationale: This metric captures how often a process is part of a multi-step interaction or data flow between other system resources. This is useful to identify malware aiming at man-in-the-middle attacks to e.g. intercept the communication of a benign process with a socket, or to manipulate the information that a benign process reads into memory, to e.g. infect that process with malicious code at runtime.

   Computation: The function $sp(x, y, G)$ returns the number of shortest paths between the nodes x and y in a graph G; $sp_z(x, y, G)$ the ones that pass through node z.

   $$\phi^5(n, G) := \sum_{n', n'' \in N : n \neq n' \neq n''} \frac{sp_n(n', n'', G)}{sp(n', n'', G)}$$

3.2 Training and Model Building Phase

We can now establish statistical profiles for the discrimination between benign and potentially malicious process nodes in a graph. A concrete instantiation of this training procedure with real-world data will be discussed in Sect. 4.2. The training procedure consists of four activities: (i) event log generation; (ii) graph generation; (iii) feature extraction; (iv) classifier training.

Event Log Generation. Using a user mode Windows API monitor from the literature [33], we log a defined amount of calls of processes to the Windows API to capture the activity and interaction of all processes within a system for a certain period of time. The monitor intercepts process calls to the Windows API and stores data flow relevant information like event name, parameter values, and name of the issuing process along with additional context information like a time-stamp to an event log.

Graph Generation. We then extract the data flow related information from the event logs. This is done by an *event data flow interpreter* component that maps raw events to the semantic model discussed in Sect. 2.2. The *graph builder* then generates one QDFG per event log as described in Sect. 2.1. In order to reduce noise, instead of storing the complete QDFG for training, we generate so-called reachability graphs for all process nodes in the base QDFGs. Such reachability graphs contain all nodes and edges that are directly or indirectly connected to the starting node. By this means we ensure, that the training graphs only contain activities that are actually triggered by a certain process or of processes that it directly or indirectly influenced, ignoring all activities that are conducted by non-related processes.

Feature Extraction. The *feature extractor* computes all graph features from Sect. 3.1 for all process nodes of the graphs in the training graph repository. This yields a set of feature values for different benign and malicious process. Recall that we labeled the known malicious process and thus also the corresponding graph nodes. We are hence able to label the resulting process node feature sets as belonging to a known malicious/benign process, which is a necessary precondition for later using a supervised machine learning algorithm.

Classifier Training. After the feature extraction phase, we feed the obtained features into a machine learning algorithm for training.

To this end, we construct a feature vector for each process node of the training set. Each element of this vector is one of the considered QDFG metrics from Sect. 3.1, plus one label element representing the known classification (benign or malign) of the respective process. Each feature vector is thus of size $|\Phi| + 1$.

Note that we only compute feature vectors for process nodes as we are solely interested in determining whether a specific process that originated from a executed binary is malicious or not; we thus do not classify a binary itself, but its runtime representation, i.e. the respective process or its children[1].

Considering the high dimensionality and diversity of the value space of the selected training features we need a machine learning algorithm that is robust

---

[1] By examining the reachability graph associated with a node, it is possible for analysts to investigate the root cause of an infection.

towards training set diversity and scales well with respect to the number or training features. Initial attempts to use simple classifiers like naïve Bayes yielded poor performance in terms of detection precision. We hence explored more complex algorithms like support vector machines and meta-learners. Particularly good results were achieved with the Random Forest (RF) algorithm. RF is a meta- or ensemble-learner, which means that it uses several distinct, potentially imprecise, classification models and merges their decisions to form a more precise combined decision. RF constructs many individual decision trees, called decision forest, based on random selection of limited feature subsets of the feature space.

3.3 Detection Phase

We now have a classifier that can predict the class (malicious or benign) of an unknown process node based on its characteristic local and global graph features. In a nutshell, for the detection phase we thus only need to build the graph of a potentially infected system at runtime based on captured events, compute the characteristic features for each process node in the graph, and match the resulting feature set against the classifier.

Like for the training phase, we intercept relevant system events at runtime, interpret them in terms of their data flow semantics, and then build the corresponding (reachability) QDFGs for each process. We then compute the characteristic feature sets for the process nodes of the generated reachability graphs and match them against the classifier, using the classification model that was generated as result of the training phase.

Consequently, all process nodes of these reachability graph are classified into benign or potentially malicious ones.

4 Evaluation

We implemented the detection framework and captured activities of a representative and diverse set of known benign and malicious software to assess the effectiveness and efficiency of our approach.

4.1 Prototype

Our prototype is a distributed system as shown in Fig. 3. We used and extended a user mode Windows API runtime monitor [33] to intercept system activities relevant in terms of data flows of all processes running within the evaluation system. For the training phase we used the Random Forest implementation of the Weka machine learning framework [15], configured to build a forest of 10 distinct decision trees using the a random feature subsets.

To be able to analyze a large body of malware samples it was necessary to automate the different analysis steps. For this purpose we customized the open-source malware sandbox framework Cuckoo[2] by replacing its function call

---

[2] http://www.cuckoosandbox.org/.

hooking module with our hooking module. Each Cuckoo sandbox VirtualBox instance was running a clean installation of Windows 7 SP1 and assigned two 2,4GHz cores and 2 GByte of RAM. The generation of the QDFGs, computation of the corresponding graph features, and the classification of process samples performed on a 2,8 GHz quadcore i7 system with 8 GByte of RAM.

4.2   Effectiveness

As data source for our experiments we used 6994 different known malicious programs and 513 different known benign applications.

The malicious program samples were taken from a subset of the Malicia malware data set, i.e. all samples that were executable in the considered evaluation environment, that comprises of real-world malware samples from more than 500 drive-by download servers [24]. The respective malware set consists of samples from 12 malware families, including families like zeus, spyeye, and ramnit.

The goodware set was composed of a selection of popular applications from http://download.com and a wide range of standard windows programs, including popular email programs like ThunderBird, browsers like FireFox, video and graphics tools like Gimp, or VLC Player, and security software like Avast.

We generated about 7500 event logs and converted them into QDFGs, each capturing activities of the sandbox machines for a time interval of 5 min.

With this data and the procedure explained in the previous section we obtained a total of 8648 (i.e. 1654 goodware and 6994 malware) QDFG feature sets. The reason for the set of goodware features being bigger than the set of executed goodware samples is that for each execution of a goodware sample we did not only capture the behavior of the goodware sample itself, but also the interaction with all simultaneously running standard Windows processes.

To evaluate the detection performance of our approach on the obtained feature set we first performed ten times a 10-fold cross validation test. For this tests we split the entire feature set into two parts, using 90 % of the set for training and the remaining 10 % for testing. The sets were randomly generated and the splitting repeated 10 times for each test to limit bias from specific set compositions. For each run we built a classification model on basis of the training data and used it for classifying the remaining test set. To avoid training bias due to unbalanced feature sets we in addition applied a SMOTE oversampling [8] on the training sets to approximately balance the distribution of malware and goodware samples. To express the effectiveness, we computed the following quality metrics. True positives (TP) refer to malware samples (MW) that have been correctly classified as malicious, true negatives (TN) to goodware samples (GW) that were correctly classified as benign, false positives (FP) to goodware samples incorrectly classified as malicious, and false negatives (FN) malware samples that were mistakenly labeled as benign:

$$\text{Detection Rate (DR)} : \frac{TP}{MW} \qquad \text{False Positive Rate (FPR)} : \frac{FP}{GW}$$
$$\text{Precision} : \frac{TP}{TP+FP} \qquad \text{F-Measure} : \frac{2*TP}{2*TP+FP+FN}$$

Table 1. Effectiveness quality metrics

	(a) Real	(b) Fixed	(c) Random
Avg. Det. Rate (Std. Dev.)	98.01 % ($\sigma = 0.51$ %)	98.00 % ($\sigma = 0.57$ %)	95.23 % ($\sigma = 0.90$ %)
Avg. FP Rate (Std. Dev.)	0.48 % ($\sigma = 0.34$ %)	0.85 % ($\sigma = 0.35$ %)	1.08 % ($\sigma = 0.41$ %)
Precision	99.62 %	99.32 %	99.12 %
F-Measure	98.81 %	98.65 %	97.13 %

Table 1(a) depicts the average *effectiveness quality metrics* of the cross validation experiments. As we can see, our approach at average can correctly detect 98 % of the provided malware set with a low false positive rate of only about 0.5 %. The low standard deviations furthermore indicates a good stability of the results.

Impact of Quantities. To evaluate our hypothesis, that the consideration of quantities has a significant impact on the effectiveness of the classification, we performed two more tests. For the first test we replaced the real quantities associated to the edges of the QDFGs with a globally fixed value of 1. For the second test we performed the edge quantity replacement by associating varying random quantities to the edges. With this we effectively destroyed the inherent quantitative information of the QDFGs. For both experiments we again performed 10-fold cross validation tests to ensure stability of the results. Table 1(b) and (c) depicts the average detection and false positive rates for both settings.

To calculate the relative impact of quantities on the detection effectiveness we divided the false positive and false negative rate (which is the dual of the detection rate) for the fixed and randomized quantities experiment by the respective rates of the experiment with the real quantities.

As we can see, fixing the quantities to a constant value increases the false positives by a factor of 1.8 ($\frac{.0085}{.0048}$). For the randomized quantities experiment we could observe an even bigger loss of effectiveness. Here the false positives increased by a factor of 2.3 ($\frac{.0108}{.0048}$), while also the false negatives increased by a factor of 2.4 ($\frac{1-.9523}{1-.9801}$) with respect to the experiments with the actual quantities.

These observations thus support the hypothesis about the utility of quantitative information for malware detection. To verify the statistical significance of these finding we performed a two-tailed t-test on the detection and false positive rates of the different experiments. The resulting p-values were all far below 0.01 %, which indicates a high statistical significance of our observation.

Ability to Detect New Malware. For evaluating our second hypothesis, i.e. that we are able to detect new malware, we performed an additional classification experiment. For each experiment run we split our data set into two parts. The first part, which we used for training, contained all goodware samples and the samples of all malware families except for one. The second set correspondingly contained all samples from the remaining family and was used as test set.

With this strategy we ensured that the training set did not contain any samples from the same family that was used for testing. In consequence the classifier could not gain any knowledge about the to be classified malware family.

With this test procedure we simulated the real-world scenario that our approach faced a sample from a new malware type that was never seen before and thus could not be used for training the detection model.

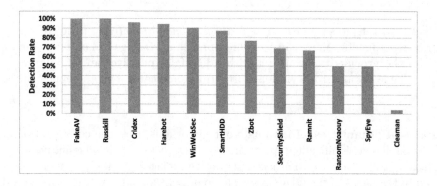

Fig. 4. Detectability of new malware

Figure 4 depicts the detection rates that could be achieved for the different malware families. Each bar shows the percentage of all malware samples of a specific family that could be detected using a classifier that was trained on the samples from the remaining malware families.

As we can see, our approach in all cases was able to detect samples from unknown malware families. On average our approach was able to correctly identify 73.68 % of the new malware samples; some malware families could even be classified with 100 % correctness. These results for this experiment supports our hypothesis that our approach is capable of detecting new unknown malware and goodware. Although further investigation is needed to understand why, we speculate that this is the case because malware behavior is often not too different, even between distinct malware families.

Obfuscation Resilience. Approaches that obfuscate the binary image of malware through build-time code encryption and run-time decryption or code diversification barely have any influence on the detectability through behavior-based detection approaches as such code transformations typically do not alter the externally observable program behavior. In consequence, our approach is likely to be widely robust to such used code obfuscation. This assumption is supported by the ability of our approach to detect variants of malware families that were obfuscated through code transformations. Our evaluations for instance show that we were able to detect 96 of 101 variants of the Harebot trojan from our data set, which is known to employ different forms of code obfuscation.

On the other hand, if malware e.g. non-deterministically executes bogus non-malicious activities or randomly alters between semantically equivalent system calls to achieve the same behavior, it is intuitive to think that it can effectively trick common behavioral approaches that base on n-grams profiling and re-identification as consequence on the unpredictable diverse resulting n-grams. The same holds for most call-graph based approaches as call-graphs can be easily obfuscated by altering or reordering system calls.

Our approach is by construction more robust against call reordering or substitution approaches. This is because reordering of system calls does not alter the corresponding QDFGs, and because semantic substitutions of system calls typically exhibit similar data flow properties that result in similar QDFG updates. Moreover, the injection of bogus calls can change QDFGs, in particular if new edges are created in consequence of e.g. previously untouched system entities being read or written to, or if certain operations are repeated such that the edge weights are altered.

To empirically evaluate the absolute effects of different types of behavioral obfuscation techniques on the effectiveness of our approach we thus set up a series of additional experiments.

First, we picked a set of 100 malware and 100 goodware samples as baseline for our experiments. To reason about the obfuscation resilience of our approach and related behavioral detection approaches like n-gram based ones we then step-wise applied behavioral obfuscation transformations on the call traces of these samples to achieve two typical types of behavior obfuscation, namely re-ordering of calls and injection of bogus calls. We did so by applying a behavior obfuscation tool [2] to the baseline malware set. This tools obfuscates commodity malware by randomly reordering its issued, or injecting new, system calls.

To investigate the effect of increasing degree of behavior obfuscation, we repeated these obfuscation steps 360 times with different configurations for call reordering and injection probabilities, as well as different upper bounds for to be reordered or injected calls. We represented the degree of obfuscation as Levenshtein Distance between the obfuscated and the non-obfuscated baseline call traces. More specifically, we computed the average number of insertions, deletions, and substitutions needed to transform the non-obfuscated call traces into the respectively obfuscated ones. To also get a relative comparison with other behavioral, raw system call based detection approaches, we conducted these experiments with measuring both, the detection effectiveness of our approach and the effectiveness of a typical behavioral detection approach based on n-grams of unordered system calls without arguments with varying n-gram sizes as e.g. discussed in [6].

As we can see in Fig. 5, the ability of the n-gram based approach to correctly identify malicious processes significantly dropped with increasing obfuscation degree. In particular, higher-order n-grams seem to be more sensitive to behavioral obfuscation than lower-order ones. In contrast to n-gram based approaches, our approach seems to be considerably more robust and stable towards behavioral obfuscation. While the effectiveness of the n-gram approaches quickly dropped quadratically and lost prediction stability when obfuscation transformations where applied, the effectiveness of our approach at the same time remained rather stable and only slowly dropped linearly.

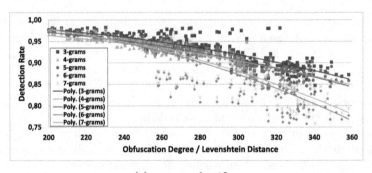

(a) n-gram classifier

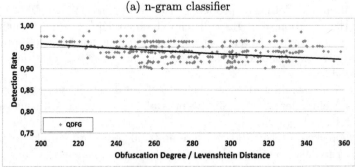

(b) QDFG metric classifier

Fig. 5. Obfuscation experiments

In sum, our evaluation indicates that we are rather robust with respect to realistic behavior obfuscation such as random bogus call injection or reordering, whereas we could show that common n-gram based approaches are considerably challenged by such obfuscation techniques.

4.3 Efficiency

The generation of Random Forest classification models took between 55.21 and 75.38 s. The size of the generated models was between 16 and 19 MBytes. As the training and model generation phase is only conducted once, this overhead does not contribute to the overhead during the detection phases.

As we can see in Fig. 6 the overall detection time seems to increase quadratically with respect to the graph size. The bottom-most part of the area stack refers to the time it took to generate a QDFG from a given event log, the area on top of that indicates the time needed to compute the local graph metrics, and the top-most area expresses the time spent for computing the global metrics. This is not surprising, as most graph algorithms such the used centrality metrics have a theoretical complexity of $\mathcal{O}(n^2)$ to $\mathcal{O}(n^3)$, with n being the number of nodes in the graph [5]. On the other hand, the overhead for graph generation and computation of local features only grows linearly with respect to the graph size.

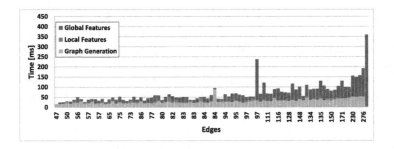

Fig. 6. Computation time vs. graph complexity

The overhead induced by matching the generated graph features against the classification model was below the evaluation precision threshold of 1 ms and thus ignored for this analysis as it has no noticeable impact on the overall overhead. The size of the QDFGs used for our evaluation ranged from 47 to 330 edges resulting in an overall detection time between 24 ms and 412 ms. On average, generating a QDFG, computing its local and global features, and matching it against the trained classifier took 71.213 ms.

4.4   Summary and Threats to Validity

In sum, we have shown our approach to be highly effective; to yield these results, among other things, on the basis of quantities; to be able to detect malware families for which it has not been trained; to be robust w.r.t. obfuscation – in particular more robust than n-grams; and to be efficient.

Naturally, these results need to be put in the context of our study. The evaluation results were obtained on the basis of a proof-of-concept prototype with event logs generated in a controlled lab environment. The obtained insights might not generalize to the application of our approach in real-world settings.

We tried to limit the risk of over-fitting the model to specific sub-sets of the training data by pro-actively diversifying the training set by selecting a wide and diverse range of popular malware and goodware samples for our training set. Furthermore, the fact that our cross-validation results show a very low standard deviation supports the assumption that we did not over-fit our models.

We executed and sampled the evaluation malware in a virtualized sandbox environment. It is known that modern malware often includes functionality to detect virtualization. There hence is a risk that we train our classification models on unrealistic malware behavior and thus are not able to detect their behavior in real-world scenarios. Even though we did not explicitly address this threat, for the future we plan to generate malware event data on realistic bare-metal environments and re-run the experiments to find out if this has any effect on the performance of our approach.

Because current malware still mainly focuses on avoiding detection by signature-based approaches, it rarely employs advanced behavior obfuscation techniques. Although we applied as much randomization as possible for our obfuscation it can of course not be excluded that the simulations do not adequately reflect real-world obfuscation techniques, or that adversaries might come up with more complex behavioral obfuscation operators and advanced mimicry attacks (for instance by learning benign flows and trying to reproduce them). Also, for this study we logged malware behaviour for a fix period of time, which might invalidate our result for purposefully stalling malware. A study of such attacks is left for future work.

5   Related Work

While behavior-based detection algorithms can still not be considered standard for commercial products, they have a long history in academia, especially in the intrusion detection domain. We do not perform a full literature survey on this topic here but focus on dynamic behavior-based malware detection.

A seminal idea of Forrest et al. [11] for behavior-based analysis was to profile benign and malign processes on the basis of characteristic system call sequences (n-grams). This approach was later refined and combined machine learning methods to improve classification effectiveness [14,19,21,23,31]. Similar ideas were also used to classify malware w.r.t. behavioral similarities [1,28,29].

Our system also intercepts and processes system calls. However, while the previously mentioned approaches directly use sequences of raw system calls, we use *a data flow abstraction* of these calls. This distinction is important as approaches that base on raw system call data are often significantly challenged by malware that use behavioral obfuscation techniques [4,30,35]. Such obfuscations for example target at breaking n-gram based approaches by reordering or randomizing system call sequences. As we base our analysis on a (quantitative) data flow abstractions of the system calls, which is independent of sequence order, our approach is, by construction, more robust to such obfuscation attempts.

Besides those detection approaches that use non-interpreted sequences of raw system calls, a separate line of research performs intermediate interpretation steps. A common approach is to extract semantic dependencies between different system calls of a process to form characteristic profiles for known goodware and malware. Popular examples represent system call dependency profiles in form of data or control flow graphs [13,18,20,26], or assign high-level semantics to known graphs [9,10,27]. (Sub-)graphs that pertain to known malicious behavior are then used to re-identify malicious behavior of system processes at runtime. Due to the used intermediate abstraction steps such approaches also appear more robust to behavioral obfuscation attempts. Unfortunately, they are also challenged in terms of identifying previously unknown malicious behavior for which detection profile graphs have not yet been extracted.

In particular, from the data flow perspective, close to ours is the work of Park et al. [26]. They construct Data Flow Graphs based on system calls, where entities are processes, child processes and files. Based on the DFGs of variants of a given malware family, they compute a common sub-graph called a *HotPath*. This process can be repeated for sets of variants of different malware families, and the resulting sub-graphs can be used to classify the DFG of a given process: it will be a variant of a known malware family if it contains a similar sub-graph or goodware otherwise. Different from our work, they do not consider quantities in their graph representation (which we have shown to be an important discriminating factor) and by construction their approach is tailored to recognize mutations of known malware families. They discuss the robustness of their approach against similar obfuscation techniques as the ones we consider, but opposed to our work their approach is challenged by the injection of arbitrary bogus system calls.

Other approaches [17, 34] share similar drawbacks, as they depend on explicit definitions of malicious behavior. Our approach in contrast does not rely on fixed detection patterns. Due to the generic high-level nature of the used data flow graph features, it is more likely to also be able to detect new attacks and malicious behavior that deviate from the ones that were used for training. The use of statistical graph-based metrics for detection instead of fixed data flow patterns also differs from previous work on malware detection through quantitative data flow graphs [32]. The main difference to related work that leverage taint analysis for anomaly-based malware detection [3, 7] is that we leverage quantitative data flow aspects without using comparably expensive taint tracking.

The recently published work of Jang et al. [16] relates to our work in that they also leverage graph metrics to discriminate malware from goodware. But, in contrast to our work, they base the computation of those metrics on system call dependency graphs, while our model is based on quantitative data flow graphs. As we could show, this abstraction increases the robustness towards behavioral obfuscation which gives us better resilience than approaches that directly base on raw system calls. Mao et al. [22] also leverage graph metrics on system entity dependency graphs for malware detection. Similarly, in contrast to us they do not incorporate any quantitative flow information for which we could show that it has an considerable impact on detection precision.

In sum, the main technical difference between our work and related contributions is that we leverage QDFG features rather than raw system calls or system entity dependency graphs. This makes our approach fast and robust against common types of behavioral obfuscations, and, due to the additional quantitative dimension, we achieve a good detection precision.

6   Discussion and Conclusion

We have presented a novel approach to perform graph metric based malware detection on the basis of quantitative data flow analysis. We intercept system calls issued by system processes, interpret them in terms of their data flow semantic and build quantitative data flow graphs. These are used to identify graph nodes that represent potentially malicious system processes.

To this extent, we compute sets of characteristic graph features, such as centrality metrics, for each process node in the graph to discriminate between benign and potentially malign nodes through a machine learning classifier.

Using this classifier, trained on feature sets of known goodware and malware, we are able to discriminate unknown process samples.

It is difficult to objectively compare the effectiveness of different malware detection approaches presented in literature, due to varying evaluation baselines and used assessment procedures. However with respect to closely related dynamic malware detection approaches [13,18,34], our approach has similar or better detection effectiveness, while achieving a significantly better efficiency.

In contrast to previous QDFG-based work [32] and related rule-based approaches [34], our approach is able to detect novel malware samples that exhibit unknown behavior with better detection effectiveness and efficiency. In comparison to related metric-based approaches [16,22] we could show that the quantitative aspect significantly improves detection precision.

Moreover, we have shown that our approach is robust to certain classes of behavioral obfuscation: by construction the *order* of system calls is irrelevant, since they produce the same QDFGs, and more interestingly, random injection of system calls that potentially modify both the structure and the original quantities does not significantly alter the detection effectiveness either.

In conclusion, we showed the usefulness of quantitative data flows for malware detection and established a foundation for further research in the area of QDFG based malware detection models. We plan to perform further tests on the robustness of our approach: try to generalize our approach to non-sandbox settings, explore the usage of more stealthy monitors (i.e. at kernel-level), test the ability to correctly classify new goodware and to improve effectiveness through additional graph features.

References

1. Bailey, M., Oberheide, J., Andersen, J., Mao, Z.M., Jahanian, F., Nazario, J.: Automated classification and analysis of internet malware. In: Kruegel, C., Lippmann, R., Clark, A. (eds.) RAID 2007. LNCS, vol. 4637, pp. 178–197. Springer, Heidelberg (2007)
2. Banescu, S., Wüchner, T., Guggenmos, M., Ochoa, M., Pretschner, A.: FEEBO: an empirical evaluation framework for malware behavior obfuscation. CoRR, arXiv:1502.03245 (2015)
3. Bhatkar, S., Chaturvedi, A., Sekar, R.: Dataflow anomaly detection. In: S&P, pp. 15. IEEE (2006)
4. Borello, J.-M., Me, L.: Code obfuscation techniques for metamorphic viruses. J. Comput. Virol. 4, 211–220 (2008)
5. Brandes, U.: A faster algorithm for betweenness centrality. J. Math. Sociol. 25(2), 163–177 (2001)
6. Canali, D., Lanzi, A., Balzarotti, D., Kruegel, C., Christodorescu, M., Kirda, E.: A quantitative study of accuracy in system call-based malware detection. In: ISSTA. ACM (2012)
7. Cavallaro, L., Sekar, R.: Taint-enhanced anomaly detection. In: Jajodia, S., Mazumdar, C. (eds.) ICISS 2011. LNCS, vol. 7093, pp. 160–174. Springer, Heidelberg (2011)

8. Chawla, N.V., Bowyer, K.W., Hall, L.O., Kegelmeyer, W.P.: Smote: synthetic minority over-sampling technique. J. Artif. Intell. Res. **16**(1), 321–357 (2002)
9. Christodorescu, M., Jha, S., Kruegel, C.: Mining specifications of malicious behavior. In: India Software Engineering Conference, pp. 5–14 (2008)
10. Christodorescu, M., Jha, S., Seshia, S., Song, D., Bryant, R.: Semantics-aware malware detection. In: S&P 2005, pp. 32–46 (2005)
11. Forrest, S., Hofmeyr, S., Somayaji, A., Longstaff, T.: A sense of self for Unix processes. In: S&P, pp. 120–128 (1996)
12. Fredrikson, M., Christodorescu, M., Jha, S.: Dynamic behavior matching: a complexity analysis and new approximation algorithms. In: Bjørner, N., Sofronie-Stokkermans, V. (eds.) CADE 2011. LNCS, vol. 6803, pp. 252–267. Springer, Heidelberg (2011)
13. Fredrikson, M., Jha, S., Christodorescu, M., Sailer, R., Yan, X.: Synthesizing near-optimal malware specifications from suspicious behaviors. In: S&P, pp. 45–60. IEEE (2010)
14. Ghosh, A.K., Schwartzbard, A., Schatz, M.: Learning program behavior profiles for intrusion detection. In: Workshop on Intrusion Detection and Network Monitoring, p. 6 (1999)
15. Hall, M., Frank, E., Holmes, G., Pfahringer, B., Reutemann, P., Witten, I.H.: The weka data mining software: an update. ACM SIGKDD Explor. Newsl. **11**(1), 10–18 (2009)
16. Jang, J., Woo, J., Yun, J., Kim, H.K.: Mal-netminer: malware classification based on social network analysis of call graph. In: WWW (2014)
17. Kirda, E., Kruegel, C., Banks, G., Vigna, G., Kemmerer, R.A.: Behavior-based spyware detection. In: USENIX (2006)
18. Kolbitsch, C., Comparetti, P.M., Kruegel, C., Kirda, E., Zhou, X., Wang, X.: Effective and efficient malware detection at the end host. In: USENIX, pp. 351–366 (2009)
19. Lanzi, A., Balzarotti, D., Kruegel, C., Christodorescu, M., Kirda, E.: Accessminer: using system-centric models for malware protection. In: CCS, pp. 399–412 (2010)
20. Lee, J., Jeong, K., Lee, H.: Detecting metamorphic malwares using code graphs. In: SAC (2010)
21. Lee, W., Stolfo, S.J., Chan, P.K.: Learning patterns from unix process execution traces for intrusion detection. In: Workshop on AI Approaches to Fraud Detection and Risk Management, pp. 50–56 (1997)
22. Mao, W., Cai, Z., Guan, X., Towsley, D.: Centrality metrics of importance in access behaviors and malware detections. In: ACSAC. ACM (2014)
23. Milea, N.A., Khoo, S.C.: Nort: runtime anomaly-based monitoring of malicious behavior for windows, pp. 115–130 (2012)
24. Nappa, A., Rafique, M.Z., Caballero, J.: Driving in the cloud: an analysis of drive-by download operations and abuse reporting. In: Rieck, K., Stewin, P., Seifert, J.-P. (eds.) DIMVA 2013. LNCS, vol. 7967, pp. 1–20. Springer, Heidelberg (2013)
25. Okamoto, K., Chen, W., Li, X.-Y.: Ranking of closeness centrality for large-scale social networks. In: Preparata, F.P., Wu, X., Yin, J. (eds.) FAW 2008. LNCS, vol. 5059, pp. 186–195. Springer, Heidelberg (2008)
26. Park, Y., Reeves, D.S., Stamp, M.: Deriving common malware behavior through graph clustering. Comput. Secur. **39**, 419–430 (2013)
27. Preda, M., Christodorescu, M., Jha, S., Debray, S.: A semantics-based approach to malware detection. ACM SIGPLAN Notices, pp. 1–12 (2007)

28. Rieck, K., Holz, T., Willems, C., Düssel, P., Laskov, P.: Learning and classification of malware behavior. In: Zamboni, D. (ed.) DIMVA 2008. LNCS, vol. 5137, pp. 108–125. Springer, Heidelberg (2008)
29. Rieck, K., Trinius, P., Willems, C., Holz, T.: Automatic analysis of malware behavior using machine learning. J. Comput. Secur. **19**, 639–668 (2011)
30. Sharif, M.I., Lanzi, A., Giffin, J.T., Lee, W.: Impeding malware analysis using conditional code obfuscation. In: NDSS (2008)
31. Wressnegger, C., Schwenk, G., Arp, D., Rieck, K.: A close look on n-grams in intrusion detection: anomaly detection vs. classification. In: Workshop on Artificial Intelligence and Security, pp. 67–76 (2013)
32. Wüchner, T., Ochoa, M., Pretschner, A.: Malware detection with quantitative data flow graphs. In: ASIACCS (2014)
33. Wüchner, T., Pretschner, A.: Data loss prevention based on data-driven usage control. In: ISSRE, pp. 151–160, November 2012
34. Yin, H., Song, D., Egele, M., Kruegel, C., Kirda, E.: Panorama: capturing system-wide information flow for malware detection and analysis. In: CCS, pp. 116–127 (2007)
35. You, I., Yim, K.: Malware obfuscation techniques: a brief survey. In: BWCCA, pp. 297–300 (2010)

Binary Analysis and Mobile Malware Protection

Jackdaw: Towards Automatic Reverse Engineering of Large Datasets of Binaries

Mario Polino[⊠], Andrea Scorti, Federico Maggi, and Stefano Zanero

DEIB, Politecnico di Milano, Milan, Italy
{mario.polino,federico.maggi,stefano.zanero}@polimi.it,
andrea.scorit@mail.polimi.it

Abstract. When analyzing an untrusted binary, reverse engineers usually rely on ad-hoc collections of interesting dynamic patterns—known as behaviors in the malware-analysis community—and static patterns—known as signatures in the antivirus community. Such patterns are often part of the skill set of the analyst, sometimes implemented in manually-created post-processing scripts. It would be desirable to be able to automatically find such behaviors, present them to analysts, and create a systematic catalog of matching rules and relevant implementations. We propose JACKDAW, a system that finds interesting dynamic patterns, and ranks them to unveil potentially interesting behaviors. Then, it annotates them with static information, capturing the distinct implementations of each across different malware families. Finally, JACKDAW associates semantic information to the behaviors, so as to create a descriptive summary that helps the analysts in querying the catalog of behaviors by type. To do this, it leverages the dynamic information and an indexed Web-based knowledge databases.

We implement and demonstrate JACKDAW on the Win32 API (even if the technique can be generalized to any OS). On a dataset of 2,136 distinct binaries, including both malicious and benign libraries and executables, we compared the behaviors extracted automatically against a ground truth of 44 behaviors created manually by expert analysts. JACKDAW found 77.3 % of them and was able to exclude spurious behaviors in 99.6 % cases. We also discovered 466 novel behaviors, among which manual exploration and review by expert reverse engineers revealed interesting findings and confirmed the correctness of the semantic tagging.

1 Introduction

The increasing interest around reverse engineering complex legacy, untrusted or malicious binaries demands for automated tools that aid the analysts. Recent works such as Howard [36] or TIE [20] propose intelligent solutions to tackle some of the hard aspects of "reversing". We believe that research efforts in this direction are needed to turn reverse engineering from an art into a more structured engineering discipline with appropriate methodologies, tools and computer-supported processes.

© Springer International Publishing Switzerland 2015
M. Almgren et al. (Eds.): DIMVA 2015, LNCS 9148, pp. 121–143, 2015.
DOI: 10.1007/978-3-319-20550-2_7

Research Challenges. One of the main challenges of reverse engineering is achieving automation, in order to overcome the shortage of skilled analysts. A variety of static- and dynamic-analysis tools exist and are very useful to this end. Moreover, so-called "hybrid analysis" approaches can be used to balance their symmetric strengths and weaknesses [6,10,21,34]. We believe that hybrid approaches can be pushed forward and leveraged to obtain better reverse engineering tools.

The core aim of hybrid analysis techniques is to help bridging the semantic gap between static and dynamic analysis, using as a pivot the concept of *behavior*, expressed in different ways and abstraction levels (e.g., groups of API or system calls, instruction sequences). Thus, the automatic identification of such behaviors is an interesting and challenging research problem with immediate and profound practical impact. Such an output could, for example, be used by a plugin for reverse-engineering tools to automatically highlight and annotate certain portions of the CFG to prioritize the analysis based on the information extracted from a large, collaborative back-end database, freeing up valuable analyst time to focus on novel, interesting behaviors. Such behaviors could then be fed back into the behavior database.

Goals and Approach. We propose a practical approach to automatically extract behavior specifications. JACKDAW is based on the correlation of control- and data-flow information extracted from binaries both statically (after unpacking) and dynamically.

Under the realistic assumption that data-flow-dependent APIs or system calls are signs of strictly-related events, we can automatically recognize groups of relevant actions that could constitute a behavior, without any previous knowledge of that behavior. More precisely, if a sequence of API or system calls connected through data-flow dependency (which we call *sequence of dataflow-dependent API calls* for brevity) is recurrent within many binaries, it could constitute a meaningful and interesting behavior.

Obviously, frequency alone is not enough. We exploit the observation of previous work (e.g., [21]) that code reuse in malware is common, also across families that evolve independently. Thus, we leverage the availability of a large number of samples to find different, recurring implementations of such behaviors, which confirm their consistency. In a way, we are turning the abundance of malware variants against the adversaries.

System Overview. JACKDAW first identifies candidate behaviors as groups of API functions. The groups are formed by means of dynamically extracted data-flow dependencies, and using a similarity criterion based on the Control Flow Graph (CFG). Then, JACKDAW builds a model of each group, which essentially is the list of the most frequent function calls contained. Finally, JACKDAW leverages a knowledge base (e.g., StackOverflow) to associate function names and semantic tags.

Impact. The difference between JACKDAW and previous works that employ clustering in malware analysis is clear: JACKDAW does *not* cluster the *binaries* in any way. Instead, it uses clustering techniques to *assist the discovery* of (relevant) behaviors automatically. Clustering executable binaries based on shared, known behaviors has been already done in the past [17,33] and is not the focus of our work. In fact, our motivation is exactly the opposite, we do not assume any knowledge about behaviors. Thus, the goal is to find recurrent and correlated data-flow and CFG sub-graphs that could represent a behavior.

The output of our system (i.e., a list of high-level dynamic traces enriched with static information) could be used as input to other hybrid analysis systems that need behavior definitions to work, thus relieving the analyst from the burden of producing behavior specifications manually. It could also be used to build binary clustering or classification techniques. Finally, it could be used by a plugin for reverse-engineering tools in order to automatically annotate portions of the CFG that implement behaviors.

Evaluation Summary. We compared the behaviors extracted automatically by JACKDAW against a ground truth of 44 known behaviors constructed manually (and tediously) with the help of a malware analyst. Our results on real-world malicious and benign binaries indicate that JACKDAW finds up to 77.3 % of the ground truth behaviors, and effectively "suggests" interesting new ones: We verified this by validating novel extracted behaviors with the help of a panel of malware analysts. In a similar fashion, we were able to validate the automated semantic tagging of behaviors. Moreover, when applied across binaries of distinct categories (e.g., malicious vs. benign), we show that JACKDAW is useful to lookup in the benign binaries (only) those behaviors constructed from malicious binaries, with high precision. Indeed, when used to query a behavior catalog constructed from malicious binaries, only 0.4 % of such behaviors are found in benign binaries, showing that JACKDAW could be used to perform differential analysis and similar tasks. Finally, we show that JACKDAW can recognize (new) behaviors in binaries never seen before.

Contributions. In summary:

- We present an unsupervised approach to ease and systematize the task of reverse engineering by automatically extracting high-level behavior descriptions from a large dataset of binaries.
- We remove a time consuming manual step in hybrid static-dynamic analysis processes, namely the definition of high level behaviors.
- We propose an automatic algorithm to associate semantic tags to behaviors, allowing (inexperienced) analysts to understand their actions.

2 Binary Analysis and Reverse Engineering

Static and dynamic analysis techniques have symmetric pros and cons. The key advantage of static analysis is the good code coverage, whereas the main disadvantage is that it requires skills and time to understand the results. Moreover, these techniques suffer from compiler optimization, packing, obfuscation, polymorphism, and other code-transformation techniques applied both to good-ware, for intellectual-property protection, and to malware, for evading static signatures. Dynamic-analysis techniques are based on tracking events at differ-ent abstraction levels (e.g., machine instructions, file system writes, network activity, auto-update capabilities, registry actions) while a binary executes. The relevant events are obtained in various ways (e.g., API hooking in user or ker-nel mode, custom kernel). Symmetrically to static analysis, dynamic analysis requires significantly less skills and effort to be understood and is resilient to code transformations. The main limitation is that we can only analyze the pieces of code that are actually executed during the analysis. Therefore, some features remain hidden, either by chance or intentionally (e.g., evasion). Code coverage can be increased with proper code-stimulation techniques, at the price of an increased complexity, and by relying on hardware-level introspection. As shown by a recent quantitative analysis [40], a combination of static and dynamic analy-sis, creating so-called *hybrid* approaches, is the key to achieve the best recall and precision.

We observe that previous work revolve around the concept of *behavior* [16,26], which is leveraged as the bridge between static an dynamic techniques. This concept has been used for various purposes, ranging from classification to analysis [21] and detection. In a general meaning, a behavior is a set of events—possibly along with arguments and types (see [20,36])—observed during dynamic analysis. The classic example is a trace of system or API calls. Current approaches require that the analyst defines behaviors manually To take reverse engineering and malware analysis one step further, our first goal is to generate (candidate) behaviors in a fully automatic way. More precisely, we want to find groups of API calls that *could be* the building blocks of a higher level action, from the results of hybrid analysis. Our second goal is to reduce the gap between the API functions used to describe a behavior and their semantic meaning (i.e., what the analyst wants to understand). In other words, we want to assign a name to a behavior, and thus complete the bottom-up recognition of the top-level behavioral description in [26]. Then, we want to attach static information (e.g., basic blocks) to the extracted behaviors.

Our starting point are the data dependencies, identified through dynamic data-flow analysis (DFA). In short, DFA allows to "track" data in memory by following copy or other manipulation operations. For instance, this means that the result of an operation receives the union of labels of the operation's argu-ments. Although in principle any DFA technique could be used, we base our implementation on value-based DFA, by connecting the return values (and out-put arguments) of one API call with the input arguments of subsequent calls, creating sets of connected calls. These sets are the initial candidates to mine behavior specifications. The challenge, however, is that these sets can contain API calls that are irrelevant to defining a behavior. We want to find smaller groups of API calls that are the "core" of these sets and that frequently occur together, in a way automating the process of identifying bottom-up the "lower level" of the hierarchy explained in [26].

3   System Details

As summarized in Fig. 1, JACKDAW comprises four steps. **Step 1 (Data Collection)** collects and pre-processes static and dynamic information, **Step 2 (Clustering of Data-flow Information)** groups the sequences of dataflow-dependent API calls that have the same CFG fingerprints, and in **Step 3 (Behavior Extraction)**, the clusters are modeled by means of the representative API calls found in the sequences of dataflow-dependent API calls. **Step 4 (Semantic Tagging)** attaches meaningful tags to each extracted behavior.

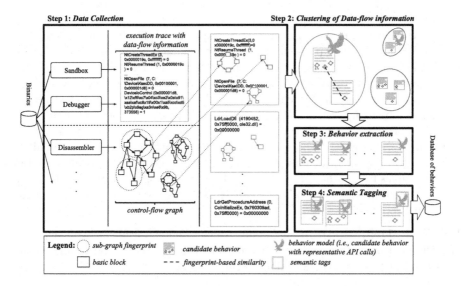

Fig. 1. Step 1: Data Collection combines static information (CFG) and dynamic information (execution traces). **Step 2: Clustering of Data-flow Information** groups the sequences of dataflow-dependent API calls that have the same CFG fingerprints. In **Step 3: Behavior Extraction**, the clusters are modeled by means of the representative API calls found in the sequences of dataflow-dependent API calls. **Step 4: Semantic tagging**, semantic tags are attached for each model.

3.1   Step 1: Data Collection

We let each binary run in a monitored environment, this preliminary execution step also unpacks packed code, if any, by letting the executable run and then dumping the process memory. Clearly, a solution to the generic and challenging problem of packing is out of the scope of this work. During execution we collect the set of sequences of dataflow-dependent API calls and map any data dependencies to the code where the API function is called. Here, we represent the *static code* by means of sub-graphs of the CFG (built from the memory dump), which we call *fingerprints*.

Introspection and DFA. In our implementation we use an introspection technique proven to work well even in case of malicious binaries [7,27,31]. During tracing, we attach labels to interesting data flows. The flow sources are the API calls (with their return values). We propagate these labels whenever they are copied or otherwise manipulated. This is essentially taint analysis, although we prefer to use the term data-flow analysis, which is more generic. Indeed, if type information is available, our technique can be easily extended. In practice, for each API function called, we extract the parameters' name and actual value at the moment of invocation. Then, we use data-flow information to connect the return values (and out-arguments) of one API call with the in-arguments of subsequent calls.

Static Information. We also map each sequence of dataflow-dependent API calls to the code that implements it. To represent (and compare) code blocks in a way that is resilient to recompilation in different contexts, we use the notion of *fingerprints*, which are sub-graphs of size k (in our work, as in previous and recent work, we use $k = 10$) of the colored CFG obtained from the unpacked binary code. The unpacking step is obviously optional. The CFG is colored according to the types of instructions contained in each basic block. Each sub-graph can be conveniently represented and efficiently matched using a hash. This technique is proven to be resilient against polymorphism [19] and was successfully used in recent samples by Comparetti et al. in [6]. Finally, we normalize the API function names (e.g., removing 'A', 'W', 'Ex' suffixes referring to different versions of the same function).

Behavior (Definition). At this point, we can define a *behavior* as a sequence of API function names and parameters, and the respective static fingerprints used to identify its implementation on the CFG.

3.2 Step 2: Clustering of Data-Flow Information

The input of this phase is a set of sequences of dataflow-dependent API calls, enriched with static information. The goal is to group sequences of dataflow-dependent API calls by their similarity. The requirements are a simple, fast clustering algorithm to keep the analysis time under control. The algorithm must be one-pass and distance-based, where clusters can evolve in an on-line mode as new samples come in. To this end, we customized the ECM algorithm [38] as explained in the reminder of this section.

Clustering Algorithm. As detailed in Fig. 2, we associate each item to the cluster with the highest (Jaccard) similarity. Recall that the items to be clustered are the sequences of dataflow-dependent API calls, each represented by their set of fingerprints. The original ECM algorithm uses average linkage to compute the distance. However, the concept of "average set of fingerprints" is meaningless in our domain. Thus, we use single linkage. For this reason, if the distance to the closest cluster s_{i*} is higher than a threshold (empirically set to $u = 0.75$, as justified in Sect. 4.2), the item is considered the first item of a new cluster.

Distance Function. Conceptually, two sequences of dataflow-dependent API calls are very similar if they share large parts of code fingerprints. Therefore, we use the fingerprints—indexed with hashes—to calculate a similarity score between each pair of sequences of dataflow-dependent API calls.

After having considered several distance metrics suitable for sets (proposed in [4]), we ended up comparing the *dice coefficient*, the *Jaccard similarity* and the *overlap coefficient*. Through a set of experiments, we concluded that Jaccard similarity works best for purposes: $J(A, B) = |A \cap B|/|A \cup B|$, where A and B are two sets of fingerprints.

```
 1: Input: dataflow_set, clusterset={c₁...cₗ}
 2: for all t ∈ dataflow_set do
 3:     for i ∈ {1...l} do
 4:         sᵢ ← J(t,cᵢ) {Jaccard similarity computation}
 5:     end for
 6:     sᵢ* ← argmax(sᵢ)
 7:     if sᵢ* > u then
 8:         cᵢ* ← cᵢ* ∪ {t}
 9:     else
10:         new cₗ₊₁
11:         cₗ₊₁ ← {t}
12:         clusterset ← clusterset ∪ cₗ₊₁
13:         l ← l + 1
14:     end if
15: end for
```

Fig. 2. Clustering algorithm based on ECM: s_{i*} is the maximum Jaccard similarity between t and all the sequences of dataflow-dependent API calls in the i-th cluster c_i.

Since our distance metric is based on the Jaccard index, alternative approaches could be used (e.g., locality-sensitive hashing). However, we consider exploring such alternatives an orthogonal aspect of our contribution, beyond demonstrating our idea.

We run a pilot experiment on a distance function based on the API calls that two sequences of dataflow-dependent API calls have in common. However, this approach would yield very sparse clustering, too biased by dormant code. Indeed, we show that different sets of APIs are found in similar portions of code (i.e., implementing the very same behavior).

3.3   Step 3: Behavior Extraction

Each cluster is now a potential candidate behavior, of which we know that all elements share similar code. The goal of this step is to create a succint cluster model that represents the sequences of dataflow-dependent API calls that it contains. For this, we need to find a small set of API calls that characterize each cluster. To this end, we propose an heuristic based on the frequency of each API call, which searches for sequences of dataflow-dependent API calls that have sub-sequences of API calls in common. Our hypothesis, validated by our experiments, is that they will also share (parts of) the implementation code.

As a result, since each cluster carries the respective fingerprints, we have obtained a *dictionary of behaviors* (i.e., set of APIs) with several implementations (i.e., CFG fingerprints). In addition to the fingerprint information that is useful for fast indexing, we store the static information associated to each behavior as a set of offsets that identify the code into the binary. Therefore, this dictionary can be used to statically match behaviors, both in new, unseen binaries, or in binaries where such behaviors are implemented but "dormant" [6]. Notably, the ability to produce both a static and dynamic description of behaviors is useful because in this way we are not bound to dynamic analysis to identify behavior in samples.

Extraction Logic. To find the set of APIs that will build a cluster model we consider an API as part of a behavior if it appears frequently within the same cluster. This means that, given the same portions of code (i.e., CFG fingerprints of a cluster), the most frequent APIs are those that are manifested during dynamic analysis. An API is representative of a cluster, and thus part of its model, if it appears more frequently than a threshold f in the cluster. We found $f = 0.75$ to be a good value empirically, as justified by our experiments. A conservative choice would be $f = 1.00$, which would mean that we use as a descriptor only APIs that appear in all the sequences of dataflow-dependent API calls of the cluster. This, however, is brittle and decreases the amounts of behaviors found (as will be evident in Sect. 4.2): Indeed, it does not take into account dormant behaviors [6], or the possibility that a behavior contains multiple branches and thus alternative portions of code.

At this point, as shown in Fig. 1 (right), we merge the behaviors that have the same API function names, thus enriching the set of fingerprints (i.e., code fragments) associated to each behavior. Two clusters are merged if their have the same model (i.e., same set of representative APIs). Recall that although the cluster modeling is done at behavioral level, the clustering is obtained based on a distance function calculated on the CFGs (i.e., static code level). Therefore, merging these models will produce clusters that contains several sets of these fingerprints, each representing a specific implementation of the behavior. Consequently, distinct clusters could yield the very same model.

As a result, we obtain a linked graph (excerpt in Fig. 10). This creates our catalog of behaviors. In this graph we show the inclusion relationships, to show which behaviors depend on which behaviors, pretty much like the behavior graphs produced by [26].

Type Information. If type information is available from **Step 1**, we take into account also the arguments of the representative APIs. To this end, we ported to Win32 the well-known, robust models implemented in [24,29] for the most common data types of Linux system calls. We focused on the four most common types of parameters in our proof of concept implementation: strings, tokens, IP addresses and transport protocols. The first two are precisely the same present in [24], while the latter two are just specializations of the token model.

3.4 Step 4: Semantic Tagging

The goal is now to tag candidate behaviors with human-readable semantic descriptions. The rationale is that each API call has a role in building the overall behavior. The final result is a set of candidate behaviors and dictionaries of their implementations, and tagged with keywords that can help the analyst in determining their semantics.

Sources of Semantic Tags. We first explored the official MSDN documentation. However, it considers the API functions when used alone, not in various combinations. Therefore, we exploited the abundant, structured information available nowadays in community-driven websites. As a proof of concept, we obtained data from StackOverflow, a popular community-based Q&A website extensively used by programmers. Questions about programming problem often include code snippets, and are always tagged as enforced by the site. In principle, any of such knowledge databases could be used, including custom ones built by the analyst over time, which makes JACKDAW fairly flexible.

Tagging Algorithm. For each element of the power set of the set API function names and parameters of each behavior, we search our dump of StackOverflow for questions that contain that element and extract title, body and tags. For example, given a behavior that contains Connect Port 25, for each StackOverflow result[1] we extract the title (e.g., "Send mail through gmail SMTP server using Win API"), body and tags (e.g., "winapi", "smtp", "gmail"). For each post, we compute Score(*post*) from two configurable lists:

- **Interesting tags list**: we add +1 for each word of this list contained in a post; this (extensible) list currently contains ^c$, c\+\+, c\#, win in order to lookup posts strictly related to Windows APIs.
- **Trifling tags list**: we add −1 for each word of this list contained in a post; this (extensible) list currently contains words such as php, python, and other language names, which suggest that the post is related to a specific programming language or context, not to the Win API.

These lists are an important customization aspect of a reverse-engineering product based on our technique: Indeed, the analyst should be able to tailor her lists based on the focus, which can obviously change.

Any post with a positive overall score is marked as relevant. We then weight the resulting relevant tags and posts with

$$\text{Score}(tag, post) = \frac{\text{Score}(post)}{N} \cdot \text{Found}(post, tag)$$

where Found(*post*, *tag*) $\in$ 0, 1 is 1 only if the *post* contains the given *tag*, N is the number of relevant posts. With this, we can calculate a vote for each tag as

$$\text{Vote}(tag) = \sum_{post \in \text{All posts}} \text{Score}(post)$$

---

[1] http://stackoverflow.com/questions/3281260/send-mail-through-gmail-smtp-server-using-win-api.

which we use to build a ranked list of tags. The human analyst can choose how many suggestions (s)he wishes to see for each behavior. Thanks to our experimental results (Sect. 4.4) we discuss the quality of the suggestions, and show that applicable clues to the behavior semantic meaning show up very early in the list. Our experiment shows that tags are already a useful means to create a succinct description of a behavior. Moreover, indexing and querying tags is space and time efficient. Therefore, we leave more complex techniques borrowed from natural language processing field as future improvements, as discussed in Sect. 5.

4   Experimental Evaluation

Our main goal is to validate the behaviors produced by JACKDAW. We apply it to both malicious and benign binaries. We first show that behaviors extracted from a large corpus of real-world malware samples from different families are consistent with those that an analyst would have found via manual analysis. In addition, we show that these behaviors are found on new malware families, never seen before by our system. Secondly, we show that the behavior catalog so produced does not include spurious behaviors. In fact, we show that the behaviors extracted from malicious binaries are not found in benign binaries. Clearly, some behaviors can be in common between different classes of binaries, but their implementation usually differs. JACKDAW carries such (static) information with each behavior, and thus makes this type of reasoning feasible. As a side result, our findings suggest that the behaviors discovered by JACKDAW may be used to some extent to classify binaries on a per-behavior basis, although this should be done cautiously because behaviors could be shared. Last, we conduct a survey from which we obtained 71 responses from a pool of expert reverse engineers that provided positive feedback on the usefulness of the behaviors produced by JACKDAW.

We hosted JACKDAW on an Intel Core i7 CPU Q 720 @ 1.60 GHz, with 4 GB of RAM, running Linux. We obtained access to the Anubis [1] sandbox for **Step 1**.

4.1   Dataset and Ground Truth

We collected 1,272 (about 10 GB of data flow traces) samples belonging to 17 malware families (Banload, Cycbot, Dapato, Gamarue, Generic Downloader, Generic Trojan, Graftor, Kelihos, Llac, OnlineGames, ZangoHotbar, and ZeuS). Additionally, for the experiment described in Sect. 4.4 we used a dataset comprising 864 distinct benign binaries (e.g., PE32 executables and DLL libraries) extracted randomly from the Windows/ sub-directory of a clean computer.

To validate our system we needed *known* behaviors. For this, we manually reverse engineered one sample from each family and, in addition, we manually inspected the sequences of dataflow-dependent API calls, extracted through **Step 1**, from randomly picked samples. With the help of a malware analyst, we ended up creating 44 ground truth behaviors, subsequently validated by other two distinct reverse engineers. We included behaviors in the following categories: network activity, download & execute, file harvesting, history harvesting, disabling task manager, browser hijacking, disabling an AV, autorun, disabling Windows firewall, unpacking. In Sect. 4.3 we use these behaviors as a reference to tune our parameters, in Sect. 4.4 we use these behaviors as an oracle to determine if JACKDAW would be able to find them automatically.

4.2 Parameter Estimation

In **Step 2** and **3** (Sect. 3.2 and 3.1) we introduced two parameters. One of these parameters is the threshold u used by the clustering algorithm to decide to split an incoming item and form a new cluster around it. High values of u yield many clusters (i.e., candidate behaviors), with representative sets that would have a large number of API calls, which then the merging step would hardly be able to merge again.

A second parameter, f, determines how frequent an API needs to be in a cluster to be considered a representative. A conservative choice would be $f = 1.00$, which would mean that only APIs that appear in all of the sequences of dataflow-dependent API calls of the cluster would be a descriptor. This would create very small descriptions, and decrease the numbers of behaviors found: Some clusters may not have APIs that appear in all sets at all; some others may been implemented using different APIs. On the other hand a lax choice would generate "representative sets" that would contain spurious APIs, and thus not match any real behavior.

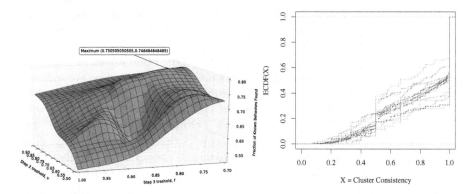

Fig. 3. Selection of the parameters used in **Step 2** and **Step 3** by optimization of the number of behaviors found in a labeled portion of the dataset.

Fig. 4. Cluster consistency distribution of all families (one line per family).

Since their effects interfere, it is necessary to jointly estimate these parameters. To do so, we exploit the availability of a ground truth of known, manually

Table 1. Results of similarity metric selection (**Step 2**).

Family	Dice Coefficent		Jaccard Similarity		Overlap Similarity	
API sequence →	#	%	#	%	#	%
Banload	63	75	63	78	87	51
	21	25	18	22	82	49
Dapato	97	86	97	86	6	03
	16	14	16	14	191	97
Gamarue	16,411	53	15,142	53	13,634	34
	14,416	47	13,583	47	25,940	66
Llac	412	90	412	91	209	86
	43	10	41	09	34	14
Gen.Downloader	8,676	64	8,211	72	12,095	29
	4,807	36	3,216	28	29,193	71

labeled behaviors. In Fig. 3 we plot, on the x and y axes, the two parameters, respectively, and on z the fraction of the ground truth behaviors extracted by JACKDAW with that combination of parameters. This surface has a global maximum in $f = 0.75$ and $u = 0.75$. It should be noted that the sensitivity with respect to this choice is not high (because of the smoothness of the surface), so we can use these parameter values safely.

4.3   Clustering Validation (Step 2)

The first set of experiments is targeted to validating the sequence of steps we designed and the assumptions we took for each step.

Similarity Metric Selection. In order to select the best similarity metric for sequences of dataflow-dependent API calls, we want our clustering to be able to group sequences of dataflow-dependent API calls that belong to the same behavior together. We used our 44 ground-truth behaviors as a reference exploring metrics chosen in [4] .

In Table 1, sequences of dataflow-dependent API calls that are similar according to each metric and that belong to the same reference behaviors are marked in white (correct), whereas the sequences of dataflow-dependent API calls that are similar only according to the metric but that belong to different behaviors are marked in gray (incorrect). To minimize such misclassification, we can use either the Dice or Jaccard distance with similar performance, whereas the overlap coefficient consistently perform worse. According to these results, we chose the Jaccard similarity for all of our next experiments, which is also fast to compute.

Consistency. The aim of this experiment is to verify whether the clusters obtained using fingerprints are consistent with their representative API functions. In other words, we want to verify our assumption that if we cluster samples using only static features (i.e., CFG fingerprints), and then cluster the same samples using only dynamic feature (i.e., API calls), we end up obtaining consistent clusters (i.e., basically the same clusters).   To verify this, we proceeded as follows. Operating on each cluster, we applied the same clustering algorithm, first on (sets of) fingerprints then on (sets of) API function names. In an optimal case, such algorithm should generate the same clustering. To visually represent this, in the examples on Fig. 5 we plot each cluster in a separate bar (white), and we superimpose the largest sub-cluster in that cluster according to the APIs (gray). On the y-axis there is the number of sequences of dataflow-dependent API calls in the cluster. Figure 5 shows the results for Banload and Graftor, respectively. The results are good, because in almost all clusters the largest sub-cluster contains well above 50 % of the sequences of dataflow-dependent API calls, and in some cases up to 100 %. This means that our clusters are eligible for a further API functions extraction. The results on this experiment on all the malicious binary families are very similar, as summarized in Fig. 4 by means of the empirical cumulative distribution function $CDF(X)$, where X is the percentage of containment (gray bars): Most of the values are high (notice the significant density around 1.00), showing good consistency overall. Thus, we conclude that our hypothesis is empirically correct. Therefore, we can safely use the static fingerprints (i.e., implementation of a behavior) as features of a behavior.

4.4 Behavior Evaluation (Step 3)

We assess whether the behaviors extracted by our approach (1) are meaningful, (2) can be recognized in unknown binaries, and (3) correctly tagged.

Evaluating the results of JACKDAW is challenging, because it produces novel knowledge (i.e., new behaviors) using unsupervised methods. The reason is that we could not possibly have (found) all these behaviors in our ground truth, and they would require an analyst to manually verify if they are reasonable, and if tags are consistent with API functions contained therein. Having considered these aspects, in addition to compare our behaviors against the 44 behaviors defined by an expert we perform a one-off cross-validation of our behaviors.

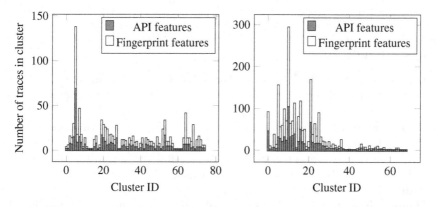

Fig. 5. Consistency of clustering (Banload left, Graftor right). Each cluster is plotted in a separate bar. In white we plot the code clusters, and in gray we superimpose the largest sub-cluster according to the APIs. On the y-axis there is the number of sequences of dataflow-dependent API calls contained in the cluster.

Comparison Against Ground Truth. We compared the behaviors extracted automatically by JACKDAW, against our ground truth of 44 behaviors built manually. This is of course not a comprehensive test of effectiveness, but rather a test of quality and precision. Overall, in about half hour JACKDAW processed our dataset was able to find, among the extracted behaviors, 34 (77.3 %) of the 44 ground-truth behaviors, which would have required days of tedious reverse engineering.

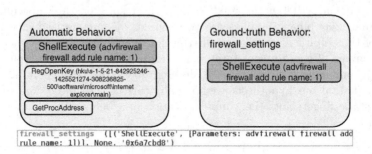

Fig. 6. Comparison of handwritten rule for a `Firewall settings` behavior and of automatically extracted specification (on the top left).

From our dataset of 1,272 malicious binaries we automatically generated 607 distinct behaviors with 2 to 3 average API functions each. Of these, 172 (28.3 %) were known to the analyst. Notably, the behaviors that we extracted are even more informative than those extracted manually: They contain more contextual information, as depicted in Fig. 6. In some cases JACKDAW reports more details that the analyst was able to specify manually (e.g., the `RegOpenKey` and `GetProc address` in Fig. 6). This useful information is part of the behavior.

Remarkably, by a manual analysis of the 435 remainder behaviors[2],which size is summarized in Fig. 7, we were able to find interesting, unknown behaviors.From this experiment we can conclude that JACKDAW is able to find, in our database, the ground-truth behaviors.

Matching Behaviors in Unknown Binaries. Besides proving that JACKDAW extracts behaviors that match those specified by expert reverse engineers, we show that the behaviors and their implementations that JACKDAW builds are useful to analyze previously unseen binaries. To do so, we create a catalog of behaviors on the malware dataset, excluding one family at a time. Then, we draw random binaries from the excluded family and verify whether they contain the behaviors from our catalog. Note that the family labels are needed only for validating the results, not for our system to work.

Figure 8 shows the fraction (in $[0, 1]$) of behaviors found in each family. The high values demonstrate that JACKDAW is able to automatically construct behaviors that have high recall in other binaries. Thus, a reverse engineer equipped

---

[2] https://gist.github.com/anonymous/6129d822af1bf299ca8a.

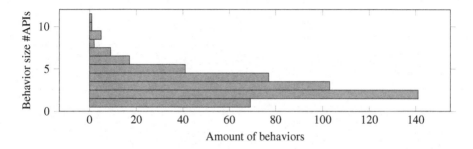

Fig. 7. Number and size (#APIs) of the new behaviors in the catalog (i.e., those not matching the behaviors specified manually by our reverse engineers).

with a dataset such as ours to run JACKDAW on, would have high chances to find behaviors in future instances of malicious binaries. As a side result, not only this is consistent with previous work [21], which demonstrated code reuse within the same malware family, but it also shows that malware developers tend to include similar behaviors across different families.

Behaviors Matching Across Classes of Binaries. We show that the behaviors catalog constructed on a dataset of a given class of binaries (i.e., malicious, in our case) does not include spurious behaviors. Spurious behaviors are essentially "noise" for the reverse engineer that want to focus on behaviors typically found in malicious programs. Notably, the results of this experiment show that JACKDAW can be used to "subtract" such noise (e.g., removing instances of behaviors extracted by benign binaries from the behaviors extracted by malicious binaries). The reason is because these behaviors describe code that is typically found in benign programs. To this end, we picked 864 Windows portable executables and libraries chosen at random from a real system and we used the (static) fingerprints extracted from such benign executables to query our behavior catalog. We searched each of the 607 behavior against every 864 benign file, obtaining 524,448 comparisons. Of these comparisons, only 2169 (0.4 %) were matching. Thus, only a minimal fraction of behaviors from our malicious binaries were found in a benign dataset. This proves that the behaviors that we have extracted from malicious binaries are very useful for a reverse engineering to focus her analysis.

Interestingly, in those 2,169 matching comparisons we were able to find instances of behaviors that JACKDAW extracted from malicious binaries. More precisely, the downloading and execution of an EXE file was found in a malicious binary, and shared 88.46 % of the code of a behavior found in the Adobe Updater. Indeed, the download-and-execute behavior is typical of benign software too.

Quality of Behavior Tagging. To evaluate the quality of behavior tagging, we took 300 extracted behaviors, tagged them with **Step 4** (Sect. 3.4), and chose the first 40 tags from our ranking and manually analyzed the results. Let us discuss emblematic examples.

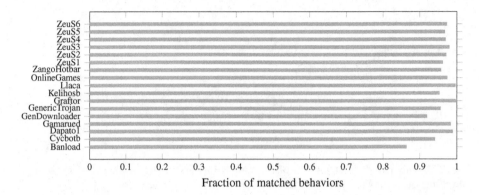

Fig. 8. Matching behaviors in unknown malware (Sect. 4.4). Each bar shows the fraction of behaviors found in each malware family, obviously we deliberately excluded the samples of that family to build the behavior catalog used for matching.

Figure 9 shows what, at first sight, is a behavior that adds a rule to a firewall—as evident by looking at the parameter of `ShellExecute`. Interestingly, within the first 5 tags there are `netsh` and `firewall`. The tag `netsh` is the command name of the NetShell utility, which is used as a scripting interface for monitoring and configuring Microsoft Windows. These tags are very close to what the behavior does.

```
ShellExecute(File: netsh, Parameters:
    advfirewall firewall add rule
    name)

RegOpenKey(hku\s
    -1-5-21-842925246-1425521274...
\software\microsoft\internet explorer\
    main)

GetProcAddress
```

Position	Tag (hint)	Score
1	netsh	71
2	registry	67
3	getprocaddress	49
4	dll	47
5	firewall	40
6	loadlibrary	19
7	installer	11
8	networking	10
9	wcf	8.1
10	mfc	8

Fig. 9. Automatically extracted behavior (a change in firewall settings), and ranking of tags.

Survey on Behaviors Quality. We asked expert reverse engineers to assign a score to randomly chosen behaviors. The scores were: "*correct*", if they understand the behavior and find it useful; "*complex*", if the behavior contains many APIs and should probably be split in sub-behaviors; "*no-sense*", if they think that the model of the behavior is wrong or useless. We obtained 71 answers: 67.71 % (48) correct, 16.90 % (12) complex, and 15.49 % (11) no-sense. These results are promising and show that the approach on which JACKDAW is based can lead to better reverse-engineering programs that suggest interesting behaviors for the analyst. The low fraction of negative feedback that we obtained from the experts is an indication that not all the extracted behaviors are useful, which is expected from a fully automated system that requires no prior knowledge.

5   Limitations and Future Work.

Despite the good results that we obtained, JACKDAW has some limitations.

First, our system shares a common limitation with all VM-based dynamic analysis tools: some binaries adopt anti-debugging or anti-virtualization techniques. This problem was first addressed in [14], which raised the problem of malware capable of fingerprinting honeypots and similar environments. It has been further shown that creating a VM or sandbox which cannot be distinguished from a real system is impractical or impossible [13]. In 2009, according to [2] 0.3 to 12.5 percent of the samples submitted to Anubis were able to detect the sandbox and refuse to run. In [22] it is shown that evasive malware was being actively developed and distributed in 2011. While overcoming this limitation is beyond the scope of our work, we can note that the problem of evasive malware is well mitigated by collecting data outside the malware execution scope. Current research focuses on using virtual machine introspection [9,12,30] instead of kernel- or user-space hooking, or work on the bare metal [8,18,39] so as to leave the ring 0 (and above) unaltered, thus limiting the malware environment fingerprinting possibilities.

A second, evident issue is that we need to unpack malware for our static analysis approach to work. We use a pragmatic approach to deal with packing: We let the executable unpack, de-obfuscate and run for at least 15 min and work on the memory snapshot. Defeating packing is not the focus of our work, and any of the more advanced unpacking techniques in the literature [15,25,34] can be used to augment our prototype.

Another limitation is the simple technique that we use to find the set of APIs that characterize a cluster. It works reasonably well, but we are considering a more complex heuristic that uses propositional logic to find whether there are (sequences of) API calls that perform similar actions but have different names and can be substituted for each other. An excerpt of an interesting case is depicted in Table 2. The analyst can easily spot that there is a rule hidden in this example: $Z =$ OpenProcess $\land$ EnumProcess $\lor$ CreateTollhelp32Snapshot $\land$ Process32First $\land$ Process32Next. More formally, we want to extract and-or rules in the form Behavior $= \bigvee_i \bigwedge_j API_{i,j}$, where $API_{i,j} \equiv API_{i,j'}$ for all $j \neq j'$, for each i. The symbol $\equiv$ indicates that two API calls can be considered equivalent because, in all the sequences of all the clusters examined, they appear always together. On the one hand, being able to extract such rules would increase the generality of the extracted behaviors by composition of two existing behaviors. On the other hand, some preliminary tests suggest that the added complexity does not pay off in terms of effectiveness. This is due to the fact that to construct these propositional-logic rules we need an exhaustive search in the power set of the API function calls that are within each cluster, which does not scale in principle.

Table 2. Each row shows the API calls found in a sequence of dataflow-dependent API calls. The names of the functions are split for space reasons.

Trace	API calls (excerpt)				
	Open-Process	Enum-Processes	CreateTool-help32-Snapshot	Process32-First	Process32-Next
1	☑	☑	☐	☐	☐
5	☑	☑	☐	☐	☐
6	☐	☐	☑	☑	☑
8	☐	☐	☑	☑	☑

Another future extension is to extract more generic behaviors by leveraging a concept that we call "behavior graph", a direct acyclic graph (DAG) where each node represents a behavior, and an edge exist between nodes if all of the APIs of a node (source) are included in the APIs of the other (destination). Nodes without incoming edges represent the most "general" behaviors. In many cases, they are composed by a single API, so they are so general that they do not really give useful information per se: we show this in Fig. 10 which magnifies a small portion of the graph to make it readable. However, by looking at behaviors "closely connected" to general behaviors (green nodes) we can see a broad classification of the behaviors in clusters such as "networking", registry, file operations, etc. Each behavior can belong to one or more of such groups. An interesting consequence that we are currently exploring is that it is possible to use this topological property to actually generate "missing" generalized behaviors.

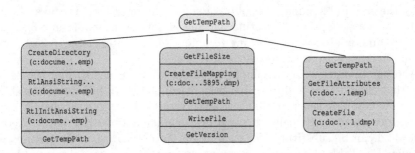

Fig. 10. Example of behavior. The `GetTempPath` API calls alone are rather useless: Instead, behaviors connected to it highlight filesystem-related actions that are useful to the analyst.

6 Related Work

Dynamic Binary Analysis. Dynamic analysis approaches are based on sandboxes or otherwise instrumented environments. Some notable sandboxes are Anubis[3], to which we obtained access for our work, TEMU [37], CWSandbox[4],

---

[3] http://anubis.iseclab.org.
[4] http://www.cwsandbox.org.

and Cuckoo[5]. Once the interesting events are collected, various post-processing techniques can be applied, for example to discover if the program is performing malicious actions. A recent, relevant work based on Anubis is [1], which extracts dynamic features and uses them to cluster similar malware samples together. We recall that this is the key difference with our work: They focus on finding groups of similar binaries, whereas we find relevant behaviors through clustering based on both dynamic and static features. Their aim is classification of malware, whereas ours is to use behaviors to aid reverse engineering.

Static Binary Analysis. Classic static analysis approaches on binary executables are based on disassembling the binary to obtain a higher-level representation based on the CFG, which has been shown to be abstract enough and resistant to obfuscation [3,19]. We use the CFG fingerprints defined in [19] as a mean to find recurring code across malware variants. In this specific part, our approach is similar to [5], which however focuses on detecting variants, whereas we provide a way to extract behaviors automatically, map them onto code, and find that code across variants.

More recent works such as [35] strive to push the abstraction further by leveraging the knowledge of the execution machine to obtain a de-compiled source code, which in principle carries more semantic than plain assembly code.

We focus specifically on explaining the reasons why an executable is malicious, by extracting the malicious behaviors and tag them semantically. Despite the good amount of research in this area, static analysis require manual work to interpret the results.

Obfuscation, Packing and Polymorphism. As shown in [28], and as motivated by the subsequent research in the field, the main drawback of static analysis arise when the malware authors transform their code [41], which is a longstanding effective practice to fool static signatures employed by current detectors deployed on the market.

Several approaches have been proposed to counteract obfuscation [23] and polymorphism. An example relevant to our work is [19], which shows that the connected sub-graph of a given size of the CFG are robust against polymorphism. We use a variant of this technique in our own work.

Binary Analysis. A significant example of hybrid analysis is Reanimator [6], which finds implementations of a dynamically observed behavior in samples that did not exhibit it, to unveil the so-called "dormant" functionalities. Relevant behaviors are detected by means of manually-written specifications. Reanimator creates a model of the identified code regions using the same CFG fingerprints we use [19]. With these hybrid models Reanimator statically checks whether another (unpacked) binary contains similar code. The key difference of our system is that we extract (relevant) high-level behavior graphs automatically, without needing manually-written specifications.

Another relevant work is Beagle [21], where the authors observe that malware authors regularly update their software in order to beat defenses, improve their

---

[5] http://cuckoosandbox.org.

capabilities or change their business model. The goal of Beagle is to observe the evolution of a malware family over time. For this, it regularly downloads new versions of the same malware, then compares them with the older ones through a series of static and dynamic diffing techniques. Then, Beagle maps found differences back to the implementation code for further analysis. Beagle also assumes that a set of high-level behaviors are available, which the authors must define manually.

We cited earlier [22]. Central to this work is once again the concept of behavior: The authors collect multiple execution traces on different environments and deem a malware as evasive if such traces differ. From this work, we can conclude that inferring *differences* between unknown behaviors automatically is feasible, whereas detecting *behaviors* automatically is still unexplored.

Analysis and Detection. An interesting approach that exploits dynamic analysis for malware detection is Panorama [42]. It executes unknown programs in a out-of-the-box installation of Microsoft Windows, using scripts to introduce sensitive information in the system. Then, it tracks propagation of this information, thanks to dynamic analysis, summarizing it in so called taint graphs. Panorama discerns malicious from benign behavior by manually defined detection policies. This and similar works are complementary to JACKDAW, since our goal is defining interesting behaviors automatically.

Behavior Extraction. The work described in [11] has a similar goal to ours. However, they concentrate on the dynamic aspect of behaviors: our behavior specifications are richer and more contextualized, as they include static information obtained by correlating many variant implementations of the same behavior. Moreover, the static information allows static matching, which is faster and, more importantly, accounts for dormant code. Another difference is that they focus on malicious binaries, whereas we do not make any apriori assumption on the intent of a program. From a technical viewpoint, their approach is to build a dependency graph from dynamic analysis of malicious and benign binaries. Then, they exploit structural leap mining to discern between malicious and benign behaviors using dependency graph built running benign code. Finally, concept analysis is used to synthesize the rule that will represents behaviors that are in malicious software e not in benign ones.

A recent related work [32] proposes to extract behaviors as significant subgraphs of the system call dependency graph. The key intuition is that graphs of goodware and malware will exhibit substantially different features, which can be used train a classifier able to extract both known and unseen behaviors from new binaries. Although this approach is related to ours, we leverage the arguments and the return values of the API calls to find interesting sub-graphs and provide a semantic meaning of the behavior extracted.

7   Conclusions

JACKDAW is able to automatically find groups of API calls that represent high-level actions, which we call behaviors, exploiting hybrid analysis on a large dataset of binaries. It maps such behaviors on the code, using fingerprints suitable for subsequent static analysis and resilient to basic code transformations. We leverage web knowledge bases to annotate behaviors with a series of hints about their nature, by means of semantic tags that support analysts in understanding what they are seeing.

We showed auto-consistency between static and dynamic components of such behaviors. Also, we showed that automatically-generated behaviors could be matched against a ground truth defined with the helps of expert analysts, resulting in 34 out of 44 manually defined behaviors being matched and automatically discovered by JACKDAW. Then, we verified by manual inspection and by means of a panel of experts that extracted behaviors are meaningful, and that their semantic tags are consistent.

As a future research direction, the outputs of our system can be used as an input to other hybrid analysis systems, or to augment reverse-engineering tools in order to automatically annotate the portions of the CFG that implement behaviors.

References

1. Bayer, U., Comparetti, P.M., Hlauschek, C., Kruegel, C., Kirda, E.: Scalable, behavior-based malware clustering. In: NDSS (2009)
2. Bayer, U., Habibi, I., Balzarotti, D., Kirda, E., Kruegel, C.: Insights into current malware behavior. In: LEET (2009)
3. Caselden, D., Bazhanyuk, A., Payer, M., McCamant, S., Song, D.: HI-CFG: construction by binary analysis and application to attack polymorphism. In: Crampton, J., Jajodia, S., Mayes, K. (eds.) ESORICS 2013. LNCS, vol. 8134, pp. 164–181. Springer, Heidelberg (2013)
4. Cesare, S., Xiang, Y.: Software Similarity and Classification. Springer Briefs in Computer Science. Springer, London (2012)
5. Cesare, S., Xiang, Y., Zhou, W.: Control flow-based malware variant detection. IEEE Trans. Dependable Secure Comput. **11**(4), 307–317 (2014). doi:10.1109/TDSC.2013.40
6. Comparetti, P.M., Salvaneschi, G., Kirda, E., Kolbitsch, C., Kruegel, C., Zanero, S.: Identifying dormant functionality in malware programs. In: SP, pp. 61–76. IEEE Computer Society, Washington, DC (2010)
7. Crandall, J.R., Wu, S.F., Chong, F.T.: Minos: architectural support for protecting control data. TACO **3**(4), 359–389 (2006)
8. Deng, Z., Zhang, X., Xu, D.: Spider: stealthy binary program instrumentation and debugging via hardware virtualization. In: ACSAC, New York, NY, USA (2013)
9. Dolan-Gavitt, B., Leek, T., Zhivich, M., Giffin, J., Lee, W.: Virtuoso: narrowing the semantic gap in virtual machine introspection. In: SP, pp. 297–312 (2011)
10. Eskandari, M., Khorshidpour, Z., Hashemi, S.: Hdm-analyser: a hybrid analysis approach based on data mining techniques for malware detection. JCV **9**(2), 77–93 (2013)
11. Fredrikson, M., Jha, S., Christodorescu, M., Sailer, R., Yan, X.: Synthesizing near-optimal malware specifications from suspicious behaviors. In: SP, pp. 45–60. IEEE Computer Society, Washington, DC (2010)

12. Fu, Y., Lin, Z.: Space traveling across vm: automatically bridging the semantic gap in virtual machine introspection via online kernel data redirection. In: SP, pp. 586–600 (2012)
13. Garfinkel, T., Adams, K., Warfield, A., Franklin, J.: Compatibility is not transparency: Vmm detection myths and realities. In: HOTOS, pp. 6:1–6:6. USENIX Association, Berkeley (2007)
14. Holz, T., Raynal, F.: Detecting honeypots and other suspicious environments. In: 6th IEEE SMC Information Assurance Workshop (2005)
15. Jacob, G., Comparetti, P.M., Neugschwandtner, M., Kruegel, C., Vigna, G.: A static, packer-agnostic filter to detect similar malware samples. In: Flegel, U., Markatos, E., Robertson, W. (eds.) DIMVA 2012. LNCS, vol. 7591, pp. 102–122. Springer, Heidelberg (2013)
16. Jacob, G., Debar, H., Filiol, E.: Behavioral detection of malware: from a survey towards an established taxonomy. JCV 4(3), 251–266 (2008)
17. Jang, J., Woo, M., Brumley, D.: Towards automatic software lineage inference. In: USENIX Security, pp. 81–96. USENIX Association, Berkeley (2013)
18. Kirat, D., Vigna, G., Kruegel, C.: Barebox: efficient malware analysis on baremetal. In: ACSAC, pp. 403–412. ACM, New York (2011)
19. Kruegel, C., Kirda, E., Mutz, D., Robertson, W., Vigna, G.: Polymorphic worm detection using structural information of executables. In: Valdes, A., Zamboni, D. (eds.) RAID 2005. LNCS, vol. 3858, pp. 207–226. Springer, Heidelberg (2006)
20. Lee, J., Avgerinos, T., Brumley, D.: Tie: principled reverse engineering of types in binary programs. In: NDSS (2011)
21. Lindorfer, M., Federico, A.D., Maggi, F., Comparetti, P.M., Zanero, S.: Lines of malicious code: insights into the malicious software industry. In: ACSAC, pp. 349–358. ACM, New York (2012)
22. Lindorfer, M., Kolbitsch, C., Milani Comparetti, P.: Detecting environment-sensitive malware. In: Sommer, R., Balzarotti, D., Maier, G. (eds.) RAID 2011. LNCS, vol. 6961, pp. 338–357. Springer, Heidelberg (2011)
23. Linn, C., Debray, S.: Obfuscation of executable code to improve resistance to static disassembly. In: CCS, pp. 290–299. ACM, New York (2003)
24. Maggi, F., Matteucci, M., Zanero, S.: Detecting intrusions through system call sequence and argument analysis. TODS 7(4), 381–395 (2008)
25. Martignoni, L., Christodorescu, M., Jha, S.: Omniunpack: fast, generic, and safe unpacking of malware. In: ACSAC, pp. 431–441. IEEE (2007)
26. Martignoni, L., Stinson, E., Fredrikson, M., Jha, S., Mitchell, J.C.: A layered architecture for detecting malicious behaviors. In: Lippmann, R., Kirda, E., Trachtenberg, A. (eds.) RAID 2008. LNCS, vol. 5230, pp. 78–97. Springer, Heidelberg (2008)
27. Moser, A., Kruegel, C., Kirda, E.: Exploring multiple execution paths for malware analysis. In: SP (2007)
28. Moser, A., Kruegel, C., Kirda, E.: Limits of static analysis for malware detection. In: ACSAC, pp. 421–430 (2007)
29. Mutz, D., Valeur, F., Vigna, G., Kruegel, C.: Anomalous system call detection. TISSEC 9(1), 61–93 (2006)
30. Nance, K., Bishop, M., Hay, B.: Virtual machine introspection: observation or interference? IEEE Secur. Priv. 6(5), 32–37 (2008)
31. Newsome, J.: Dynamic taint analysis for automatic detection, analysis, and signature generation of exploits on commodity software. In: NDSS. Internet Society (2005)
32. Palahan, S., Babic, D., Chaudhuri, S., Kifer, D.: Extraction of statistically signicant malware behaviors. In: ACSAC, New York, NY, USA, December 2013

33. Rieck, K., Trinius, P., Willems, C., Holz, T.: Automatic analysis of malware behavior using machine learning. JCS **19**(4), 639–668 (2011)
34. Royal, P., Halpin, M., Dagon, D., Edmonds, R., Lee, W.: Polyunpack: automating the hidden-code extraction of unpack-executing malware. In: ACSAC, pp. 289–300. IEEE Computer Society, Washington, DC (2006)
35. Schwartz, E.J., Lee, J., Woo, M., Brumley, D.: Native x86 decompilation using semantics-preserving structural analysis and iterative control-flow structuring. In: USENIX Security (2013)
36. Slowinska, A., Stancescu, T., Bos, H.: Howard: a dynamic excavator for reverse engineering data structures. In: NDSS. Citeseer (2011)
37. Song, D., Brumley, D., Yin, H., Caballero, J., Jager, I., Kang, M.G., Liang, Z., Newsome, J., Poosankam, P., Saxena, P.: BitBlaze: a new approach to computer security via binary analysis. In: Sekar, R., Pujari, A.K. (eds.) ICISS 2008. LNCS, vol. 5352, pp. 1–25. Springer, Heidelberg (2008)
38. Song, Q., Kasabov, N.: Ecm - a novel on-line, evolving clustering method and its applications. In: Posner, M.I. (ed.) Foundations of Cognitive Science, pp. 631–682. The MIT Press, Cambridge (2001)
39. Willems, C., Hund, R., Fobian, A., Felsch, D., Holz, T., Vasudevan, A.: Down to the bare metal: using processor features for binary analysis. In: ACSAC, pp. 189–198. ACM, New York (2012)
40. Yan, G., Brown, N., Kong, D.: Exploring discriminatory features for automated malware classification. In: Rieck, K., Stewin, P., Seifert, J.-P. (eds.) DIMVA 2013. LNCS, vol. 7967, pp. 41–61. Springer, Heidelberg (2013)
41. Yetiser, T.: Polymorphic Viruses, Implementation, Detection, and Protection (1993)
42. Yin, H., Song, D.X., Egele, M., Kruegel, C., Kirda, E.: Panorama: capturing system-wide information flow for malware detection and analysis. In: Ning, P., di Vimercati, S.D.C., Syverson, P.F. (eds.) CCS, pp. 116–127. ACM, New York (2007)

Fine-Grained Control-Flow Integrity Through Binary Hardening

Mathias Payer[1]([envelope]), Antonio Barresi[2], and Thomas R. Gross[2]

[1] Purdue University, West Lafayette, USA
mathias.payer@nebelwelt.net
[2] ETH Zurich, Zürich, Switzerland

Abstract. Applications written in low-level languages without type or memory safety are prone to memory corruption. Attackers gain code execution capabilities through memory corruption despite all currently deployed defenses. Control-Flow Integrity (CFI) is a promising security property that restricts indirect control-flow transfers to a static set of well-known locations.

We present Lockdown, a modular, fine-grained CFI policy that protects binary-only applications and libraries without requiring source-code. Lockdown adaptively discovers the control-flow graph of a running process based on the executed code. The sandbox component of Lockdown restricts interactions between different shared objects to imported and exported functions by enforcing fine-grained CFI checks using information from a trusted dynamic loader. A shadow stack enforces precise integrity for function returns. Our prototype implementation shows that Lockdown results in low performance overhead and a security analysis discusses any remaining gadgets.

1 Introduction

Memory corruption vulnerabilities are still one of the most critical types of bugs found in modern software systems. The majority of code running on current systems is written in C or C++. It is simply impossible to rewrite all these applications in a memory safe language due to the large amount of existing code. In addition, the problem of memory corruption is not restricted to low-level languages as safe languages are often implemented using low-level languages (e.g., the HotSpot Java virtual machine is implemented in C++, the CPython Python runtime is implemented in C, and Perl is implemented in C) or use native runtime libraries. Since 2006, a number of defense mechanisms like Address Space Layout Randomization (ASLR) [35], Non-Executable Memory (W⊕X)/Data Execution Prevention (DEP) [46], stack canaries [18], and safe exception handlers have been deployed in practice to limit the power of attacker-controlled memory corruption. Unfortunately, all commonly deployed defense mechanisms can be circumvented as shown by current control-flow hijack attacks.

Control-Flow Integrity (CFI) [1,4,12,16,27,33,34,38,45,47,49–52] is a security property that restricts the set of targets that can be reached by any

© Springer International Publishing Switzerland 2015
M. Almgren et al. (Eds.): DIMVA 2015, LNCS 9148, pp. 144–164, 2015.
DOI: 10.1007/978-3-319-20550-2_8

control-flow transfer to a statically determined control-flow graph. Current implementations share one or more drawbacks: (i) binary-only approaches [50–52] are restricted in their precision due to an over-approximation of the target sets where too many targets are allowed (these coarse-grained CFI policies can be exploited by attackers [8, 14, 17]), (ii) the need to recompile applications [4, 16, 34, 38, 45, 47, 49], (iii) no support (or protection) for shared libraries [1, 4, 16, 33, 38, 47], or (iv) no stack integrity protection [12, 34, 45, 48, 51, 52]. Modular CFI (MCFI) [34] recently added support for shared libraries but a recompilation of the application and all libraries is required. Furthermore, MCFI might require source code changes in the application, comes with its own `libc` implementation, which makes it less flexible, and does not support C++ code. COOP [40] presents an attack against CFI mechanisms that are unaware of C++ semantics for virtual function calls. Both MCFI and COOP were developed concurrently with Lockdown.

This paper presents Lockdown, a modular fine-grained CFI policy that supports any legacy binary. All indirect control-flow transfers are instrumented with security checks through dynamic binary translation. The target-sets for fine-grained CFI are approximated based on import and export definitions used in applications and libraries and a dynamic on-the-fly binary analysis for addresses of function pointers that are taken during the execution of the application. Using this approach, Lockdown adjusts the control-flow graph at runtime as code is being executed, growing the CFG when new code is executed, shrinking the CFG when libraries are unloaded. To protect against all forms of Return-Oriented Programming (ROP), Lockdown employs a shadow stack that enforces precise integrity of return instruction pointers. A shadow stack is stricter than a CFI check as the CFI check would allow the return instruction to target any possible call site of the current function while the shadow stack only allows the return to target the actual caller (by keeping state through the call/return relationship). A prototype implementation of our fine-grained CFI policy results in 19 % average performance overhead for SPEC CPU2006 (which is on the same order as fine-grained source-level CFI implementations) and the performance overhead for Apache 2.2 is between 1.83 % and 7.87 % (depending on the configuration). This paper makes the following contributions:

1. Demonstration that CFI handles dynamic loading without recompilation; Lockdown is the first binary-only, modular, fine-grained CFI solution that supports dynamic loading and prevents real-life control-flow hijack attacks.
2. A performance evaluation of Lockdown. Lockdown results in low performance overhead of 19.09 % on average for SPEC CPU2006 and between 1.83 % and 7.86 % on average for different Apache 2.2 configurations.
3. A CFI effectiveness and security evaluation of our fine-grained CFI approach going beyond the traditional quantitative methods. Our qualitative security evaluation method can be used to evaluate future CFI implementations.

2   Attack Model

Lockdown protects applications against control-flow hijack attacks under a powerful attack model: an attacker has read and write capabilities of the program's data regions and read capabilities of the program's code regions. This attack model reflects common efforts to circumvent deployed defenses on modern systems. The attacker uses memory corruption vulnerabilities present in the application or any of the loaded libraries to modify the program's data, thereby affecting the control-flow and execution of the program.

The attacker can neither modify the code region of the program nor inject additional code into the program. This assumption is fulfilled by current systems that enforce a W⊕X [46] strategy, where any memory area is either writable or executable (and never both at the same time). Also, the attacker cannot forcefully load attacker-controlled libraries. To achieve code execution capabilities the attacker must therefore reuse existing code sequences available in some code region of the program or its libraries [3,5,6,9,31,39,43]. As with any other CFI defense mechanism, non-control data attacks [10] are out of scope.

Using these given (practical) capabilities an attacker will try to (i) overwrite a code pointer, (ii) prepare a set of invocation frames for a code-reuse attack, and (iii) force the program to dereference and follow the compromised code pointer to achieve code execution.

3   Background and Related Work

A variety of defense mechanisms exist that protect against control-flow hijack attacks (see [44] for a systematization of attacks and defense mechanisms). Existing defense mechanisms stop control-flow hijack attacks at different stages by: (i) retrofitting type/memory safety onto existing languages [20,30], (ii) protecting the integrity of code pointers (i.e., allowing only valid code locations to change the memory area of a code pointer) [2,22,28,29], (iii) randomizing the location of code regions or code blocks (ASLR or code diversification are examples of probabilistic protections) [11,18,23,35], or (iv) verifying the correctness of code pointers when they are used, e.g., Control-Flow Integrity (CFI) [1]. CFI does not prevent memory corruption but detects corrupted values when they are used in indirect control-flow transfers. Unfortunately, CFI has not yet seen widespread use as existing implementations either affect the software development process (for source-based, fine-grained policies) or were shown to be insecure.

3.1   Control-Flow Integrity

Control-Flow Integrity (CFI) [1] and its extension XFI [16] restrict the control-flow of an application to a statically computed control-flow graph. Each indirect control-flow transfer (an indirect call, indirect jump, or function return) is allowed to transfer control at runtime only to the set of statically determined targets of this code location.

CFI relies on code integrity (i.e., an attacker cannot change the executed code of the application). Under this assumption, an attacker can only achieve code execution by controlling code pointers. CFI checks the integrity of code pointers at the location where they are used in the code. Using memory corruption vulnerabilities, an attacker may change the values of code pointers (or any other data). The attack is detected (and stopped) when the program tries to follow a compromised code pointer that refers to a location that is not in the set of allowed targets for a specific control-flow transfer instruction.

The effectiveness of CFI relies on two components: (i) the (static) precision of the control-flow graph that determines the upper bound of precision, and (ii) the (dynamic) precision of the individual runtime checks. First, CFI can only be as precise as the control-flow graph that is enforced. If the control-flow graph is too permissive, it may allow illegal control transfers. All existing CFI approaches rely on two phases: an explicit static analysis phase and an enforcement phase that executes additional checks. Most compiler-based implementations of CFI [1,2,4,16,33,38,47,49] rely on a points-to analysis for code pointers at locations in the code that execute indirect control-flow transfers. A severe limitation of these approaches is that all the protected code must be present during compilation as they do not support modularity or shared libraries. Implementations based on static binary analysis [13,27,48,50,51] either rely on relocation information (e.g., in the Windows PE executable format) or reconstruct that information using static analysis [27,52]. MCFI [34] is a recent compiler-based CFI tool that stores type information and dynamically merges points-to sets when new libraries are loaded (but does not support library unloading). Second, the initial upper bound for precision is possibly limited through the implementation of the control-flow checks (see [17] for common limitations in CFI implementations). Coarse-grained policies maintain few global sets of possible targets instead of one set per control-flow transfer: one target set each for indirect jumps, indirect calls, and function returns. The control-flow checks restrict the transfers to addresses in each set. This policy is an improvement compared to unchecked control-flow transfers but overly permissive as an attacker can hijack control-flow to any entry in the set. As demonstrated in recent work [8,14,17] these coarse-grained CFI implementations still allow attackers to successfully mount code-reuse attacks by making the exploits CFI aware, i.e., hardening them to just use gadgets still allowed in the limited set of valid targets. COOP [40], developed concurrently with our work, presents such an attack, leveraging virtual calls in C++ programs to circumvent CFI mechanisms that do not restrict call targets for virtual calls based on a type-based analysis. Recovering such precise information is hard (and often infeasible) for a binary analysis. The precision of the Lockdown CFI policy relies on the shared libraries that are used. If the same amount of code is broken into smaller libraries then the precision of Lockdown increases, limiting attacks like COOP to call targets that are imported in the current object.

Lockdown is a dynamic fine-grained CFI approach for unmodified binary-only applications (i.e., no source access is needed) that enforces a stricter, dynamically constructed *modular* control-flow graph using CFI checks and stack integrity using a shadow stack, than obtained in earlier approaches. Lockdown ensures code integrity, adds a shadow stack that protects against ROP attacks, and enforces dynamic control-flow checks for all indirect control-flow transfers.

3.2 Dynamic Binary Translation

Software-based Fault Isolation (SFI) protects the integrity of the system and/or data by executing additional guards that are not part of the original code. Dynamic Binary Translation (DBT) allows the implementation of SFI guards on applications without prior compiler involvement by translating code on the fly. The DBT system can dynamically enforce security policies by collecting runtime information and restricting capabilities of the executed code [21].

Several DBT systems exist with different performance characteristics. Valgrind [32] and PIN [25] offer a high-level runtime interface resulting in higher performance costs while DynamoRIO [7] and libdetox [36] support a more direct translation mechanism with low overhead, translating application code on the granularity of basic blocks. Lockdown builds on libdetox, which has already been used to implement several security policies.

A security policy can only be enforced if the translation system itself is secure. Libdetox splits the user-space address space into two domains: the untrusted application domain and the trusted and protected binary translator domain. This design protects the binary translation system against memory corruption attacks. Libdetox uses a separate translator stack and separate memory regions from the running application. Libdetox protects the trusted domain by randomizing address locations[1] and enforces the following properties: (i) all code is translated before execution; (ii) translated code can only access the application domain; (iii) no pointer to the trusted domain is ever stored in the application domain, protecting the trusted domain against information leakage. The application traps into the trusted domain when (i) it executes a system call, (ii) reaches untranslated code, or (iii) a full (non-inlined) security check is triggered. Libdetox relies on a trusted loader [37], protecting the DBT system from attacks against the loader when loading or unloading shared libraries.

Lockdown gives the following security guarantees: a *shadow stack* protects the integrity of return instruction pointers on the stack at all times; the *trusted loader* protects the data structures that are used to execute functions in other loaded libraries at runtime; and the *integrity* of the security mechanism is guaranteed by the binary translation system. The shadow stack is implemented by translating call and return instructions [36]. Translated call instructions push the return instruction pointer on both the application stack and the shadow stack in the trusted domain. Translated return instructions check the equivalence between the return instruction pointer on the application stack and the shadow stack; if the pointers are equivalent then control is transferred to the translated code

---

[1] The trusted domain is small both regarding code and data. An alternative implementation uses SFI and mask operations (added by the binary translator to any read/write in the application domain) to protect against information side channels [42], resulting in higher overhead.

block identified by the code pointer on the shadow stack. The existing version of libdetox supports the full x86 instruction set (including SSE extensions).

4   Lockdown Design

Lockdown enforces a fine-grained, dynamic, modular CFI policy at the granularity of individual Dynamic Shared Objects (DSO) (a DSO is an individual ELF file like the program or any used shared library) and symbols (applications or libraries for calls, symbol definitions for jumps). Lockdown restricts (i) inter-module indirect calls to functions that are exported from one object and imported in the other object, (ii) intra-module indirect calls to valid functions, (iii) indirect jump instructions to valid instructions in the same function and valid call targets for tail calls, and (iv) return instructions to the precise return address (with a special handler for exceptions). Figures 1 and 2 show examples for call and jump restrictions. The per-object target sets are adapted

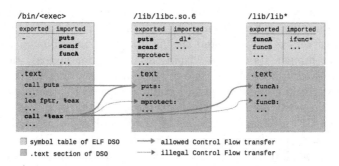

Fig. 1. Call restrictions for an executable and two libraries. DSOs are only allowed to call imported function symbols. Local function calls may only transfer to local function symbols.

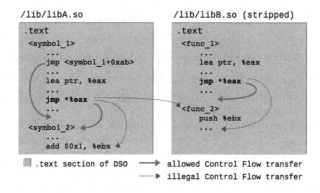

Fig. 2. Restrictions for jump instructions within two different libraries. Jumps may only target locations within the same symbol. Inter-DSO jumps are not allowed in general. If stripped, jumps have to stay within the bounds of the nearest symbol definitions.

dynamically whenever libraries are loaded or unloaded. The integrity of return instructions is enforced at all times using a shadow stack. Indirect call instructions and indirect jump instructions execute a runtime check that validates the current target according to the current location and the object's sets.

The ELF format [15, 41] specifies the on-disk layout of applications, libraries, and compiled objects. ELF files contain symbol information with different level of detail. The ELF section dynsym provides the required symbol information for inter-module calls and the optional symtab ELF section contains information about all symbols. Lockdown uses both symbol tables to construct the per-object target sets (and to infer function boundaries to restrict jumps). If only the coarse-grained dynsym table is available, e.g., because the library is stripped, then Lockdown falls back to a coarser-grained protection for intra-object calls and jumps. The policies for inter-object transfers and return targets are not affected. On current Ubuntu systems (and other popular Linux distributions) the full symtab information is available and easily installable for user-space applications and all common libraries.

In contrast to other binary CFI solutions where only one global static set of valid targets per indirect control-flow type exists (e.g., one global set for all return instructions), Lockdown provides a finer-grained approach where the set of valid targets is dynamic and specific to the instruction type, its object (for calls and jumps), its symbol within the object (for jumps), and the currently active stack frames at the time of the control-flow transfer (for returns). This setup results in a fine-grained CFI policy compared to other coarse-grained approaches that solely use (few) global sets for all valid targets. The precision of the Lockdown CFI mechanism depends on the modularity of the application. If the same amount of code is split across more libraries (e.g., one library is split into multiple libraries) then the precision of our CFI mechanism increases and becomes finer-grained. Modern applications are often implemented in a highly modular way with, e.g., LibreOffice using 297 libraries, Chromium-browser using 194 libraries, or Firefox using 29 libraries.

4.1 Rules for Control Transfers

Three different forms of indirect control transfers exist, call, jump, and return instructions. The rules for different control transfers are as follows:

1. Call instructions must always target valid functions. The set of valid functions is specific for each object. Only functions that are defined or imported in the current object are allowed as targets;
2. The target of a jump instruction must (i) target a valid instruction inside the current function (according to a linear disassembly from function beginning) or (ii) target a valid function target (due to tail call optimizations);
3. Return instructions must always transfer control back to the caller (or to one of the previous callers in exceptional cases). The DBT system transparently keeps a shadow stack data structure in the trusted domain (not visible to the application) to verify return addresses on the stack before they are dereferenced. Therefore, Lockdown always enforces the precise return target.

Additionally, Lockdown implements a set of special handlers for control-flow particularities in low-level libraries (e.g., libc) as discussed in Sect. 5.2.

4.2   Control Transfer Guards

Generally, the target of an indirect control-flow transfer is not known in advance. Therefore, a runtime check is needed and the binary translator emits a guard that executes these dynamic checks when an indirect control-flow transfer executes. Conceptually, each indirect control-flow transfer traps into the Lockdown domain and verifies that the current target is allowed according to the current location and the rules defined in Sect. 4.1. To avoid unnecessary resolutions, differents are implemented. For each DSO a lookup table is used to cache already verified transitions that can be used in the fast path. Further optimizations are described in Sect. 5.1.

Return instructions are translated to check the shadow stack. The added guard verifies that the current return address on the application stack is the same as the address that was pushed by the last call instruction. The shadow stack in the Lockdown domain keeps track of valid return targets. To allow different exceptional cases (e.g., tail calls, or C++ exception handling) the shadow stack can be resynchronized with the application stack by unwinding shadow stack frames until the frames match again. Shadow stack frames can only be *removed* by exceptions (never added), resulting in sound behavior.

4.3   Handling Stripped Binaries

For many systems, full symbol information is available (e.g., the symbol tables of all common libraries for Ubuntu 12.04 are available as separate packages). Yet, some binaries are only available in stripped form. Even if binaries are stripped, imported and exported symbols are always available and Lockdown enforces a policy that is fine-grained even without full symbol tables. The same strong CFI policy is enforced for all inter-module transfers as all required information remains available. For intra-module transfers we currently rely on heuristics (see Sect. 5.3) that detect valid transfers. A more detailed (static or dynamic) binary analysis could recover function prologues more precisely, increasing the intra-module protection to the level where full symbol information is available.

5   Prototype Implementation

The prototype implementation (Fig. 3) builds on libdetox and secuLoader [36,37]. The DBT embeds the control-flow checks during the translation of individual basic blocks. All static control-flow transfers are verified during translation and indirect (dynamic) control-flow transfers are instrumented to execute an inlined dynamic guard depending on the control-flow transfer type.

For all DBT systems, one of the biggest performance overheads is the translation of indirect control-flow transfers. Such transfers cannot be translated ahead

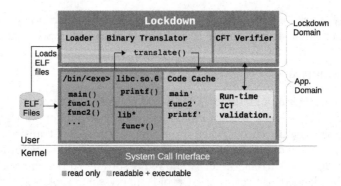

Fig. 3. Overview of the Lockdown approach. (CFT: Control-Flow Transfer, ICT: Indirect Control-Flow Transfer, ELF: Executable and Linkable Format)

of time and always incur a runtime lookup to consult the mapping between the original code and the translated code blocks before transferring control-flow to the translated code. Lockdown executes dynamic CFI checks right before the runtime lookup. To reduce the overhead of these indirect control-flow transfers Lockdown implements a set of optimizations that cache data at different levels (e.g., a cache for each indirect control-flow transfer location, a cache for lookup values in the mapping table, and a cache for frequently used symbols).

The prototype is released as open-source and is implemented in less than 24 k loc (C code mixed with a small amount of inline assembly): 2 k loc for Lockdown, 15 k loc for the binary translator and 7 k loc for the trusted loader.

5.1   Runtime Optimizations

Achieving low overhead when running binary-only applications is a challenging problem: to support dynamic CFI policies, Lockdown needs to run the binary analysis alongside the executing application. We have implemented a set of optimizations to achieve low overhead without loss of precision or security. The libdetox DBT engine already implements a set of optimizations like local inline caches for indirect control-flow transfers. We extend these lookups by a control-flow transfer check. The validation uses a lookup table for already verified {source, destination} pairs and recovers if this fast check fails (e.g., on a hash miss in the lookup table).

Furthermore, Lockdown uses inlined optimizations for different guards to avoid the validation path whenever possible. To understand indirect control-flow behavior we measured a large set of applications. Out of all indirect control-flow transfers, 51.04 % are intra-DSO calls, 19.88 % are inter-DSO calls, 28.99 % are intra-DSO jumps with only 0.09 % inter-DSO jumps. Inlined CFI checks for indirect jumps (i) check if the target stays inside the same symbol, (ii) execute a fast, direct lookup for intra-DSO targets, or (iii) redirect to a slow path. Inlined CFI checks for indirect calls (i) consult a local cache if the current target equals the last target, or (ii) redirect to the slow path that executes a full validation and updates the local cache as a side effect. Lockdown calculates symbol boundaries at translation time. Correctness of inlined checks follows due to immutability of symbol definitions and code (given by W⊕X). These optimizations effectively avoid the slow path (and full table lookup) and therefore reduce the performance overhead introduced by the control-flow transfer checks significantly.

5.2   Control-Flow Particularities

Control-flow transfers in off-the-shelf binaries do not always adhere to the rules listed in Sect. 4.1 and Lockdown catches this behavior and recovers using a set of handlers. ELF implements calls to other libraries as a call to the PLT section of the current module and an indirect jump to the real function [15]. As Lockdown can only rely on binaries (a source code approach could implement this differently) it replaces such calls with a direct call to the loaded function, removing the indirect jump and needed CFI guard. Some special cases are specific to low-level libraries like the libc runtime support functions, e.g., inter-module calls to symbols that were not imported, intra-module cross function jumptables, inter-module callback functions, or even inter-module calls targeting PLT entries which would bypass our PLT inlining if not handled correctly. Lockdown also allows indirect jumps as tail calls to the beginning of other functions in the set of currently allowed call targets. Although a variety of these special cases exist, our experience shows that they can all be handled by a small set of handlers without compromising the CFI security properties.

High-level application code (i.e., all code that is not the libc or other low-level functionality like the loader) adheres to the rules listed in Sect. 4.1 and therefore does not require special handling, except callback functions (function pointers), which are discussed in the next section.

5.3   Implementation Heuristics

Binaries have little information about the types that are used at runtime and it is not always possible to recover information precisely. To support callback functions (i.e., a function in a library returns a function pointer that is later called from a different library; if this function is not exported/imported then the CFI guard would fail), Lockdown implements a dynamic scanning technique that is similar in design to the static analysis of Zhang and Sekar proposed in [52].

Lockdown uses the following patterns to detect pointers to callback functions on the fly (i) `push imm32`, where a function pointer is pushed onto the stack, (ii) `movl imm32, rel(%esp)`, where rel references a local variable on the stack, and (iii) `leal imm32(%ebx), %e*x`, where a function pointer is moved from memory into a general purpose register relative to GOT.PLT [15], or (iv) relocations that are used to define pointers for many callbacks (e.g., R_386_RELATIVE). In addition, Lockdown scans data sections (`.data` and `.rodata`) to detect static code pointers. Lockdown's dynamic analysis allows us to use the actual values and hard-code references in our guards. Each code pointer is verified to target a valid code location. These heuristics detect code pointers at the source where they are either encoded in instructions or stored in read-only data. Such heuristics will miss pointers that are modified using pointer arithmetic or taken from attacker-controlled, writable memory. We verified that these heuristics are sufficient to protect a large set of common Unix applications. To prevent attacker-controlled manipulation of our pointer detection heuristics we ensure that code pointers detected by heuristics can only come from read-only data or the trusted loader (e.g., through the GOT.PLT section). Our heuristics purposely only detect *few* targets that can be called from any module. Note that using heuristics to find *all* possible targets would degenerate to a weak CFI policy that is open to existing attacks. A finer-grained attribution of targets to modules through a data-flow analysis remains an interesting research question.

5.4 Binary Compatibility

Binary compatibility is a challenge for approaches like Lockdown, and using heuristics leads to a formally unsound approach. We successfully tested our implementation with a large set of applications, compilers, and optimization levels without problems. Our experience shows that low-level particularities (e.g., of the libc) can be handled in an automated and efficient way. As a dynamic approach, there are few limits to implement special handling and therefore Lockdown can easily be extended to account for possibly remaining special cases where binary compatibility is broken. An example concern might be that `ret` instructions are implemented as `pop;jmp*;` sequences. We did not experience this potential issue in any of our tests, but such sequences can be handled by simulating a `ret` instruction. Furthermore, all recently proposed CFI approaches [34,50–52] come with either a binary or source code compatibility risk and none of them can guarantee full compatibility. Even MCFI [34] cannot guarantee full C source code compatibility and requires source code changes within the SPEC CPU2006 benchmark suite. Under Lockdown, no binary compatibility issues where encountered for tested applications (including SPEC CPU2006), and no source-code changes were necessary.

The current prototype supports arbitrary user-space x86 code, shared libraries, signals, setjmp/longjmp, and multi-threaded applications. Self-modifying code or dynamic code generation is not supported. This is not a general limitation as a dynamic approach like Lockdown can detect runtime code generation and translate this new code alongside regular application code. A challenge for the binary translator is to detect if the dynamic code was generated by the benign application or by the attacker.

6   Evaluation

We evaluate Lockdown in the following areas: (i) performance using the SPEC CPU2006 benchmarks, (ii) real-world performance using Apache 2.2,

(iii) a discussion of the security guarantees according to the implemented security policy, and (iv) remaining attack surface.

We run the experiments on an Intel Core i7 CPU 920@2.67 GHz with 12 GiB memory on Ubuntu Linux 12.04.4 LTS (on 32-bit ×86). Lockdown and the SPEC CPU2006 benchmarks are compiled with GCC version 4.6.3 and -O2 optimization level. The full set of security features of Ubuntu Linux 12.04.4 LTS is enabled (ASLR, W⊕X, stack canaries, and safe exception frames).

6.1   Performance

We use the SPEC CPU2006 benchmarks to measure CPU performance and to evaluate the performance impact of (i) Lockdown and (ii) binary translation only, both compared to native execution, in Fig. 4. Due to issues with the trusted loader [37] combined with new versions of the libc we were unable to run omnetpp and dealII. The binary translation column includes the overhead from the trusted loader. The additional average overhead introduced by Lockdown for CFI enforcement (compared to binary translation) is 4.45 %, and the average overhead for Lockdown in total is 19.09 %. Only five benchmarks have a total overhead of more than 45 % if run under Lockdown. The majority of benchmarks face a reasonable performance overhead of less than 10 %.

An average overhead of 19.09 % may seem high, but we point out that Lockdown enforces a purely dynamic binary-only fine-grained CFI policy that runs the binary analysis alongside the executed application whilst supporting dynamic library loading. Other fine-grained compiler-based CFI policies report comparable overhead of 20 % overhead for SPEC CPU2006 [49] . MCFI, a compiler-based solution, recently reduced this overhead to 5–6 % for a subset of SPEC CPU2006 benchmarks [34] without enforcing stack pointer integrity (which is essential to protect against ROP attacks).

A dynamic, binary-only, fine-grained CFI policy faces several challenges: (i) type information must be recovered using binary analysis and (ii) the analysis must be low-overhead and carried out alongside the executed application. The overhead of Lockdown currently includes 14.64 % for the shadow stack, trusted loader, and binary translation as well as 4.45 % for the CFI target analysis and dynamic checks. A combination of static and dynamic binary rewriting may reduce the performance impact further.

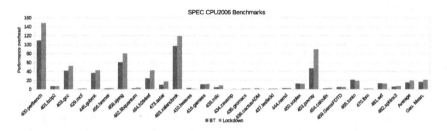

Fig. 4. SPEC CPU2006 overhead for binary translation only and Lockdown (full CFI protection including shadow stack).

6.2   Apache Case Study

We evaluate the performance of a full Apache 2.2 setup running under Lockdown. Apache is set up in the default configuration. To test the performance of the web server we use an HTML file (56 KB) and a jpg image (1054 KB). The file sizes correspond to average HTML and image sizes [19]. We used ab (Apache benchmark tool) to send 15,000,000 requests for each file in 3 configurations (single threaded, 10 concurrent connections, 10 concurrent connections with keep-alive) and measured the overall time required to respond to these requests.

Table 1. Apache 2.2 benchmark results.

Configuration	Small file	Image	Combined
Single threaded	30.41 %	1.94 %	7.87 %
Concurrent	6.27 %	1.09 %	1.83 %
Concurrent with keep-alive	15.80 %	3.00 %	4.36 %

Table 1 shows the overhead of running Apache 2.2 under the Lockdown CFI policy. The overhead for smaller files is generally higher due to the additional context switches between translator domain and application domain for file and network operations. Apache sends files using as few I/O operations as possible and with small files there is not enough computation that is executed to recover from the performance hit of the context switch. In the single-threaded configuration the overhead is high compared to the concurrent configurations due to additional translation and lookup overhead as threads are not reused as many times as for the concurrent configuration. This case-study shows that the overhead for Lockdown is small in real-world contexts.

6.3   Security and CFI Effectiveness Case-Study

Evaluating the effectiveness of a CFI implementation in terms of security is nontrivial. Running a vulnerable program with a CFI mechanism and preventing exploitation using one specific vulnerability does not guarantee that the vulnerability is not exploitable under other circumstances (hijacking a different indirect branch instruction, overwriting other control-flow sensitive data, or just using different gadgets in a code-reuse attack).

We make the following observations: (i) in our attack model a successful attacker needs to hijack the control-flow to already executable code within the process, (ii) the probability of success for an attacker depends on the ability to find a sequence of reusable code (gadgets) that (executed in the right order) accomplishes the intended malicious behavior (e.g., spawning a shell).

The effectiveness of a CFI implementation therefore depends on how effectively an attacker is restrained in the ability to find and reuse already available code. This directly translates to the *quantity* and *quality* of the remaining indirect-control flow targets of the enforced CFG.

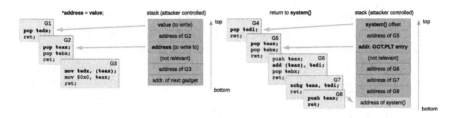

Fig. 5. Gadgets in our nginx 1.4.0.0 exploit (on Ubuntu Linux 12.04.4 LTS). G1–G3 implement a write primitive and G4–G8 transfer control to an arbitrary libc function.

CFI Effectiveness with AIR. Zhang and Sekar [52] propose a metric for measuring CFI strength called Average Indirect target Reduction (AIR). AIR exclusively focuses on the quantity of remaining gadgets ignoring quality and therefore fails to capture the effectiveness of CFI policies regarding security. This limitation is underlined in recent work [8,14,17] where coarse-grained CFI implementations proved to be ineffective while having very high AIR values (>99 %).

For a program like LibreOffice, which maps at least 56,417,429[2] bytes of executable memory, for a CFI solution with AIR of 99 % the remaining 1 % of valid targets still consist of 564,174 potential targets. An attacker needs to find only a handful of gadgets within this set of valid targets to successfully exploit a vulnerability. Hence, there is no AIR threshold that indicates if a CFI policy is secure or not; we present AIR numbers only to allow comparison with related work. Lockdown enforces a dynamic policy which extends and shrinks target sets depending on the executed code, we therefore report numbers at the end of execution. Lockdown achieves an AIR value of *99.88* % for SPEC CPU2006 (*99.84* % with stripped libraries) and 99.55 % for an application set of LibreOffice, Apache, Vim, and xterm. In comparison, static CFI implementations have AIR values for SPEC CPU2006 of 99.13 % (CFI reloc) or 98.86 % (CFI bin) [52].

CFI Security Effectiveness Case Study. We provide an in-depth analysis of the effectiveness of Lockdown by looking at CVE 2013-2028, a memory corruption vulnerability for nginx. Modern attacks exploiting memory corruption vulnerabilities rely on code-reuse techniques. The widespread deployment of W⊕X does not allow to execute memory areas like the stack or the heap. A code-reuse attack [3,5,6,9,31,39,43] combines already executable code snippets (gadgets) found in the executable area of a program or libraries to realise attacker desired behavior. Return-Oriented Programming (ROP) uses gadgets ending with a return instruction while Jump-Oriented Programming (JOP) and Call-Oriented Programming (COP) use gadgets ending with indirect jumps and indirect calls. Most real-life code-reuse attacks rely on return gadgets.

---

[2] We looked at LibreOffice 3.5 on Ubuntu Linux 12.04.4 LTS and added all the initial executable ELF segments, i.e., of the soffice.bin and all its library dependencies.

CVE 2013-2028 reports a signedness bug in nginx before 1.4.0.0. The vulnerability can be exploited by overflowing the stack [26] or corrupting heap data [24]. ASLR and stack canaries are bypassed by server-side heap spraying and brute-forcing. The gadgets in Fig. 5 can be used to exploit the vulnerability and to execute a remote bind shell. Gadgets 1–3 (G1–G3) are used to implement a "write value to address" primitive and gadgets 4–8 (G4–G8) are used to load a GOT.PLT entry into a register, add an offset to it, push it onto the stack and transfer control it. The "write value to address" primitive is used several times to copy a sequence of 4 byte values to a writeable memory area (somewhere within the .data section) and then gadget sequence 4–8 is used to perform an arbitrary function call. More specifically the copied data will be used as the function argument to libc's **system()** function. This technique allows an attacker to execute arbitrary commands (e.g., a remote shell).

An attacker needs only a small number of gadgets that, when chained together, allows the implementation of the desired behavior. To assess the security effectiveness of a CFI implementation a detailed *application specific* analysis is required. We implemented a gadget finder tool that identifies potential gadgets within the set of valid target locations for a particular indirect control-flow transfer, returning all potential gadgets (according to additional filter criteria).

A filter criterion for gadgets is the type of indirect branch instruction at the end of the gadget: return (ret), indirect jump (jmp), or indirect call (call). We consider gadgets up to a length of 30 instructions. In practice, gadgets are short (up to 5 instructions). Longer gadgets might be used to bypass ROP heuristics [14,17] but are harder to control due to unwanted side effects. We allow conditional and unconditional jumps within gadgets. Jumps to (i) locations outside of the gadget, (ii) illegal instructions, or (iii) instructions not allowed in user mode are not allowed in a gadget. We further introduce a *system gadget* (sys) type that ends with a system call (i.e. **int 0 x 80** or **sysenter**). These gadgets are used to construct syscall primitives.

To reliably perform JOP or COP attacks [5,9] certain types of gadgets are needed. We follow the terminology from [5]. Gadgets are either initialization, dispatcher, or functional gadgets: An *initialization gadget* (init) contains a **popa** instruction or allows to pop or move at least three values from the stack into registers. Such gadgets allow the initialization of registers. Initialization gadgets in our evaluation can be return, jump, or call gadgets. *Dispatcher gadgets* (disp) are jump or call gadgets that change the target used for the indirect jump or call at the end of the gadget. Not all gadgets that fulfil this criterion are feasible dispatcher gadgets, providing an over-approximation of available gadgets. *Functional gadgets* (func) are the opposite of dispatcher gadgets, they do not change the content of the register later used for addressing of the indirect jump or call. The idea is to have a register holding the address of the dispatcher gadget so at the end of a functional gadget we can jump or call the dispatcher gadget to load and dispatch the next gadget. We refer to related work [5,9] for details on gadget chain construction. Attacks that rely *exclusively* on JOP and COP (i.e., no return gadgets are used) need at least one initialization gadget (that initializes a set of registers from attacker supplied memory), one dispatcher gadget (that implements the 'load and branch' sequence to dispatch execution to the next gadget), and a set of functional gadgets (e.g., to move a value to a register).

We analyse remaining gadgets in nginx for (i) Lockdown and (ii) a coarse-grained CFI policy using the filtering described above. The coarse-grained CFI policy follows a conservative and strict static CFI policy where returns and jumps can target call sites (call preceded locations) and where calls are allowed to target only symbol addresses (beginning of functions). The coarse-grained CFI policy is stricter than the combined static CFI policy described in [14,17]. Such an overly-strict CFI policy results in a lower bound of total targets that *must* be allowed by any coarse-grained CFI policy. Real policies must over-approximate this set of targets due to imprecisions in the analysis, therefore this policy is strictly stronger than any coarse-grained policy. We show that an attacker can achieve arbitrary computation for this overly strict policy that under-approximates the valid targets and thereby over-approximates the protection capabilities of all coarse-grained CFI policies, therefore all coarse-grained CFI policies are broken, generalizing prior attacks against coarse-grained CFI [8,14,17].

We provide a precise analysis of the remaining gadgets (which we inspected manually) for Lockdown and we show that no usable gadgets remain. Filtering the valid targets of the vulnerable 'ret' and 'call' instruction in nginx 1.4.0.0 under Lockdown (L_{ret}, L_{call}) and under the coarse-grained CFI policy (S_{ret}, S_{call}), results in the number of gadgets presented in Table 2. These are the only gadgets available for exploit construction.

Lockdown greatly reduces the available attack surface. For the vulnerable return instruction only 3 gadgets with a maximum size of 5 instructions are available (7 gadgets if longer sequences are considered). The set of valid targets only contains return gadgets, prohibiting a transition to JOP or COP. A further restriction is that the 7 gadgets can only be executed in a certain order, namely from top of the shadow stack down. Therefore, every gadget can only be executed once. Manual analysis of the specific instructions within the available gadgets shows limited computational abilities, making successful exploitation highly unlikely. We therefore conclude that Lockdown effectively prevents attacks targeting the vulnerable return instruction (for this vulnerability). The second possible exploitation vector of CVE 2013-2028 uses an indirect call instruction. Manual analysis of the gadgets available for the specific vulnerable indirect call instruction again shows limited computational abilities, making successful exploitation highly unlikely as well. First, only JOP-only or COP-only attacks are possible. Using return gadgets is no longer possible due to the strictness of Lockdown's policy for return instructions (the number of reachable return gadgets is shown in parentheses). For long gadgets we get few initialization or dispatcher gadgets but no functional gadgets. Longer gadgets come with an increasing risk of unwanted (and unrecoverable) side effects and/or loss of control-flow from the attacker's perspective. Even if one of the call gadgets could (hypothetically) be used as an arbitrary call, Lockdown always enforces a least-privileges policy for inter-DSO calls (if a symbol is not explicitly imported, the call is not allowed). Therefore even in the most extreme case where the

Table 2. Gadgets found at valid return and call locations when protecting the vulnerable return and indirect call instruction in nginx 1.4.0.0 for Lockdown (L_{ret} and L_{call}) and the strict static CFI policy (S_{ret} and S_{call}).

	Length	Total	ret	jmp	call	sys	init	disp	func	Protected?
L_{ret}	5	3	3	0	0	0	0	0	0	✓
	10	6	6	0	0	0	1	0	0	✓
	15	7	7	0	0	0	1	0	0	✓
	30	7	7	0	0	0	1	0	0	✓
L_{call}	5	20 (97)	0 (77)	0	17	3	0	13	0	✓
	10	53 (270)	0 (217)	0	50	3	9	45	0	✓
	15	65 (392)	0 (327)	1	61	3	31	56	0	✓
	30	99 (586)	0 (487)	2	94	3	125	85	0	✓
S_{ret}	5	2037	1295	440	294	8	2	216	50	×
	10	3741	2662	536	533	10	261	326	69	×
	15	4622	3330	583	698	11	516	375	97	×
	30	6209	4450	763	980	16	1072	558	117	×
S_{call}	5	99	97	0	0	2	4	0	0	×
	10	401	391	0	4	6	9	4	0	×
	15	635	617	0	12	6	68	12	0	×
	30	954	922	0	24	8	268	24	0	×

redirection over a call gadget to a specific function would be sufficient, the called function must also be imported (for nginx, e.g., `system` or `mprotect` are not imported).

Looking at the results for the coarse-grained CFI policy shows that, despite the high AIR value, thousands of gadgets remain readily available. Most gadgets are return gadgets, allowing flexible ROP chains. In fact, we easily find a set of gadgets that implements the same primitives needed for successful exploitation even if the coarse-grained CFI policy is enforced. For the indirect call exploitation vector we simply fall back to ROP by using a stack pivot and one of the available return gadgets. Falling back to ROP is not possible for Lockdown because the shadow stack enforces stack integrity.

We conclude that Lockdown indeed prevents exploitation of CVE 2013-2028 for both exploitation vectors (while coarse-grained CFI fails to protect both exploitation vectors). Lockdown's strength originates from the combination of a precise policy for return instructions and a fine-grained policy for call/jump instructions. In contrast, our analysis for a representative coarse-grained CFI policy shows that despite high AIR values such policies are unable to effectively prevent code-reuse attacks, further questioning the effectiveness of existing coarse-grained CFI techniques. In fact, current binary-only CFI implementations are even more permissive than the strict coarse-grained CFI policy discussed here. A common problem is the missing (strong) protection against ROP attacks.

Table 3 shows remaining gadgets under Lockdown for the vulnerable call instruction if *nginx and all libraries are stripped*. Due to the limited symbol information, more targets are reachable for the vulnerable call instruction compared to the unstripped binary. This leaves the attacker with several gadgets to choose from. As the shadow stack does not rely on symbol information, the precision for the stack remains the same as in Table 2 and the attacker must exclusively rely on COP or JOP. The majority of the available gadgets are intra-DSO targets as the information needed for inter-DSO control transfers is always available. While the attacker can construct Turing-complete computation inside one DSO, executing arbitrary system calls is only possible if the desired libc functions are imported into the DSO or an exploitable call or jump instruction inside libc is found. Therefore, even if binaries are stripped the Lockdown policy offers protection for transfers between objects and against ROP attacks. Here, an attacker is restricted to the few functions imported in the vulnerable object (therefore the protection is partial), e.g., in the case of libc as the destination DSO the list of allowed functions from a source DSO to libc is generally limited. If a security sensitive function (like `system()`) is still within the allowed targets then data validation guards could be emitted to detect attacks.

Our analysis shows that the combination of a strong policy for returns and a fine-grained CFI policy for indirect jumps and calls is key in preventing attacks. Missing only one of these fine-grained policies for either of the indirect branch instructions would already open up the attack surface for successful exploitation.

6.4   Security Guarantees

Lockdown enforces a strict, modular, fine-grained CFI policy for executed code combined with a precise shadow stack, resulting in the following guarantees: (i) the DBT always maintains control of the control-flow, (ii) only valid, legitimate instructions are executed, (iii) function returns cannot be redirected, mitigating ROP attacks, (iv) jump instructions can target only valid instructions in the same function or symbols in the same module (DSO), (v) call instructions can target only valid functions in the same module (DSO) or imported functions, (vi) all signals are caught by the DBT system, protecting from signal oriented programming, (vii) all system calls go through a system call policy check. Due to the modular implementation, individual guarantees build on each other: the

Table 3. Gadgets found at valid call locations when protecting the vulnerable indirect call instruction in nginx 1.4.0.0 for Lockdown (L_{call}) *without debug symbol information*.

	Length	Total	ret	jmp	call	sys	init	disp	func	Prot.?
L_{call}	5	4016 (20388)	0 (16372)	804	3203	9	2	563	403	(✓)
	10	6129 (34885)	0 (28756)	906	5206	17	1446	1323	565	(✓)
	15	6961 (45209)	0 (38248)	947	5990	24	3880	1707	618	(✓)
	30	10109 (64695)	0 (54586)	1017	9062	30	10932	3294	760	(✓)

binary translator ensures the SFI properties that only valid instructions can be targeted, the shadow stack protects return instructions at all times, the trusted loader provides information about valid targets for `call` and `jmp` instructions, and the dynamic control-flow transfer checks enforce dynamic CFI.

7   Conclusion

This paper presents Lockdown, a fine-grained, modular, dynamic control-flow integrity policy for binaries. Using the symbol tables available in shared libraries and executables we build a control-flow graph on the granularity of shared objects. A dynamic binary translation based system enforces the integrity of control-flow transfers at all times according to this model. To counter recent attacks on coarse-grained CFI implementations, we use a shadow stack that protects from all ROP attacks.

Our prototype implementation shows low performance overhead of 19.09 % on average for SPEC CPU2006. In addition, we reason about CFI effectiveness and the strength of Lockdown's dynamic CFI approach, which is more precise than other CFI solutions that rely on static binary rewriting. Our security evaluation goes beyond AIR metrics and we provide an in-depth analysis of our implementation's security effectiveness using real exploits that demonstrates a strong policy for returns must be combined with a fine-grained CFI policy for indirect jumps and calls if we want to prevent attacks.

Lockdown enforces strong security guarantees for current systems in a practical environment that allows dynamic code loading (of shared libraries), supports threads, and results in low overhead.

Acknowledgements. We thank Andreas Follner, Volodymyr Kuznetsov, Per Larsen, Kaveh Razavi, our shepherd Cristiano Giuffrida, and the anonymous reviewers for feedback and discussions. This research was supported, in part, by a grant from NSF.

References

1. Abadi, M., Budiu, M., Erlingsson, U., Ligatti, J.: Control-flow integrity. In: CCS 2005 (2005)
2. Akritidis, P., Cadar, C., Raiciu, C., Costa, M., Castro, M.: Preventing memory error exploits with WIT. In: SP 2008 (2008)
3. Bittau, A., Belay, A., Mashtizadeh, A., Mazieres, D., Boneh, D.: Hacking blind. In: SP 2014 (2014)
4. Bletsch, T., Jiang, X., Freeh, V.: Mitigating code-reuse attacks with control-flow locking. In: ACSAC 2011 (2011)
5. Bletsch, T., Jiang, X., Freeh, V.W., Liang, Z.: Jump-oriented programming: a new class of code-reuse attack. In: ASIACCS 2011 (2011)
6. Bosman, E., Bos, H.: Framing signals - a return to portable shellcode. In: SP 2014 (2014)
7. Bruening, D., Garnett, T., Amarasinghe, S.: An infrastructure for adaptive dynamic optimization. In: CGO 2003 (2003)

8. Carlini, N., Wagner, D.: ROP is still dangerous: breaking modern defenses. In: SSYM 2014 (2014)
9. Checkoway, S., Davi, L., Dmitrienko, A., Sadeghi, A.R., Shacham, H., Winandy, M.: Return-oriented programming without returns. In: CCS 2010 (2010)
10. Chen, S., Xu, J., Sezer, E.C., Gauriar, P., Iyer, R.K.: Non-control-data attacks are realistic threats. In: SSYM 2005 (2005)
11. Crane, S., Liebchen, C., Homescu, A., Davi, L., Larsen, P., Sadeghi, A.R., Brunthaler, S., Franz, M.: Readactor: practical code randomization resilient to memory disclosure. In: SP 2015 (2015)
12. Criswell, J., Dautenhahn, N., Adve, V.: KCoFI: complete control-flow integrity for commodity operating system kernels. In: SP 2014 (2014)
13. Davi, L., Dmitrienko, R., Egele, M., Fischer, T., Holz, T., Hund, R., Nuernberger, S., Sadeghi, A.: MoCFI: a framework to mitigate control-flow attacks on smartphones. In: NDSS 2012 (2012)
14. Davi, L., Sadeghi, A.R., Lehmann, D., Monrose, F.: Stitching the gadgets: on the ineffectiveness of coarse-grained control-flow integrity protection. In: SSYM 2014 (2014)
15. Drepper, U.: How to write shared libraries, December 2010. http://www.akkadia. org/drepper/dsohowto.pdf
16. Erlingsson, Ú., Abadi, M., Vrable, M., Budiu, M., Necula, G.C.: XFI: software guards for system address spaces. In: OSDI 2006 (2006)
17. Göktaş, E., Athanasopoulos, E., Bos, H., Portokalidis, G.: Out of control: overcoming control-flow integrity. In: SP 2014 (2014)
18. Hiroaki, E., Kunikazu, Y.: ProPolice: improved stack-smashing attack detection. IPSJ SIG Notes pp. 181–188 (2001)
19. HTTP Archive: Http archive - interesting stats - average sizes of web sites and objects (2014). http://httparchive.org/interesting.php?a=All& l=Mar%201%202014
20. Jim, T., Morrisett, J.G., Grossman, D., Hicks, M.W., Cheney, J., Wang, Y.: Cyclone: a safe dialect of C. In: ATC 2002 (2002)
21. Kiriansky, V., Bruening, D., Amarasinghe, S.P.: Secure execution via program shepherding. In: SSYM 2002 (2002)
22. Kuzentsov, V., Payer, M., Szekeres, L., Candea, G., Song, D., Sekar, R.: Code pointer integrity. In: OSDI (2014)
23. Larsen, P., Homescu, A., Brunthaler, S., Franz, M.: SoK: automated software diversity. In: SP 2014 (2014)
24. Le, L.: Exploiting nginx chunked overflow bug, the undisclosed attack vector (CVE-2013-2028) (2013)
25. Luk, C.K., Cohn, R., Muth, R., Patil, H., Klauser, A., Lowney, G., Wallace, S., Reddi, V.J., Hazelwood, K.: Pin: building customized program analysis tools with dynamic instrumentation. In: PLDI 2005 (2005)
26. MacManus, G., Saelo, H.: Metasploit module nginx chunked size for CVE-2013-2028 (2013). http://www.rapid7.com/db/modules/exploit/linux/http/ nginx_chunked_size
27. Mohan, V., Larsen, P., Brunthaler, S., Hamlen, K.W., Franz, M.: Opaque control-flow integrity. In: NDSS 2015 (2015)
28. Nagarakatte, S., Zhao, J., Martin, M.M., Zdancewic, S.: SoftBound: highly compatible and complete spatial memory safety for C. In: PLDI 2009 (2009)
29. Nagarakatte, S., Zhao, J., Martin, M.M., Zdancewic, S.: CETS: compiler enforced temporal safety for C. In: ISMM 2010 (2010)

30. Necula, G., Condit, J., Harren, M., McPeak, S., Weimer, W.: CCured: type-safe retrofitting of legacy software. ACM Trans. Program. Lang. Syst. (TOPLAS) **27**(3), 477–526 (2005)
31. Nergal: the advanced return-into-lib(c) exploits. Phrack 11(58), November 2007. http://phrack.com/issues.html?issue=67&id=8
32. Nethercote, N., Seward, J.: Valgrind: a framework for heavyweight dynamic binary instrumentation. In: PLDI 2007 (2007)
33. Niu, B., Tan, G.: Monitor integrity protection with space efficiency and separate compilation. In: CCS 2013 (2013)
34. Niu, B., Tan, G.: Modular control-flow integrity. In: PLDI 2014 (2014)
35. PaX-Team: PaX ASLR (Address Space Layout Randomization) (2003). http://pax.grsecurity.net/docs/aslr.txt
36. Payer, M., Gross, T.R.: Fine-grained user-space security through virtualization. In: VEE 2011 (2011)
37. Payer, M., Hartmann, T., Gross, T.R.: Safe loading - a foundation for secure execution of untrusted programs. In: SP 2012 (2012)
38. Philippaerts, P., Younan, Y., Muylle, S., Piessens, F., Lachmund, S., Walter, T.: Code pointer masking: hardening applications against code injection attacks. In: Holz, T., Bos, H. (eds.) DIMVA 2011. LNCS, vol. 6739, pp. 194–213. Springer, Heidelberg (2011)
39. Pincus, J., Baker, B.: Beyond stack smashing: recent advances in exploiting buffer overruns. IEEE Secur. Priv. **2**, 20–27 (2004)
40. Schuster, F., Tendyck, T., Liebchen, C., Davi, L., Sadeghi, A.R., Holz, T.: Counterfeit object-oriented programming. In: SP 2015 (2015)
41. SCO: System V Application Binary Interface, Intel386 Architecture Processor Supplement (1996). http://www.sco.com/developers/devspecs/abi386-4.pdf
42. Seibert, J., Okhravi, H., Soederstroem, E.: Information leaks without memory disclosures: remote side channel attacks on diversified code. In: CCS (2014)
43. Shacham, H.: The geometry of innocent flesh on the bone: return-into-libc without function calls (on the x86). In: CCS 2007 (2007)
44. Szekeres, L., Payer, M., Wei, T., Song, D.: SoK: eternal war in memory. In: SP 2013 (2013)
45. Tice, C., Roeder, T., Collingbourne, P., Checkoway, S., Erlingsson, Ú., Lozano, L., Pike, G.: Enforcing forward-edge control-flow integrity in GCC & LLVM. In: SSYM 2014 (2014)
46. van de Ven, A., Molnar, I.: Exec shield (2004). https://www.redhat.com/f/pdf/rhel/WHP0006US_Execshield.pdf
47. Wang, Z., Jiang, X.: Hypersafe: a lightweight approach to provide lifetime hypervisor control-flow integrity. In: SP 2010 (2010)
48. Xia, Y., Liu, Y., Chen, H., Zang, B.: CFIMon: detecting violation of vontrol flow integrity using performance counters. In: DSN 2012 (2012)
49. Zeng, B., Tan, G., Erlingsson, U.: Strato: a retargetable framework for low-level inlined-reference monitors. In: SSYM 2013 (2013)
50. Zhang, C., Wei, T., Chen, Z., Duan, L., McCamant, S., Szekeres, L.: Protecting function pointers in binary. In: ASIACCS 2013 (2013)
51. Zhang, C., Wei, T., Chen, Z., Duan, L., Szekeres, L., McCamant, S., Song, D., Zou, W.: Practical control flow integrity and randomization for binary executables. In: SP 2013 (2013)
52. Zhang, M., Sekar, R.: Control flow integrity for COTS binaries. In: SSYM 2013 (2013)

Powerslave: Analyzing the Energy Consumption of Mobile Antivirus Software

Iasonas Polakis[1], Michalis Diamantaris[2], Thanasis Petsas[2],
Federico Maggi[3]([⊠]), and Sotiris Ioannidis[2]

[1] Columbia University, New York, USA
polakis@cs.columbia.edu
[2] FORTH, Heraklion, Greece
{diamant,petsas,sotiris}@ics.forth.gr
[3] Politecnico di Milano, Milan, Italy
federico.maggi@polimi.it

Abstract. Battery technology seems unable to keep up with the rapid evolution of smartphones and their applications, which continuously demand more and more energy. Modern smartphones, with their plethora of application scenarios and usage habits, are setting new challenges and constraints for malware detection software. Among these challenges, preserving the battery life as much as possible is one of the most pressing. From the end users' perspective, a security solution, such as an antivirus (AV), that significantly impacts the battery's life is unacceptable. Thus, the quality and degree of adoption of malware-detection products is also influenced by their energy demands.

Motivated by the above rationale, we perform the first fine-grained measurement that analyzes, at a low level, the energy efficiency of modern, commercial, popular AVs. We explore the relations between various aspects of popular AVs, when handling malicious and benign applications, and the resulting energy consumption. Even though we focus on energy consumption, we also explore other dimensions such as the discrepancies between scanning modes, the impact of file size and scan duration. We then translate our findings into a set of design guidelines for reducing the energy footprint of modern AVs for mobile devices.

1 Introduction

The popularity of mobile devices has also resulted in them being heavily targeted by malware authors. Their built-in billing system, along with the plethora of personal information and account credentials that can be found on such devices, render them a highly profitable resource. According to practically every threat report (e.g., [24]), the amount of malware against Android, the most popular smartphone platform, is a real problem. The ample literature on the subject also confirms the importance of defending smartphones from these threats.

The vast amount of malicious software has resulted in most antivirus (AV) vendors releasing mobile versions of their software. Consequently, a wide range of free and paid solutions is readily available. Interestingly, several of the most

© Springer International Publishing Switzerland 2015
M. Almgren et al. (Eds.): DIMVA 2015, LNCS 9148, pp. 165–184, 2015.
DOI: 10.1007/978-3-319-20550-2_9

popular AV apps available on the Google Play Store are from new vendors [15]. Apart from the detection techniques and capabilities, the mobile nature of these devices introduces an important performance requirement for security solutions; energy consumption [12]. Understanding the energy consumption of a mobile security app is a key area of interest for end users, as well as developers [19]. An extra half hour of battery life really makes a big difference for the end user, and sets a strong decision boundary on whether or not to install a security app. Previous work investigated the energy efficiency of mobile browsers [25], among the most extensively used mobile apps, focusing on how the various components of a site (e.g., HTML, JavaScript) affect battery usage. Other work [26] explored whether battery usage can be leveraged as an early indicator of potential infection, despite previous work [13] demonstrating that a smart malicious app can circumvent such indicators by carefully diluting energy-intensive tasks over long time spans.

In this paper, we evaluate the energy efficiency of current AV tools on the Android platform, and explore whether the energy consumption is correlated to their detection quality. As the overall energy consumption of an AV is dominated by scanning benign apps during everyday use, a complete evaluation of the energy efficiency of AV engines mandates including benign apps as well. To this end, we conduct accurate and manually validated experiments on a real device, with a set of 250 malware samples and 250 goodware apps, on 6 of the most popular AVs. We measure the energy consumption during various scanning operations: (i) scanning the app upon installation, (ii) scanning the entire device, and (iii) scanning the SD card. We go beyond quantifying energy efficiency; we design and calculate metrics that quantify and "visualize" the relation between energy consumption and detection outcome. We break the energy consumption down to the energy consumed by each of the device's components. Finally, we provide a series of recommendations for designing the functionality and graphical interface of AV apps so as to minimize unnecessary energy consumption.

Our findings show that when handling benign apps, all but one of the AVs consume more energy than with malicious apps. One of the AVs consumes 8 times more energy, rendering usage under normal conditions considerably expensive in terms of energy. Our results also show that the most accurate AV is also efficient, consuming 46–65 % less energy than half of the AVs we tested. In most cases, size does matter, as larger apps will result in higher amounts of consumed energy. The AVs that rely heavily on hash-based signature matching techniques are an exception, and consume less energy for large apps compared to the others. The drawback of such AVs, however, is that their signatures can be easily bypassed. Furthermore, we find that design characteristics of the AV apps' graphical interfaces can significantly impact the overall energy consumption. Overall, the main contributions of this work are:

- We perform the first fine-grained, low-level study that quantifies the energy consumption of AV software in Android, which reveals the inefficiency of existing solutions and the impact on battery life.

- Our metrics and their visualization provide a detailed analysis of the energy consumption behavior of various aspects of AV software.
- We derive insights from our measurements and translate them into guidelines for the design of more energy-efficient security solutions.

2   Energy Measurements

The generation of energy-consumption traces that are accurate enough for our study require a framework that is sufficiently precise and fine grained, which will allow us to separate the consumption per application and per device component.

Software-Based Measurements. We reviewed, and tested when publicly available, several options that have been used in previous research. PowerTutor [29] works in user space and is designed to measure the cumulative energy consumed by a device within a time window. Unfortunately, this is not suitable for fine-grained measurements, i.e.,for measuring the energy consumption of each process or application individually. Any irregular, non-scheduled activity (that cannot be prevented or predicted due to the asynchronous nature of the Android runtime) may result in severely skewed readings. Moreover, the energy consumption readings returned by PowerTutor also contain the energy it consumes, which further skews results. Eprof [21] is an accurate fine-grained energy profiler for Android apps with routine level granularity. It is able to analyze the asynchronous energy state of an app, and model the tail-state energy characteristics of the hardware components appropriately. Unfortunately, this software is not publicly available. Yoon et al. proposed AppScope [28], which is designed to accurately estimate the energy consumed by each device component (CPU, display, wireless, GPS) per application and process, through monitoring of the Android kernel at a microscopic level. By following an event-driven approach that analyzes the traces of all system calls, along with any messages that pass through the Binder (used for inter-process communication in Android), AppScope is able to provide fine-grained readings at the process level. Additionally, AppScope is applicable to any Android device, without modification of system software, since it is implemented using a dynamic module in the Linux kernel. It has been calibrated for the power model of a specific device (HTC Google Nexus One), resulting in very accurate readings for experiments conducted on that device.

Hardware-Based Measurements. Many approaches have tried to perform accurate energy measurements on mobile devices based on readings from external hardware [8,9,11,23], e.g.,by using oscilloscopes and low current sensors. Even though such approaches can provide accurate energy measurements for the total power dissipation, none of them can provide fine-grained energy consumption information at an application or process level granularity.

For the aforementioned reasons, we selected AppScope for our experiments.

3   Experimental Setup and Datasets

Measurement Environment. AppScope best supports HTC Google Nexus One, as it is calibrated based on the power model of this specific device. We prepared our device by first unlocking the boot-loader through a standard rooting procedure, and installing the AppScope kernel module. Moreover, we implemented a custom component that parses the AppScope logs and extracts the energy samples for a specific process or app. During our experiments, the device had no SIM plugged in and WiFi was disabled (unless stated otherwise).

Measurement Unit. The power readings produced by AppScope every second are in units of Watts. Since a Watt expresses energy per time unit (Joules per second), we transform these samples to energy samples with $E(t) = P \cdot t$, as the goal of our experiments is to compute the total energy consumption of specific apps. In the rest of the paper, we use the energy unit in milli-Joules (mJ) to express the energy consumption of an app.

Measurements Automation. We automate our measurements through user interface (UI) actions, using the MonkeyRunner [1] API to produce specific actions (e.g., tapping on UI elements) on the device. We can perform actions such as installing-uninstalling an APK, rebooting the device, starting-stopping a scan. For this, we identify the main activity name of each AV and extract the package name of each malware, from their bytecode representation, obtained through reverse engineering using the `apktool` [3].

Antivirus Apps. We evaluate the 6 AVs listed in Table 1, which we obtained from the Google Play Store, on August 1st 2013. Most of the AVs are in the top ten list, with downloads ranging from 100K to 500M, and we denote their relative popularity within our selected set; as an exact number is not provided, but rather a range of downloads, two apps are tied for 1st and two for 4th place. The "Signature-based" column indicates whether the AV relies mainly on easily evaded hash- or package-name-based signatures for detecting malware. We provide more details on this aspect of the AVs in Sect. 4.2.

Even though some AVs offer in-the-cloud scanning (NQ and Sophos state it explicitly), our goal is to explore the energy consumption of the actual

Table 1. List of AV products tested in our study. Rank refers to the respective rank among the tested AVs based on their downloads in Google Play.

Product	Rank	Downloads	Updated	Signature-based
AVG Antivirus Free (2.12.3)	1	100–500M	05/03/13	✓
Symantec Norton Mobile (3.5)	4	10–50M	25/06/13	✗
Dr.Web (8.0)	3	50–100M	27/02/13	✗
Avast Mobile (2.0.4)	1	100–500M	09/05/13	✗
Sophos Mobile (2.5.1009)	6	100–500K	09/04/13	✓
NQ Mobile (6.8.6)	4	10–50M	21/05/13	✗

offline detection process. In addition, uploading times can significantly fluctuate depending on network conditions, causing non-negligible deviations on the usage and, thus, energy consumption of the wireless module. Last, we wanted to maintain the malware definitions stable for the duration of the experiments. Thus, we disabled Internet access to avoid updates, and selected AVs that also work in an offline mode. In Sect. 4.6 we provide preliminary insights on the influence of WiFi connectivity as a concluding experiment. Given the complexity introduced by this variable, our results pave the way for further research.

Malware Dataset. We select a set of 250 malware samples, collected from the Contagio Mini Dump [4] and the Android Malware Genome Project [2]. Note that, as the size of a malware sample may influence the overall energy consumption during the scanning process, we opt for a collection with a variety of sizes, ranging from 12.9 KB to 24.2 MB. The overall detection capability of each AV is reported in Table 2.

Goodware Dataset. We collected a benign set consisting of 250 apps from the Google Play Store. Specifically, we selected apps from the list of the most popular in the Google Play Store. The size of the apps ranges from 92.1 KB to 40.2 MB. Again, Table 2 summarizes the overall detection outcome.

Device Setup. Based on our requirements and experimental parameters, we use the following device setup for our experiments:

- *Snapshots.* We removed unnecessary, pre-installed apps (e.g., Youtube) and created a backup of a clean state of the device (one with each AV installed), containing AppScope components for determining the energy consumption.
- *Revert.* After each malware sample is installed and scanned, we revert to the clean state and erase the SD card.
- *Run.* We repeat each test five times in a row, and calculate the average energy consumed per device component (e.g., CPU, display) and time taken.
- *Luminosity.* We set the display luminosity to a fixed amount.

Measurement Methodology. Malware can infect the device internal storage (e.g., via simple copy operation during installation) or the external SD card (e.g., via simple copy operation). The per-app isolation security model of Android is such that an app—including AVs—can only read certain portions of the filesystem, unless granted root privileges. Regardless of the permission, no AV can possibly perform dynamic analysis of (malicious) apps at runtime, as Android exposes no system-level auditing API at the app level. The SD card filesystem is universally readable. As a result, AVs are designed to look for malware using a combination of the following access modes. As explained in [15], the *On Demand* mode scans the readable portions of the filesystem (internal or external), whereas in *Upon Installation* mode, the AV scans any APK being installed. Based on the these observations, we conduct two different experimental procedures, which we automate via MonkeyRunner:

1. *Device (Internal):* We install each APK individually and scan the app installed on the device's internal storage through two methods:

(a) On Demand. After installing an APK, we perform a full scan of the device.
(b) Upon Installation. After installing an APK, the AV automatically scans the installed app (e.g., with a `PACKAGE_ADDED` broadcast receiver).
2. *SD Card (External):* Copying (via `adb push`) all the APKs to the SD card, without installing them, and then scanning the entire SD card partition.

We extract the following data: (1) *time* taken to perform a scan, (2) *energy consumed* by the specific process for each device's component, and (3) whether or not the AV identified the malware or goodware correctly.

4 Experimental Results

We explored, with specific experiments, the relation between energy consumption and scan duration (Sect. 4.1), detection outcome (Sect. 4.2), on-demand or upon-installation scan (Sect. 4.3), app size (Sect. 4.4), use of display (Sect. 4.5), and, preliminary, the usage of Internet connectivity (Sect. 4.6).

4.1 Energy Consumption vs. Scan Duration

Once the scanning has completed, the AVs include a message in Android's logging system (which we fetch through `logcat`), enabling us to calculate the exact duration of the scan. Table 2 shows the aggregated results for each AV, and reports the minimum and maximum scan duration for both goodware and malware. The scan duration coincides fairly accurately with the aggregate energy consumption, with a few exceptions; Norton has a comparatively small duration for the energy it consumes, while Dr. Web exhibits the opposite behavior with a relatively small consumption and a long duration.

We present the duration statistics for the "On Demand" scan and not the "Upon Installation". Whenever an app—during installation—is flagged as a threat, the AV produces feedback (i.e., a pop-up). This enables us to check at which point the AV has finished scanning the app, and calculate the duration. However, we can not extract the time for false negatives, because there is no feedback. One could count the number of seconds for which AppScope returns an energy consumption reading since the installation. This, however, only allows readings at a granularity of seconds, which can introduce significant error in these experiments. For example, if a scan lasts 3.1 s, we would retrieve readings for 4 s from AppScope, and calculate a significantly skewed energy consumption rate. As such, despite the "On Demand" scan lasting significantly longer than the "Upon Installation", it is useful for comparing the AVs in terms of time performance.

4.2 Energy Consumption vs. Detection Outcome

Malware. We explored the relation between energy consumption and the detection outcome. Our experiments show that there is not a restricting correlation

Table 2. Detection outcome for all scanning modes, and duration of the "On Demand" scan (Sect. 4.1). The "Correct" and "Error" columns refer to correct and erroneous labelling by the AV for the apps being scanned. The "Energy Penalty" expresses the percentage of energy wasted due to the AV misclassifying a malicious app as benign.

AV	Detection rate [%]				Energy Penalty [%]	Scan duration [s]			
	Malware		Goodware		Malware	Malware		Goodware	
	Device	SD	Device	SD		Correct	(Error)	Correct	(Error)
Norton	98.8	98.8	4.8	0.0	+20.00	22–28	(22–28)	23–31	(23–28)
Avast	98.0	98.0	0.0	0.0	+6.500	30–34	(33–36)	23–38	-
Sophos	97.2	97.2	0.0	0.0	+1,023	18–38	(18–24)	11–27	-
Dr. Web	96.4	96.0	1.2	1.2	+31.40	30–107	(30–43)	30–169	(33–80)
NQ	95.2	95.6	0.0	0.0	+49.00	26–50	(23–53)	25–54	-
AVG	94.8	72.0	0.0	0.0	−73.90	9–13	(10–13)	9–13	-

between the two, as can be seen in Fig. 1(a). For example, while AVG is the most energy-efficient and also achieves the lowest detection rate, we find that the most effective AV engine in terms of detecting malicious apps (Norton) is also highly efficient in terms of energy consumption. Specifically, while achieving a 98.8 % detection rate, it consumes 46.2 %–65 % less energy than three of the other AVs. Thus, our findings show that security vendors have the potential to create AVs that *achieve high detection rates, while maintaining reasonable energy consumption profiles.* Sophos exhibits the highest consumption of all, consuming 22.2 % more energy than Avast that has the second highest consumption. Compared to the remaining apps, Sophos consumes 53.8 % more than NQ, 185 % more than Norton, 215 % more than Dr. Web, and over 326 % more than AVG that is the most efficient.

Signature-Based Heuristics. As the type of heuristics employed by an AV can impact certain aspects of its energy consumption, we run the following experiment for identifying the AVs that rely heavily on signatures that detect specific package names or hash values. We altered the package name (and thus the file hash) of the malware samples using an automated process built on `apktool`, and repeat the scans for all the AVs. Sophos failed to detect a single sample, indicating that the effectiveness of its detection engine relies significantly on signatures that can be trivially evaded, all the while exhibiting the highest energy consumption out of all the AVs. AVG is also severely impacted, detecting only 30.2 % of the malware samples. As can be seen in Table 1 the remaining AVs were not impacted, and achieved the same detection rate as before.

Note that there are several ways to evade signatures and, in general, to stress test the obfuscation resilience of AVs, as demonstrated in previous work [22,30]. This specific point falls out of the scope of our paper, as our goal was to explore the correlation, if any, between signatures sophistication and energy consumption.

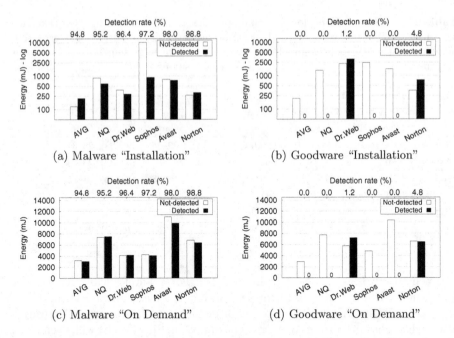

(a) Malware "Installation"   (b) Goodware "Installation"

(c) Malware "On Demand"   (d) Goodware "On Demand"

Fig. 1. Aggregate energy consumption by CPU during the "Upon Installation" and "On Demand" scan (Sect. 4.2).

Goodware. The majority of apps installed by users are benign. As such, a significant aspect of the energy consumption of AVs is how they handle such apps. When scanning an app, if one of the heuristics is triggered, the AV can flag the app as malicious and save energy by not executing the remaining heuristics. On the other hand, when scanning a benign app, no heuristics will be triggered (unless there is a false positive), resulting in all of them being executed, which will also result in a higher energy consumption.

Figure 1(a) and (b) shows the results for the CPU energy consumption for both app collections during the "Upon Installation" scanning. Our results demonstrate that most AV engines exhibit this behavior, apart from AVG where the energy consumption is approximately the same for malware and benign apps. Dr. Web presents the largest increase, with 8 times more energy consumed when scanning goodware. The higher average consumption for the 3 falsely detected apps, compared to the other benign apps, is in part due to their large size which affects the scanning process of Dr. Web as we discuss later on (we found that when scanning apps of comparable size, benign ones tend to have a higher consumption).

NQ, Sophos and Avast consume 64 %–169 % more energy for goodware. Norton is the most efficient with a 12.9 % increase, which may be correlated to the high false positive rate: in an effort to maintain a low energy consumption, they may employ a more "superficial" heuristic that is prone to false positives.

Table 3. Detection outcome and energy consumption of the seven malicious apps not detected by Sophos (Sect. 4.2).

Sample	Size	Energy Consumption (mJ)					
		Sophos	AVG	NQ	Avast	Dr. Web	Norton
thespyja	15.5 KB	9,748.3	102.4	612.9	202.1	314.3	111.9
vending.sectool.v1	96.37 KB	9,676.1	196.4	543.2	580.8	87.9	254.8
androiddefender	1.5 MB	9,834.5	184.4	895.9	568.4	384.7	211.3
carrierig.trial	1.69 MB	9,825.4	96.6	717.9	894.1	585.6	253.2
dropbox.android	3.03 MB	12,410.2	232.3	787.5	738.1	580.7	468.7
apps.DWBeta	4.28 MB	9,838.2	298.1	580.5	664.2	363.3	573.9
appgame7.candystar	5.76 MB	9,942.3	99.2	2,182.5	1,540.4	779.4	520.7

not detected — detected

Application Whitelisting. We explore whether any of the AVs employ whitelisting for popular apps (i.e., if really popular apps are matched against a simple signature and are not scanned in depth). We select the 10 most popular apps (e.g., Instagram, WhatsApp) and repeat the previous experiments. Results are in line with our previous measurements for each AV, with the app sizes once again affecting the energy consumption for certain AVs. There were no instances of an app being processed in a significantly faster manner or consuming less energy, indicating the lack of some form of whitelisting.

False Classification. We calculate the penalty, in terms of "wasted" energy consumption, that occurs when the AV misclassifies a malicious app as benign. As can be seen in Table 2, AVG is the only AV engine to actually benefit in terms of energy consumption when failing to detect a malicious app, with a 73.9 % decrease in consumption. While consuming more energy is, obviously, a negligible side-effect of a malicious app going undetected, in our case it serves as a potential indicator of instances where an AV exhibits strange behavior.

Indeed, one can see that Sophos exhibits a strange behavior and has the largest increase with 1023.8 % compared to the malware samples that are detected, and has a consumption 4–6 times larger than when scanning benign apps. As shown in Table 3, all of the malware samples have a significant impact on Sophos in terms of the amount of energy consumed when scanning them. We also explore the effect of those seven malicious apps on the other AV engines. Although 3 samples are not detected by any of the AVs, 2 of them were detected by all but Sophos. None, however, present the same effect on all of the remaining AVs. While some result in higher consumption than the average for the specific AV, they do not present a consistent effect on all AVs. This indicates that this is most likely caused by the internal implementation of Sophos, and not the malware employing detection or analysis evasions technique.

Regarding the undetected samples, we found that dropbox.android and thespyja remain undetected by several AV engines, as shown by popular online scanning services. Indeed, `dropbox.android` was detected by only one AV engine (out of 52 in VirusTotal, and 7 in AndroTotal [15]), while `thespyja` was detected by 11 (~21%) in VirusTotal and 2 (~28%) in AndroTotal, which are still quite low. This could be attributed to AVs intentionally not labelling a sample as a threat after some time. However, in the case of the third sample (`androiddefender`), VirusTotal and AndroTotal report detection by 61.5 and 85.7% of the AVs respectively.

To gain a better understanding of the behavior of `thespyja`, which has a size of merely 15.5 KB and is characterized as Spyware, we reverse engineer the app. We first obtain the Java bytecode using `apktool` and then get the actual source code (Java files) using `dex2jar` [5] and `JD-GUI` [6]. The source code is constituted by only two Java files, one Android Activity file and a graphical layout file. By inspecting the code of the activity file we found that the app's logic is simplistic. It opens a web view and transfers the user to a web page. Evidently any malicious action occurs when the user visits the page. The app does not contain any other functionality and only requires the INTERNET permission.

4.3 Upon Installation vs. on Demand Detection

Figure 1(c) and (d) shows the average energy consumed by the CPU for each AV when scanning the whole device "On Demand". As expected, the "Upon Installation" method consumes less energy than the "On Demand" method as it only scans the app being installed and not the entire device. Sophos exhibits the smallest increase for the "On Demand" consuming 4.5 times more energy for malware and 2 times more for benign apps. Norton has the largest increase, with a 20 times larger consumption for malware and 18 for goodware. The remaining AVs have an increased energy consumption by 12–14 times for malware and 3–6 for benign apps. AVG and Sophos remain fairly consistent, with the energy consumption being the same whether an app is malicious or benign, for both the "On Demand" and "Upon Installation" scanning modes. This can be attributed to our finding that both AVs rely heavily on hash-based signatures for detection. Overall, the "On Demand" scan proves to be a very expensive activity in terms of energy consumption, even when not taking into account the energy consumption from the device's display.

4.4 Size Does Matter

The app's size may affect the energy consumption of the AV, depending on the type of heuristics employed. One would expect larger apps to result in longer scans and increased consumption. However, as our experiments show, that is not always the case. Figure 2 plots the aggregate energy consumed by each AV, and the size of the scanned app. Dr. Web clearly exhibits a strong correlation between the two, and Avast mostly for benign apps. For the remaining AVs size does not seem to be a dominating factor. The lack of correlation may be attributed to fingerprinting techniques that create a compact signature without processing the entire file, or may leverage some indexing technique to speed up

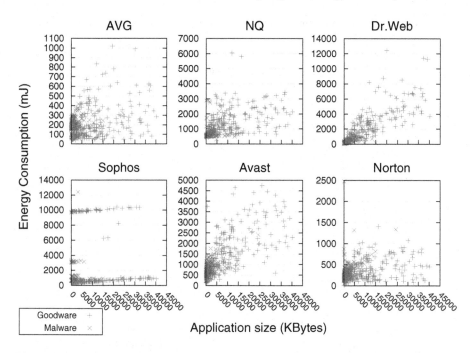

Fig. 2. Size and aggregate energy consumption for "Upon Installation" scan (Sect. 4.4).

matching. Sophos presents no correlation at all, as there are three clusters of consumption, which remain consistent regardless of app size. The three clusters of consumption suggest three sets of heuristics and termination of the scan upon detection by a set of heuristics.

To verify our analysis, we also calculate the Pearson's correlation coefficient, a value between $[-1, 1]$, between app size and energy consumption; 1 denotes perfect linear correlation between two variables, 0 denotes no correlation and -1 shows total negative correlation. Table 4 shows that for Dr. Web we have a correlation value of over 0.7 for both benign and malicious apps verifying our previous observations. Avast also demonstrates a strong correlation for benign apps but not for malicious ones. Furthermore, Sophos presents almost no correlation with 0.012 for benign apps and 0.098 for malware. Norton is the only AV to exhibit a higher correlation for the malicious apps compared to the benign, suggesting extensive heuristics that analyze the app, justifying its high detection rate. Interestingly, the two AVs with the lowest correlation between size and consumption, namely AVG and Sophos, are also the two apps that rely heavily on package name or hash-based signatures for detection.

To further explore the correlation, we plot the duration of the "On Demand" scan for Dr. Web, correlated to the app's size in Fig. 3. While it is evident that the size has an impact on the scan's duration, it is not the only factor. Whereas in the case of malware the duration is fairly comparable for samples of a similar size (apart from a few exceptions), things are more complicated for benign apps,

Table 4. Correlation between energy consumption and size (Sect. 4.4).

Antivirus	Pearson's correlation coefficient	
	Goodware	Malware
AVG	0.402	0.349
NQ	0.420	0.085
Dr.Web	0.793	0.721
Sophos	0.012	0.098
Avast	0.673	0.493
Norton	0.402	0.510

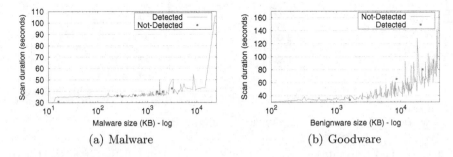

(a) Malware   (b) Goodware

Fig. 3. Duration of the scan vs. size of the app for Dr. Web (Sect. 4.4).

with large fluctuations for almost identical sizes. In one case, an app with a 0.3 %
increase in size from the previous app, presents a 150 % increase in duration.
Thus, the scanning process can be greatly influenced by the internals of each
app and the type of code and system calls included.

4.5 Display vs. CPU Energy Consumption

The energy consumption of a display is not determined only by the choice of colors. It is also heavily influenced by the amount of text, animations, and the general design of the layout. We found that while some of the AVs we tested adopt a
darker design which consumes less energy [10], they consume more energy than
others that use white but follow a more minimalistic design. We were not able
to collect information about the energy consumption of the display for NQ, as
AppScope is not able to collect that information for the specific app, due to a
bug of the app.

Figure 4(a) shows the average energy consumption per second for the display.
Results exhibit a significant disparity between certain AVs. Specifically, Dr. Web
is the least efficient, consuming 25.4 % more energy than AVG that is the most
efficient. The app's energy consumption behavior is completely different for the
CPU and display, as Dr. Web was the second most efficient for the CPU experiments, while AVG was the second least effective. Figure 4(b) shows the aggregate

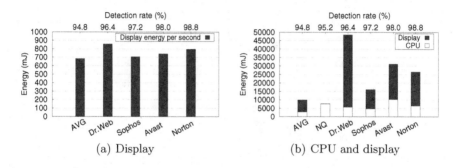

Fig. 4. Average energy consumed per second during "On Demand" scan (Sect. 4.5).

consumption of the CPU and display. The apps' consumption is heavily dominated by the display, with the CPU accounting for 11.9 %–33.3 % of the overall consumption, leaving room for significant improvement. The aggregate energy consumption during the "On Demand" scan by Dr. Web is 5 times larger than AVG. This is due to both the scan duration being comparatively much longer, as well as specific design aspects of the Dr. Web app that we describe in Sect. 5.

Note that during "Upon Installation" scans, the AV runs in the background, and does not use the display. Consequently, the contribution of the AV to the display energy consumption is dominated by the foreground app, not by the on-screen notifications—visualized only in cases of detected malware. Thus, we measured the energy consumption for the "On Demand" scan only, which keeps the AV's view in the foreground, and provides a better baseline for comparison.

Impact on Battery Life. We calculate the effect of an "On Demand" scan (CPU and display) on the battery life for each AV, i.e., what percentage of the battery is consumed by a single scan. We calculate a lower bound based on the value for the specific battery (the value will be higher for older batteries with decreased duration). Dr Web presented the largest impact by consuming 0.19 % of the total capacity of the battery, whereas AVG has the smallest impact with 0.05 %. The remaining AVs consume 0.10–0.18 % of the battery's energy.

4.6   Internet Connectivity (WiFi)

We conducted a preliminary experiment to investigate the impact of Internet connectivity during the "Upon Installation" scans of the 250 malicious samples. Even though such a study needs a large number of runs to eliminate any discrepancies in the energy consumption readings due to unpredictable external factors (e.g., network load, uploading times), our goal was to test whether the detection rates were affected, and to provide an estimation of the consumption. Our experiments reveal some interesting results.

Detection Rate. Given the availability of cloud-based scanning, we expected much higher detection rates. However, that was not the case. Specifically, we turned on the WiFi antenna, which triggered a signature update for Dr. Web,

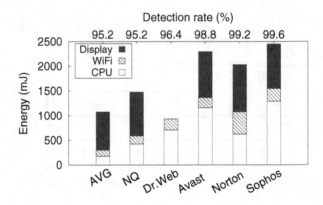

Fig. 5. Aggregate energy consumed by CPU, WiFi and display for malware detected "Upon Installation" (Sect. 4.6).

Sophos, Norton and AVG (experiment conducted late May 2014). Even though we recorded slight improvements in Sophos (+2.4 %) and Norton (+0.4 %), still none of the AVs was able to reach 100 % detection rate, verifying previous results [18]. After this upgrade, we recorded no further increase, neither due to subsequent upgrades, nor in-the-cloud scanners.

Energy Consumption. Figure 5 shows the average consumption per component for "Upon Installation" scans, calculated only for the malware samples for which each AV used the network. The display's energy consumption is from the pop-up informing the users of the detected threat. Dr.Web uses the Android notification system and, thus, presents no consumption for the display. Our results show that the energy consumption for the WiFi component is always smaller than the other components. There is also significant deviation between the WiFi energy consumption of each AV. Norton has the highest consumption, being 79 % higher than that of Sophos. As further motivated in Sect. 6, these findings support our initial decision of conducting our measurements offline, and to postpone an in-depth exploration of WiFi connectivity for future research.

5   Efficiency Guidelines

Here we present a series of guidelines for designing more energy-efficient AVs, based on the insights from our results. Most AVs adopt some of the techniques we propose, indicating that efficient power consumption is an important and relevant aspect of their design. All of them, however, could significantly improve their power consumption behavior by following the guidelines we propose.

5.1   Detection Heuristics and Behavior

Our experimental findings negate concerns of a strong correlation between security and efficiency. Norton had the highest detection rate, yet was quite efficient

Table 5. Visual characteristics of each AV (sorted in descending order of consumption).

Antivirus	Colors	Design	Text	Animation
AVG	White	Minimal	Scarce	×
Sophos	White	Minimal	Scarce	×
Avast	Grey/Orange	Normal	Substantial	✓
Norton	Dark/Blue	Normal	Substantial	✓
Dr. Web	Green/Orange	Heavy	Excessive	✓

in terms of energy consumption. We suggest the adoption of the following optimizations for further reducing the power consumption of the scanning process:

- *Early termination:* Norton and AVG consume essentially the same energy for detected malware and undetected benign apps, suggesting that all the heuristics are executed in both cases instead of stopping after a heuristic is triggered. The remaining AVs present lower consumption for detected malware, indicating that this is a feasible technique. While running all the heuristics may in principle help minimize false positives, our experiments demonstrated that 3 of the 4 AV apps that adopt an "early stop" strategy do not present any false positives, while Norton has a 4.8 % false positive rate.
- *Whitelisting*[1]: whitelists can be used to avoid scanning known benign apps. The AV will have a list of signatures for popular benign apps. If the user installs an app contained in the list, the AV simply has to match it to the signature and can avoid all the intensive, energy consuming heuristics that analyze the app in depth. The list should be updated periodically to include the latest versions of apps, and add new and popular apps that are released. Such a mechanism does not affect the detection accuracy of the AV. Even if a malware author releases a sample that exhibits a dual behavior, as demonstrated in [27], if the sample has been previously detected by the vendor it will not be whitelisted but detected as a threat. If the sample has not been previously detected, the whitelisting does not change the outcome, as it would have not been labelled as a threat regardless of the whitelisting. Furthermore, the whitelisting should only be employed for very popular apps, rendering the scenario of a whitelisted malware sample unlikely.
- *Background tasks:* Run "On Demand" scans in the background to minimize the rendering of visual components, as is done for the "Upon Installation" scans, which leverage the notification system when necessary.

5.2   Visual Design

While not pertinent to the security aspect of our study, we also provide a series of guidelines regarding the design of the apps, for reasons of completeness.

---

[1] Not to be confused with application whitelisting (e.g., [7]), where only known applications are allowed to be executed on the system.

Our results revealed that the energy consumption of an AV is largely affected by the display. Minimizing the energy consumption of the display will significantly reduce the app's consumption and minimize the impact on the battery's life.

Table 5 provides details of the visual design of each AV, which directly affect the energy consumption. Most of the design elements of the apps we tested could easily be changed towards minimizing the consumption. Even though appearance is an important aspect of apps, which can affect their popularity, AVs present a "special" case, because their success is based on their functionality (i.e., good detection accuracy, low CPU load and energy consumption), rather than their look and feel. This, of course, is more constraining for other categories, such as websites [25], as they have to be visually appealing and entice users. On the other hand, the popularity of AVs is primarily affected by their ability to detect malware, regardless of their visual design. This could be further supported by the fact that AVG, which is one of the two most popular AV apps, is also the most energy-efficient one. Nonetheless, even though AVG follows the most "clean" visual design, it also relies heavily on bright colors, significantly draining more energy than dark ones. Overall, taking into account the current hype about "green" or "sustainable" designs, following our guidelines and advertising its power efficiency, may further boost the popularity of an AV app.

We propose the following guidelines in terms of visual design:

- *Colors:* Maximize the dark areas (e.g., backgrounds). In OLED displays black pixels are produced by turning them off, which greatly reduces consumption.
- *Text:* Reduce text to bare essential (e.g., result of analysis).
- *Design:* Follow minimalistic and clear designs. Animations and "heavy" designs unnecessarily increase energy consumption.

Note that the default theme for system apps (e.g., system settings) in vanilla Android is dark and minimalistic. Indeed, development guidelines encourage the adoption of built-in widgets, which ensure a memory-efficient, fast and sleek UI.

6   Limitations and Future Work

Multiple Devices. All experiments have been conducted on a specific smartphone model, as AppScope's power consumption model has been calibrated for this specific device. Building models for AppScope and calibrating them for other devices is out of the scope of this work. While the power consumption of these AVs might present differences on other devices (e.g., devices with larger displays), their inherent behavior will remain the same across devices. Furthermore, our study is comparative, and all measurements are completed on the same model. Thus, the insights we derive are not bound to the specific device, and our design guidelines will improve energy consumption regardless of the device.

WiFi. Apart form the preliminary WiFi experiment, our study has been conducted with the WiFi connectivity disabled. Several reasons guided that choice, with the inability to maintain all aspects of the experiments constant for the entirety of their duration being the most significant. Fluctuations of uploading times and differences in network loads can significantly alter the duration and, thus, energy consumption of the experiments. Furthermore, the apps may "silently" update certain aspects of their functionality or signature database. As the experiments are conducted on a real device and not within a simulator, reverting the device to a clean state after every sample installation significantly increases the duration of each experiment. Taking into account the number of apps explored, and the multiple iterations per sample, it is possible that before a set of experiments has completed, the AV engines might have updated, thus creating different "testing environments" within a single experiment. As such, we plan to explore methods to enable us to include WiFi connectivity, while maintaining a constant testing environment across all experiments.

7 Related Work

Battery-Based Malware Detection. Hoffmann et al. [13], proposed the idea that every action performed drains a specific amount of energy from the battery. As such, they performed tests to check whether they could analyze the behavior of benign and malware applications in terms of energy consumption. They used PowerTutor to conduct their experiments. First they conducted tests on different components (CPU, Display, 3G, WiFi) on a clean device and compared the results with experiments on 2 malware samples. According to their results, they could not identify the malicious activity from the energy traces due to the high "noise" ratio. All the experiments, were conducted on two different Android devices.

Merlo et al. [17] contradicted the conclusions drawn in [13], arguing that it is possible to identify malicious activity by monitoring the energy consumption of a device. To show the correctness of their proposal, they analyzed two different approaches to the problem. First, with a high level approach similar to [13], they attempted to measure the energy consumption based on hardware resources usage counters. They found that this approach provides inaccurate results, not capable of identifying a crafted network attack. Then, with a low level approach based on energy measurements at the battery level, they found the produced results reliable for identifying the aforementioned attack. However, this approach induces a high level OS intrusiveness that considerably limits its portability.

Additionally, Truong et al. [26] recently found that the in-the-wild malware is not sophisticated enough, or simply does not bother, to hide the extra energy consumption. To this end, they used MIT's Carat infrastructure to conduct a large-scale infection-rate measurement on 55,000 real devices.

In an older study, Hahnsang et al. [14], developed a framework for detecting energy-greedy anomalies based on power measurements, performed on a device running Windows Mobile OS. Their framework consists of two basic components: a power monitor that collects power samples of a candidate application and a data analyzer that generates power signatures from those samples. The detection is performed through comparing the generated signatures with a predefined database. The framework was evaluated on custom worms and proven to successfully detect samples sharing common behavior with known malware variants, as well as applications exhibiting unknown energy-greedy anomalies.

Previous studies [16,20] have focused on the detection of battery exhaustion attacks on mobile devices. In [16], Marting et al., presented a list of methods that an attacker can use to drain the battery of a device, along with a power-secure architecture to thwart those attacks. In [20], Nash et al., proposed an IDS for battery exhaustion attacks based on power consumption estimations as derived from several parameters of the system, such as CPU load and disk accesses.

Security vs. Energy Efficiency. Bickford et al. [8] studied the potential trade-offs between security monitoring and energy consumption for a specific class of malware detectors: rootkit detectors. They propose a framework to asses security versus energy tradeoffs along two axes, attack surface and malware scanning frequency. Their results demonstrate that protection against code-driven attacks is relatively cheap, while protection against all data-driven attacks is prohibitively expensive. Their study was performed on a mobile device running a version of Linux, and was limited for a specific class of malware (rootkits) which currently does not constitute a threat for mobile devices. In contrast, our study was performed on a mobile device running the Android OS and we use popular commercial AVs and real malware samples which pose a significant threat.

Android AV Evaluation. Rastogi et al. in [22], performed an evaluation, in the most popular AVs, regarding malware evasion techniques. They developed DroidChameleon a framework which transforms malware from different malware families by changing the package name, renaming the files and the identifiers, reordering code etc. They tested the new transformed malware samples in ten AV products. Results indicate that all the tested AV products are susceptible to common evasion techniques. In a similar work [30], Zhen et al. present an automated and extensible platform, called ADAM, which evaluates the detection of Android anti-malware tools through different static transformation techniques. applied on a number of malicious apps. They tested their repackaged malware samples on a popular analysis service and found that the detection rates dropped compared to the original samples.

8   Conclusion

Battery technology seems unable to keep up with the rapid evolution of smartphones and their applications, which demand more and more energy. The popularity of external power banks and slim batteries camouflaged as covers are a sign that smartphone users do need extra power for their devices. In a similar vein, the rise of applications that promise to make the battery draining slower (e.g., by killing processes) show that users are concerned about this aspect. Security is generally a cost, and in the case of mobile AVs, the risk is that users may decide to uninstall an AV because it drains too much battery. In other words, the less energy an AV consumes, the more usable it is.

Research efforts such as the one presented in this paper are preparatory for building design methodologies and tools that enable application vendors and developers to balance the trade off existing between security effectiveness, user experience and speed. We derived our design guidelines from thorough measurements obtained on a real-world device running the most popular mobile operating system and, thus, we believe they offer an accurate reference for practitioners and future researchers.

In particular, our measurements show that there are significant deviations of CPU energy consumption among different AV products. Interestingly, the energy consumed by the CPU due to the AV is 3–4 times lower when compared to other hardware components, which are energy greedy. This means that there is room for increasing the detection accuracy, for example by running more energy greedy algorithms. Indeed, we found that no correlation exists between the detection accuracy and energy consumption of AV applications on mobile devices. Moreover, in most AV products a pattern can be seen: the bigger the size of an application, the higher the energy consumption required for scanning it, but that depends on the AV and the specific scanning technique. Clearly, energy efficiency and complex detection algorithms can coexist only if the UI designers are cautious and create UI components that minimize the illumination of the pixels. Indeed, the display is the most energy greedy component.

Based on our findings, we argue that security vendors are not bound by an "Efficiency vs Accuracy" trade off, and can produce antivirus apps that are effective while maintaining modest energy consumption profiles.

Acknowledgements. This work was supported in part by DARPA through Contract FA8750-10-2-0253, with additional support by Intel Corp. It was also supported by the FP7 project NECOMA, funded by the European Commission under Grant Agreement No. 608533, and the MIUR FACE Project No. RBFR13AJFT. Any opinions, findings, conclusions, or recommendations expressed herein are those of the authors, and do not necessarily reflect those of the US Government, DARPA, or Intel.

References

1. Android developers - monkeyrunner. http://developer.android.com/tools/help/monkeyrunner_concepts.html
2. Android malware genome project. http://www.malgenomeproject.org/
3. Apktool. https://code.google.com/p/android-apktool/
4. Contagio - mobile malware. http://contagiominidump.blogspot.com
5. Dex2jar. https://code.google.com/p/dex2jar/
6. Java decompiler. http://jd.benow.ca/
7. Beechey, J.: Application whitelisting: Panacea or propaganda (2010). http://www.sans.org/reading-room/whitepapers/application/application-whitelisting-panacea-propaganda-33599
8. Bickford, J., Lagar-Cavilla, H.A., Varshavsky, A., Ganapathy, V., Iftode, L.: Security versus energy tradeoffs in host-based mobile malware detection. In: MobiSys (2011)
9. Carroll, A., Heiser, G.: An analysis of power consumption in a smartphone. In: USENIX ATC (2010)
10. Chen, X., Chen, Y., Ma, Z., Fernandes, F.C.A.: How is energy consumed in smartphone display applications? In: HotMobile (2013)

11. Friedman, R., Kogan, A., Krivolapov, Y.: On power and throughput tradeoffs of wifi and bluetooth in smartphones. In: INFOCOM (2011)
12. Harlalka, R.: How to stop your mobile app from being a serious battery drain (2013)
13. Hoffmann, J., Neumann, S., Holz, T.: Mobile malware detection based on energy fingerprints — a dead end? In: Stolfo, S.J., Stavrou, A., Wright, C.V. (eds.) RAID 2013. LNCS, vol. 8145, pp. 348–368. Springer, Heidelberg (2013)
14. Kim, H., Smith, J., Shin, K.G.: Detecting energy-greedy anomalies and mobile malware variants. In: Proceedings of the 6th International Conference on Mobile Systems, Applications, and Services, MobiSys 2008 (2008)
15. Maggi, F., Valdi, A., Zanero, S.: Andrototal: a flexible, scalable toolbox and service for testing mobile malware detectors. In: CCS SPSM (2013)
16. Martin, T., Hsiao, M., Ha, D., Krishnaswami, J.: Denial-of-service attacks on battery-powered mobile computers. In: Proceedings of the Second IEEE International Conference on Pervasive Computing and Communications(PerCom 2004) (2004)
17. Merlo, A., Migliardi, M., Fontanelli, P.: On energy-based profiling of malware in android. In: HPCS (2014)
18. Mohaisen, A., Alrawi, O.: AV-meter: an evaluation of antivirus scans and labels. In: Dietrich, S. (ed.) DIMVA 2014. LNCS, vol. 8550, pp. 112–131. Springer, Heidelberg (2014)
19. Nacci, A.A., Trovò, F., Maggi, F., Ferroni, M., Cazzola, A., Sciuto, D., Santambrogio, M.D.: Adaptive and flexible smartphone power modeling. Mob. Netw. Appl. 18(5), 600–609 (2013)
20. Nash, D.C., Martin, T.L., Ha, D.S., Hsiao, M.S.: Towards an intrusion detection system for battery exhaustion attacks on mobile computing devices. In: PerCom Workshops. IEEE Computer Society (2005)
21. Pathak, A., Hu, Y.C., Zhang, M.: Where is the energy spent inside my app? Fine grained energy accounting on smartphones with eprof. In: EuroSys (2012)
22. Rastogi, V., Chen, Y., Jiang, X.: Droidchameleon: evaluating android anti-malware against transformation attacks. In: ASIA CCS (2013)
23. Rice, A.C., Hay, S.: Decomposing power measurements for mobile devices. In: PerCom (2010)
24. Symantec: Android Madware and Malware Trends (2013)
25. Thiagarajan, N., Aggarwal, G., Nicoara, A., Boneh, D., Singh, J.P.: Who killed my battery? Analyzing mobile browser energy consumption. In: WWW (2012)
26. Truong, H.T.T., Lagerspetz, E., Nurmi, P., Oliner, A.J., Tarkoma, S., Asokan, N., Bhattacharya, S.: The company you keep: mobile malware infection rates and inexpensive risk indicators. In: WWW (2014)
27. Wang, T., Lu, K., Lu, L., Chung, S., Lee, W.: Jekyll on iOS: when benign apps become evil. In: Proceedings of the 22Nd USENIX Conference on Security, SEC 2013 (2013)
28. Yoon, C., Kim, D., Jung, W., Kang, C., Cha, H.: Appscope: application energy metering framework for android smartphones using kernel activity monitoring. In: USENIX ATC (2012)
29. Zhang, L., Tiwana, B., Qian, Z., Wang, Z., Dick, R.P., Mao, Z.M., Yang, L.: Accurate online power estimation and automatic battery behavior based power model generation for smartphones. In: CODES/ISSS (2010)
30. Zheng, M., Lee, P.P.C., Lui, J.C.S.: ADAM: an automatic and extensible platform to stress test android anti-virus systems. In: Flegel, U., Markatos, E., Robertson, W. (eds.) DIMVA 2012. LNCS, vol. 7591, pp. 82–101. Springer, Heidelberg (2013)

Social Networks
and Large-Scale Attacks

The Role of Cloud Services in Malicious Software: Trends and Insights

Xiao Han[1,2(✉)], Nizar Kheir[1], and Davide Balzarotti[2]

[1] Orange Labs, Issy Les Moulineaux, France
{xiao.han,nizar.kheir}@orange.com
[2] EURECOM, Sophia Antipolis, France
davide.balzarotti@eurecom.com

Abstract. In this paper we investigate the way cyber-criminals abuse public cloud services to host part of their malicious infrastructures, including exploit servers to distribute malware, C&C servers to manage infected terminals, redirectors to increase anonymity, and drop zones to host stolen data.

We conduct a large scale analysis of all the malware samples submitted to the Anubis malware analysis system between 2008 and 2014. For each sample, we extracted and analyzed all malware interactions with Amazon EC2, a major public cloud service provider, in order to better understand the malicious activities that involve public cloud services. In our experiments, we distinguish between benign cloud services that are passively used by malware (such as file sharing, URL shortening, and pay-per-install services), and other dedicated machines that play a key role in the malware infrastructure. Our results reveal that cyber-criminals sustain long-lived operations through the use of public cloud resources, either as a redundant or a major component of their malware infrastructures. We also observe that the number of malicious and dedicated cloud-based domains has increased almost 4 times between 2010 and 2013. To understand the reasons behind this trend, we also present a detailed analysis using public DNS records. For instance, we observe that certain dedicated malicious domains hosted on the cloud remain active for an average of 110 days since they are first observed in the wild.

1 Introduction

Public infrastructure-as-a-service (IaaS) clouds have rapidly expanded in the recent years, with almost half of US businesses now using cloud computing in some capacity [10]. IaaS offer a straightforward *pay-as-you-go* pricing model where users dynamically create virtual machines at will, provide them with public IP addresses and on-demand compute and storage resources, and then delete them without any sustainable cost. Major providers of IaaS clouds, such as Amazon EC2 [2] and Microsoft Azure [4], also propose scalable services and default configuration options that contributed to the wide adoption of cloud services.

Unfortunately, the rapid growth of cloud services has also attracted cyber-criminals, paving the way to an active underground economy. As a result,

© Springer International Publishing Switzerland 2015
M. Almgren et al. (Eds.): DIMVA 2015, LNCS 9148, pp. 187–204, 2015.
DOI: 10.1007/978-3-319-20550-2_10

Los et al. [17] list the abuse of cloud services among the top nine critical threats to cloud computing. In fact, public IaaS clouds provide users with virtually unlimited network, compute, and storage resources. These are coupled with weak registration processes that facilitate anonymity, and so anyone with a valid credit card can easily register and use cloud services. For example, an early case of cloud service abuse was publicly uncovered in 2009, where a Zeus command and control (C&C) server was found to be hosted on Amazon EC2 [11]. More recent examples include the SpyEye banking trojan that was found to be using Amazon S3 storage [7], Android malware that exploited the Google Cloud Message service [21], and more advanced persistent attacks that used Dropbox and Wordpress services as a cover [14]. Despite these multiple examples, we are unaware of any existing study that measures the extent at which public cloud services are being abused by cyber-criminals. Such study would advise the design and implementation of future cloud monitoring and accountability services. More precisely, we do not know if cyber-criminals use cloud-based servers only as redundant components of their malware infrastructure, or whether they *specifically* use cloud services to achieve a better sustainability. Besides, we do not know if public clouds add more resilience to malware infrastructures, what is the time it takes to detect a malicious server hosted on a public cloud, as well as the time required to take down this server after it was first discovered.

In this paper we present a framework to measure and analyze malicious activity that involves public cloud services. Unlike previous work that actively probed public cloud IP addresses [22] or only use passive DNS records [13], we directly collect malware communications by analyzing the network traffic recorded by the Anubis dynamic analysis system [6]. Anubis is a publicly accessible service that analyzes malware samples in an instrumented sandbox. As part of its analysis, the system also records which domains and IP addresses are contacted by each malware sample, and part of the data that is transferred through the connection. Unfortunately, malware can communicate with the cloud for multiple reasons, including malicious activities but also other innocuous connections which range from simple connectivity checks, to the use of public benign services. This greatly complicated the analysis, and required the development of several heuristics to discard malware samples using public services hosted on the cloud, as this cannot be considered an abuse of the cloud itself.

In our experiments, we analyzed the network communication of over 30 million samples, submitted between 2008 and 2014. Our system identified 1.08 million (roughly 3.6 %) that connected to at least one publicly routable Amazon EC2 IP address. These IPs were associated to 12,522 distinct cloud-based domains. Interestingly, we observed that over the same period, only 32,225 samples connected to Microsoft Azure. Due to the relatively low number of samples that interacted with Azure, we only focused our study on Amazon EC2.

To summarize, the paper makes the following contributions:

- We present the first systematic, large scale study on the use of public cloud services by malicious software.

- We perform a precise categorization of each cloud access, separating the cases in which the malware samples simply rely on legitimate services which happen to be hosted on the cloud, from the cases in which part of the malware infrastructure is hosted on the cloud.
- We study the evolution of cloud adoption over the past six years, and identify an increasing trend that affects many different categories of malware.
- We present some general observations and insights about the global picture. For instance, while the recent efforts towards enhancing malware detection capabilities have contributed to considerably reduce the detection time for malicious hosts and domains, we were unable to observe a similar effect in the domains pointing to machines hosted on the cloud.

The rest of the paper is structured as follows. Section 2 provides an overview of our approach. We then describe our experiments in Sect. 3, and summarize and discuss the major findings in Sect. 4. Finally, Sect. 5 presented an overview of the related work in the area and Sect. 6 concludes the paper.

2   Approach

To identify malicious servers hosted on Amazon EC2, we first collected the range of IP addresses assigned to the cloud images, as reported by the Amazon website[1]. Moreover, to account for possible yearly changes, we also retrieved previous versions of the page from the web archive project[2]. We then extracted and analyzed the network traffic generated by all the malicious samples that have been collected and executed in Anubis, a popular malware analysis sandbox [6], over the past six years.

The main goal of our study is to verify the way miscreants make use of cloud services, whether they specifically target cloud infrastructures, and measure the time it takes for the provider to detect and drop malicious services hosted on EC2. To do so, our system tracks all domain names associated with the EC2 IP addresses that were contacted at least once by a malicious sample. Then, it further extracts and analyzes the DNS features and the content of network communications between the malware and the EC2 machines.

A major challenge in our study is that domain names extracted from the Anubis database do not only include dedicated malicious servers, and so we cannot simply mark as suspicious every connection toward a cloud-based IP address. In fact malware often contacts other public and benign cloud-based services, such as IP lookup services, advertisement websites, and URL shortening. These services are not part of the malicious activity and therefore need to be identified and discarded from our subsequent analysis.

On the other hand, real malicious domains may have been *sinkholed* by security organizations at the time the malware was analyzed in Anubis. Malware will be thus redirected towards sinkhole services that are sometimes hosted on EC2,

---

[1] http://docs.aws.amazon.com/general/latest/gr/aws-ip-ranges.html.
[2] https://archive.org/web/.

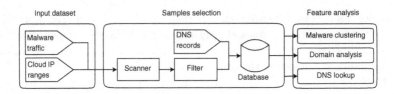

Fig. 1. Architecture of our platform

even though the original domains may have not been hosted on the cloud. Our system filters these cases and does not consider them as cloud-related malicious activities. Finally, in our experiments we discovered that many malware samples were *adwares* that leverage pay-per-install (PPI) services hosted on Amazon or other cloud providers. PPI services allow software publishers to pay affiliates by the number of installations that they perform on target machines. Caballero et al. analyze in [8] the *modus-operandi* of PPI services and measure their use for malware distribution. Although the use of PPI services to distribute malware still constitutes a malicious activity, PPI services are not malicious *per-se*, and so they need to be discarded from our dataset as we only focus in this paper on dedicated malicious services that were hosted on EC2.

2.1 Platform Description

To setup our experiments, we designed and implemented the platform illustrated in Fig. 1. Our system consists of two main components: the samples selection and the feature analysis modules. The first extracts from the Anubis database all malware samples that exhibited at least one network connection towards the Amazon cloud. During the period of our study, we identified 1.08 million malware samples that satisfied this criterion. The samples selection module further discards samples that have contacted benign public services hosted on EC2, and *keeps only dedicated malicious services* as input to the feature analysis module. Finally, the feature analysis module classifies the remaining malware samples and analyzes their dedicated malicious services hosted on cloud.

Samples Selection. The samples selection module aims at building a database of malware samples that, during their analysis, connected to malicious services hosted on EC2 – as well as the domain names or IP addresses that were associated with these services.

Malware Scanner: This module first extracts from Anubis all malicious samples that interacted with EC2 machines. We seed this module with the list of publicly routable IP ranges that were associated to the Amazon cloud in the year in which the analysis was performed. During the six years of our study, we identified 1,079,318 distinct samples that connected to EC2.

The first thing we noticed in our experiments is that a large number of samples in our dataset were executables that leveraged pay-per-install (PPI)

Table 1. Top 20 PPI services in our dataset

PPI Domain name	Samples	PPI Domain name	Samples
getapplicationmy.info	116306	torntv.net	16578
sslsecure1.com	71965	powerpackdl.com	15586
oi-imp1.com	68255	oi-config3.com	15578
secdls.com	52857	webfilescdn.com	14050
oi-config1.com	43526	torntvz.com	12440
ppdserver.com	39434	premiuminstaller.com	11879
optimum-installer.com	38777	ppdistro.us	10463
optimuminstaller.com	35510	bestringtonesmaker.com	10136
leadboltapps.net	31918	baixakialtcdn2.com	9946
xtrdlapi.com	18615	oi-config2.com	9601

services hosted on EC2. PPI services have recently emerged as a key component of modern cybercrime and miscreants often refer to these services to outsource the global distribution of their malware. They supply PPI services with malware executables, which in turn charge them for successful installations based on the requested features for the desired victims. PPI service providers operate directly or through affiliate programs. They develop downloaders that retrieve and run the requested software (possibly malware) upon execution on the victim computer.

To identify PPI downloaders in our dataset, we refer to multiple public sources such as PPI forums [1] and public PPI web sites. The main challenge in our case was to identify the different PPI brands, since there are new brands that constantly appear over time. In order to address this challenge, we analyzed the public PPI services that were mostly contacted by the samples in our dataset, and we tried to infiltrate these services by supplying a small program we developed for distribution. By testing and manually reverse engineering the resulting installer we developed a set of 13 distinct network signatures that match the download URLs associated with different families of PPI services. By using these signatures on the malware traffic we could further discard their associated samples in our dataset. As illustrated in Fig. 2, we were able to discard 1, 003, 289 PPI downloaders, which corresponds to up to 93.2 % of our initial dataset. Table 1 summarizes the top 20 PPI domain names that were contacted by malware in our dataset and the number of samples that were associated with each service.

In addition to PPI downloaders, our dataset also includes benign files that were submitted for analysis in Anubis. In fact Anubis is a public service where Internet users freely submit suspect files for analysis. These files may turn out to be benign files that connect to benign cloud-based services and so they also need to be discarded from our dataset as they do not belong to the malware category. Since our dataset covers a period where the most recent samples are few months old, we use anti-virus (AV) signatures to identify and discard benign

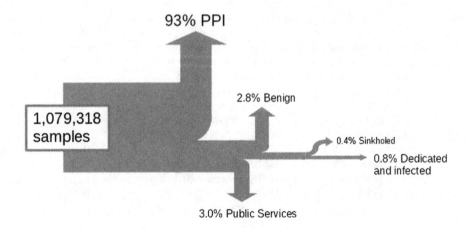

Fig. 2. Composition of our malware dataset

samples. We refer to public services such as VirusTotal[3] to scan our dataset, and we consider as benign files all samples that are detected by less than five AV editors. Our dataset finally includes 45,422 confirmed malicious malware samples. The remaining 30,607 samples (2.83 % of the initial malware dataset) were discarded as we do not have enough confidence about the malicious nature of these files.

Domain Filter: The domain filter module further discards from our dataset all domains that are associated with benign cloud-based services. Although these domains supply public Internet services that can be used by malware, they are not part of dedicated malicious services. Out of the initial set of 12,522 distinct EC2-based domain names or IP addresses, the malware scanner discarded 8,619 associated to PPI services or that were also contacted by benign programs. The domain filter classifies the remaining 3,903 domains into four categories, as illustrated in Table 2.

The first category includes public benign services that were contacted by malware. We found multiple examples in this category, including public IP resolvers (e.g. `hostip.info`), advertising and affiliate services, file sharing (e.g. `dropbox`), URL shortening (e.g. `notlong.com`), and multiple other free services (e.g. `about.me`, `spring.me`). To identify known public services in our dataset, the domain filter leverages multiple sources such as the Alexa list of top domains, public repositories that provide URL shortening services (e.g. `bit.do`) and file sharing[4]. We also refer to AV labels in VirusTotal in order to identify generic adwares. The domain filter module identifies as advertisement services all domains that were only contacted by Adwares samples. To be conservative, these domains were classified by our system into the public services category.

---

[3] http://www.virustotal.com.

[4] http://online-file-sharing-services-review.toptenreviews.com/.

Table 2. EC2-based service categories

Service		Domain Names	Malware Samples
Public Services	Advertising	930	22,216
	File sharing	796	7,657
	Domain redirection	270	479
	Others	211	1,723
Sinkholed		26	4,249
Infected		22	231
Dedicated		1,648	7,884
		N/A	983
Total		**3,903**	**45,422**

The second category includes domain names that have been sinkholed, and so they were redirected to sinkhole destinations that are hosted on the cloud. EC2 hosts multiple sinkhole destinations that are used to subvert BOT communications with their remote C&C domains. These domains were not originally hosted on EC2, and so they need to be discarded from our dataset. We leverage the X-sinkole HTTP header[5] in order to identify sinkhole destinations in our dataset.

The last two categories include both dedicated malware domains and domains that were once infected and temporarily used as part of the malicious infrastructure. The separation between these two categories is more difficult and more prone to errors. Our system relies on multiple empirical observations in order to discriminate between the two cases. First, we assume that dedicated malware machines that were hosted on EC2 more than one year ago have all been detected or abandoned at the time we run our experiments. We show in Sect. 3 that this is a reasonable assumption, consistent with the average lifetime of dedicated malicious domains hosted on EC2. Based on this assumption, the domain filter module actively probes all the domains and if the domain is still in use and points to a populated web page, we classify it as an infected host. Unfortunately, domain name vendors often return a HTML page to sell expired domains. Therefore, to correctly identify these domains, we parsed the HTML response page using multiple keywords (e.g. 'domain expired', 'domain for sale') and we removed these domains from the infected domains category. On top of this first heuristic, we also leveraged the history of DNS requests towards expired domains in order to assess the average lifetime of these domains. We use for this purpose DNS records that we extracted from DNSDB, a passive DNS duplication service[6]. In this case, our assumption is that infected domains usually have a longer turnover than other dedicated malicious domains. In other terms, infected domains are expected to appear in DNS records a long time before the

---

[5] http://www.iss.net/security_center/reference/vuln/HTTP_Malware_XSinkhole.htm.
[6] https://www.dnsdb.info/.

associated malware first appears in the wild. Dedicated domains instead, usually appear a short time before the malware is released and go offline a short time after the malware has been detected. By combining these two heuristics we were able to identify 22 infected services hosted on EC2 over the six years of observation. The remaining 1,648 domain names were identified by our system as being associated with dedicated malicious services.

Most of the connections were initiated using a domain name, but 983 malware samples directly connected to EC2-based IP addresses that were hard-coded in the malware itself, without any prior DNS request. To summarize, 8,867 of the 45,422 samples used at least one dedicated server hosted on Amazon EC2. For these, we also analyzed the content of their network communications. Almost 90.3 % of these samples used the standard HTTP protocol (either GET, POST, or HEAD methods). Few samples were IRC bots (19 distinct samples) and spam bots (136 distinct samples) that connected to malicious IRC and SMTP servers hosted on EC2. The remaining samples belonged to the Zeus version 3 and the Sality peer to peer (P2P) malware families, and were using the UDP protocol to connect to malicious P2P services hosted on EC2.

Feature Analysis. The analysis module processes the output dataset provided by the feature extraction module in order to extract main trends. First, it clusters malware families according to their antivirus labels, in order to figure out whether there exists a general trend towards moving malware infrastructures into the cloud, or whether this phenomenon is limited to some specific malware families. Second, it analyzes the network activity of each malware sample, computing the distribution of IP addresses and the domain flux to tell if miscreants specifically target cloud services, or if they use these services as part of their redundant malware infrastructure. Third, the feature analysis module observes the average duration a dedicated malicious server remains publicly accessible on the cloud. This can be used to estimate how effective are cloud providers in detecting abuse of their services, and whether malware writers sustain long lived malicious activities through the use of public cloud services. The following section provides the details and the main results of our experiments.

3   Experiments

The dataset provided by the feature extraction module (as described in Table 2) allows us to analyze both the malware families that are using EC2 cloud services in some capacity, as well as the distribution and lifetime of malicious domains that are hosted on EC2. Therefore, a first question that we would like to address in this section is whether the use of public cloud services is still limited to a small set of malware families, or whether it can be generalized to different families of malware. A straightforward approach to answer this question is to analyze the 8,867 distinct malware samples that we found to be connecting to dedicated malicious EC2 machines.

Since our dataset includes malware samples that are at least few months old at the time we run our analysis, we believe it is reasonable to use AV labels

Table 3. Top 20 malware family

AV label	# samples	AV label	# samples
Downloader Fosniw	1249	Trojan Kryptik	160
Worm Vobfus	909	Ramnit	129
Android DroidAp/SmsSend	634	Downloader Banload/Zlob	128
Downloader Murlo/Renos	567	Trojan Kazy	127
Backdoor QQRob	528	Downloader Virut/Virtob	127
Downloader Small BKY	208	Zbot	117
Delf Downloader	196	Malware SoftPulse	108
Trojan Injector	194	Downloader Karagany	90
Downloader 8CCBF09D99CF	186	Trojan Krap	89
Clicker Agent	172	Downloader Cutwail	80

as a reference to understand and classify our dataset. More complex behavioral clustering mechanisms, as proposed for instance by Bayer et al. [5] and Perdisci et al. [19], could be applied to refine the classification. However, since we only need a broad understanding of the major malware families that use cloud services and we can tolerate few misclassification errors, a simple AV-based solution is better suited for our study.

It is well known that different AV vendors assign different labels for the same malware sample. For example, the SpyEye malware can be identified by Kaspersky as `Trojan-Spy.Win32.SpyEyes`, and by McAfee as `PWS-Zbot.gen.br`. To limit the impact of such inconsistencies, we applied a majority voting to assign the labels to our dataset. In order to do so, we pre-process each label by splitting it in multiple elementary keywords according to non-alphanumeric characters We then discarded common prefixes such as `W32`, `Mal` and `Trojan`, as well as Generic malware identifiers, such as `Heur`, `Worm`, `Gen`, and `malware`. To handle malware aliases, we referred to multiple public sources such as the spywareremove website[7] to group together all aliases of a given malware family. For example, the labels `win32.spammy` by Kaspersky and `W32/Sality` by McAfee were identified as aliases for the same sality malware, and therefore grouped as part of the same family.

Cloud-Based Malware Families: We mainly focus in this paper on malware that uses dedicated malicious services hosted on EC2. Therefore, we build clusters of malware families for our dataset including 8, 867 distinct samples that belong to this category. Using our approach, we are able to identify 377 distinct malware families. As clearly illustrated in Table 3, which provides the list of top 20 malware families, we were not able to identify a predominant malware family that uses dedicated malicious cloud services. More interestingly, our dataset includes malware that uses different topologies, including also decentralized peer-to-peer networks such as the Sality malware. Clearly the use of dedicated malicious

---

[7] http://spywareremove.com/.

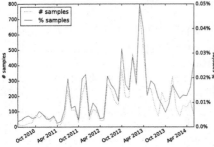 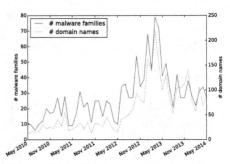

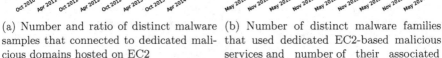

(a) Number and ratio of distinct malware samples that connected to dedicated malicious domains hosted on EC2

(b) Number of distinct malware families that used dedicated EC2-based malicious services and number of their associated malicious domain names

Fig. 3. Malware dataset analysis

cloud services is not limited to a small set of malware families, but it could be generalized to all categories of malware.

Time Evolution: Since the hosting and usage of malicious services on public cloud infrastructures such as EC2 is not limited to specific malware families, our next goal is to identify if there is a clear trend on the amount of malicious software that make use of cloud services. Figure 3a illustrates the number of distinct samples that connected to dedicated malicious domains hosted on EC2 during the period of our observation. To account for changes in the overall number of submissions, the figure also shows the percentage of distinct samples compared to the total number of samples submitted to Anubis in the same period. Figure 3b shows instead the number of distinct malware families, and the number of their associated malicious domains that were found to be hosted on EC2 over the same period.

On average, the number of malware that uses dedicated cloud-based malicious services has grown by almost 4 times between 2010 and 2013. The overall trend also includes multiple peaks, that after a manual analysis resulted to be associated with multiple instances of malicious servers found to be temporarily hosted on Amazon EC2. While the fast growing number of malware samples that use cloud-based services may appear as a natural consequence of the general increase in the number of malware attacks [3], Fig. 3a shows that this is not the case and that the ratio between these malware samples and the total number of malware submitted to Anubis has been increasing at the same rate. As illustrated in Fig. 3b, this trend can be generalized to all malware families, which means there is a growing appetite towards using cloud infrastructures to host malicious servers. This could be due to multiple elements, including the fact that cloud services have been rapidly expanding in the past few years, and the fact that they are ease to access and still lack a strict accountability and control over their hosted machines [15].

3.1   Role of Public Cloud Services in Malware Infrastructures

In this section we describe the different ways malicious software makes use of public cloud services. In particular, we are interested in understanding whether miscreants specifically target cloud services or whether they use these services as small parts in a much larger redundant infrastructure.

For this purpose, we measured the ratio of remote malicious destinations that were hosted on EC2, compared to all malicious destinations contacted by the malware during the analysis. Then, for those malicious services that were hosted on EC2, we determined if they were hosted on EC2 only as part of a redundant mechanism. In this case, we extracted the DNS requests executed by the malware and we monitored the DNS records history using DNSDB service in order to compute the ratio of IP addresses that belong to the EC2 IP range, compared to all IP addresses associated with that malicious domain in other moment in time. This technique works particularly well in the presence of round-robin DNS and DNS fast-flux techniques that are often adopted by botnet herders. For instance, miscreants can associate different IP addresses with the same malicious domain name, where only some of these IPs may be hosted on EC2.

Figure 4 presents the average distribution of the ratio of remote malicious destinations that were hosted on EC2, compared to all malicious destinations contacted by all malware samples. We present our findings as a box plot where malware samples are classified according to their submission date to Anubis. The Y-axis characterizes the ratio of dedicated malicious domains that were hosted on EC2, with respect to all malicious domains contacted by malware. Since we included in this experiment only malware samples that used dedicated malicious services on the Cloud, the percentage is always greater than 0 %. On the other hand, a malware would fit into the 100 % category in case all dedicated malicious domains that were contacted by the malware were strictly found to be hosted on EC2.

As shown in Fig. 4, miscreants mostly use public cloud services in order to host only certain components of their malware infrastructures. Note that while in 2010, and for malware that uses EC2 to host its dedicated malicious services, only few components of its malware infrastructures were found to be hosted on EC2 (less than 40 % of remote malicious domains in average); the use of public clouds to host dedicated malicious services has rapidly evolved in the recent years, including malware samples that were found to be exclusively communicating with dedicated cloud-based malicious domains in years 2013 and 2014. In other terms, miscreants have been recently referring to public cloud services in order to setup and manage their entire malware infrastructure. Therefore, although the use of public cloud services is still limited to only specific components of malware infrastructures, we observe an increasing appetite for miscreants towards using public cloud services to setup and manage additional components of their malware infrastructures.

Since most miscreants refer to public cloud services to host only certain components of their malware infrastructure, the second question we would like to answer is whether they specifically refer to public cloud services for this purpose,

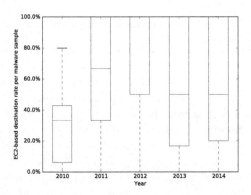

Fig. 4. Rate of dedicated malicious EC2-based domains contact per malware sample

or whether they use these services as redundant or failover components. We observed for this purpose the history of DNS records for all dedicated malicious EC2-based domains in our dataset until they were blacklisted, then we identified all IP addresses that were associated with these domains and their registrars in the DNSDB service. The results of our investigation were compelling. Out of the initial 1,648 dedicated malicious EC2-based domains that constitute our dataset, 1,620 domains (almost 98.3% of our dataset) were exclusively associated with IP addresses that belong to the EC2 IP range. Note that while 87.5% of dedicated malicious domains were associated with only a single EC2-based IP address, another 10.8% where found to be associated with multiple IP addresses that all belong to the EC2 IP range. In other terms, miscreants were specifically using public cloud infrastructures such as EC2 to host their dedicated malicious services.

While the use of public cloud services to host dedicated malicious domains is still limited to only certain components of today's malware infrastructures, miscreants appear to be specifically targeting cloud infrastructures for this purpose, and do not use public clouds only as redundant components of their malware infrastructures.

3.2 Dedicated Domains Lifetime Estimation

In the last part of our study, we tried to estimate the average time that malicious domains persist on EC2 cloud. Our approach leverages the lifetime of the EC2-based malicious domains in order to estimate whether the use of public cloud providers such as EC2 adds more resilience to malware infrastructures.

In the following, we refer to the lifetime of a EC2-based malicious domain as the duration when it was consecutively associated with EC2 cloud IP address in the passive DNS records. Note that the use of passive DNS service only provides an estimation of the real lifetime of these domains but this is an approximation that is often used for this type of measurements [16]. Since domains first appear in the passive DNS services when they are actively requested on the Internet,

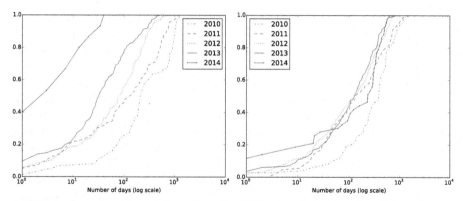

(a) Time elapsed until a dedicated malicious EC2-based domain was first observed
in Anubis

(b) Time until a edicated malicious domain
was no longer hosted on EC2, after it was
observed in Anubis

Fig. 5. Lifetime of dedicated malicious EC2-based domains

we consider that the use of this service provides a reliable estimation of the real
duration in which a given domain remained active and accessible on the wild. In
this section, we observe only dedicated malicious domains that were hosted on
EC2, and that were contacted by our malware dataset collected over a period
that ends by June 2014. Hence, we only consider historical DNS records associated with malicious servers that are no longer hosted on EC2 cloud at the
time of writing. Note that these domains may be still accessible but no longer
associated with any EC2 IP address.

We defined two metrics for our experiments. First of all, we measured the
time between the domain first appeared in the passive DNS service and the
time the malware was analyzed by Anubis. Second, we extract the time when
a dedicated malicious domain is no longer associated with an EC2 IP address,
after the malware was first submitted to the Anubis service.

The results of our experiment are summarized by the cumulative distributions
that are illustrated in Fig. 5. The graphs separately illustrate the results of our
experiments for the last five years since 2010, in order to extrapolate some trends
and assess the efficiency of security measures implemented by Amazon over time.
The first graph shows that the distribution is clearly moving toward the top-left
corner, meaning that each domain was observed in Anubis soon after it first
appeared in the wild. For instance, while in 2011 around 50 % of the domains
were already present in the passive DNS service (and therefore active in the wild)
for 100 days before some malware in Anubis contacted them, in 2014 they had
only been active for two days. In other words, the security community became
very efficient to promptly detect, collect, and submit malware samples.

Unfortunately, Fig. 5b shows that the time these domains were hosted on
EC2 *after* the malware was analyzed remained stable over the same period.
While many factors are involved in this process, this seems to suggest that Cloud

providers did not improve their ability to detect and report abusive behaviors. In other words, our observations suggest that the security mechanisms implemented by public cloud service providers have not contributed to reducing the lifetime of malicious domains hosted by these providers.

In order to confirm these findings, and since cloud providers may take-down malicious IPs and not their associated domain names, we analyzed the way malicious EC2 domains resolve to different IP addresses over time. We wanted to evaluate how long malicious machines remain active on EC2 before they are taken down by the cloud provider, and so miscreants may be forced into migrating their malicious domains towards other IP addresses. We monitored for this purpose all DNS records in the DNSDB service, searching for different IP addresses that were associated with every malicious domain in our dataset. Confirming our hypothesis, we found multiple instances of malicious machines that remained active on EC2 even for several months before they were migrated towards other IP addresses in the cloud.

Table 4. Examples of domains that rotated their IP addresses on EC2 over time

Id	Domain	IP address	First seen	Last seen	Duration (months)
1	09sp.co.tv	174.129.222.176	August 2010	October 2010	3
		174.129.242.247	January 2011	November 2012	22
2	47gr.co.tv	174.129.222.176	July 2010	July 2010	1
		174.129.242.247	February 2011	November 2012	21
3	dl.ka3ek.com	107.20.206.69	January 2013	November 2013	11
		54.209.129.218	January 2014	January 2014	1
4	hightool.com	107.20.206.69	January 2013	December 2013	12
		54.209.168.250	March 2014	September 2014	7
		54.208.247.222	September 2014	September 2014	1
5	hzmksreiuojy.com	54.241.7.53	April 2013	April 2013	1
		50.18.179.196	April 2013	October 2013	7
		50.17.195.149	July 2014	July 2014	1

As illustrated by the examples in Table 4, the first two malicious domains were associated with the same EC2 IP address for up to twenty consecutive months before they went out from the EC2 IP ranges. Interestingly, certain malicious domains, such as domains 1 and 2, as well as domains 3 and 4 in Table 4, were associated with the same IP address during the same period of time, which seems to indicate that miscreants may associate different domain names with their malicious machines in the cloud in order to obtain a better resilience against domain blacklisting. Moreover, they also seem to benefit from the flexibility offered by the cloud in order to migrate towards new IP addresses in

EC2 as soon as their current IP addresses have disappeared from the active DNS records, which may suggest that their malicious machines have been identified and taken down by the cloud provider (EC2 in our study). In total, we observed similar behaviors in over 240 malicious domains in our dataset.

4   Discussion

When we started our experiments, we were surprised to discover that over 3.5 % of the malware samples in our dataset exhibited at least one network connection with a machine hosted on the Amazon cloud. However, as clearly depicted in Fig. 2, the vast majority of these connections had nothing to do with the fact that criminals were intentionally using the Cloud as part of their infrastructure. In fact, once PPI and other benign services were filtered out, we discovered that less than 1 % of the traffic toward Amazon involved a malicious EC2 machine.

Even though this number may seem incredibly small (roughly one every 3200 malicious samples), it is still relevant when scaled to the entire dataset containing tens of millions of malicious samples. Moreover, our experiments show that the use of public cloud services by malicious software has been increasing over the last six years, despite the measures taken by certain cloud providers to limit the extent of these abuses. It also seems that the use of dedicated malicious cloud services is not limited to a small set of malware families, but it can be generalized to most of the malware categories – as summarized by Table 3.

The final observation of our study is related to how the cloud providers, Amazon in our case, respond to this threat. Even though we did not have a direct way to observe their reaction, we were able to measure for how long – after the malware was publicly known – the malicious domains it contacted were resolving to IPs hosted on EC2. While the absolute value is not very important, the fact that it remained constant over the past four years seems to indicate that the cloud provider did not make any substantial improvement in detecting and taking down malicious machines.

5   Related Work

Prior abuse cases of public cloud providers have attracted a lot of interests in the recent years [7,11,14,21]. For instance, cloud services are listed by Solutionary [20] among the major components of modern cybercrime, and attackers seem to use these services the same way and for the same reasons as legitimate customers. Despite this popularity, we are aware of only few research studies that managed to evaluate the real extent of this phenomenon.

Hamza et al. [12] presented a survey of possible techniques to abuse cloud services in modern cybercrime. They provide interesting insights on the way cyber-attacks are perpetrated from within cloud platforms, including examples such as host hopping attacks and abuse of privileges. However, this survey only focuses on strong attack signals, and does not consider other weak signals that determine the way cloud services are being used as part of the attackers command and control infrastructures.

In [18], Nappa et al. analyze drive-by download attacks and exploit servers that are managed by the same organizations. They found that 60 % of the exploit servers are hosted by public cloud service providers. More interestingly, they evaluated the abuse report procedures implemented by public cloud service providers. They realized that out of 19 abuse reports they have submitted, only 7 were investigated by cloud providers. Moreover, the authors computed that it takes on average 4.3 days for a cloud provider to take down an exploit server after it has been reported. It is important to note that the authors of this study only focus on drive-by-download attacks that involve cloud services. Although drive-by-download servers constitute a major component of a modern malware infrastructures, we go beyond this unique use case in order to provide in this paper a more comprehensive assessment about the way cloud services are being integrated in malware infrastructures in modern cybercrime. We also try to understand whether clouds constitute core elements of the malware structure, or whether they are only used as redundant or failover components.

In [9], Canali et al. propose an active approach to evaluate the security mechanisms implemented by web hosting providers. They installed vulnerable web services on 22 distinct hosting providers, and triggered multiple attacks to leverage the reaction capabilities of these providers. To test the security mechanisms implemented by cloud service providers we adopt a less intrusive approach where we only observe malware interactions with the cloud. In our study we only focus on Amazon EC2. While this choice may limit the extent of our observations, at the same time eliminate as much as possible the impact of rogue or other hosting providers that do not guarantee minimal security SLA requirements to their users. We believe that focusing only on the biggest cloud providers in terms of market share also shed light on the limits of current security and accountability mechanisms implemented by today's cloud providers.

Finally, Wang et al. [22] propose a system that measures the churn rates in EC2 and Azure in order to evaluate the efficacy of IP blacklists for malicious activity in the cloud. The authors actively probed the EC2 and Azure IP ranges, and proposed a clustering mechanism that groups together IP addresses implementing the same services. They also observed all web services hosted by cloud providers, spanning both benign and malicious activities. The results of their experiments show only small amounts of malicious activity (mostly phishing and malware hosting) by comparing data from their system with public blacklists. We propose in this paper a complementary approach that observes only malware interactions with the cloud in order to leverage the true extent of the malicious activity hosted by public cloud providers.

6   Conclusion

Public cloud services have rapidly expanded in recent years, yet they have attracted cyber criminals because of the wealth of resources they make available, and the lack of accountability over the usage of these resources. In order to measure the extent at which public cloud services are being abused by cyber-criminals, we conducted a longitudinal study of malware in order to better understand the way it interacts with public cloud services.

In particular, in this paper we study several characteristics of the traffic observed between malicious samples and the Amazon EC2 cloud. Based on our measurements, we discuss the evolution of this phenomenon over the past six years, and we present few key observations and insights into this growing problem.

We hope that our study can shed some light on a key component of the modern cyber crime infrastructure, and would provide useful input to devise appropriate mitigation strategies.

Acknowledgments. We would like to thank the reviewers for their valuable comments that allowed us to improve the quality of this paper. This research was partly funded by the French Ministry of education and research under Cifre grant given to Xiao Han, and by the European Unions Horizon 2020 project SUPERCLOUD under grant agreement 643964.

References

1. Best pay-per-install affiliate program reviews. http://pay-per-install.com. Accessed December 2014
2. Amazon, E.: Amazon elastic compute cloud (amazon ec2) (2010). http://aws.amazon.com/ec2/
3. AVTest Institute. Malware statistics & trends report. http://www.av-test.org/en/statistics/malware/
4. Azure, W.: Microsofts cloud platform (2013). http://azure.microsoft.com/
5. Bayer, U., Comparetti, P.M., Hlauschek, C., Kruegel, C., Kirda, E.: Scalable, behavior-based malware clustering. NDSS **9**, 8–11 (2009)
6. Bayer, U., Kruegel, C., Kirda, E.: Ttanalyze: a tool for analyzing malware. In: 15th European Institute for Computer Antivirus Research (EICAR 2006) Annual Conference (2006)
7. Bestuzhev, D.: Financial data stealing malware now on amazon web services cloud (2011). http://www.securelist.com/en/blog/208188099/Financial_data_stealing_Malware_now_on_Amazon_Web_Services_Cloud. Accessed 15 May 2014
8. Caballero, J., Grier, C., Kreibich, C., Paxson, V.: Measuring pay-per-install: the commoditization of malware distribution. In: 20th USENIX Conference on Security (2011)
9. Canali, D., Balzarotti, D., Francillon, A.: The role of web hosting providers in detecting compromised websites. In: Proceedings of the 22nd International Conference on World Wide Web, International World Wide Web Conferences Steering Committee, pp. 177–188 (2013)
10. Cohen, R.: The cloud hits the mainstream: more than half of u.s. businesses now use cloud computing. In: Forbes Magazine (2013)
11. Ferrer, M.C.: Zeus in the cloud. http://community.ca.com/blogs/securityadvisor/archive/2009/12/09/zeus-in-the-cloud.aspx

12. Hamza, Y.A., Omar, M.D.: Cloud computing security: abuse and nefarious use of cloud computing. Int. J. Comput. Eng. Res. **3**, 22–27 (2013)
13. He, K., Fisher, A., Wang, L., Gember, A., Akella, A., Ristenpart, T.: Next stop, the cloud: understanding modern web service deployment in ec2 and azure. In: ACM Internet Measurement Conference (IMC) (2013)
14. Higgins, K.J.: Dropbox, wordpress used as cloud cover in new apt attacks (2013). http://www.darkreading.com/attacks-breaches/dropbox-wordpress-used-as-cloud-cover-in-new-apt-attacks/d/d-id/1140098?. Accessed 15 May 2014
15. Ko, R.K., Jagadpramana, P., Mowbray, M., Pearson, S., Kirchberg, M., Liang, Q., Lee, B.S.: Trustcloud: a framework for accountability and trust in cloud computing. In: 2011 IEEE World Congress on Services (SERVICES), pp. 584–588. IEEE (2011)
16. Li, Z., Alrwais, S., Xie, Y., Yu, F., Wang, X.: Finding the linchpins of the dark web: a study on topologically dedicated hosts on malicious web infrastructures. In: 2013 IEEE Symposium on Security and Privacy (SP), pp. 112–126. IEEE (2013)
17. Los, R., Shackleford, D., Sullivan, B.: The notorious nine cloud computing top threats in 2013. In: Cloud Security Alliance (2013)
18. Nappa, A., Xu, Z., Rafique, M.Z., Caballero, J., Cyberprobe, G.Gu.: Towards internet-scale active detection of malicious servers. In: Network and Distributed System Security Symposium (NDSS) (2014)
19. Perdisci, R., Lee, W., Feamster, N.: Behavioral clustering of http-based malware and signature generation using malicious network traces. In: USENIX Symposium on Networked Systems Design and Implementation (NSDI) (2010)
20. Solutionary. Security Engineering Research Team (SERT) Quarterly Threat Intelligence Report (2014). http://www.solutionary.com/_assets/pdf/research/sert-q4-2013-threat-intelligence.pdf. Accessed 15 May 2014
21. Unuchek, R.: Gcm in malicious attachments (2013). http://www.securelist.com/en/blog/8113/GCM_in_malicious_attachments. Accessed 15 May 2014
22. Wang, L., Nappa, A., Caballero, J., Ristenpart, T., Akella, A.: Whowas: a platform for measuring web deployments on iaas clouds. In: ACM Internet Measurement Conference (IMC) (2014)

Capturing DDoS Attack Dynamics Behind the Scenes

An Wang[1]([✉]), Aziz Mohaisen[2], Wentao Chang[1], and Songqing Chen[1]

[1] Department of Computer Science, George Mason University, Fairfax, USA
{awang10,wchang7,sqchen}@gmu.edu
[2] Verisign Labs, Reston, USA
amohaisen@verisign.com

Abstract. Despite continuous defense efforts, DDoS attacks are still very prevalent on the Internet. In such arms races, attackers are becoming more agile and their strategies are more sophisticated to escape from detection. Effective defenses demand in-depth understanding of such strategies. In this paper, we set to investigate the DDoS landscape from the perspective of the attackers. We focus on the dynamics of the attacking force, aiming to explore the attack strategies, if any. Our study is based on 50,704 different Internet DDoS attacks. Our results indicate that attackers deliberately schedule their controlled bots in a dynamic fashion, and such dynamics can be well captured by statistical distributions.

1 Introduction

Internet Distributed Denial of Service (DDoS) attacks have been a challenge for many years. Today, many DDoS attacks are launched via different botnets. Recent years have witnessed the rapid increase of such DDoS attacks in terms of both the number and the volume. For example, according to a recent report by Verisign on DDoS trends [1], the duration, intensity, and diversity of attacks are on the rise: a year-over-year analysis shows that the average DDoS attack size has increased by 245 % in the fourth quarter of 2014, compared to the same quarter of 2013, and by 14 % from the previous quarter of the same year, with an average attack of 7.39 Gbps. Furthermore, the same report shows that all industry verticals are targeted by attacks. As a matter of fact, today botnet DDoS attacks have become a mainstream commodity in the cybercrime ecosystem, where they could be rented or loaned to facilitate such increasing attacks.

To understand the fundamentals of DDoS attacks and defend against them, enormous efforts are continuously made from both academia and industry [4,9,17,22]. Driven by the underlying profits and the lifted bar by the ever-improving defense mechanisms, DDoS attacking strategies are becoming increasingly sophisticated in order to evade various detection systems. Therefore, a timely and in-depth understanding of latest DDoS attack strategies is a key to improve the existing defenses. However, most of our understanding of DDoS attacks is based on the indirect traffic measures and static characterization of

© Springer International Publishing Switzerland 2015
M. Almgren et al. (Eds.): DIMVA 2015, LNCS 9148, pp. 205–215, 2015.
DOI: 10.1007/978-3-319-20550-2_11

DDoS attacks [6, 7, 9, 15, 16, 22]. For example, our previous study shows that most DDoS attacks today are not widely distributed, but highly regionalized [22]. Most of such characterizations only touch the surface of attackers' strategies, which is far from sufficient for us to design more effective defenses against many attacks.

To win the arms race, we set out to investigate the attacking strategies behind the scenes. For this purpose, we aim to explore the attackers' strategies in deploying the attack force, focusing on the dynamic control of the attack forces in different DDoS attacks. Our study is based on a DDoS dataset collected for a period of 7 continuous months. Our dataset was collected using passive and active techniques from multiple anchor points. The data was collected from August 28, 2012 to March 24, 2013, a total of 209 days (about seven months of valid and marked attack logs). In this seven-month period, a total of 50,704 different DDoS attacks were observed—more details are in [5]. Also, this work focuses on the analysis of dynamic patterns of DDoS attacks. More static analysis of the attacks could be found in [21]. Through our analysis, we find several interesting results. We find that a botnet family often uses a limited number of sophisticated patterns in dynamically scheduling bots to participate in various DDoS attacks. This dynamic scheduling is indicated by the shifting patterns of participating bots. Further, the bot shifting pattern in different botnet families can be well captured by statistical distributions, with parameters depending on the corresponding family.

The preliminary findings in this study not only refresh our understanding of today's Internet DDoS attacks, but also offer new insights for security analysts to identify botnet families and help predict how the attacking forces evolve over time during attacks.

The rest of the paper is organized as follows. In Sect. 2, we describe our dataset including the overall data statistics and the data fields we utilized for our analysis. In Sect. 3, we study the bot shifting pattern of each botnet family, the basic characteristics of each pattern We discuss related work in Sect. 4 and conclude with a concise summary of our analyses and their implications in Sect. 5.

2   Dataset Collection

As mentioned earlier, the dataset is based on constant monitoring of Internet critical infrastructure to aid intelligence gathering concerning the state of the art of attack posture, using both active and passive measurement techniques.

Even though there might be some potential skews in our dataset, our preliminary studies [5, 6, 22] suggest that our dataset still preserves the geographical features of botnet families. The unit constantly monitors Internet attacking traffic to aid the mitigation efforts of its customers, using both active and passive measurement techniques. For active measurements and attribution, malware families used in launching the various attacks are reverse engineered, and labeled to a known malware family using best practices. An enumeration technique, similar to the one proposed by Kang et al. [10], is used enumerate bots participating in the particular botnet. As each botnet evolves over time, new generations are marked by their unique hashes.

Traces of traffic associated with various DDoS campaigns are then collected at various anchor points across the globe in cooperation with various ISPs. The traces are then analyzed to attribute and characterize attacks on various targets. The collection of traffic is guided by two general principles: (1) that the source of the traffic is an infected host participating in a DDoS campaign, and (2) the destination of the traffic is a targeted client, as concluded from eavesdropping on C&C of the campaign using a live sample, or where the end-host is a customer of the said DDoS mitigation company.

The analysis is high level in nature to cope with the high volume of ingest traffic at peak attack times—as shown later, on average there were 243 simultaneous verified DDoS attacks launched by the different botnets studied in this work. High level statistics associated with the various botnets and DDoS attacks are recorded every one hour. The workload we obtained ranges from August 28, 2012 to March 24, 2013, a total of 209 days (about seven months of valid and marked attack logs). In the log, a DDoS attack is labeled with a unique DDoS identifier, corresponding to an attack by given DDoS malware family on a given target. We cannot reveal the capability of the capturing facility because attackers would learn such information, which is also critical to the business of the data source.

Table 1 sums up some statistics of our dataset, including information from both the attacker and the target sides. Over a period of 28 weeks, 50,704 different DDoS attacks were observed. These attacks are launched by 674 different botnets. These attacks targeted victims located in 84 different countries, 616 cities, involving 1074 organizations, residing in 1260 different autonomous systems. In our analysis, we focus on the botnets involved in DDoS attacks. However, [5] contains more detailed information about botnet family activities and patterns.

Table 1. Summary of the workload information

Summary of attackers		Summary of victims	
Description	Count	Description	Count
# of bot_ips	310950	# of target_ip	9026
# of cities	2897	# of cities	616
# of countries	186	# of countries	84
# of organizations	3498	# of organizations	1074
# of asn	3973	# of asn	1260

The attackers' IP information enables us to study the geolocation distribution of each botnet family. Contrary to the traditional understanding of DDoS attacks, the attacks are not very distributed but rather highly regionalized [22]. Each family has its own geolocation preferences. Among all the families, *Dirtjumper* covers the largest number of countries: 164. A comparable coverage is Optima's: 153. Even though these families have very broad country coverages, the average number of bots participating in each attack pertaining to those botnets is small.

3   Attack Dynamics

To seek an in-depth understanding of attackers' strategies, we set to explore attacks from the adversary's perspective. By doing that, we are motivated to find out how their controlled bots are scheduled to participate in attacks. To this end, we use the IP information of the bots captured in our dataset. Our analysis starts off from two different perspectives, namely the bot shift pattern dynamics and the multi-owned bot attacking interval, both of which are related to DDoS attack strategies.

For any DDoS attack, it evolves over time in terms of the attacking force. In our dataset, each entry represents a snapshot of the DDoS attacks captured at that time point. As a result, each DDoS can be represented by a chronological sequence of snapshots. Dynamic characterizations can be captured by analyzing each data record.

For each entry in our dataset, we have the IP information of all the bots participating in that DDoS attack at that moment, of which the country code (cc) could also be obtained from such information (the snapshots are updated hourly). Thus, the dataset contains all the IP information of bots involved. After further organizing the bots based on their country code, each entry in the dataset can be denoted by $< cc_1 : n_1, cc_2 : n_2, \ldots, cc_m : n_m >$ where each $cc_i, i \in [1 \ldots m]$ represents the country code where the bots locate; while for each $n_i, i \in [1 \ldots m]$ denotes the number of bots located in $cc_i, i \in [1 \ldots m]$. Since each of such vector represents a snapshot, so if we line up all the vectors belonging to the same DDoS attack together, we can observe the deployment differences by comparing the number of bots in each country and the number of countries involved. For example, if we have two such records, denoted by vec_1 and vec_2, the change can be denoted by $vec_2 - vec_1 = < cc_1 : \Delta_1, cc_2 : \Delta_2, \ldots, cc_j : \Delta_j > = vec_{\Delta_v}$. Notice that the lengths of vec_1 and vec_2 may not be equal and the length of vec_{Δ_v} will be the same as the longer one. Thus, the difference vector reflects the changes of the bots numbers at the country level for the given attack, which is defined as *shift* in our analysis.

To further quantify such changes, we use the notion of *shift expectation* to represent each attacking force shift. In another word, each vector described above will be denoted by a single value called *shift expectation*, whose calculation will be elaborated later. In this way, each DDoS attack can be denoted by a vector whose elements are shift expectation, i.e. $< E_{shift_1}, E_{shift_2}, \ldots, E_{shift_m} >$, since each DDoS attack can be denoted by a time series of snapshots. And the length of this vector is determined by both the number of magnitude changes happened in each attack as well as the number of snapshots taken for each attack.

The *shift expectation* is calculated as $\sum_{i=1}^{m} p_i \times \Delta_i$, where Δ_i is obtained from vec_{Δ_v} and p_i denotes the probability estimator of the shift. And p_i is computed as follows. From our dataset, we obtain the geolocation information of all bots involved in the DDoS attacks. For each family, we generate a table that has two columns; the first column contains all the country codes that are covered by this family while the second one has the corresponding number of bots that locate in that country. So each entry in this table is denoted by (cc_i, n_i), for $i \in [1 \ldots l]$. On the other hand, $p_i, i \in [1 \ldots l]$, is calculated as $\frac{n_i}{\sum_{j=1}^{l} n_j}$. With both p_i and Δ_i, the expectation of each shift E_{shift} can be calculated. After converting each DDoS attack into a time series vector, we have all the vectors with various lengths for all the DDoS attacks in our dataset. Our following analyses will be built on top of these vectors.

3.1 Bots Shift Pattern Analysis

First, we use the K-means clustering on all attack vectors of each family. Since the lengths of vectors may vary, we cannot calculate the Euclidean distance between vectors directly. The Dynamic Time Warping (DTW) has been widely used for shape matching and time series classification. Accordingly, we use DTW to calculate the distance and similarity between attack vectors. To reduce the distortion under the influence of attack magnitude, we normalize the vector before we calculate the DTW distance on them.

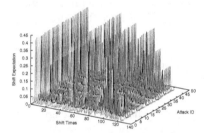

Fig. 1. *Dirtjumper:* attacks with same bot shift pattern

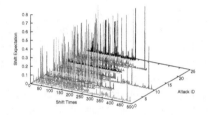

Fig. 2. *Dirtjumper:* attacks with similar bot shift pattern

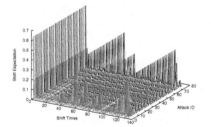

Fig. 3. *Pandora:* attacks with same bot shift pattern

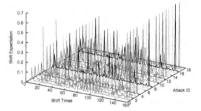

Fig. 4. *Pandora:* attacks with similar bot shift pattern

The results are shown in Figs. 1, 2, 3, and 4. In these figures, x-axis represents Shift Times, which is determined by the number of snapshots belonging to each DDoS attack; y-axis represents Attack ID, which is used to differentiate different DDoS attacks; z-axis represents the calculated Shift Expectation values. Figures 1 and 2 illustrate two of the four largest clusters discovered by the K-means algorithm of the *Dirtjumper* family, where $K = 10$. We cluster these vectors into 5, 10, and 20 clusters. It is shown that clustering them into 10 clusters yields better results. So, we present the two largest clusters of the 10 clusters for brevity. The two clusters contain 54 and 24 attacks, respectively. In each figure, the x-axis represents the length of the attack vector, i.e., the shifts happened in a single attack; the y-axis represents the unique DDoS ID; and the z-axis represents the shift expectation of each shift. Note that since *Dirtjumper* has too many DDoS attacks with different lengths of shifts, we first group the attacks by size. In this study, we focus on the analysis of attack vectors that have more than 100 shifts, which include 242 attacks launched by *Dirtjumper*. Our following analyses are based on this subset of our dataset as well.

In these figures, the expectations should be discrete values. To more clearly show the changes, we use lines to connect these dots. Figure 1 shows that in these attacks, bots are being scheduled with the exact same pattern in different attacks, while Fig. 2 indicates a similar pattern—although not identically—in different attacks. With further inspection, we find that in Fig. 1 there are 46 simultaneous DDoS attacks ongoing towards the same target located in Finland, which is a company providing communication services from basic broadband to high-speed fiber connections.

These results suggest that the attacking forces are not randomly scheduled by the attackers in *Dirtjumper*. Also, simultaneous attacks cannot be arranged by a completely random deployment strategy. There has to be certain strategies behind DDoS attacks launched by each family. To see if such a pattern is specific to *Dirtjumper* or generalizable to others, we examine other families. Figures 3 and 4 illustrate two clusters of another active botnet family *Pandora*. We use the same K-means clustering with 10 clusters for attacks and more than 100 shifts as before. We have similar observations on *Pandora* as on *Dirtjumper*. While other families show similar results, we omit them due to page limit. These findings also suggest that there might be a way to detect DDoS attacks based on these shift behaviors. But this only will be possible if we can precisely model these pattern, which is the aim of our next step.

3.2   Mathematical Representation of Shift Patterns

To further explore the pattern behind these vectors, we first find the centroid vector of each cluster and then calculate the distance between each attack vector in that cluster and the centroid. The centroid vector cannot be calculated simply by averaging all the vectors involved since they are of different length. We define centroid vector as the vector that has the smallest total distance to all other vectors. And all the distances involved are measured by DTW distance. We use *Dirtjumper* as an example since it is the most active family.

The CDF of the distance distribution for *Dirtjumper* is shown in Fig. 5. In this figure, each curve represents a cluster. If we observe these curves, the distances seem to follow the normal distribution very well except for cluster-1. To verify the distribution, we further fit the data into multiple distributions, including

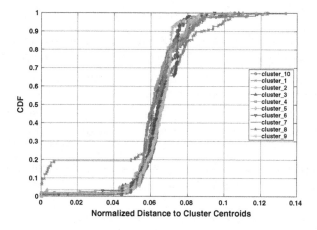

Fig. 5. Vector distances CDF

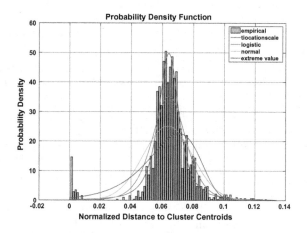

Fig. 6. Distribution fit

tlocationscale distribution, normal distribution, logistic distribution and *extreme value distribution.* The fitting results are shown in Fig. 6.

Except for the *extreme value distribution*, all other distribution functions are symmetric distributions. Figure 6 shows that the data fit the *tlocationscale distribution* best. *tlocationscale distribution* is the generalized *Student's t-distribution* into location-scale family. Location-scale family is a family of univariate probability distributions parameterized by a location parameter and a non-negative scale parameter. The *tlocationscale distribution* is useful for modeling data distribution with heavier tails than the *normal distribution*, meaning that it is more prone to producing values that fall far from its mean. This makes it useful for understanding the statistical behavior of certain types of ratios of random quantities. In this case, the distribution describes the distances between multiple shift

Table 2. Statistic information of *Pandora* cluster

Size	Max_Diss	Avg_Diss	Diameter	Separation	Avg_Exp	Max_Exp	Std
97	3.69	0.18	3.73	3.46	0.03	0.74	0.076
74	0.06	0.02	0.09	3.62	0.03	0.63	0.08
20	4.52	1.46	4.99	2.39	0.025	0.88	0.073
17	3.48	0.41	3.48	2.39	0.028	0.68	0.075
7	4.18	1.06	4.30	3.57	0.03	0.88	0.08

patterns of botnets. It means that if we use the centroids of different clusters as a baseline, we can learn and predict how the bots are going to shift based on this distribution.

To this end, it is likely that attackers are utilizing this feature to arrange and control bots during attacks, especially with a large number of bots. From a defense perspective, such information can be very useful. On one hand, with this information—even though there might be more than one shift pattern per family—we can predict how attacks shift based on the distribution. On the other hand, we can simulate DDoS attacks behaviors, not only based on traffic volume but also by incorporating dynamics behind them.

Similar to Fig. 5, we also plotted a CDF for *Pandora*'s clusters, which confirmed the similar behavioral patterns. However, compared to *Dirtjumper*, *Pandora* exhibits a slight deviation in the distribution, perhaps due to the smaller number of attacks in *Pandora* compared to *Dirtjumper*. Results obtained by analyzing other families reveal similar findings.

Besides the pattern clustering graphs, Table 2 summarizes some statistical information about *Pandora* clusters. In this table, *Size* shows the size of each cluster; *Max_Diss* represents the maximum distance between any two vectors in the same cluster; *Diameter* represents the largest dissimilarity between any two pairs of the observations within the same cluster; *Separation* represents the minimal dissimilarity between an observation of the cluster and an observation of another cluster; *Avg_Exp* shows the average shift expectation of each cluster and *Std* is the standard deviation of expectations of each cluster. Statistically speaking, the smaller the *Diameter*, the better the cluster. From this table, we can see that the second cluster is the best, which also conforms with Fig. 3. Another observation from this table is that for most clusters, the *Diameter* is larger than *Separation*, meaning that these clusters are not totally isolated. The total isolation means that the patterns might be attack-specific. However, results show the opposite: each cluster still shares some similarities with other clusters. This further indicates that there might be certain dynamic mechanisms behind each family.

4   Related Work

DDoS attacks have been intensively investigated and numerous measurement works have been done to help achieve better understanding of them. In 2006,

Mao et al. [17] presented their measurement work of DDoS attacks relying on both direct measurement of flow-level information and more traditional indirect measurements using backscatter analysis. Moore et al. [18] conducted a backscatter analysis for quantitatively estimating DoS activity in the Internet based on a three-week dataset. Due to the growth of network address translation and firewall techniques, much of the Internet was precluded from the study by the traditional network measurement techniques. Thus, in the early days, the work [4] proposed an opportunistic measurement approach that leverages sources of spurious traffic, such as worms and DDoS backscatter, to unveil unseen portion of Internet. In 2010, a more recent study [24] revisited the same topic and characterized the current state of background radiation specifically highlighting those which exhibit significant differences. Our work serves as a revisit to those studies with new insights. Bailey et al. [2] designed and implemented the Internet Motion Sensors (IMS), a globally scoped Internet monitoring system to detect Internet threats, which includes a distributed blackhole network with a lightweight responder and a novel payload signature and caching mechanism. Xu et al. [25] presented a general methodology to build behavior profiles of Internet backbone traffic in terms of communication patterns of end-hosts and services.

In our work, we focus on DDoS dynamics. We use several techniques including K-means clustering and Dynamic Time Warping (DTW). DTW was first introduced in the data mining community in the context of mining time series proposed by Berndt et al. [8]. Several techniques have been introduced to speed up DTW and to reduce the space overhead [12,13]. The K-means clustering methods we use were first proposed by Lloyd et al. [19]. And it remains a very popular method of clustering after many years perhaps due to the simplicity of the algorithm and its effectiveness in practice. These techniques successfully helped us discover the principles of the dynamics behind the scenes. Several other works focused on DDoS dynamics analysis as well, including Arne et al. [23], Armin et al. [3], Mohammad et al. [11], Kührer et al. [14]. In Stringhini et al. [20], a similar approach was proposed to model the country distribution of bots and cluster together botnets.

5   Conclusion

DDoS attacks remain one of the most challenging threats on the Internet, despite numerous efforts to characterize, model, and defend against them. This indicates that increasingly sophisticated strategies are being employed by the DDoS attackers. Successful defenses demand in-depth understanding of their strategies. In this work, we have conducted a preliminary analysis on a large scale DDoS dataset, aiming to understand the dynamics of the DDoS attack strategies behind the scenes. With the help of Dynamic Time Warping and clustering, we have found that attackers are deliberately and dynamically deploying their attack forces in individual or collaborative attacks, indicating the strong bond and organization of different botnet families in various attacks. Furthermore, such dynamics can be well captured by statistical distributions. These results add to the existing literature of DDoS characterization and understanding. More importantly, they lay a promising foundation for us to predict the dynamics during a DDoS attack in the future, which could be utilized to enhance existing defenses.

Acknowledgment. This work is partially supported by National Science Foundation (NSF) under grant CNS-1117300. The views and opinions expressed in this paper are the views of the authors, and do not necessarily represent the policy or position of NSF or VeriSign, Inc.

References

1. Verisign distributed denial of service trends report. http://www.verisigninc.com/en_US/cyber-security/ddos-protection/ddos-report/index.xhtml, February 2015
2. Bailey, M., Cooke, E., Jahanian, F., Nazario, J., Watson, D., et al.: The internet motion sensor-a distributed blackhole monitoring system. In: NDSS (2005)
3. Büscher, A., Holz, T.: Tracking DDoS attacks: insights into the business of disrupting the web. In: Proceedings of the 5th USENIX Workshop on Large-Scale Exploits and Emergent Threats (LEET), San Jose (2012)
4. Casado, M., Garfinkel, T., Cui, W., Paxson, V., Savage, S.: Opportunistic measurement: extracting insight from spurious traffic. In: Proceedings of the 4th ACM Workshop on Hot Topics in Networks (Hotnets-IV) (2005)
5. Chang, W., Mohaisen, A., Wang, A., Chen, S.: Measuring botnets in the wild: some new trends. In: ACM ASIACCS (2015)
6. Chang, W., Wang, A., Mohaisen, A., Chen, S.: Characterizing botnets-as-a-service. In: Proceedings of the ACM SIGCOMM (poster) (2014)
7. Feinstein, L., Schnackenberg, D., Balupari, R., Kindred, D.: Statistical approaches to DDoS attack detection and response. In: DARPA Information Survivability Conference and Exposition (2003)
8. Berndt, D.J., Clifford, J.: Using dynamic time warping to find patterns in time series. In: KDD Workshop (1994)
9. Jin, S., Yeung, D.: A covariance analysis model for ddos attack detection. In: IEEE International Conference on Communications (2004)
10. Kang, B.B., Chan-Tin, E., Lee, C.P., Tyra, J., Kang, H.J., Nunnery, C., Wadler, Z., Sinclair, G., Hopper, N., Dagon, D., et al.: Towards complete node enumeration in a peer-to-peer botnet. In: Proceedings of the 4th International Symposium on Information, Computer, and Communications Security, pp. 23–34. ACM (2009)
11. Karami, M., McCoy, D.: Understanding the emerging threat of DDoS-as-a-service. In: LEET (2013)
12. Keogh, E., Ratanamahatana, C.A.: Exact indexing of dynamic time warping. In: Knowledge and Information Systems (2005)
13. Kim, S.W., Park, S., Chu, W.W.: An index-based approach for similarity search supporting time warping in large sequence databases. In: Proceedings of International Conference on Data Engineering (2001)
14. Kührer, M., Hupperich, T., Rossow, C., Holz, T.: Exit from hell? reducing the impact of amplification DDoS attacks. In: USENIX Security Symposium (2014)
15. Lee, K., Kim, J., Kwon, K.H., Han, Y., Kim, S.: DDoS attack detection method using cluster analysis. Expert Syst. Appl. **34**, 1659–1665 (2008)

16. Li, M.: Change trend of averaged hurst parameter of traffic under DDoS flood attacks. Comput. Secur. **25**, 213–220 (2006)
17. Mao, Z.M., Sekar, V., Spatscheck, O., van der Merwe, J., Vasudevan, R.: Analyzing large DDoS attacks using multiple data sources. In: Proceedings of ACM SIGCOMM Workshop on Large-Scale Attack Defense (2006)
18. Moore, D., Shannon, C., Brown, D.J., Voelker, G.M., Savage, S.: Inferring internet denial-of-service activity. ACM Trans. Comput. Syst. (TOCS) **24**(2), 115–139 (2006)
19. Lloyd, S.P.: Least squares quantization in PCM. IEEE Trans. Inf. Theory **IT–28**, 129–137 (1982)
20. Stringhini, G., Holz, T., Stone-Gross, B., Kruegel, C., Vigna, G.: BOTMAGNI-FIER: locating spambots on the internet. In: USENIX Security Symposium (2011)
21. Wang, A., Mohaisen, A., Chang, W., Chen, S.: Delving into internet DDoS attacks by botnets: characterization and analysis. In: IEEE International Conference on Dependable Systems and Networks (2015)
22. Wang, A., Chang, W., Mohaisen, A., Chen, S.: How distributed are today's DDoS attacks? In: Proceedings of the ACM CCS (poster) (2014)
23. Welzel, A., Rossow, C., Bos, H.: On measuring the impact of DDoS botnets. In: Proceedings of the Seventh European Workshop on System Security, p. 3. ACM (2014)
24. Wustrow, E., Karir, M., Bailey, M., Jahanian, F., Huston, G.: Internet background radiation revisited. In: Proceedings of the 10th ACM SIGCOMM Conference on Internet Measurement, pp. 62–74. ACM (2010)
25. Xu, K., Zhang, Z.L., Bhattacharyya, S.: Profiling internet backbone traffic: behavior models and applications. ACM SIGCOMM Comput. Commun. Rev. **35**, 169–180 (2005)

Quit Playing Games with My Heart: Understanding Online Dating Scams

JingMin Huang, Gianluca Stringhini$^{(\boxtimes)}$, and Peng Yong

Jiayuan Corp., University College London, London, UK
jhua8590@uni.sydney.edu.au, g.stringhini@ucl.ac.uk,
pengyong20@picc.com.cn

Abstract. Online dating sites are experiencing a rise in popularity, with one in five relationships in the United States starting on one of these sites. Online dating sites provide a valuable platform not only for single people trying to meet a life partner, but also for cybercriminals, who see in people looking for love easy victims for scams. Such scams span from schemes similar to traditional advertisement of illicit services or goods (i.e., *spam*) to advanced schemes, in which the victim starts a long-distance relationship with the scammer and is eventually extorted money.

In this paper we perform the first large-scale study of online dating scams. We analyze the scam accounts detected on a popular online dating site over a period of eleven months, and provide a taxonomy of the different types of scammers that are active in the online dating landscape. We show that different types of scammers target a different demographics on the site, and therefore set up accounts with different characteristics. Our results shed light on the threats associated to online dating scams, and can help researchers and practitioners in developing effective countermeasures to fight them.

1 Introduction

Online dating sites have become a popular solution for users to meet people and start relationships. The most popular dating sites have between 15 and 20 million active members, and the revenue of the whole online dating industry in 2012 was estimated to exceed one billion dollars [5]. As it happens for any popular online service, online dating sites attract cybercriminals too. This should not surprise, since online services are commonly plagued with spam [20] and malware [7]. Online dating sites, however, have a very different purpose than common online services: meeting people in real life and possibly starting a relationship. For this reason, such services attract more advanced scammers than other online services, who exploit the vulnerable emotional state of online dating users for financial gain [29]. As an example, scammers commonly set up fake accounts on an online dating site, start interacting with a user on the site, and then lure her into sending them money, for example to pay for the flight needed to meet in person [37]. Such scams are similar in spirit to the infamous *"419 scams,"*

© Springer International Publishing Switzerland 2015
M. Almgren et al. (Eds.): DIMVA 2015, LNCS 9148, pp. 216–236, 2015.
DOI: 10.1007/978-3-319-20550-2_12

in which scammers ask their victims to send them a sum of money to establish trust and then promise to transfer a very large sum to them [18, 19, 24, 26]. Online dating scams, however, are more insidious than "419 scams," because they target emotionally vulnerable people looking for love.

Compared to traditional malicious activity on online services, the one happening on online dating sites shows three main differences. The first difference is that malicious activity on online services (social networks, blogs, webmail services) is typically run in large-scale campaigns [14, 17]. As a result of this, malicious activity is automatically generated and can be detected by leveraging similarities across the same malicious campaign [27, 38]. When dealing with online dating sites however, this assumption does not hold anymore: scammers are usually real people, writing personalized messages to their victims [37]. The second difference is that, unlike traditional spam and malware attacks, online dating scams can develop over a long period of time. Scammers typically exchange many messages with their victims to win their trust, before performing the actual scam [37]. In some cases, the scam is performed once the victim and the scammer meet in person. The third difference is that, unlike other online services, online dating sites are designed to put in contact people who do not know each other. For this reason, the concept of unsolicited message, which is the core of traditional anti-spam systems, does not have any meaning when applied to online dating sites: all messages received on such sites are in fact unsolicited.

The landscape of online dating scams is widely unstudied by the research community. Previous research in this field focused on describing single scam schemes, and relied on descriptions of single incidents instead of performing large-scale measurements of the phenomenon [29, 37]. In this paper, we present the first comprehensive study of scams targeting online dating sites. We analyze the accounts used by scammers that have been identified over a period of one year on *Jiayuan* [1], the largest online dating site in China. We discuss the different types of scams that we identified, showing that the threats that online dating users are exposed to are usually different than the ones that are faced by the users of traditional online services (such as Online Social Networks).

Given the different nature of the threats that users face on online dating sites, current systems that detect malicious activity on online services are not enough to protect the users of such sites. This paper aims at providing the research community with insights on how online dating scammers operate, on the types of threats that users face on such platforms, and on typical traits and behaviors of the accounts that are used by scammers to perform their operations. We hope that our observations will shed some light on the problem of online dating scams, and help researchers and online dating sites operators develop better detection methods to keep their users safe.

In summary, this paper makes the following contributions:

- We discuss the threat model associated with scammers operating on online dating sites, outlining the differences between this type of malicious activity and the one that is found on other online services.

- We analyze more than 500,000 accounts used by scammers on a popular online dating site, and provide a taxonomy of the most prevalent online dating scams. In particular, we identified four types of scams. Cybercriminals performing different types of scams present a different *modus operandi* in interacting with victims, and a different level of sophistication.
- We provide detailed statistics and case studies on the detected scam accounts. We show that different types of scams target different demographics on the site, and that specific scam schemes have a higher success in receiving attention by the users of online dating sites.

2   Background and Problem Study

In this section, we first describe online dating sites in general, giving an overview of the functionalities that are typically offered by these sites to their users. Then, we describe Jiayuan, which is the online dating site that we analyzed in this paper.

2.1   Online Dating Sites

There are a wealth of online dating sites on the Internet. Some of them cater to audiences with a specific ethnic or cultural background (e.g., christianmingle.com), while some others are targeted at all types of users (e.g., match.com). Some sites just aim at making people meet, while others have specific types of relationships as a target (for example marriage).

In general, the first thing users have to do after signing up on an online dating site is setting up a profile. The profile is what other users see, and having a complete and well-written one influences the first impression that possible matches have of the person [23]. Users are encouraged to add personal pictures and a description of themselves to the profile. In addition, people can add information about their favorite activities and hobbies. Users are required to add their sexual preference as well, and can specify the age range of the people they would like to meet.

All the information that the user inputs is processed by a matching algorithm. The algorithm compares the information on the user's profile with the one on the profiles of possible matches and displays to the user the profiles of people that she would probably like. The user can then review these suggestions and contact those people with whom she wants to start a conversation. Some sites allow users to browse all profiles on the site, while others restrict them to only see those profiles that were highly ranked as possible matches for her [2].

A major difference between online dating sites is the subscription price: unlike online social networks, creating a profile on an online dating site is usually not free, and the user has to pay a monthly subscription to use the functionalities of the site. A subscription to a popular online dating site ranges from $13 and $24 per month [4]. On the other hand, a handful of online dating sites (for example okcupid.com [3]) offer free subscriptions, and their websites feature advertisements, similarly to what happens on traditional online social network sites.

The amount of effort required to create an online dating profile influences the way in which cybercriminals use these services. Intuitively, the high price of subscription to most of these websites makes is unsuitable for spammers to create fake accounts in bulk. Similarly, the high amount of information needed to create a believable profile on the free online dating sites limits the effectiveness of mass-created fake accounts. For this reason, miscreants use online dating sites to perform more advanced scams, which rely on personal interactions and social engineering. We will describe the types of scams that we identified on the online dating site Jiayuan in Sect. 4.

2.2 Case Study: Jiayuan

We performed our analysis on Jiayuan, the largest online dating site in China. Jiayuan has more than 100 million registered users (of which about 10 million logged into the site within the last six months), which gives it a comparable user base to the most successful online dating sites worldwide.

Jiayuan presents all the elements typical of online dating sites that we described. After registering, users have to set up a profile, including information such as their age, gender, education, marital status, etc. Users can then browse other users' profiles and contact people they like.

Unlike most online dating sites, users can create a profile on Jiayuan for free. This fact makes it a particularly convenient platform for scammers, who can set up their accounts at no cost. To keep their users safe from scammers, Jiayuan deployed a number of detection mechanisms that are able to flag possible scam accounts. Because the false positives of such systems are higher than what is considered acceptable in a production system, and blocking a legitimate account by mistake would be very negative for the dating site's reputation, Jiayuan employs a team of experts that vet the flagged accounts, deciding which ones actually belong to scammers. If an account is detected as controlled by a scammer, the profile is "frozen" until the user confirms her identity and is forbidden from contacting other profiles on the site. In this paper, we analyze the accounts flagged as belonging to scammers by these human specialists over a period of one year.

2.3 Threat Model: Online Dating Scams

As we mentioned earlier, the main difference between traditional online services and online dating sites is that the latter are designed to put in contact people who have no connection whatsoever. In this context, the concept of *unsolicited message*, which is a strong indicator of maliciousness on other online services, has no meaning: all messages are "unsolicited," but users are happy to receive them instead of being annoyed by them. For this reason, we need to go beyond considering any unsolicited message as malicious and formulate a more advanced threat model.

In this paper, we consider an online dating user a scammer if he/she is using the service to take advantage (often economic) of another user. A scammer will set up one or more accounts on the online dating site, and interact with the users of the site. We call such accounts *scam accounts*. Online dating scams can be more or less sophisticated. In some cases, the scam accounts are just advertising goods or services, similarly to traditional spam (for example escort services). In this case the scam content (for example the contact information of the escort agency) is sent to the victim very early, possibly in the first message that is exchanged. In some other cases, however, scammers are more sophisticated, and establish a long-distance relationship with the victim before performing the actual scam. In many cases, the scammer tries to convince the victim to continue the conversation on a different medium, for example Skype. This is an additional reason why online dating scams are difficult to the detect: often the online dating site administrators do not see the scam happening, because the scammer and the victim have moved to a different way of communicating.

In the rest of the paper we first describe the way in which we collected a set of more than 500,000 scam accounts on Jiayuan. We then present a taxonomy of the scam accounts that we observed, and discuss some typical characteristics of such accounts that could be used for detection.

3   Methodology

Given the difficulty of automatically detecting advanced scam accounts, online dating sites employ customer-service specialists who manually review suspicious profiles and suspend the ones that belong to scammers. These customer-service specialists are experts in detecting scammers, and therefore they can reliably assess the maliciousness of an account. However, it is unfeasible (and intrusive) for these specialists to analyze every single profile on the site and assess its maliciousness. For this reason, specialists are aided by automatic programs that narrow down the number of possible scammers as much as possible. Ideally, these detection systems should have high accuracy, so that the human specialists can quickly decide whether a profile belongs to a scammer. Their accuracy, however, is not high enough to justify a completely-automated scam detection system – this is due to the complex nature of online dating scams as we previously discussed. In addition, the cost of false positives for the company is very high: a user having his/her account suspended by mistake would leave the site and move to a competitor, and even ask for a refund in case of a paid dating site.

In the following, we briefly describe the four detection systems that help the customer service specialists at Jiayuan in detecting scam accounts. Two of the authors of this paper worked on the development of such systems. Because these systems resemble, in large part, anti-spam systems that have been proposed by the research community over the years, we do not claim that they are novel, and we include them for the sake of completeness, and to give the reader a better idea of how the dataset of scam accounts used in the rest of the study was collected.

3.1   Behavioral-Based Detection System

The goal of scammers on online dating sites is very different from the one of legitimate users: while legitimate users want to get to know new people, and possibly start a romantic relationship, scammers seek vulnerable and gullible victims, with the purpose of extorting money from them. For this reason, the behavior of accounts controlled by scammers is likely to show differences than the one of legitimate users. To capture these differences, Jiayuan developed a detection system that models the typical behavior of scam accounts (as opposed to legitimate accounts). This system looks at two types of account characteristics. The first one are profile traits that scam accounts typically show (as we will see in Sect. 6, specific types of scam accounts pose as a particular demographic to appeal a particular type of victim). The second type of characteristics are related to the typical behavior of scam accounts. Such characteristics include the number of conversations initiated simultaneously, the time waited between the creation of the profile and the first message, and the fraction of the received messages to which the account replies. This system is similar to other anti-spam systems that have been proposed by the research community [14,25,32].

3.2   IP Address-Based Detection System

Systems that detect automated misuse on online services often look at the reuse of IP addresses by miscreants [21,31]. This element is not as important when dealing with online dating scammers, because, as we will show in Sect. 6.2, they typically do not use high levels of automation for their operations. However, IP address reuse is still an useful indicator to detect those scammers with a lower level of sophistication, who create a number of different profiles to advertise their businesses. Similarly, some sophisticated scammers might create a handful of profiles, and access them from the same IP address or network. For these reasons, Jiayuan deployed a system that flags multiple accounts accessed by the same IP address as possibly malicious.

3.3   Photograph-Based Detection System

Previous research noted that spammers that are active on Online Social Networks typically reuse profile pictures for their fake accounts [32]. For this reason, it makes sense to look for profiles that share the same profile picture to find possible fake accounts on those platforms. We observed the same trend happening on online dating sites. Although scams are usually run by humans and do not have the scale of spam campaigns on other online services, scammers often use the same picture (typically of an attractive young woman or a handsome middle-aged man) for a multitude of accounts. Jiayuan deployed a system that is able to detect duplicated profile pictures and flag those accounts as possibly malicious. This system is based on a perceptual hashing algorithm [40], to be able to detect images that look the same, but have been re-encoded.

3.4   Text-Based Detection System

Content analysis is a popular way of fighting spam [12,30]. Such systems typically identify words that are indicative of malicious and benign content and leverage them for detection. Content analysis systems work well in automatically detecting spam. In our specific case, they can be useful in detecting scammers who employ a low level of sophistication (for example, who send a copy of the same message to many other profiles). For this reason, Jiayuan developed a system that looks for keywords in messages that are typical of scam accounts, and flag them as malicious.

Because of their differences, each detection system is more suited to detect different types of scam accounts. For example, the photograph and text based systems are more suited to detect accounts that are part of large scale campaigns and share the same picture or the same profile text. On the other hand, the behavioral-based detection system works best in detecting advanced scammers, who set up their own accounts and exchange a long series of manually-crafted messages with the victim before performing the actual scam.

4   Description of the Scam Account Dataset

Previous work showed anecdotes and case studies of scams on online dating sites [29, 37]. In this paper, we provide the first large-scale measurement of online dating scams, performed over a period of 11 months between 2012 and 2013. Our analysis is based on a set of scam accounts detected by the systems described previously on Jiayuan. In particular, we analyze a dataset composed of the scam accounts detected on Jiayuan during the period of observation. In total, the dataset is composed of 510,503 scam accounts.

Note that, since the detections performed by the detection systems were manually vetted by human analysts, we are confident that they were correct, taking aside potential mistakes made by the analysts[1]. This "clean" set of malicious accounts allowed us to come up with a taxonomy of online dating scammers. In the next section we discuss this taxonomy in detail.

5   A Taxonomy of Online Dating Scammers

With the help of the human analysts employed by Jiayuan, we further analyzed the scam accounts in our dataset. We identified four types of scammers that infest the site: "*Escort Service Advertisements*," "*Dates for Profit*," "*Swindlers*," and "*Matchmaking Services*." Although some of the scammer schemes that we identified are specific to the Chinese culture and society, we think that this taxonomy holds also for dating sites located in other countries. In the following, we describe the types of scams that we identified. In Sect. 6 we analyze the scammers that we detected in the wild more in detail, breaking them down by

---

[1] The data about the users of Jiayuan was collected according to the company's privacy policy and it was only accessed by two of the authors of this paper, who were Jiayuan employees at the time the research was conducted. The authors external to Jiayuan did not access any personal or sensitive information about any user on the online dating site, but instead worked with aggregated statistics.

scam type, and we investigate the different demographics that they use to attract victims, as well the different strategies that they use.

Escort Service Advertisements. As we said, the bulk creation of accounts with the purpose of spreading spam is not a viable solution for cybercriminals operating on online dating sites. However, this does not prevent miscreants from creating a number of accounts and sending unsolicited advertisements to the users of the dating site. Although this type of activity is not as predominant as it is on other media (such as online social networks [32] and email [34]) we still observed it on Jiayuan. It is interesting to note that, since the main purpose of an online dating site is to connect two people who do not know each other, the concept of *unsolicited messages* has little meaning on such platforms. For this reason, it is more difficult to fight spammers on online dating sites than it is on other services.

On Jiayuan, the vast majority of unsolicited advertisements promote escort agencies. In total, we detected 374,051 accounts of this type during our study. In this scheme, cybercriminals operate as follows: first, they create a profile belonging to a young woman (often including an attractive picture). Then, they start contacting other profiles, including the contact information of the escort agency in their messages. Note that considering accounts that contact a large number of profiles as malicious is usually not enough. In fact, legitimate accounts that contact many profiles, trying to establish a contact, are not uncommon on online dating sites; previous work showed that 78 % of the messages sent on online dating sites never receive a reply from the other person [15]. We confirm this low turnaround of messages in Sect. 6.2.

Dates for Profit. As we said, the purpose of using online dating sites is to meet people in person and possibly start a relationship. This opens additional possibilities for scammers, who can leverage the fact that their victims will want to meet them in person and perform the actual scam once this happens. This element has no parallel on other online services. Even in advanced "419 scams," which rely on social engineering, the only "physical" interaction between the scammer and the victim is the transfer of a sum of money.

On Jiayuan, we observed an interesting trend in scams that exploit in-person meetings. Owners of establishments such as cafes and restaurants would hire girls to create profiles on the online dating site, contact multiple victims, and ask them to meet in person at that particular establishment. Such establishments are usually very expensive, and it is customary in China for males to pay for food and drink on dates. Therefore, the owners of the establishments can make a considerable amount of money out of these scams. Obviously, after this first encounter, the victim is never contacted again. To put this type of scam in perspective, a meal at most of the rogue establishments can cost between $100 and $2,000. This amount of money is similar to what is gained by traditional "419 scams" [13]. However, the success rate of this type of scam is much higher, because the scammer leverages the desire of the victim to meet an attractive woman. In addition, it is likely that the victim will never realize that he has been scammed, since the date really happened, and the victim possibly had a good time. Therefore, there is a low chance for the owner of the establishment to get caught. In total, we detected 57,218 accounts of this type during our study.

This particular type of scam appears to be a popular scheme for scammers on Jiayuan, as we will show in Sect. 6. Although the cultural setting of China might make such scams more likely to be successful, we do not see a reason why similar scams should not be happening on dating sites based in other countries too.

Swindlers. Online dating sites are seen as a valuable resource for mid-aged people who so far have not found a partner for life. This type of person is particularly vulnerable to scams, and scammers take advantage of it. We observed multiple instances of scammers contacting mid-aged men and women, and establishing a long distance relationship with them. Over time, the trust that the victim has in the scammer would grow. After some time, the scammer will ask the victim to send him a sum of money to help in some task. The scammer might be in financial trouble or need money to buy a plane ticket to come visit the victim. At this point in the relationship, the victim is very likely to trust the scammer and send him the required money. After sending the requested amount of money, the victim will never hear back from the scammer. We call these type of scammers *"Swindlers."* Swindlers are a big problem on online dating sites. Similar scam schemes have already been studied by previous work [29,37]. In total, we detected 43,318 accounts of this type during our study.

A particular type of swindlers, which are very peculiar to the culture of certain areas of China, are what we call *"Flower-basket Swindlers."* In this particular type of scam, the scammer creates a fake profile, usually of an attractive mid-aged man, contacts a mid-aged woman, and starts exchanging messages with her. Over time, the victim will think that she is developing a romantic relationship with the scammer, and will start trusting him. After a while, the scammer will start implying that he wants to marry the victim, and that his parents need some proof of the victim's "good will." At this point the scam happens. It is customary in those areas of China to send baskets of flowers to newly-opened shops, as gifts and to wish good luck. The scammer will then pretend to be opening a new shop, and will ask the victim to send some baskets of flowers to the shop. He will also give her the contact information of a florist in his area, who is actually one of the scammer's accomplices. As for other swindler scams, once the victim buys the flowers, she will never hear from the scammer again. These shipments of flowers can be very expensive and cost up to $20,000 to the victim.

Another type of swindlers that we observed on Jiayuan are the so-called *"lottery-ticket swindlers."* This type of scams is more similar to traditional "419 scams." The miscreant establishes a romantic relationship with the victim, by pretending to be a successful businessperson in a foreign country, and lures the victim into sending him a sum of money, as part of a rewarding financial operation.

Swindlers are present on all online dating sites and are not specific to Jiayuan or the Chinese culture in particular. On the other hand, flower-basket swindlers seem to be leveraging a specific Chinese tradition, and this type of scam is probably peculiar to Chinese online dating sites.

Previous research showed that scams perpetrated by email need to narrow down the number of potential victims that will reply to their messages, because each message requires some effort on the scammer part to reply to it [22]. For this reason, the scammer sets up a story that is hardly believable to a general audience, making sure that whoever responds is already prone to fall for the scam. In the case of online dating swindlers, this does not happen. The scammer starts a long-lasting conversation with the potential victims, and the purpose of the scam is revealed very late in the relationship. A partial selection of users that are more likely to fall for the scam is performed by setting up profiles that appeal a specific audience, such as mid-aged divorced women. We will discuss more details on these strategies in Sect. 6.1.

Matchmaking Services. Before online dating sites were popular, people used to sign up for matchmaking services, which would find them a partner. We observe that agents from these matchmaking services are active on online dating sites too. They typically create fake profiles of attractive people, lure users into handing out some contact information, and then contact them directly, advertising the matchmaking agency. Although no financial scam is involved in the operation of matchmaking services, users are annoyed by them, and online dating sites see them as a competitor that is illicitly using their site to gain customers. We detected 35,916 accounts of this type during our study.

In the next section we provide more details on the scam accounts that we detected in the wild.

6   Analysis of the Scam Account Dataset

In this section we first analyze the different demographics and profile characteristics of the various types of scam accounts that we detected, comparing them to the legitimate accounts that were active on Jiayuan during the analysis period. We then study the *modus operandi* of the different types of scammers, providing new insights on how these cybercriminal crews operate.

6.1   Demographics of Different Scam Account Types

As we mentioned, the different types of online dating scammers have very different goals, and cater to a very different pool of victims. For this reason, the accounts that they use to perpetrate their scams show very different characteristics, and impersonate people with different demographics. Not only, but the population of malicious accounts for each scam type shows reasonably homogeneous characteristics, which are very different from the general population on the dating site. In this section we analyze the demographics of the different types of scam accounts that we detected.

We first analyzed the gender distribution of the different types of scam accounts. As Fig. 1 shows, legitimate accounts on Jiayuan are mostly male, with

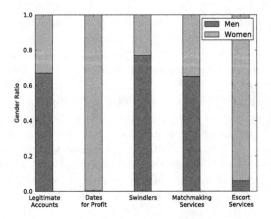

Fig. 1. Gender distribution of the different types of scam accounts, compared to legitimate accounts.

a 65 % - 35 % ratio compared to female accounts. Different types of scams, on the other hand, aim at attracting victims from a specific gender, and therefore their gender ratio is dramatically skewed. For instance, "Dates for Profit" scammers try to lure men looking for a date with an attractive lady to go to a particular establishment; therefore, the accounts performing such scams are almost entirely female. A similar situation holds for "Escort Services" scam accounts.

"Swindler" accounts, on the other hand, cater to an older audience composed mostly of divorced or widowed ladies. For this reason, this type of scam accounts is prevalently male. A similar reasoning goes for "Matchmaking Services" scam accounts. These accounts mostly try to lure older women into handing out personal information such as email addresses and phone numbers, and their gender distribution is in line with the one of the legitimate user population of Jiayuan.

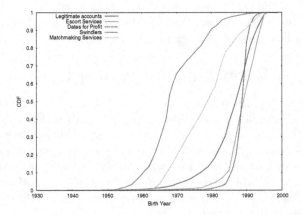

Fig. 2. Cumulative Distribution Function (CDF) of the birth years of the different types of scam accounts, compared to legitimate accounts.

The purpose of the different types of scammers is also reflected in the different ages of the profiles that they use. As Fig. 2 shows, 50 % of the legitimate users on Jiayuan are 26 years old or older. "Dates for Profit" and "Escort Services" accounts list themselves as slightly younger than average, with an average age of 25 and 24 respectively. In particular, 20 % of the "Escort Services" profile list their age as between 20 and 18 (which is the minimum age allowed on Jiayuan). In comparison, only 1 % of the normal users is younger than 20 on the site. Because they target older victims, "Swindler" profiles are a lot older on average: 50 % of these accounts pretend to be at least 46 years old, with only 3 % of them younger than the average age on the site. "Matchmaking Services" accounts are older than average as well, although not as much as "Swindler" accounts: 50 % of them are older than 35, while 18 % of them is younger than the average age on Jiayuan.

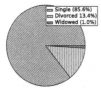

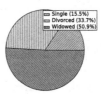

Fig. 3. Fraction of the marital status for legitimate accounts on Jiayuan.

Fig. 4. Fraction of the marital status for "Swindler" scammers.

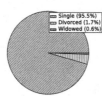

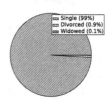

Fig. 5. Fraction of the marital status for "Dates for Profit" scammers.

Fig. 6. Fraction of the marital status for "Matchmaking Service" scammers.

Fig. 7. Fraction of the marital status for "Escort Service Advertisement" scammers.

The final element for which scam accounts differ from regular users is marital status. As Fig. 3 shows, more than 85 % of the regular users on Jiayuan are single. Scam accounts mostly list themselves as single as well, probably because they cater to the majority of the users on the site, and in general it is a more neutral connotation. Figures 5, 6, and 7 show this trend for "Dates for Profit," "Matchmaking Services," and "Escort Agencies" scam accounts respectively. A notable exception are "Swindler" scam accounts. As it is shown in Fig. 4, these accounts prevalently list themselves as widowed or divorced. The reason for that is that these accounts need to build a believable story, as we mentioned in Sect. 4,

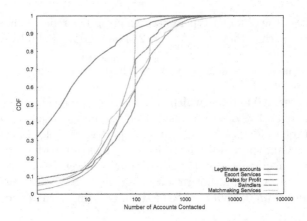

Fig. 8. Cumulative Distribution Function (CDF) of the accounts contacted by the different types of scammers, compared to legitimate users.

and being widowed is a good starting point to establish trust and a long-lasting relationship with an emotionally fragile person, and eventually steal her money.

To recap, in this section we confirmed that stereotypes do exist for each type of scammer: while "Dates for Profit" and "Escort Agency Services" mostly present themselves as young, single females, "Swindlers" present themselves as mid-aged, widowed men.

6.2   Strategies Used by Different Scam Account Types

Another interesting aspect is looking at the different strategies used by different types of scammers to reach victims. In the previous section we analyzed how different types of scammers set up their accounts to look appealing to a different audience, such as older women or younger men. After setting up a profile, a scammer needs to attract victims. This is probably the most challenging part, because replying to a number of users who are not really convinced of the authenticity of the scam profile is time consuming for the scammer. As previous research noted, it is very advantageous for a scammer to make sure that the accounts that either reach out to him or that will reply to his first message are likely to fall for the scam [22]. In this section we show that some types of scammers are more successful in doing this.

In general a scammer has two strategies while trying to attract victims: he can contact users on the dating site himself, or he can make his account so appealing that a number of potential victims will contact him themselves. To understand the typical strategies put in practice by scammers, we first looked at the number of accounts contacted by scam accounts. As Fig. 8 shows, scam accounts typically contact many more accounts than legitimate users on Jiayuan do. Legitimate accounts contact a small number of profiles: from our observations, 50 % of them contacted at most four profiles, while only 20 % accounts contacted more than 27 profiles. Conversely, the majority of scam accounts contacted 100 or more

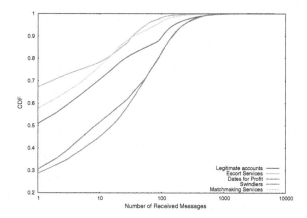

Fig. 9. Cumulative Distribution Function (CDF) of the number of messages received by different types of scammer accounts, compared to legitimate users.

profiles during their activity on Jiayuan. This shows that scam accounts are on average a lot more aggressive in contacting other people on the dating site than regular users. Note that these numbers are a lower bound, because the scam accounts in our dataset were shut down by the support people at Jiayuan, and therefore would have contacted more victims if they were left free to act.

Instead of contacting their victims, scammers can wait for users to contact them. This approach has the advantage that whoever contacts a scam account is more likely to be genuinely interested in him/her. On the scammer side, all he needs to do is setting up a profile that is appealing to potential victims. Figure 9 shows the CDF of the number of messages initiating a conversation received by different types of accounts on Jiayuan. As it can be seen, 50 % of legitimate accounts were contacted at least once by another user on the dating site. We observe a two-fold distribution in the success of scam accounts. "Escort Services" and "Matchmaking Services" are on average less successful than regular accounts in receiving attention from users on the site, although these numbers are not dramatically lower than what we observe for legitimate users. The reason for this lower turnaround might be that these profiles look phony, and they do not appear believable to many users. Also, these accounts are usually easier to recognize by the human specialists than more advanced types of scam accounts, and are therefore "frozen" quickly, so that possible victims cannot contact them anymore. This is in line with previous research, which showed that social network users are fairly good in realizing whether a profile is fake, although their detection rate is not perfect [35]. "Swindlers" and "Dates for Profit" scam accounts, on the other hand, attract more victims on average: 70 % of these accounts were contacted by at least a user on the site, while 20 % of the "Swindler" accounts were contacted by at least 90 potential victims. All together, this shows that advanced scammers are remarkably successful in setting up profiles that appeal

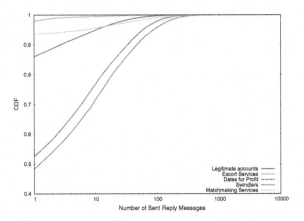

Fig. 10. Cumulative Distribution Function (CDF) of the replies sent by the different types of scammers in reply to messages they received, compared to legitimate users.

their potential victim audience, and, unlike the less sophisticated types of scams, their profiles are considered legitimate by many users.

We then analyzed how often scam accounts reply to the messages they receive from potential victims. Figure 10 shows the Cumulative Distribution Function of the number of replies that different types of scam accounts sent as responses to messages they received. As it can be seen, legitimate users rarely reply to the messages they received: only 14 % of the users ever replied to a message on the site[2], and more in general only 7 % of the messages that are sent on Jiayuan ever receive a reply. This result is in line with what was shown by previous research [15]. Looking at scam accounts, we see a clear two-fold distribution: "Escort Services" and "Matchmaking Services" reply even less than regular users. The reason for this is that these scams are typically composed of a single spam-like message, and do not involve message exchanges with their victims. In addition to that, these accounts show the tendency of being quickly abandoned by the scammers, or being shut down by the Jiayuan operators. "Swindlers" and "Dates for profit," on the other hand, are a lot more likely to start conversations with their victims: around 50 % of these accounts sent replies to potential victims after being contacted. The fact that they do not reply to about half of the messages they receive, on the other hand, shows that scammers are carefully choosing which users to engage with, favoring the ones that are more likely to fall for the scam. This shows that these scams are more sophisticated and require a longer set up (and a longer exchange of messages). For this reason, these types of scammers take the time to reply to the messages they receive, crafting them in a way that it will make them appealing and believable to potential victims.

Finally, we studied the way in which different types of scammers connected to their accounts. Previous work showed that malicious accounts on social networks are typically controlled by botnets [20,32], which are networks of compromised

---

[2] Note that this number takes into accounts also those accounts that never received a message at all on the site.

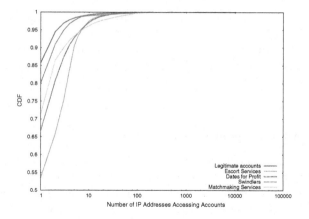

Fig. 11. Cumulative Distribution Function (CDF) of the number of other accounts of the same scam type that were accessed by a single IP address over a period of one week, compared to legitimate users.

computers acting under the same cybercriminal. Botnets provide a convenient way for cybercriminals to control their malicious accounts, and run large-scale campaigns on online services. To investigate the *modus operandi* of the connections performed by different types of scammers on Jiayuan, we studied the number of scam accounts of the same type that were accessed by single IP addresses. Although observing multiple accounts connecting from the same IP address is not suspicious per se, and it is usually an artifact of Network Address Translation (NAT) networks, having a high number of accounts accessed by the same IP address is highly suspicious. Figure 11 shows the CDF of the number of different scam accounts accessed by a single IP address on Jiayuan. As it can be seen, legitimate accounts are typically accessed by only one IP address during a period of one week (85 % of them). Although it is more common to have IP addresses that access many accounts, the ratio of scam accounts accessed by multiple IP addresses is low too: it is rare to have IP addresses that accessed more than ten scam accounts, and the majority of them accessed a single IP address. This does not give us conclusive evidence that scammers are using botnets to perform their malicious activity on Jiayuan. The reason for this is that online dating scams require quite a bit of interaction by the scammer to succeed, and are more difficult to automate than traditional spam or phishing operations. Reports by the human experts at Jiayuan, as well as by law enforcement, show that an exception to this trend are "Escort Services" scam accounts, whose accounts are usually controlled by bots. Still, these bots are typically used in isolation or in small numbers, and therefore we have no indication that these types of scammers are taking advantage of botnets.

7 Discussion

Online dating scams are a relatively new problem and present very unique aspects, compared to traditional Internet threats. In this paper we described in detail the insights that we obtained by analyzing the scam accounts detected on a large online dating site over a period of one year. Many points are open and will be the focus of future research. In this section, we first discuss the efforts needed to secure online dating sites from scammers, both from the policy and the technical side. Finally, we introduce some ideas that we are planning to pursue as future work.

7.1 Scammers Are Perseverant

According to the human experts at Jiayuan, each individual scam on the site is usually set up and performed by a small number of people, composed of two to five individuals. For example, a typical "Date for Profit" scam will involve the owner of a restaurant, a girl who agrees to go on a date with the victim, and optionally a third person who interacts with the online dating site. Similarly, a "Flower-basket swindler" scam is performed by a person interacting with the victim on the dating site and by an accomplice who pretends to own a flower shop. Optionally, other accomplices will pretend to be family members of the scammer, and contact the victim to test her "good will." This is quite different than what we observe in traditional cybercriminal schemes, in which there are many actors involved, and a complex economy exists behind these operations.

Based on the reports by the Jiayuan human experts, there are a number of scammer groups that keep using Jiayuan to perform their scams, even after their fake accounts are detected and blocked. This happens because the scams that these groups perform on the site are particularly remunerative for them. The perseverance showed by online dating scammers teaches researchers two lessons: first, better detection systems are needed, to make sure that the scam accounts are detected and shut down quicker, making life more difficult for the scammers. We hope that some of the insights provided in this paper, such as the typical demographics and behaviors showed by scam accounts will help practitioners in developing more effective detection techniques. Second, similar to other cyber-criminal operations, it is difficult to get rid of scammers by just securing the online service. In many cases, an action from law enforcement is needed to prosecute those scammers who are most dangerous. Law enforcement operations are typically difficult to coordinate when we deal with cybercriminal schemes that are spread across multiple countries, but should be more feasible in the case of Jiayuan, in which the site, the victims, and the scammers all reside in the same country. Similar law enforcement measures might get more complicated for online dating sites that have a more international user base, such as match.com or okcupid.com.

7.2 Future Work

Aside from law enforcement efforts, online dating scams can be made less success-ful by improving the effectiveness of detection systems deployed on the online dating site. As we showed in this paper, detecting the more advanced types of scammers, such as "Swindlers," is challenging, because the activity of these accounts is not automatically generated, and their scams unfold over a long period of time and several exchanges of messages with the victim. To detect the majority of these scam accounts, Jiayuan administrators decided to have a better recall over precision for their anti-scam systems, and to employ a team of human experts to vet such detections.

In this paper, however, we showed that scam accounts show differences from legitimate accounts in the way they set up their profiles, in the way they select the people they chat with, and in the way they interact with the site. Such differences could be the base for developing effective detection techniques that could work with minimal human interaction. In addition, future work could include the use of stylometry to detect message language that might be typical of scams [6].

We are aware that the insights provided in this paper are only the first step into understanding and fighting scammers on online dating sites. In particular, although many of the scams that we identified are likely to happen on other online dating sites too, our analysis is limited to Jiayuan, and therefore might be biased toward the Chinese culture. In the future, we are interested in studying online dating sites based in other countries. In particular, online dating sites with an international audience might attract scammers that are located in different countries than the victim; tracking these schemes might be challenging, but could give interesting insights on how to fight the phenomenon. In addition, we are interested in studying the underground economy behind these scams, such as tracking how much money is actually stolen as a consequence of these schemes. We would also like to study online dating sites that require users to pay a monthly subscription. We suspect that the population of scammers on such sites will be heavily skewed towards more advanced schemes.

8   Related Work

The popularity of online dating sites has attracted a wealth of research. Fiore et al. performed an analysis of the demographic characteristics of online dating users, as well as of the characteristics of the messages that those users exchange [15]. Chen et al. presented a work that analyzed the social network of the users on an online dating site [11]. Hitsch et al. looked at what characteristics influence the chance of an online dating message to receive a reply [23].

Our work is the first comprehensive study on online dating scams. A few previous papers provided case studies of single scam schemes happening on online dating sites [28,29,37], while Wang et al. observed that miscreants crawl online dating sites, and use the crawled pictures to set up fake online dating accounts, which they then use for their scams [36]. Unlike these preliminary works, our paper provides a comprehensive study of the scams that happen on a large online dating site, and gives real-world numbers on how prevalent such scams are.

Online dating scams that try to lure a victim into sending money to the miscreant have many points in common with the so-called "419 scams." This type of scams has been widely studied by the research community [13,18,19,22,24,26].

Despite the similarities, in this paper we showed that online dating scams are very different from these schemes, because they typically involve a long exchange of messages between the scammer and the victim before the actual scam is performed.

Many systems have been presented to detect spam and malicious activity on social networks. Some systems analyze the characteristics of social network accounts, looking for sign of mass-created fake accounts [8,17,25,32,41,43]. Other systems look at the social network structure of accounts, or at how the messages posted by them spread, looking for anomalies indicative of a malicious profile [9,10,16,33,39,42]. These systems work well in detecting automated activity finalized at spreading malicious content. However, they are often ineffective in detecting advanced scams, such as the ones presented in this paper. The reason is that such scams require a lot of manual effort by the attackers, and often times span through long periods of time (and multiple message exchanges between the victim and the scammer).

9   Conclusions

In this paper, we analyzed the problem of online dating scams. We analyzed a set of ground-truth scam accounts on a large online dating site, and provided a taxonomy of the different types of scams that we observed. We showed that different types of scammers targeted different audiences, and have a very different success rate in attracting victims. In particular, we showed that advanced scammers are more successful than regular users in getting attention by other online dating users, which can potentially turn into scam victims. This paper is the first large-scale measurement of online dating scams, and it sheds light on these operations and on the challenges that researchers face in fighting them. Future work will focus on developing better detection techniques to block even the stealthiest scammers, and studying new types of online dating scams.

Acknowledgments. We thank the anonymous reviewers for their comments. We would also like to thank Ali Zand, Adam Doupé, Alexandros Kapravelos, Ben Y. Zhao, and Christo Wilson for reviewing an early draft of this paper. Your feedback was highly appreciated.

References

1. Jiayuan. http://www.jiayuan.com/
2. eHarmony (2013). http://www.eharmony.com
3. OkCupid (2013). http://www.okcupid.com
4. Online dating sites pricing (2013). http://www.nextadvisor.com/online_dating/compare.php
5. Online Dating Statistics 2013. http://www.statisticbrain.com/online-dating-statistics/
6. Afroz, S., Brennan, M., Greenstadt, R.: Detecting hoaxes, frauds, and deception in writing style online. In IEEE Symposium on Security and Privacy (2012)

7. Baltazar, J., Costoya, J., Flores, R.: KOOBFACE: the largest web 2.0 botnet explained. Trend Micro Threat Research (2009)
8. Benevenuto, F., Magno, G., Rodrigues, T., Almeida, V.: Detecting spammers on twitter. In: Conference on Email and Anti-spam (CEAS) (2010)
9. Cai, Z., Jermaine, C.: The latent community model for detecting sybils in social networks. In: Symposium on Network and Distributed System Security (NDSS) (2012)
10. Cao, Y., Yegneswaran, V., Possas, P., Chen, Y.: PathCutter: severing the self-propagation path of XSS javascript worms in social web networks. In: Symposium on Network and Distributed System Security (NDSS) (2012)
11. Chen, L., Nayak, R.: Social network analysis of an online dating network. In: Proceedings of the 5th International Conference on Communities and Technologies (2011)
12. Drucker, H., Wu, D., Vapnik, V.N.: Support vector machines for spam categorization. IEEE Trans. Neural Netw. **10**(5), 988–999 (1999)
13. Dyrud, M.A.: "I brought you a good news": an analysis of nigerian 419 letters. In: Association for Business Communication Annual Convention (2005)
14. Egele, M., Stringhini, G., Kruegel, C., Vigna, G.: Compa: detecting compromised accounts on social networks. In: Symposium on Network and Distributed System Security (NDSS) (2013)
15. Fiore, A., Tresolini, R.: Romantic regressions: an analysis of behavior in online dating systems. Ph.D. thesis, Massachusetts Institute of Technology (2004)
16. Gao, H., Chen, Y., Lee, K., Palsetia, D., Choudhary, A.: Towards Online spam filtering in social networks. In: Symposium on Network and Distributed System Security (NDSS) (2012)
17. Gao, H., Hu, J., Wilson, C., Li, Z., Chen, Y., Zhao, B.: Detecting and characterizing social spam campaigns. In: Internet Measurement Conference (IMC) (2010)
18. Gao, Y., Zhao, G.: Knowledge-based information extraction: a case study of recognizing emails of nigerian frauds. In: Montoyo, A., Muñoz, R., Métais, E. (eds.) NLDB 2005. LNCS, vol. 3513, pp. 161–172. Springer, Heidelberg (2005)
19. Glickman, H.: The nigerian "419" advance fee scams: prank or peril? Can. J. Afr. Stud. **39**(3), 460–89 (2005)
20. Grier, C., Thomas, K., Paxson, V., Zhang, M.: @spam: the underground on 140 characters or less. In: ACM Conference on Computer and Communications Security (CCS) (2010)
21. Hao, S., Syed, N.A., Feamster, N., Gray, A.G., Krasser, S.: Detecting spammers with SNARE: spatio-temporal network-level automatic reputation engine. In: USENIX Security Symposium (2009)
22. Herley, C.: Why do Nigerian scammers say they are from Nigeria? In: Workshop on the Economics of Information Security (WEIS) (2012)
23. Hitsch, G.J., Hortacsu, A., Ariely, D.: What makes you click: an empirical analysis of online dating. Society for Economic Dynamics Meeting Papers (2005)
24. Isacenkova, J., Thonnard, O., Costin, A., Balzarotti, D., Francillon, A.: Inside the SCAM jungle: a closer look at 419 scam email operations. In: International Workshop on Cyber Crime (IWCC) (2013)
25. Lee, K., Caverlee, J., Webb, S.: Uncovering social spammers: social honeypots+ machine learning. In: International ACM SIGIR Conference on Research and Development in Information Retrieval (2010)
26. Park, Y., Jones, J., McCoy, D., Shi, E., Jakobsson, M.: Scambaiter: understanding targeted nigerian scams on craigslist. In: Symposium on Network and Distributed System Security (NDSS) (2014)

27. Pitsillidis, A., Levchenko, K., Kreibich, C., Kanich, C., Voelker, G.M., Paxson, V., Weaver, N., Savage, S.: Botnet judo: fighting spam with itself. In: Symposium on Network and Distributed System Security (NDSS) (2010)
28. Pizzato, L.A., Akehurst, J., Silvestrini, C., Yacef, K., Koprinska, I., Kay, J.: The effect of suspicious profiles on people recommenders. In: Masthoff, J., Mobasher, B., Desmarais, M.C., Nkambou, R. (eds.) UMAP 2012. LNCS, vol. 7379, pp. 225–236. Springer, Heidelberg (2012)
29. Rege, A.: What's love got to do with it? Exploring online dating scams and identity fraud. Int. J. Cyber Criminol. **3**(2), 494–512 (2009)
30. Sahami, M., Dumais, S., Heckermann, D., Horvitz, E.: A Bayesian approach to filtering junk e-mail. Learning for Text Categorization (1998)
31. Stringhini, G., Holz, T., Stone-Gross, B., Kruegel, C., Vigna, G.: BotMagnifier: locating spambots on the Internet. In: USENIX Security Symposium (2011)
32. Stringhini, G., Kruegel, C., Vigna, G.: Detecting spammers on social networks. In: Annual Computer Security Applications Conference (ACSAC) (2010)
33. Stringhini, G., Wang, G., Egele, M., Kruegel, C., Vigna, G., Zheng, H., Zhao, B.Y.: Follow the green: growth and dynamics in twitter follower markets. In: ACM SIGCOMM Conference on Internet Measurement (2013)
34. Symantec Corp. Symantec intelligence report (2013). http://www.symanteccloud.com/mlireport/SYMCINT_2013_01_January.pdf
35. Wang, G., Mohanlal, M., Wilson, C., Wang, X., Metzger, M., Zheng, H., Zhao, B.Y.: Social turing tests: crowdsourcing sybil detection. In: Symposium on Network and Distributed System Security (NDSS) (2013)
36. Wang, G., Wilson, C., Zhao, X., Zhu, Y., Mohanlal, M., Zheng, H., Zhao, B.Y.: Serf and turf: crowdturfing for fun and profit. In: Wold Wide Web Conference (WWW) (2012)
37. Whitty, M.T., Buchanan, T.: The online romance scam: a serious cybercrime. CyberPsychology Behav. Soc. Netw. **15**(3), 181–183 (2012)
38. Xie, Y., Yu, F., Achan, K., Panigrahy, R., Hulten, G., Osipkov, I.: Spamming botnets: signatures and characteristics. SIGCOMM Comput. Commun. Rev. **38**, 171–182 (2008)
39. Xu, W., Zhang, F., Zhu, S.: Toward worm detection in online social networks. In: Annual Computer Security Applications Conference (ACSAC) (2010)
40. Yang, B., Gu, F., Niu, X.: Block mean value based image perceptual hashing. In: International Conference on Intelligent Information Hiding and Multimedia Signal Processing (2006)
41. Yang, C., Harkreader, R.C., Gu, G.: Die free or live hard? Empirical evaluation and new design for fighting evolving twitter spammers. In: Sommer, R., Balzarotti, D., Maier, G. (eds.) RAID 2011. LNCS, vol. 6961, pp. 318–337. Springer, Heidelberg (2011)
42. Yu, H., Kaminsky, M., Gibbons, P.B., Flaxman, A.: Sybilguard: defending against sybil attacks via social networks. ACM SIGCOMM Comput. Commun. Rev. **40**(4), 363–374 (2006)
43. Zhang, C.M., Paxson, V.: Detecting and analyzing automated activity on twitter. In: Spring, N., Riley, G.F. (eds.) PAM 2011. LNCS, vol. 6579, pp. 102–111. Springer, Heidelberg (2011)

Web and Mobile Security

More Guidelines Than Rules:
CSRF Vulnerabilities from Noncompliant
OAuth 2.0 Implementations

Ethan Shernan[1], Henry Carter[1]([✉]), Dave Tian[2],
Patrick Traynor[2], and Kevin Butler[2]

[1] Georgia Institute of Technology, Atlanta, USA
eshernan3@mail.gatech.edu, carterh@gatech.edu
[2] University of Florida, Gainesville, USA
daveti@ufl.edu, {traynor,butler}@cise.ufl.edu

Abstract. OAuth 2.0 provides an open framework for the authorization of users across the web. While the standard enumerates mandatory security protections for a variety of attacks, many embodiments of this standard allow these protections to be optionally implemented. In this paper, we analyze the extent to which one particularly dangerous vulnerability, Cross Site Request Forgery, exists in real-world deployments. We crawl the Alexa Top 10,000 domains, and conservatively identify that 25 % of websites using OAuth appear vulnerable to CSRF attacks. We then perform an in-depth analysis of four high-profile case studies, which reveal not only weaknesses in sample code provided in SDKs, but also inconsistent implementation of protections among services provided by the same company. From these data points, we argue that protection against known and sometimes subtle security vulnerabilities can not simply be thrust upon developers as an option, but instead must be strongly enforced by Identity Providers before allowing web applications to connect.

1 Introduction

One of the most significant recent revolutions in web applications is the ability to combine mechanisms and data from disparate domains. So transformative is this change that a number of protocols have been proposed to encourage and facilitate such interaction. None of these protocols have been as widely adopted as OAuth 2.0 [18], an IETF standard for delegated authorization employed as a means of providing secure access to application data and user accounts. Through the use of this highly flexible standard, a wide range of domains can now build extensible tools far surpassing OAuth 2.0's original mandate, including authentication and single-sign on services.

Recent research has shown that noncompliance with the standard has led to vulnerabilities in real-world deployments. For instance, many mobile application developers have struggled to develop secure implementations of OAuth 2.0 because their use in non-web applications conflicts with assumptions made in

© Springer International Publishing Switzerland 2015
M. Almgren et al. (Eds.): DIMVA 2015, LNCS 9148, pp. 239–260, 2015.
DOI: 10.1007/978-3-319-20550-2_13

the standard [10]. Other researchers have demonstrated that a range of implementations fail to correctly implement or apply features, leaving them similarly insecure [29,39]. In particular, [39] considers a range of OAuth implementation vulnerabilities and provides recommended mitigations for each. However, these studies do not explore the root causes of these vulnerabilities in depth, and as a result advise mitigations that are ineffective in practice.

In this paper, we consider the extent to which a specific documented vulnerability is embodied in real-world implementations. Specifically, the OAuth 2.0 standard explicitly identifies the potential for Cross Site Request Forgery (CSRF) attacks, which may force an unsuspecting user to perform an "authorized" action without their knowledge (e.g., transmit financial information to a malicious third-party, modify sensitive file contents, etc.). The OAuth 2.0 standard is *absolutely unambiguous* about the danger that such vulnerabilities pose, and notes that both client and server "MUST implement CSRF protection" [18]. Unfortunately, these specific warnings are not heeded by many deployments of this protocol, leaving the implementation of protections as either a suggested task or simply an unmentioned burden for web application developers. As our experiments demonstrate, this lack of strict adherence to the standard leaves a significant portion of OAuth-enabled web applications vulnerable to CSRF attacks.

We make the following contributions:

- **Analysis of Adherence to Standard:** We evaluate 13 of the most popular OAuth 2.0 Identity Providers, including Facebook, Google, and Microsoft. We show that only four out of thirteen such providers force CSRF protections as part of their APIs, leaving the remaining nine to merely suggest or simply not mention that protection is necessary.
- **Measurement Study:** We develop a crawler and perform a depth-two analysis of the Alexa Top 10,000 websites [1], visiting more than 5.6 million URLs during our evaluation. Of those we detect as offering OAuth 2.0 services, we show that 25 % do not implement standard CSRF protections and appear vulnerable to attack.
- **Analysis of Case Studies:** We provide deeper analysis into four different specific instances in which vulnerable uses of OAuth 2.0 APIs are identified. We show that mistakes are the result of a range of factors, ranging from vulnerable sample code published by Identity Providers to inconsistencies between APIs across a large company. These contributing factors all point to Identity Providers as the logical agents to effect change by mandating compliant implementations.

From these observations, we argue that expecting web application developers to understand and implement subtle web security protection mechanisms is a design choice doomed to failure. Specifically, when a known vulnerability identified in the standard can be fixed with a known remediation technique that does not impact performance, it must be a mandatory component of any embodiment of that standard.

The remainder of this paper is organized as follows: Sect. 2 provides background information on the OAuth 2.0 protocol, and discusses CSRF attacks; Sect. 3 applies CSRF to OAuth, and demonstrates how the use of a challenge-response string can prevent such attacks; Sect. 4 offers the results of our web crawl; Sect. 5 details four case studies; Sect. 6 provides further insights and discussion; Sect. 7 examines related work; and Sect. 8 provides concluding remarks.

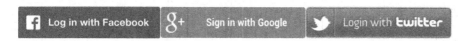

Fig. 1. Examples of popular single-sign on services that use OAuth. The presence of these buttons on a web page indicate that the domain has implemented OAuth as a single-sign on protocol.

2 Background

At its core, the OAuth protocol allows a user to grant a web application authorized access to his data on a different application [28]. Specifically, it allows a user to grant a Relying Party (RP) the ability to perform a set of operations on an account with an Identity Provider (IdP). The set of permissible actions are defined by the IdP in an API. A very common application of distributing authorization via OAuth is Single-Sign On (SSO), which allows users to connect to multiple web services (RPs) using one set of credentials from an IdP [20] (e.g., logging into Urbanspoon with Facebook). However, unlike dedicated SSO protocols such as OpenID [42] (which is built on top of OAuth 2.0), OAuth is capable of functioning as a general-purpose authorization protocol, making the impact of the protocol much more broad than a dedicated SSO application. OAuth 2.0 first authenticates users with a username and password, followed by consent given at a permissions screen for the RP to access the identity stored at the IdP [18]. The protocol relies on the use of access tokens that expire over time to authorize requests made by an RP to access data provided by an IdP on behalf of a user [25]. OAuth 2.0 has multiple forms of authentication flows to allow for use in different scenarios such as native, web, and mobile applications [18]. The significance of the OAuth 2.0 protocol is clear, as research has shown that a growing number of web applications are relying heavily on a small set of IdPs, many of which (e.g., Facebook, Google, Twitter) employ the OAuth 2.0 protocol [43] (Fig. 1). In addition, new research is proposing the use of OAuth 2.0 as a critical underlying component for authentication [12,33].

2.1 Authorization Code Flow

The OAuth 2.0 standard has multiple authorization protocols to allow for flexibility in implementation for both IdPs and RPs. These different "grant types" are

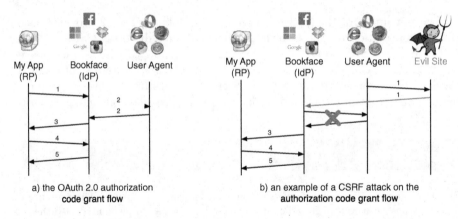

a) the OAuth 2.0 authorization
code grant flow

b) an example of a CSRF attack on the
authorization code grant flow

Fig. 2. The OAuth authorization code grant flow compared to an OAuth CSRF attack. In a normal execution, the user initiates authorization (1), grants the RP access to his IdP account (2), then forwards this approval to the RP (3). The protocol concludes with the RP authenticating and receiving and access token (4-5). In the CSRF attack, the adversary tricks the user into initiating the protocol. If the user has recently authenticated to the IdP, step 2 of the grant flow is skipped and the user agent automatically forwards the request embedded in the evil site to the IdP.

meant to enable easy implementations for a wide variety of scenarios. For example: the implicit grant flow is tailored toward client side web applications [18]. This flow involves making a single HTTP request to an IdP's authorization server and retrieving a bearer token that can be used to make subsequent authorized API calls for a specific user's data.

This paper focuses specifically on a vulnerability contained within the authorization code flow of the OAuth 2.0 standard [18]. This flow is widely implemented by IdPs and is designed for web server applications. We describe the authorization code flow when used by a client application (relying party) *MyApp* to access user data provided by an IdP (identity provider) *Bookface*. A graphical representation can be found in Fig. 2a.

1. *MyApp* sends an HTTP GET request to *Bookface*'s OAuth 2.0 endpoint containing - at minimum - the following parameters, specified in the OAuth 2.0 RFC [18]:
   (a) `client_id`: a value that determines the specific RP application utilizing the IdP's services (*MyApp* in this example)
   (b) `scope`: an IdP defined set of descriptors that describe what data the RP has access to on behalf of its users. The RP can set a combination of these descriptors to describe the scope of authorization a user must consent to.
   (c) `grant_type`: set to `code` for the authorization code grant
   (d) `redirect_uri`: the URI the IdP will redirect the *user agent* (a web browser or similar application) to where it will receive an *authorization code*. This should be a URI that the RP application can handle requests from.

2. *Bookface* responds to this request by prompting the current user of *MyApp* for their *Bookface* credentials and consent to allow *MyApp* access to their data based on the scope of the authorization. This is done by redirecting the user agent to a login page specific to the IdP.
3. If the user provides consent, *Bookface* sends an *authorization code* to the redirect_uri specified in Step 2.
4. *MyApp* receives the code at the redirect_uri and makes a POST request to *Bookface* to exchange this code for the final *authorization token* that can be used to make authorized API calls to *Bookface*. This request should include - at minimum - the following parameters in its POST data [18]:
   (a) client_id: the same value as used in the request in step 1
   (b) client_secret: a password to authenticate *MyApp*
   (c) redirect_uri: the URI to be redirected to with the *authorization token*
   (d) grant_type: set to code for the authorization code grant
   (e) code: the authorization code received with the result of step 3
5. *Bookface* exchanges the authorization code with an *authorization token* and delivers it to the redirect_uri.

The *authorization token* can now be used by *MyApp* to make authorized and authenticated requests to *Bookface's* APIs to retrieve specific user data. This authorization protocol differs from the OAuth 2.0 implicit grant flow in that it grants an authorization code before the authorization token, while the implicit grant flow directly grants the authorization token in step 3. This ensures that only the RP authenticated in step 4 is granted access to the API. By contrast, the implicit grant flow allows *any* party holding the authorization token to access the API. It should be noted that in both steps 2 and 5 there are optional parameters that may be included according to the standard, but not required for implementations of OAuth 2.0 [18]. One parameter that is critical for CSRF prevention is the state parameter. This parameter can hold any optional state required by the RP application. The value of this parameter is then echoed back to the RP by the IdP in any response in which it was included in the initial HTTP request.

2.2   Cross Site Request Forgery

A cross site request forgery attack (CSRF) is a common form of *confused deputy* attack where a user's previous session data is used by an attacker to make a malicious request on behalf of the victim [19,27]. CSRF attacks involve an attacker performing an HTTP request on behalf of a victim who logs into a website using stored session data (usually a cookie). CSRF attacks leverage the commonly used paradigm of storing session data about a user to make HTTP requests as if the victim actually authorized the request [26]. CSRF vulnerabilities were long ignored by web developers, and prominent websites such as The New York Times and YouTube have had significant CSRF vulnerabilities in the past [49]. While developers have historically considered this a low-risk vulnerability, the security community has considered the attack as a serious threat. Allowing non-expert software developers to make security assumptions can potentially lead to unexpected system behavior and vulnerabilities, so understanding CSRF and developing better means for enforcement remains a critical research area.

The malicious URL used in a CSRF attack is often embedded within an <img> HTML tag on an innocent looking web page so that a web browser will automatically perform a GET request to the URL without user consent. However, an attack requiring POST data can also be performed by tricking a victim into submitting form data to a maliciously formed URL on an honest web site. If a user has previously logged into the honest web application the attacker is targeting, a session cookie is automatically sent along with the malicious HTTP request, thereby authenticating the user. If the user is authorized to make the request, the honest web application processes the request as normal, even if the victim's user agent has actually just been tricked into making it.

A concrete example of this attack is described as follows: Alice logs into her bank website bank.example.com. This site allows users to make transfers by performing a GET request to the following endpoint: https://bank.example.com/transfer?src=alice&dest=bob&amt=500. The amt parameter is the amount to transfer, the src and dest parameters are the source and destination of the transfer.

An attacker, Eve, can perform a CSRF on Alice by embedding a malicious form of the previous URL in an <img> tag on her website (e.g., "https://bank.example.com/transfer?src=alice&dest=eve&amt=1000").

If Eve can get Alice to visit her website, Alice's web browser will automatically perform a GET request to the transfer endpoint at bank.example.com. If Alice has previously logged in with bank.example.com, her cookie will automatically be sent along with this request that authenticates her, and as long as she is authorized to make a transfer, bank.example.com will process the request as normal. If bank.example.com instead had the transfer operation as a POST request, a similar attack could be made but with Eve tricking Alice into submitting a form that points to the transfer endpoint of bank.example.com.

CSRF attacks can be prevented in different ways [6,31]. One simple protection scheme uses a randomly generated token that synchronizes a specific request with a specific user session [2]. Requests are disallowed unless a token is included and matches the user's current session token as remembered by the server. In the above example, bank.example.com could include on their website a hidden HTML field that includes a token that is randomly generated each time Alice visits their website. This token can then be included along with every HTTP request and identifies Alice's session with the sequence of requests. When Alice visits Eve's website, the malicious HTTP request is made as before. However this request will not include the same synchronizing token that bank.example.com now requires, and the request is rejected even if Alice was previously authenticated. As long as the token cannot be guessed by Eve, a CSRF attack will not be possible [49].

3   Attack

In this section, we describe a CSRF attack that can be launched on an incorrectly-implemented OAuth 2.0 connection. This attack is well-known and discussed in the OAuth RFC, but does not appear in a majority of live developer documentation. We close the section with a discussion of documented mitigation techniques and other mitigations that appear in practice.

3.1   CSRF in OAuth

The CSRF attack on the authorization code grant flow of OAuth 2.0 involves four parties, as shown in Fig. 2b. In this scenario, a victim user has accessed an RP at some point in the past, and has granted that RP access to his account on an IdP. While the user may have logged out of the RP application, we assume that he is still logged into his account with the IdP. While both the RP and the IdP are honest players, the RP must have a vulnerable implementation of the authorization code grant flow. The adversary is assumed to have no control over the RP or the IdP, but is capable of launching requests from the user agent. This action could be performed in practice by luring the user to click a malicious link in a phishing email or as a part of a clickjacking attack. This link could then load a malicious HTML <img> tag or other malicious code on a web page.

The attack proceeds as follows: If the adversary recognizes a vulnerable OAuth URL in an RP application, she can initiate the authorization code grant flow by luring the user to load the URL from their user agent (step 1 in Fig. 2b). When the victim loads this URL, their browser will automatically submit a GET request to this vulnerable OAuth URL. Because the victim is still logged in with that OAuth IdP, the pop-up request for user authorization in step 2 will be bypassed, and the IdP will proceed to issue the authorization token to the RP.

The result of the attack is that the RP now has authorization to access the user's IdP account *without the user having granted consent for this session*. The OAuth authorization token allows an RP to execute any operation in the IdPs API, potentially accessing and modifying private user information.

The RFC defining OAuth 2.0 provides an entire subsection detailing the potential for CSRF attack in the authorization code grant flow. After detailing how the attack proceeds, the RFC expressly states that:

> *The client MUST implement CSRF protection for its redirection URI... The authorization server MUST implement CSRF protection for its authorization endpoint...* [18]

The specification clearly requires that CSRF protection be implemented to prevent the attack described above. However, upon investigating the OAuth policy and implementation of 13 major IdPs, we discovered that CSRF prevention tools are only required by 4 of the 13 IdPs (Table 1). The documented policies of the rest of the IdPs either recommend but do not require CSRF defenses, or completely ignore them. This lack of proper enforcement of the OAuth 2.0

Table 1. A table of major OAuth Identity Providers. Regarding the prevention of CSRF attacks, this table describes if the IdP forces CSRF prevention, suggests it, or makes no mention of implementing it. Note that only 4 of the 13 IdPs require that RPs implement protections that are mandated by the OAuth 2.0 standard.

Provider	CSRF Protection	Provider	CSRF Protection	Provider	CSRF Protection
Battle.net	Forced	Dropbox	Suggested	AOL	No Mention
Github	Forced	Facebook	Suggested	Microsoft	No Mention
LinkedIn	Forced	Google	Suggested	Salesforce.com	No Mention
Reddit	Forced	Instagram	Suggested		
Amazon	Suggested	PayPal	Suggested		

standard indicates that there is a dangerous potential for RP developers to implement OAuth 2.0 requests in a vulnerable manner that will still be accepted by the IdP.

3.2 Developer Implementation Problems

The OAuth 2.0 standard contains an entire section entitled "Security Considerations" that is dedicated to specific security concerns when implementing OAuth [18]. Given that developers appear to be ignoring the subsection regarding CSRF, we examined the other considerations to determine if the problem of noncompliant implementation is widespread or if CSRF presents a unique challenge in correct implementation.

The section covers 16 different security concerns and mitigations for each attack. Many of these mitigations are standard good security practice, with examples including not storing or sending passwords in plaintext, sanitizing all data fields, and securing connections with TLS. A smaller subset of considerations deal with server back-end implementations, such as preventing brute-force login attempts and choosing secure cryptographic values. Finally, there are a few considerations warning against using deprecated flows and encouraging proper user education on strong password creation and identifying phishing attacks.

The most important take away from the documentation is that throughout the entire section, the client (i.e., the RP initiating the request) is only tasked with implementing three security mechanisms. Those mechanisms are:

- Validating the server TLS certificate
- Sanitizing all data fields received during the protocol
- Implementing CSRF protection

While many server-based applications have been found to improperly validate TLS certificates, these problems are largely a result of errors and poor design in the underlying TLS libraries, not application code itself [13]. Likewise, sanitizing

data is a well-studied security problem with extensive documentation on mitigation techniques to check the format of incoming data. However, implementing
CSRF protection mechanisms according to the OAuth standard slightly increases
the complexity of application code. This increase in complexity appears to have
the strong side effect of discouraging developers from implementing protections
at all. Even when developers are only tasked with managing a handful of security
concerns, requiring even a small amount of security expertise appears to be an
impediment to proper implementation.

3.3   Mitigation

The OAuth specification explicitly identifies the use of the OAuth `state` parameter in the section defining necessary CSRF protection mechanisms:

> *This is typically accomplished by requiring any request sent to the redi-
> rection URI endpoint to include a value that binds the request to the
> user-agent's authenticated state (e.g., a hash of the session cookie used
> to authenticate the user-agent). The client SHOULD utilize the "state"
> request parameter to deliver this value to the authorization server when
> making an authorization request.*

By requiring a non-guessable value that binds the request to a specific,
authenticated state, an adversary is prevented from constructing a valid malicious request to then lure the victim into launching through his user agent.

Given this advised policy, we next examined the CSRF prevention techniques
employed by a selection of common RPs, shown in Table 2. We found a variety
of different CSRF prevention techniques exist in practical deployments. The
varying CSRF prevention techniques implemented by RPs tended to correspond
with the CSRF policy of the IdP they were accessing.

The four IdPs listed in Table 1 as forcing CSRF protection all required that
connecting RPs implement protection using the `state` parameter as documented
in the OAuth standard. RPs sending connection requests to these services without the `state` parameter defined are denied authorization. This strict adherence
to the standard forces developers to implement protection correctly, preventing the CSRF attack described above when accessing these IdPs. For example,
Battle.net provides a comprehensive developer guide to properly generating and
using the `state` variable [7].

However, a small selection of IdPs that do not explicitly require CSRF protection offered non-standard protection mechanisms. As an example, the RPs
listed under "secure protocol" use a modified OAuth flow or completely different protocol for authorizing IdP access. In particular, the use of the OAuth 2.0
implicit grant flow by OneNote and OneDrive prevents this particular CSRF
attack by requiring more specific user agent interaction that is difficult for an
adversary to initiate without the user's knowledge. Other IdPs provided propri-
etary authentication or non-standard variables to prevent CSRF attacks. Unfortunately, because these mechanisms do not conform to the CRSF protection

Table 2. A listing of RPs and their means of preventing CSRF attacks. Without a single mandatory technique for CSRF prevention, RPs have developed a wide variety of protection schemes.

Technique and App	Web/Desktop	IdP	Details
CSRF Token			
Spotify	Desktop	Facebook	Extra CSRF token
TheVerge.com	Web	Google, Facebook	Google suggests state parameter, Facebook suggests the Facebook SDK
Secure Protocol			
OneNote	Desktop	Microsoft	Uses the implicit OAuth 2.0 flow
Google	Desktop (OS X)	Google	Uses the (deprecated) ClientLogin flow
OneDrive	Desktop	Microsoft	Uses the implicit OAuth 2.0 flow
LinkedIn	Desktop (OS X)	LinkedIn	Uses an undocumented method in OAuth 1.0
Other			
Spotify	Web	Facebook	Uses protection mechanism included in the Facebook SDK
OneNote	Web	Microsoft	Uses proprietary Microsoft authentication
Huffington Post	Web	Facebook	Facebook SDK mechanism
Hulu	Web	Facebook	Facebook SDK mechanism
ESPN.com	Web	Facebook	Facebook SDK mechanism
MLB.com	Web	Facebook	Facebook SDK mechanism
Facebook	Desktop (OS X)	Facebook	Uses the auth.login method from the Facebook API

specified in the standard, they may not offer the necessary protection against attack. Ultimately, the lax and variable standards for implementing CSRF protection in a majority of the IdPs leaves extreme potential for developers to bypass or incorrectly implement CSRF protection in their OAuth applications.

4   CSRF in the Wild

While the attack described in Sect. 3 is well understood with known mitigation strategies, our goal is to learn how often mitigations are correctly implemented in practice. To achieve this goal, we first performed an analysis of the Alexa top 10,000 websites to ascertain the breadth of the problem. We then performed in-depth analyses of four high-profile case studies to learn the underlying issues that cause developers to incorrectly implement OAuth 2.0.

4.1   Web Crawler Design and Implementation

Popular web crawler frameworks such as Scrapy [37] and Crawler4j [41] have been developed to provide robust web scraping functionality. However, these frameworks are heavy-weight compared to our needs for OAuth URL detection, and only provide limited URL crawling front-end capability. For these reasons, we implemented our own web crawler, which we entitled the OAuth Detector (OAD).

OAD is a light-weight, multi-threaded, high-performance web crawler, with an OAuth-specific data collection back-end. We implemented the crawler using the Beautiful Soup library [36]. OAD supports raw URL crawling using Python urllib2 [35]. For our application, raw URL crawling offers the best speed. Once the list of websites to crawl is loaded, OAD divides these sites according to the target thread requested. Any remaining sites are distributed to different threads in an round-robin fashion, balancing the workload across all threads. As our goal is to determine if the website contains vulnerable OAuth URLs, OAD allocates the minimum memory used to store these URLs for each website. If additional analytic information is needed, it is easy to extend the current data structure to save extra information. The OAD source code is available at https://bitbucket.org/uf_sensei/oadpublic.

4.2   Data Collection Setup

To approximate the number of occurrences of this vulnerability in the wild, we used OAD to analyze the Alexa top 10,000 websites. For each site, we analyzed two points: First, we checked whether the website makes any OAuth requests. Second, we checked to see if the website implemented the OAuth authorization code grant flow correctly (i.e., implemented CSRF protection in the state para-meter). To do this, our crawler iteratively examined links found in each site's source code. To identify an OAuth URL, we checked that the client_id and grant_type parameters were defined. If an OAuth URL was found, it was exam-ined to identify the grant flow, determine whether the vulnerability existed, and logged. The metric used to determine vulnerability was the existence or absence of a state variable in the URL. While it is possible for developers to implement CSRF protection outside of the state variable, this constitutes a non-standard CSRF protection technique not advised by the OAuth standard. If the link was not an OAuth URL, the crawler followed the link, and the process recursively repeated on the next page. Each link on the main page was followed up to depth-two, inspecting all links on the main page and the links on each page linked from the main page. In the Alexa top 10,000 websites, we crawled a total of 5,671,022 URLs.

Our results provide a conservative count for OAuth use in the Alexa top 10,000. Because OAD scans URLs in the page source, is not capable of finding URLs that are produced after executing Javascript on each page. As a result, it is possible that more domains exist that are vulnerable to CSRF or implement a non-standard CSRF protection mechanism. This makes our vulnerability estimate conservative.

4.3   Results

On the websites crawled, OAD found 302 domains that implement OAuth 2.0 in some form. Of those domains, 77 implemented at least one OAuth connection without CSRF protection. This result conservatively shows that as many as 25 % of RPs do not correctly implement CSRF protection. To determine how these vulnerabilities are distributed among domains, we broke the top 10,000 sites into five groups of 2,000 sites. When we considered the number of vulnerable domains placed in these buckets of 2,000 sites each, the CDF in Fig. 3b shows that the vulnerable implementations are evenly distributed across the top 10,000. To further determine how many vulnerable connections each domain implements, we also analyzed the total number of vulnerable URLs. Figure 3a shows that the vulnerable URLs roughly follow the same distribution as the vulnerable domains, indicating that these domains are erroneously implementing OAuth 2.0 at a similar rate.

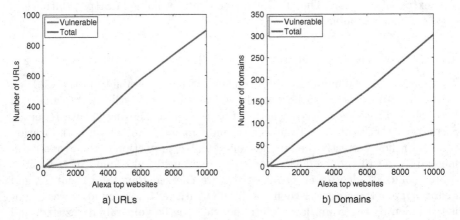

a) URLs   b) Domains

Fig. 3. CDFs showing the number of vulnerable URLs and domains in the top Alexa web pages. These plots show that vulnerable domains and URLs are evenly distributed throughout the top 10,000 websites.

To statistically demonstrate that this vulnerability is occurring consistently regardless of the popularity of the website, we performed a statistical analysis on the CDFs in Fig. 3. We divided the vulnerable URLs and domains into two sets, the lower and upper 5,000 websites of the Alexa top 10,000. We then applied Fisher's exact test to the hypothesis "website ranking correlates with the likelihood of website vulnerability", where our null hypothesis is that the two statistics are not correlated. For the vulnerable URLs, we demonstrated that the correlation is statistically not significant with $p = 0.065 > 0.05$. While this value appears to approach significance, we found even lower correlation when we applied the same test to the vulnerable domains, with $p = 0.229 > 0.05$. Both experiments strongly imply the null hypothesis, that vulnerabilities occur at a rate that does not correlate with the Alexa ranking of the website. This clearly demonstrates that correctly implementing CSRF protection is uniformly problematic for developers of both low-traffic and high-profile web applications.

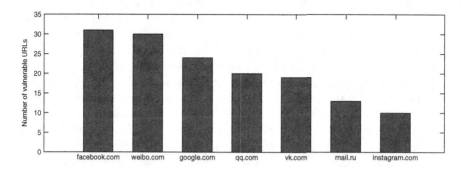

Fig. 4. The most common IdPs contacted using vulnerable OAuth URLs with the number of vulnerable URLs accessing each.

In addition to examining the distribution of vulnerabilities among RPs, we divided the number of vulnerable URLs down by which IdP they connect to. Figure 4 shows that of the vulnerable URLs, the most common IdP accessed with these vulnerable connections is Facebook. In addition, the problem is evident across IdPs from different countries as well. IdPs serving Europe (vk.com), China (weibo.com, qq.com), and Russia (mail.ru) all have RPs that are improperly implementing OAuth connections.

5 Case Studies

To identify the reasons why this well-documented vulnerability still exists at such a scale in live deployments, we selected four examples from our crawl data that represent high-profile services. We selected these examples for two reasons. First, they represent high profile web applications with significant corporate support, and should be expected to have high quality production code. Second, each subsequent example demonstrates that incremental increases in support for developers still allow for significant failures in implementation security, and that nothing short of IdPs mandating compliance will completely repair the vulnerability. We have notified each IdP that allows vulnerable connections of this potential attack prior to publishing this work.

5.1 Missing Documentation

If This Then That (IFTTT) is a popular website that connects Web APIs together to create interactions between two distinct services. This service leverages third party web APIs like Microsoft's OneNote, Salesforce.com's Chatter and Instagram to create unique alert combinations for users. For example, a user can allow IFTTT to automatically save New York Times articles to their OneNote notebook [22]. In the background, it uses OAuth 2.0 to authenticate itself with these third party identity providers provided IFTTT users give consent.

IFTTT allows connections to a range of IdPs, and accurately follows the documentation of each IdP with regards to using OAuth. We observed that if the IdP provided documentation or code to implement CSRF protection (e.g., the Facebook SDK), IFTTT correctly and securely implemented OAuth connections to those IdPs. However, IdPs like Microsoft, Salesforce.com and Instagram do not require the use of the `state` variable and do not provide developer tools for securely implementing OAuth 2.0 protocols for preventing CSRF attacks [34]. As a result, IFTTT implements OAuth connections to all three of these services that were vulnerable to CSRF attacks, allowing an attacker to authorize IFTTT to access a user's account on these services without their consent.

This example of the OAuth CSRF attack indicates that developers will simply omit CSRF protection if the implementation is left to their discretion. However, developers connecting to IdPs that provide CSRF documentation are much more likely to build their web applications correctly.

```
/**
 * Obtain a Live Connect authorization endpoint URL based on configuration.
 * @returns {string} The authorization endpoint URL
 */
this.getAuthUrl = function () {
    var scopes = ['wl.signin', 'wl.basic', 'wl.offline_access', 'office.onenote_create'];
    var query = toQueryString({
        'client_id': clientId,
        'scope': scopes.join(' '),
        'redirect_uri': redirectUrl,          no "state" parameter
        'display': 'page',
        'locale': 'en',
        'response_type': 'code'
    });
    return oauthAuthorizeUrl + "?" + query;
};
```

Fig. 5. Example code for connecting to Microsoft's live connect services. Note that there is no random token to help protect against a CSRF attack made on the URL generated by this function.

5.2 Incorrect Code Samples

The previous case study showed that without proper documentation or requiring CSRF protection, developers are prone to implementing OAuth 2.0 in an insecure manner. Our second case study revealed that this problem is often exacerbated by IdPs who provide tools that encourage insecure implementations.

To assist developers with implementing OAuth connections, it is common for IdPs to provide sample code demonstrating how to properly use their OAuth 2.0 implementations. These code samples are meant to show complete and correct examples for connecting to the IdP's API. Microsoft and AOL are two such IdPs that post sample code for developers to reference. AOL provides sample PHP code [3] hosted on their own developer website, and Microsoft publishes sample code [32] in a variety of languages on Github. Figure 5 shows a snippet of Javascript code provided by Microsoft, and Fig. 6 shows a PHP code sample provided by AOL. The Javascript function provided by Microsoft is used to build an OAuth 2.0 URL to request access to Microsoft's Live Connect services. A user accessing the URL generated by this function will be prompted for their username and password. They will then be asked for access to the security scopes provided by the scopes list on line 28. Given this client-side information, the function fills in the necessary URL fields to make a valid OAuth request to access the Microsoft API. If access is granted, the RP will receive an access token (see Sect. 2) that is used to access the user's protected resources. The PHP code provided by AOL serves the same purpose. This code builds up the parameter list of the URL used to initiate AOL's OAuth 2.0 authorization code flow. An RP implementing this code would simply need to specify its client_id (registered with AOL) and the redirect_url to return to after the authentication is complete.

```
else{//for simplicity force thru to authorization but often flows would use
    something like the HTML example with a popup
    $authorizationReq = $aolAuthorizeUrl."?
client_id=".$clientId."&response_type=code&redirect_uri=".$callbackUrl;
    header("Location: $authorizationReq");
    die();
}
```

no "state" parameter

Fig. 6. Example code for connecting to AOL's OAuth services. Notice that like Microsoft, there is no random token to protect against CSRF.

Neither of these code samples contains example code for properly implementing CSRF protection. Given that these code samples can be cut and pasted into a developer's implementation and will produce a functioning OAuth connection back to the IdP, it is not surprising that developers consistently implement the example code as is, without CSRF protection. Until IdPs remedy the vulnerabilities in their example code, these same vulnerabilities will continue to propagate into live RP implementations.

5.3   Inconsistent Requirements

While some IdPs provide insecure examples of OAuth code, there are examples of IdPs that provide helpful developer tools for correctly implementing OAuth 2.0.

One example of this is Facebook, which provides a comprehensive Javascript SDK that contains built-in protection against CSRF attacks. However, other services offered by the same company fail to provide any developer assistance in proper OAuth implementation. Now owned by Facebook for nearly three years, Instagram also provides its own API for single sign on, allowing websites to access their services. One common use of this API is to build third-party "web viewers" for Instagram accounts, such as ink361.com [23]. A user can sign onto this service using either their Instagram or Facebook account, then access their Instagram albums for online viewing. This authorization and authentication is handled by the OAuth 2.0 protocol. Upon examining the OAuth URL used to connect to these IdPs, we discovered that the Facebook connection was securely implemented using the Facebook SDK, while the Instagram implementation was vulnerable to CSRF attack.

After investigating the Instagram OAuth 2.0 documentation [24], we found that the IdP recommends CSRF protection with the following warning: "You may provide an optional **state** parameter to carry through any server-specific state you need to, for example, protect against CSRF issues." However, unlike Facebook, Instagram does not provide any tools for correctly implementing the **state** parameter, nor documentation for how to do so. Without proper enforcement from the OAuth specification itself, IdPs are unable to consistently document and implement correct OAuth implementation tools, *even within the same managing corporation.*

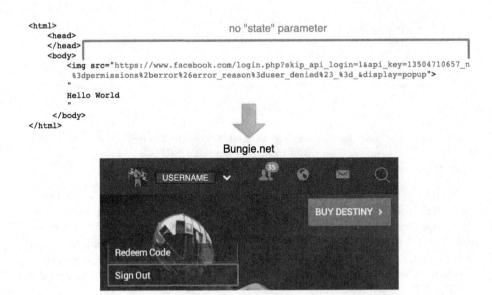

Fig. 7. An example of malicious HTML and the resulting CSRF attack. The code sample above contains a vulnerable OAuth URL. When a victim loads the URL, they are logged into the RP Bungie.net without being prompted for consent by the IdP, Facebook.

5.4   Lack of Enforcement

Given that our previous case studies showed that many IdPs are poorly documenting proper OAuth implementation or not providing developers with usable tools for implementing CSRF protection, Facebook appeared to have solved the issue by providing a comprehensive SDK. However, their implementation does not force any CSRF protection to be implemented. Our crawl revealed that of the vulnerable OAuth URLs found, almost 20 % connected to the Facebook API. One of these vulnerable URLs is implemented on the website of popular video game developer Bungie. Bungie is best known for the development of the Halo franchise and most recently the first-person shooter Destiny. They provide an online service for collecting and presenting in-game data and providing opportunities for social interactions between players, with single-sign on options for connecting to Facebook. Bungie uses OAuth 2.0 to connect to Facebook, implementing the authorization code grant flow. However, instead of using the Facebook SDK and implementing the built-in CSRF protection mechanism, Bungie implemented the OAuth protocol from scratch. Their ability to implement a functioning OAuth implementation *without* CSRF protection indicates that while Facebook provides developer tools for implementing CSRF protection, they do not require connection requests to actually use this protection. The resulting CSRF attack is illustrated in Fig. 7.

This example shows that even when developer tools are provided to assist in correct, secure implementation, developers may still choose to build their own insecure implementations. Our crawl results show that, in fact, a large number of developers are doing this. Ultimately, if correct security protection mechanisms are not mandated by the protocol, developers will only meet the minimum functional standards, even if these standards are not secure.

5.5   Recommended Approaches to Mitigation

To effectively mitigate the problem of CSRF, these case studies all point to the IdPs as the logical party to effect change. While previous studies have recommended mitigation techniques that expect RPs to implement a range of security constructions [39], our results show that even when RPs are given effective developer tools, they *still fail to correctly implement constructions as simple as a random token*. Without the ability to entrust the RPs with correctly managing their implementations, the onus lies on the IdPs to force proper implementation through a) providing *correct* and *complete* developer tools for implementing OAuth, and more importantly b) forcing correct RP implementations by rejecting OAuth requests that do not contain all necessary authenticating tokens. While it is possible that an RP could include these tokens and willingly not verify their validity after the IdP responds, our observations of the four IdPs that force CSRF protection using the `state` parameter show this is not a common case. When these IdPs mandate the use of the `state` parameter and provide proper documentation, RPs largely provide correct and secure implementations and effectively mitigate CSRF attacks. However, until more IdPs begin enforcing this level of strict adherence to the OAuth specification, RPs will continue to produce vulnerable implementations and expose their customers to attack.

6   Discussion

6.1   Comparison to HTTPS Use

Another possible conclusion for why CSRF protection is not correctly implemented in a large number of RPs is that developers are cutting corners in an attempt to develop a more efficient authorization connection. To further explore this possibility, we examined another security feature that is sometimes optionally implemented: HTTPS. Upon examining the 180 vulnerable OAuth URLs found by OAD, we discovered that 146 (81 %) of the URLs connected to the IdP over an HTTPS connection. The process of establishing a secure channel for communication requires significantly more time and bandwidth than generating and transmitting a short random token to maintain state. However, our results show that the overwhelming majority of RPs implementing CSRF-vulnerable connections *do not* cut corners when it comes to using HTTPS. This seems to indicate that the lack of CSRF protection is not an attempt to preserve efficiency.

Upon examining which IdPs were contacted over the insecure HTTP connections, we noted that 15 connected to qq.com, 8 connected to vk.com, 1 connected to Facebook, and the rest to small IdPs. Since most of the large IdPs represented in our study were never connected to over an insecure connection, this would seem to indicate that strong IdP policy ensures that developers implement HTTPS. Were the same strong enforcement on CSRF protection in place, we hypothesize that the occurrence of vulnerable OAuth connections would also appear at a similarly low rate.

6.2   OAuth 1.0

The OAuth 1.0 protocol is described in RFC 5849 [17]. This RFC was originally released in 2010 and is the original incarnation of the OAuth protocol. We elected not to focus on this particular version as it has been deemed "obsolete" by the OAuth 2.0 RFC [18]. The OAuth 1.0 RFC mentions in Sect. 4.13 that CSRF attacks are possible on OAuth URIs, and specific preventions are "beyond the scope of this specification."

7   Related Work

Single Sign-On systems have been extensively studied in general, and have been shown to exhibit a variety of vulnerabilities. Like our work, some of these vulnerabilities stem from poor implementation and unclear developer guidelines [5,45], while others are a result of flawed protocols [38,44]. In addition, a variety of automated tools exist to analyze the security of SSO implementations in the wild. However, the tools that are currently available either target more generic vulnerabilities [4, 46] or vulnerabilities of a different nature [50] than the CSRF attack that we describe here.

Since its release, OAuth 2.0 has received mixed evaluations on the security of the protocol. Formal analysis of the protocol has shown that under specific assumptions and correct implementation, OAuth 2.0 provides secure authentication. However, the same analyses point out that the prioritization of simple implementation over security has left significant potential for incorrectly implementing the protocol [9, 11, 14, 16, 21]. In practice, relying parties have been found to have implementations that fail to protect against common web attacks such as cross site scripting and click-jacking [39]. In addition, OAuth 2.0 has also been shown to be susceptible to attacks relating to all forms of SSO [40, 45], such as phishing or eavesdropping on an unprotected communication channel [8, 15, 48]. Finally, mobile applications of OAuth 2.0 have been found to be particularly vulnerable due to developer confusion [10].

Previous studies have shown that CSRF vulnerabilities could exist in OAuth 2.0 [5, 29, 39, 47]. The official threat model contains two sections dedicated to potential implementation vulnerabilities in the implicit grant and authentication code flows [30]. These sections recommend that the `state` parameter of the OAuth 2.0 protocol be used as a pseudorandom token (as recommended in [49]). However, neither the threat model nor the standard requires the use of this parameter as a synchronizer token. Other studies have been done to exploit these documented CSRF vulnerabilities in OAuth 2.0 on the relying party side [39]. However, the extent to which these vulnerabilities exist in the wild has not yet been shown. Furthermore, there has not been a study on the variations of implementations of identity providers and how these differences can actually cause these critical vulnerabilities. This paper aims to show that because the OAuth 2.0 standard does not require certain precautions such as a synchronizer token, IdPs are providing vulnerable implementations of "the standard" to unknowing relying parties.

8   Conclusion

As an increasing number of web applications require the exchange of user data between services, OAuth 2.0 provides a convenient framework for authorization between accounts. While the standard contains explicit instructions for implementing security protection mechanisms, these standards do not always translate into real-world implementations. This work demonstrates that the documented CSRF vulnerability in particular is often not defended against in practical deployments. Our OAD crawler was able to show that 25 % of the domains using OAuth in the Alexa top 10,000 do not properly implement CSRF protection mechanisms. After examining four high-profile vulnerabilities, we demonstrate that the reason for this lack of compliance is because IdPs do not require developers to implement the protocol with CSRF protection according to the RFC. This lack of enforcement shows that we cannot rely on developers to properly implement optional security controls, but must strongly enforce their use within the protocol and developer tools.

Acknowledgements. This work is based upon work supported by the U.S. National Science Foundation under grant numbers CNS-1118046, CNS-1245198, and CNS-1464087.

References

1. Alexa Internet, Inc.: Alexa top sites (2014). http://www.alexa.com/
2. Alur, D., Crupi, J., Malks, D.: Core j2ee patterns: best practices and design strategies (2001). http://www.corej2eepatterns.com/Design/PresoDesign.htm
3. AOL Inc.: Php sample (2014). http://identity.aol.com/documentation/start/oauth2/web-site-integration/php-sample/
4. Bai, G., Lei, J., Meng, G., Venkatraman, S.S., Saxena, P., Sun, J., Liu, Y., Dong, J.S.: Authscan: automatic extraction of web authentication protocols from implementations. In: Proceedings of the Network and Distributed System Security Symposium (2013)
5. Bansal, C., Bhargavan, K., Maffeis, S.: Discovering concrete attacks on website authorization by formal analysis. In: Proceedings of the IEEE Computer Security Foundations Symposium (2012)
6. Barth, A., Jackson, C., Mitchell, J.C.: Robust defenses for cross-site request forgery. In: Proceedings of the ACM Conference on Computer and Communications Security (2008)
7. Blizzard Entertainment, Inc.: Using OAuth (2014). https://dev.battle.net/docs/read/oauth
8. Cao, Y., Shoshitaishvili, Y., Borgolte, K., Kruegel, C., Vigna, G., Chen, Y.: Protecting web-based single sign-on protocols against relying party impersonation attacks through a dedicated bi-directional authenticated secure channel. In: Stavrou, A., Bos, H., Portokalidis, G. (eds.) RAID 2014. LNCS, vol. 8688, pp. 276–298. Springer, Heidelberg (2014)
9. Chari, S., Jutla, C., Roy, A.: Universally composable security analysis of OAuth v2.0. Cryptology ePrint Archive, Report 2011/526 (2011). http://eprint.iacr.org/
10. Chen, E., Pei, Y., Chen, S., Tian, Y., Kotcher, R., Tague, P.: OAuth demystified for mobile application developers. In: Proceedings of the ACM Conference on Computer and Communications Security (2014)
11. Cherrueau, R.-A., Douence, R., Royer, J.C., Südholt, M., de Oliveira, A.S., Roudier, Y., Dell'Amico, M.: Reference monitors for security and interoperability in OAuth 2.0. In: Garcia-Alfaro, J., Lioudakis, G., Cuppens-Boulahia, N., Foley, S., Fitzgerald, W.M. (eds.) DPM 2013. LNCS, vol. 8247, pp. 236–249. Springer, Heidelberg (2014)
12. Ferreira, H.G.C., de Sousa Junior, R.T., de Deus, F.E.G., Canedo, E.D.: Proposal of a secure, deployable and transparent middleware for internet of things. In: Proceedings of the Iberian Conference on Information Systems & Technologies (CISTI) (2014)
13. Georgiev, M., Iyengar, S., Jana, S., Anubhai, R., Boneh, D., Shmatikov, V.: The most dangerous code in the world: validating SSL certificates in non-browser software. In: Proceedings of the ACM Conference on Computer and Communications Security (2012)
14. Gibbons, K., Raw, J.O.: Security evaluation of the OAuth 2.0 framework. Inf. Manage. Comput. Secur. **22**(3), 1–8 (2014)
15. Hammer, E.: OAuth 2.0 (without signatures) is bad for the web (2010). http://hueniverse.com/2010/09/15/oauth-2-0-without-signatures-is-bad-for-the-web/

16. Hammer, E.: OAuth 2.0 and the road to hell (2012). http://hueniverse.com/2012/07/26/oauth-2-0-and-the-road-to-hell/
17. Hammer-Lahav, E.: The OAuth 1.0 protocol. RFC 5849, RFC Editor, April 2010. http://tools.ietf.org/html/rfc5849
18. Hardt, D.: The OAuth 2.0 authorization framework. RFC 6749, RFC Editor, October 2012. http://tools.ietf.org/html/rfc6749
19. Hardy, N.: The confused deputy: (or why capabilities might have been invented). SIGOPS Operating Syst. Rev. **22**(4), 36–38 (1988)
20. Hhnlein, D., Wich, T., Schmlz, J., Haase, H.M.: The evolution of identity management using the example of web-based applications. Inf. Technol. **56**(3), 134–140 (2014)
21. Homakov, E.: OAuth1, OAuth2, OAuth...? (2013). http://homakov.blogspot.jp/2013/03/oauth1-oauth2-oauth.html
22. IFTTT Inc.: If this then that (2014). https://ifttt.com/
23. INK361: Instagram web viewer - ink361 (2014). http://ink361.com/
24. Instagram: Authentication (2014). http://instagram.com/developer/authentication/
25. Jones, M., Hardt, D.: The OAuth 2.0 authorization framework: bearer token usage. RFC 6750, RFC Editor, October 2012. http://tools.ietf.org/html/rfc6750
26. Jovanovic, N., Kirda, E., Kruegel, C.: Preventing cross site request forgery attacks. In: Proceedings of the International Conference on Security and Privacy in Communication Networks (Securecomm) (2006)
27. Käfer, K.: Cross site request forgery (2008). http://dump.kkaefer.com/csrf-paper.pdf
28. Kaur, G., Aggarwal, D.: A survey paper on social sign-on protocol OAuth 2.0. J. Eng. Comput. Appl. Sci. **2**(6), 93–96 (2013)
29. Li, W., Mitchell, C.J.: Security issues in OAuth 2.0 SSO implementations. In: Chow, S.S.M., Camenisch, J., Hui, L.C.K., Yiu, S.M. (eds.) ISC 2014. LNCS, vol. 8783, pp. 529–541. Springer, Heidelberg (2014)
30. Lodderstedt, T., McGloin, M., Hunt, P.: OAuth 2.0 threat model and security considerations. RFC 6819, RFC Editor, January 2013. http://tools.ietf.org/html/rfc6819
31. Mao, Z., Li, N., Molloy, I.: Defeating cross-site request forgery attacks with browser-enforced authenticity protection. In: Dingledine, R., Golle, P. (eds.) FC 2009. LNCS, vol. 5628, pp. 238–255. Springer, Heidelberg (2009)
32. Microsoft: liveconnect-client.js (2014). https://github.com/OneNoteDev/OneNoteAPISampleNodejs/blob/master/lib/liveconnect-client.js
33. Nauman, M., Khan, S., Othman, A.T., Musa, S.U., Rehman, N.U.: POAuth: privacy-aware open authorization for native apps on smartphone platforms. In: Proceedings of the International Conference on Ubiquitous Information Management and Communication (2012)
34. Patterson, P.: Digging deeper into OAuth 2.0 on force.com (2014). https://developer.salesforce.com/page/Digging_Deeper_into_OAuth_2.0_on_Force.com
35. Python Software Foundation: urllib2 (2015). https://docs.python.org/2/library/urllib2.html
36. Richardson, L.: Beautiful soup (2014). http://www.crummy.com/software/BeautifulSoup/
37. Scrapinghub: Scrapy (2015). http://scrapy.org/
38. Somorovsky, J., Mayer, A., Schwenk, J., Kampmann, M., Jensen, M.: On breaking saml: be whoever you want to be. In: Proceedings of the USENIX Security Symposium (2012)

39. Sun, S.T., Beznosov, K.: The devil is in the (implementation) details: an empirical analysis of OAuth SSO systems. In: Proceedings of the ACM Conference on Computer and Communications Security (2012)
40. Sun, S.T., Pospisil, E., Muslukhov, I., Dindar, N., Hawkey, K., Beznosov, K.: Investigating users' perspectives of web single sign-on: conceptual gaps and acceptance model. ACM Trans. Internet Technol. **13**(1), 2:1–2:35 (2013)
41. The crawler4j community: crawler4j (2015). https://code.google.com/p/crawler4j/
42. The OpenID Foundation: OpenID (2015). http://openid.net/
43. Vapen, A., Carlsson, N., Mahanti, A., Shahmehri, N.: Third-Party identity management usage on the web. In: Faloutsos, M., Kuzmanovic, A. (eds.) PAM 2014. LNCS, vol. 8362, pp. 151–162. Springer, Heidelberg (2014)
44. Wang, R., Chen, S., Wang, X.: Signing me onto your accounts through facebook and google: a traffic-guided security study of commercially deployed single-sign-on web services. In: Proceedings of the IEEE Symposium on Security and Privacy (2012)
45. Wang, R., Zhou, Y., Chen, S., Qadeer, S., Evans, D., Gurevich, Y.: Explicating SDKs: uncovering assumptions underlying secure authentication and authorization. In: Proceedings of the USENIX Security Symposium (2013)
46. Xing, L., Chen, Y., Wang, X., Chen, S.: Integuard: toward automatic protection of third-party web service integrations. In: Proceedings of the Network and Distributed System Security Symposium (2013)
47. Yang, F., Manoharan, S.: A security analysis of the OAuth protocol. In: IEEE Pacific Rim Conference on Communications, Computers and Signal Processing (PACRIM) (2013)
48. Yue, C.: The devil is phishing: rethinking web single sign-on systems security. In: Proceedings of the USENIX Workshop on Large-Scale Exploits and Emergent Threats (LEET) (2013)
49. Zeller, W., Felten, E.W.: Cross-Site Request Forgeries: Exploitation and prevention. Princeton University, Tech. rep. (2008)
50. Zhou, Y., Evans, D.: SSOScan: automated testing of web applications for single sign-on vulnerabilities. In: Proceedings of the USENIX Security Symposium (2014)

May I? - Content Security Policy Endorsement for Browser Extensions

Daniel Hausknecht[1]([✉]), Jonas Magazinius[1,2,3], and Andrei Sabelfeld[1]

[1] Chalmers University of Technology, Gothenburg, Sweden
`daniel.hausknecht@chalmers.se`
[2] CISPA, Saarland University, Saarbrucken, Germany
[3] Assured Security AB, Gothenburg, Sweden

Abstract. Cross-site scripting (XSS) vulnerabilities are among the most prevailing problems on the web. Among the practically deployed countermeasures is a "defense-in-depth" Content Security Policy (CSP) to mitigate the effects of XSS attacks. However, the adoption of CSP has been frustratingly slow. This paper focuses on a particular roadblock for wider adoption of CSP: its interplay with browser extensions.

We report on a large-scale empirical study of all free extensions from Google's Chrome web store that uncovers three classes of vulnerabilities arising from the tension between the power of extensions and CSP intended by web pages: third party code inclusion, enabling XSS, and user profiling. We discover extensions with over a million users in each vulnerable category.

With the goal to facilitate a wider adoption of CSP, we propose an extension-aware CSP endorsement mechanism between the server and client. A case study with the Rapportive extensions for Firefox and Chrome demonstrates the practicality of the approach.

1 Introduction

Cross-site Scripting (XSS) [27] vulnerabilities allow attackers to inject malicious JavaScript for execution in the browsers of victim users. XSS vulnerabilities are among the most prevailing problems on the web [28]. The *World Wide Web Consortium (W3C)* [38] has proposed a "defense-in-depth" *Content Security Policy (CSP)* [36] to mitigate the effects of XSS attacks. A CSP policy lets websites whitelist a set of URIs which are accepted as the sources for content on a web page. The standard defines CSP to be transmitted in an HTTP header to the client, where it is enforced by a CSP compliant user agent. The browsers enforce the policy by disallowing communication to the hosts outside the whitelist. The majority of the modern browsers support CSP [35].

The web application security community largely agrees on the usefulness of CSP [26,40] as an effective access control policy not only to mitigate XSS but also other cross-domain attacks such as *clickjacking* [25]. However, the adoption of CSP has been frustratingly slow. Major companies lead the way, e.g. with Google introducing CSP for Gmail in December 2014 [14], yet, currently, only 402 out of the top one million websites actually specify a policy for their websites [6].

© Springer International Publishing Switzerland 2015
M. Almgren et al. (Eds.): DIMVA 2015, LNCS 9148, pp. 261–281, 2015.
DOI: 10.1007/978-3-319-20550-2_14

CSP and Browser Extensions: This paper focuses on what we believe is a serious roadblock for wider adoption of CSP: its interplay with browser extensions. Browser extensions often rely on communication with websites, fetching their own scripts, external libraries, and integrating independent services. For example, the extension *Rapportive* [20], with over 320,000 users, shows information from LinkedIn about the contacts displayed in Gmail. The functionality of this extension depends on the ability to communicate with LinkedIn. This is in dissonance with Gmail's CSP, where, not surprisingly, LinkedIn is not whitelisted.

As mentioned above, Google recently started enforcing a CSP policy for Gmail. To be more precise, Google changed CSP from *report-only* to enforcement mode [14]. This resulted in immediate consequences for both the Firefox and Chrome versions of the Rapportive extension. Interestingly, the consequences were different for Firefox and Chrome. The Firefox extension no longer runs. As we will see later in the paper this is related to Firefox' conservative approach to loading external resources by extensions. After an update, the Chrome version of the extension has been adapted to the change that allows it to run. It is possible because the new CSP for Gmail includes neither a `connect-src` nor a `default-src` directive, which allows scripts injected by browser extensions to open connections to remote servers. Rapportive uses this permissiveness in Gmail's CSP to load the LinkedIn profile information into the web page rendered in Chrome. This different behaviors of Rapportive with Firefox and Chrome exemplify the differences in the browser extension frameworks, motivating the need to investigate these differences deeper.

The above highlights the tension between the power of extensions and CSP intended by web pages. Website administrators are in a difficult position to foresee what browser extensions the users have installed. This indeed hampers the adoption of CSP.

Research Questions: The paper focuses on two main research questions: Q1: What is the state of the art in resolving the tension between the power of browser extensions and restrictions of CSP? and Q2: How to improve the state of the art as to leverage the security benefits of CSP without hampering the functionality of browser extensions?

The State of the Art: To answer Q1, we perform an in-depth study of practices used by extensions and browsers to deal with CSP. Within the browser, browser extensions have the capabilities to modify HTTP headers and content of the page. Injecting content to the page is common among extensions to add features and functionality. CSP applies also to this injected content, which may break or limit the functionality of the extension. To maintain the functionality and added user experience, extensions require the needs for relaxing the policy of the page. Because extensions have the capability to modify page headers, and to execute before a page is loaded, extensions have the window of opportunity to relax or even disable the CSP policy before it is applied. Changing the CSP header undermines high security requirements of a web service, e.g. for online banking, or simply bypass the benign intentions of a web application provider. Relaxing or removing the CSP of a web page disables this last line of defense.

Empirical Study: We address Q1 by a large-scale empirical study of all free 25835 extensions from Google's Chrome web store [10]. We have analyzed how browser extensions make use of their capability to modify the CSP header. We are also interested in how the presence of a CSP header affects content injection through browser extensions, i.e. the practical effects of CSP on extensions.

To understand the prevalence of invasive modifications, we have developed tools to identify such extensions and analyze their behavior in the presence of a CSP policy. The results are two-fold, they show that invasive modifications are very common in extensions, but at the same time manipulation of the CSP headers are still rare.

Vulnerability Classes Uncovered: With the insights from the empirical study at hand, we categorize the findings to identify three classes of vulnerabilities that arise from invasive modifications that relax or disable the CSP policy. First, the extension injects *third party content* that increases the attack surface and introduces attack vectors that can be used for further attacks previously not present in the page. Second, it opens up for *XSS attacks* that would have been mitigated in otherwise hardened web pages. Third, the extension injects code that allows its developer to perform *user tracking* during the browser session. The invasive modifications described in these scenarios constitute a risk to both the user and the web service. Because extensions are applied either to a specific set of pages or all browsed pages, the impact varies. Naturally, an extension that is applied to every page puts the user at greater risk.

There exist, however, cases of content injections with which a web service would comply. For example, a web service provider that trusts the provided content of another service agrees to allow the modified CSP. By default the service does not include the third party content and therefore does not include the origin of the content in its CSP to be as restrictive as possible and thus to obtain the best protection for the web page. In this case, a relaxation of the CSP made by an extension would be acceptable. This brings out to the second research question and motivates a mechanism for detecting and endorsing CSP modifications to detect and agree on a policy acceptable by the web service.

CSP Endorsement: To address Q2, we propose a mechanism that enables extension-aware CSP endorsement by the server of the client's request to modify CSP. We expand the event processing of extensions in web browsers to detect CSP modifications made by an extension. On detection, the browser collects the necessary information and sends a request to the server which decides over accepting or rejecting the CSP modification. The browser eventually enforces the CSP policy respecting the server's decision. Additionally to the basic mechanism, we also propose an optimization with which the browser itself is able to make decisions based on origins labeled as acceptable by the web server, in order to obviate the need of sending CSP endorsement messages.

Note that the mechanism provides higher granularity than simply including a whitelist in the original CSP that attempts to foresee what extensions might be installed and relax CSP accordingly. Such an over-approximating whitelist would not be desirable to transport for performance reasons. Instead, our CSP endorsement allows making on-the-fly decisions by the server depending on the context and grants the flexibility of not having to send a complete whitelist in the first phase. We have implemented the CSP endorsement mechanism for Firefox and Chrome, and an endorsement server using *Node.js* [17].

Rapportive Case Study: We have conducted a case study to analyze the usefulness of the CSP endorsement mechanism. For this, we have implemented a Firefox and a Chrome extension that models the behavior of Rapportive and used it to report the performance of the prototype implementation.

Contributions: In summary, the paper's contributions are as follows:

- Large-scale empirical study to analyze the behavior of Chrome browser extensions in the context of CSP (Sect. 2).
- Identification of vulnerability classes stemming from modifications of CSP policies by extensions (Sect. 2).
- Analysis of browser extension framework behavior and the implications for resource loading in the presence of a CSP (Sect. 3).
- Development and prototype implementation of an extended CSP mechanism which allows the endorsement of CSP modifications (Sect. 4).
- Case study with the Rapportive extension to demonstrate the practicality of the approach (Sect. 5).

The program code for our prototype implementation is available online[1].

2   Empirical Study

Browser extensions are pieces of software that can be plugged into web browsers and extend its basic functionality. Depending on the development interfaces and used technologies, the capabilities of extensions vary depending on the respective browser but powerful in general. For example, all major browsers enable extensions to intercept HTTP messages and to modify their headers, or to tweak the actual page content. Though this allows of course augmenting a user's browsing experience, this can willingly or unwillingly affect a web page's security.

In the following section, we analyze all 25835 free extensions from Google Chrome store in order to learn how browser extensions modify web pages in practice and how these modifications affect a page's security, in particular with respect to CSP policies. We classify our findings and identify popular real world examples while following the principle of responsible disclosure.

---

[1] http://www.cse.chalmers.se/~danhau/csp_endorsement/.

2.1 Extension Analysis

Many extensions modify the browsed page when loaded, however some do it more invasively than others. In order to understand how web pages are affected by extensions and their relation to CSP we perform an empirical study. The aim of the study is to see how many extensions are doing invasive modification to the web page source. An invasive modification is here defined as injecting content that poses a threat to the confidentiality or integrity of the page in the relation to user assets. Examples of such invasive modification are inclusion of scripts referring to potentially malicious external code, inclusion of scripts designed to track the user's browsing habits, and modifications that disable the browser's built in protection, e.g., against cross-site scripting attacks.

Large-Scale Study. This study was performed by downloading (on December 20, 2014), extracting, and analyzing the source of each of the complete set of free extensions available in the Google Chrome store at the time of the analysis.

To perform the study we developed simple tools to automate the process of downloading extensions from the store and extracting their sources.

Only the scripts of the extension itself (called *content scripts*) can do invasive modifications to page content. Therefore, the analysis was limited to the subset of extensions that had content scripts defined. For each extension in this set each individual content script was analyzed to find invasive modifications that manifest themselves by injecting scripts or references to external resources. At last, we split the set into those that are applied to specific pages, versus every page. Due to the large number of extensions that modify the page, the analysis was to a large part automated.

To find extensions that modifies the CSP the set of extensions that in any form mentions *content security policy* or *CSP*. Each of these were manually inspected to see exactly how CSP is used. Because these extensions were manually inspected the numbers are exact.

A total of 25853 extensions were downloaded and analyzed. Out of these, about 1400 (5 %) of the existing extensions do invasive modifications to browsed pages, less than 0.2 % of all downloaded extensions take CSP into consideration. This suggests that the currently low adoption of CSP among major web sites makes invasive page modifications relatively rare and modification of the CSP header largely superfluous. If the technology reaches more wide-spread use, this will pose an issue for the large part of these extensions, who would in turn have to adapt. Figure 1 summarizes these results.

Extension Categories. The results have been categorized in two main categories: extensions that invasively modify pages, and extensions that modify the CSP-header. The first category includes extensions that modify pages in a way that is restricted by the CSP policy if one is in place. In the later category we distinguish between different ways in which the CSP policy is modified, restricting, relaxing, replacing, or removing the policy, as can be seen in Fig. 1.

	Specific pages	All pages	Total
Modify page	651	781	1432
Modify CSP	20	25	45
- Restrict	1	4	5
- Relax	11	18	29
- Replace	2	2	4
- Remove	6	1	7

Fig. 1. Extension behavior with respect to page content and CSP modification

The main set of extensions that modify the CSP relaxes the policy to include a few additional domains. This is typically required for the extension to load external resources from these sources. A small number of extensions were found to make the policy stricter. These restrictions are generally made by extensions that allow the user to control what resources should be loaded and allowed to execute. Some extensions replace the policy. Here the new policy were either an "allow all" or "allow none" policy. Lastly, some extensions removed any CSP policy entirely. This allows the extension to add any content without restrictions.

Taking into account that extensions can be applied to different pages differently, the categories are further divided into the set of extensions that perform modifications on a single or small number of pages, and those that apply themselves to every page. The latter set of extensions are more of a concern as they potentially introduce vulnerabilities on every page visited by the user.

Vulnerability Classes. Many extensions rely on being able to inject content in the pages they are applied to. For these extensions a restrictive CSP policy prevents them from functioning as intended. Some of them bypass this restriction by modifying the policy to suit their needs. Extensions that modify the CSP header can inadvertently, or intentionally, weaken the security of a web page. Attacks that would have been prevented by the policy again pose a threat as a result of disabling or relaxing the policy.

We identify three classes of vulnerabilities to potentially expose web pages, and in that also the user, as a direct result of installing an extension that modifies the CSP. All three cases can be mitigated by a solid CSP policy.

Third Party Code Inclusion: As documented by Nikiforakis et al. [24], including third party code weakens the security of the web page in which it is included. A real-life example is the defacement of the Reuters site in June 2014 [31], attributed to "Syrian Electronic Army", which compromised a third-party widget (Taboola [34]). This shows that even established content delivery networks risk being compromised, and these risks immediately extend to all web sites that include scripts from such networks.

Upon loading a page, certain extensions inject and load third party code in the page itself, out of the control of the page. The included third party code can be benign in itself, but broadens the attack surface in an unintended way.

Or, it contains seemingly benign code that may be malicious in the context of a specific page. For external resources the included code may change over time, making it next to impossible to tell for certain what code will actually execute.

A prominent example of such an extension has at present around 1.9 million users. The extension allows the user to select a section of the page to be saved for viewing offline at a later point. In order to do so, it injects a script tag in every browsed page from a domain under the control of the developers. Should the developer have malicious intentions, or the domain be hacked, it would take no effort to exploit every web page visited by their 1.9 million users. By inspecting its code and stated purpose, it is most certainly believed to be benign, yet it displays the vulnerable behavior described above.

Enabling XSS: Recall that CSP is intended to be a "last line of defense" against XSS attacks by optionally disabling inline code and restricting resource origins to a small set of trusted domains. Extensions that modify the CSP policy open up for otherwise prevented attacks, in particular extensions that add the `unsafe-inline` or `unsafe-eval` to the `script-src`, `style-src` or even `default-src` directives. This allows to directly inject arbitrary code into the web page and to execute it.

One high-profile extension, at the time of writing having more than 2.8 million users, allows the user to define scripts that will execute when certain pages are browsed, e.g., to load aggregated information or dynamically set the background color of pages during night time. To allow the user defined scripts full freedom to execute, the extension removes the CSP-header on every browsed page. While perhaps written with good intentions, the extension subjects the user to additional exposure on pages that are normally protected by a CSP policy.

User Profiling: Profiling a user's habits can be a lucrative source of information. A large number of extensions add content that allows its developer to track the user's movements across the Internet, page by page. In an extreme form of tracking, some extensions add Google Analytics to *every* browsed web page with their own Google Analytics ID, enabling comprehensive user profiling.

One extension, with possibly unsuspecting 1.2 million users, stands out in this respect. The official description states that the extension offers an extended set of smileys on a small and specific hardcoded set of web pages. Aside from this, the extension injects itself in every page and adds a Google Analytics script with own ID.

3   Extension Framework Analysis

An important goal for our work is understanding the behavior of extensions in different browsers. Our attention is focused on the current stable release versions of Firefox (v35.0.1), Chrome (v40.0.2214.111), Opera (v27.0.1689.66) and Safari (v8.0.3) whose extensions are especially popular. In particular, we want to know how browsers restrict loading of resources initiated by an extension.

In this respect, we first describe in this section a simple scenario for loading a sequence of different resources which we use to examine the behaviors of the afore mentioned browsers. We then demonstrate the real world implications of the different browser behaviors with a case study on LinkedIn's browser extension Rapportive for Firefox and Chrome.

3.1   Resource Loading Through Content Scripts

There are two ways of loading resources: first, the content is loaded by the extension itself directly into the extension. Second, a target web page is modified to load the content as part of the page itself. In Chrome, e.g., loading a script is done by injecting an HTML element either in the extension's internal background page or the web page, respectively. Loading within an extension is in Chrome restricted through a CSP defined in its manifest file [12]. This CSP is defined by the developer herself and applies only to the extension, not to browsed web pages. Since extension security is already extensively discussed in literature [1,4, 5,7,18,32], we focus on loading of resources in the context of web pages deploying CSP policies.

We have set up a simple scenario in various browsers to test possible content script behavior. We illustrate the setup in Fig. 2. In the first step, an extension injects an HTML script element with a script `script1.js` from a server `server1` into the visited web page's DOM. This causes the browser in a second step to load the script from the given URI. Third, the code of `script1.js` injects yet another HTML script element with a script `script2.js` from a server `server2` into the same web page (step 3). The browser again loads the script from the server (step 4) but this time generates a dialog message indicating that the loading of `script2.js` was successful (step 5).

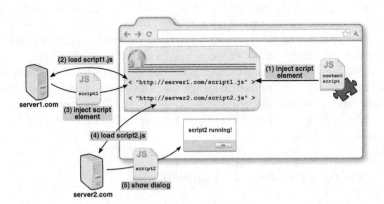

Fig. 2. Experiment set-up for evaluating the behavior of browsers for resource loading initiated by extensions

We have implemented the same scenario for various browsers and have tested the content script behavior of the respective extensions in the presence of CSP. We have chosen `example.com` as our target page. Since it does not define a CSP, we have added the most restrictive policy `default-src'none'` to the HTTP headers. The content scripts of Firefox extensions become part of the web page they are injected in. Consequently, the page's CSP directly applies to the content scripts and the loading of `script1.js` (step 2) is already blocked. We have observed a different behavior for Chrome, Opera and Safari. In these browsers, the content script successfully injects and loads the first script (steps 1-3). Step 4 and 5, however, are not executed since `script1.js` is full part of the web page and thus requesting `script2.js` is blocked by its CSP. Surprisingly, this behavior has been observed regardless of the web page's or the extension's internal CSP. This implies that even with a most restrictive CSP policy for the web page and browser extensions, an extension is always able to send requests to arbitrary servers, potentially leaking sensitive user information. Thus, extensions for these browsers can actively circumvent the CSP security mechanism. We show our results in Fig. 3.

Browser	script1.js form server1.com	script2.js from server2.com
Firefox	blocked	blocked
Chrome/Opera	loaded	blocked
Safari	loaded	blocked

Fig. 3. Different browser behavior for content loading in the scenario from Fig. 2

3.2   Case Study: Rapportive

Rapportive [20] is LinkedIn's browser extension which augments Google's email service Gmail [13] with LinkedIn profile information. This extension modifies the Gmail web page such that when a user composes an email, it automatically tries to look up the recipient's LinkedIn account information and presents it as part of the Gmail web page to the user. More technically, Rapportive dynamically loads scripts from LinkedIn within the extension and injects them through a content script into the Gmail web page. The injected scripts are then responsible for fetching the addressee's LinkedIn profile information.

Rapportive as an extension contains only scripts to dynamically download other scripts from `rapportive.com`, `linkedin.com` and LinkedIn subdomains, which provide the actual functionality of the extension, the fetching and displaying of profile data. In Rapportive for Firefox and for Chrome, user scripts are responsible for injecting HTML elements which load the respective online code into the web page. In case of Firefox, this is done by injecting an HTML `script` element from `rapportive.com`. However since content scripts are treated as part of the web page, Firefox immediately blocks its loading and consequently breaks the functionality of Rapportive. Ironically, users blamed LinkedIn, not Gmail, for breaking the extension [30]. Rapportive for Chrome, on the other hand, has been updated in reaction to Gmail's deployment of a CSP. The extension makes active use of Chromes behavior to load resources directly injected by user scripts and injects an iframe with a resource from `api.linkedin.com`. In accordance with the standard, the CSP of a host page does not apply to the content of an iframe. Therefore, every subsequent loading is done within the iframe.

4   CSP Endorsement

The implementations of Rapportive relies on the fact that the CSP policy of Gmail only restricts script, frame and plugin sources but is otherwise fully permissive, e.g. it does not hinder loaded script code to load resources from servers through, e.g., `XMLHttpRequest`. A web page's CSP policy is, however, most effective only if it is most restrictive. This can conflict with the injection behavior of extensions and eventually break their functionality. In this section we develop a mechanism that allows web applications to deploy a most restrictive CSP policy while guaranteeing the full functionality of browser extensions which inject resources from trusted domains into a web page. We first introduce a general mechanism to allow requesting endorsement of a new CSP by a web server if it is required for the seamless functioning of installed extensions. After that, we present our prototype implementation for Firefox and the Chrome browser.

4.1   Endorsement Workflow

A web browser's main purpose is to request web pages usually via HTTP or HTTPS from a web server. In most major web browsers, these requests as well as their respective responses can be intercepted by extensions. In order to do so, an extension registers a callback function for the respective events, e.g. the event that occurs on receiving a response message. An extension can then modify the HTTP CSP header in any possible way or even remove it from the HTTP response. But since browsers are responsible for calling an extension's registered event handler function, the browser can also analyze their returned data. In particular, a browser can detect when the CSP header in an HTTP response was modified by an extension. On detection, we want to send a message to a specified server to inform about the CSP modification and request a server-side decision if the change is acceptable. This of course requires a server mechanism that allows the processing of CSP endorsement requests. In the following, we describe the workflows and interplay of both, the web browser and the web server, for CSP endorsements.

Browser Improvement. On detection of a CSP header modification, we need to notify the server which accepts and processes CSP endorsement requests. To make use of existing features and to ensure backwards compatibility with the current standard, we use the URI provided in the existing CSP directive `report-uri` for determining the CSP endorsement server. Additionally, we introduce a new keyword 'allow-check' that can be added to the report-uri directive. If this keyword is set, the HTTP server notifies the browser that the report server is capable of handling endorsement request messages. Otherwise, the browser behaves as without the endorsement mechanism in place.

The overall extended browser behavior is as follows: if the CSP is set to be enforced in the browser and the 'allow-check' flag is set in the report-uri directive, the browser sends a CSP endorsement request message to the report server whenever a CSP modification has been detected. In case the flag is missing, it is assumed that the server does not accept endorsement requests and the browser falls back to the current standard behavior. The same fall-back behavior is applied in report-only mode, even when the flag is set. The reason is, because the CSP is not enforced, the extension functionality is not affected by the CSP and endorsement requests are thus redundant. Note that in any case the standard behavior for CSP is not affected at all. For example even when 'allow-check' is defined, reports are sent out for every CSP violation as defined by the standard.

We show the basic workflow for the browser and the endorsement server in Fig. 4. For our protocol to work, we assume a browser that implements our endorsement mechanism and additionally has at least one extension installed that modifies the CSP in the HTTP headers of received messages. The initial situation is that the browser sends a page request to an HTTP server and receives a response including a CSP header. The browser checks the CSP in the received header if the policy is enforced, if it includes the report-uri directive with a report URI and the 'allow-check' directive. In case of a positive check, the browser stores a copy of the received CSP. Subsequently, the browser triggers the *on-headers-received*[2] event which allows the installed extensions to access and modify the header fields. If any of the checks so far has been negative, the browser continues just as without the endorsement mechanism. If however all checks before the event call have been positive, the modified CSP headers are compared with the original ones. When a CSP modification is detected, the browser sends the updated CSP policy to the endorsement server. The server's URI is retrieved from the report-uri of the original CSP to prevent malicious extensions from redirecting endorsement requests to the attacker's server. The endorsement server decides whether to accept or reject the CSP modification and transfers the result back to the browser. In case the modified CSP is accepted, the browser continues with the new policy. In case of rejection, the browser falls back to the initially received CSP and discards the modifications. Any subsequent page handling, e.g. the page rendering, is kept unchanged regardless the server's decision. This means in particular that the CSP is enforced normally and violations are reported as defined by the current standard.

Endorsement Server. The endorsement server is the entity which accepts messages reporting CSP policy modifications and makes the decision if the modified

---

[2] The actual name of the event depends on the browser implementation.

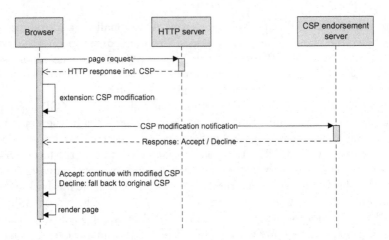

Fig. 4. CSP endorsement workflow

policy should be applied or discarded by the browser. On receiving an endorsement request message, the server must return a message containing either `Accept` or `Reject`. Otherwise, there are no restrictions on how to implement the server's decision making process. However, we suggest a server-side whitelisting as an intuitive and relatively easy to implement concept as the basis for the decision making process. For the remainder of this paper, we assume a server implementation using the whitelisting strategy.

One possible way to obtain a proper whitelist is to evaluate received CSP violation reports and endorsement request messages. A server administrator can, for example, extract the most frequent domains and analyze them in terms of trustworthiness. Depending on the administrator's decision, she can then update the whitelist with the validated domains. This method allows a half-automated and incremental maintenance of the CSP endorsement whitelist.

Optimization. The CSP policy is read out and fixed before page rendering. This implies that the modification and endorsement of CSPs must be finished before page rendering, i.e. the browser must interrupt the page loading process until a decision is made. This blocking behavior comes with an obvious performance and user experience problem. Intuitively, the loading is delayed for a full round-trip time (endorsement request message plus server response) and the computation time for making the decision itself.

To address this issue, we optimize the endorsement approach by introducing a separate whitelist sent in addition to the CSP policy. This allows for decision making in the browser on behalf of the endorsement server. The whitelist reflects in essence the list used for server-side decision making. But since the server-side whitelist might be relatively large, it is sufficient to send only a sublist with the most frequently endorsed trusted domains. Before sending an endorsement request, the browser is now enabled to accept or reject a CSP modification itself based on this list. The main motivation for a separate list and for not including trusted domains directly in the CSP, is to keep the actual CSP policy as restrictive as possible while still informing the browser which URIs are acceptable to be added to the CSP.

We do not require the whitelist to be complete. Therefore, if a modification is rejected by the browser, it must still send the endorsement request to the server because the rejected domains might be included in the complete server-side list. In case the modification is accepted, the whitelist is sufficient and the browser can immediately proceed with processing the page. Thus, for a positive client-side evaluation of CSP modifications the endorsement request must not be sent resulting in an effective performance gain. We evaluate the performance of our prototype implementation and the improvement through the optimization in Sect. 5.

4.2   Prototype Implementation

Browser Modification. We have implemented our approach for Firefox Nightly version 38 [23] and Chrome version 41 [11]. For Firefox, we have adjusted the browser's observer mechanism to detect CSP header modifications, to store the original header for potential later client-side decision making and to subsequently trigger the CSP endorsement mechanism. For Chrome, we have modified the browsers event handler in a way that it triggers our mechanism on returns of the `onHeadersReceived` event. The return value of this API function contains the modified CSP header value. The storage of the initially received header for later comparison is done automatically by Chrome. Both browser implementations have in common that whenever a CSP header has been modified, they check for the CSP enforcement mode and the presence of the 'allow-check' flag in the `report-uri` directive of the original CSP. If both checks succeed, the browsers try too extract the whitelist from the `csp-whitelist` HTTP header. If one is provided, the browsers try to make a decision without any further server requests. However if the check is negative, a CSP endorsement request is sent to the first server given in the `report-uri` directive. On receiving a reply from the server with `Accept`, the browsers proceeds as without our code extension and eventually replace the initially received CSP with the modified version. Otherwise, the CSP header is modified in the usual way.

The implementation of the browser internal decision making expects a JSON formatted whitelist in which the attributes match the directive names and their values define a list of URIs which are accepted to be added to the respective directive in the CSP. Additionally, there can be the attribute `general` which value denotes a list of URIs accepted to be added to any directive in the CSP. If any of the attributes is missing it is treated as it would contain an empty list, i.e. no modification is permitted for the respective directive. We show whitelist examples in Listing 1.1 and 1.2. The first example allows adding https://platform. linkedin.com/ to every directive and defines specific URIs allowed to be added to the `script-src` and the `frame-src` directive, respectively. The second example does not allow any URI to be added to any directive which effectively rejects all

CSP modifications. Note that removing URIs from the policy is not forbidden since that would make the policy only more restrictive but does not introduce any potential security risks.

Listing 1.1. Whitelist policy accepting CSP modifications for Rapportive

```
1  {"general":  ["https://platform.linkedin.com/"],
2
3     "script-src":  ["https://rapportive.com/",
4                      "https://www.linkedin.com/"],
5
6     "frame-src":  ["https://api.linkedin.com/"] }
```

Listing 1.2. Modification acceptance policy rejecting any modification

```
1  {  "general":  [] }
```

Endorsement Server Implementation. We have implemented a CSP modification endorsement server using the Node.js [17] runtime environment. We have implemented the same whitelist behavior as for the client-side decision making in the browser. This means that the server implementation accepts the same JSON formatted whitelist as the server configuration and uses the same algorithm to decide whether to accept or reject a policy modification.

5 Evaluation

We have used Rapportive in a case study to empirically gain experience regarding the applicability and effectiveness of our approach. In the following, we introduce the general setup and report on the results collected from our experiments.

5.1 Experiment Set-Up

For all our experiments we have used a Dell Latitude with an Intel i7 CPU and Ubuntu 14.10 operating system. Since we have implemented our approach for Firefox and Chrome, we have been able to analyze the implementations of Rapportive for both browsers.

In reaction to Gmail's CSP change from report-only to enforcement mode [14], LinkedIn has adjusted Rapportive for Chrome to not conflict with the policy. However, at the time of writing the paper, the Firefox counterpart has no longer been functioning since the dynamic loading of the necessary scripts is blocked by the CSP policy. We have implemented extensions for both browsers with the exact same functionality as Rapportive, except that our extension also modifies the CSP header and adds the necessary URIs to the policy. For convenience, we refer to our extension implementations as "Rapportive" in the remainder of this paper since they behave otherwise exactly the same.

Gmail deploys a CSP policy whitelisting resources for the `script-src`, `frame-src` and the `object-src` directive, respectively. The policy does not include the `default-src` directive which implies that there are no restrictions on other ways of loading content than the just mentioned ones, e.g. loading of content with `XMLHttpRequest`. Violation reports are sent to the URI defined in the CSP's `report-uri` directive. The complete CSP policy which had been in place during our experiments is provided in Appendix A.

The implementation of our approach uses the first report URI as the URI of the CSP endorsement server. In order to conduct experiments with Gmail, we have therefore installed a local proxy server, using mitmproxy [22], which replaces Gmail's report URI with the one of our CSP endorsement server and appends the 'allow-check' keyword. Depending on the experiment, we have also added the `csp-whitelist` header with the respective whitelist. Any other header, including the rest of the CSP header, has been left unchanged and forwarded to the browsers.

As the endorsement server, we have installed our Node.js based server implementation on the same machine as we have run our browser experiments. This allows easier repetition of the experiments and avoids misleading network latencies. At the same time we believe this set-up to be sufficiently expressive for analyzing the general performance of our implementation.

5.2   Results

We have conducted experiments with the three possible execution modes of our approach: sending of endorsement requests with full server-side decision making, receiving the modification acceptance whitelist with full client-side decision making, and mixed decision making, i.e. the additional whitelist sent with the HTTP response is not sufficient for making a client-side decision and an endorsement request is sent subsequently.

In all experiments, Rapportive relaxes Gmail's CSP by adding the three URIs https://rapportive.com/, https://platform.linkedin.com/ and https://www.linkedin.com/ to the `script-src` directive, and to the `frame-src` directive the URI https://api.linkedin.com/.

For each scenario we have measured the time overhead of the overall endorsement process, the browser internal decision making process and the round-trip time needed to request a decision from the CSP endorsement server. The results for both browsers are summarized in Fig. 5 and depict the average times of 200 samples.

Server-Side Decision Making: In our first experiment the endorsement server accepts all CSP modifications using the policy shown in Listing 1.1. The main observation is that the most time is consumed by the server-side processing which itself is almost completely the time for sending and receiving the endorsement messages. For Firefox, the browser internal processing is even so small that it is hardly noticeable. Note that the transmission times are relatively short because all components are located on the same machine. For an external endorsement

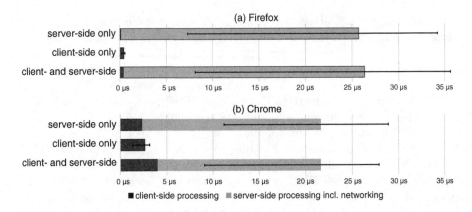

Fig. 5. Time overhead of client-side only, server-side only, and server-and client-side decision making with the respective standard deviations

server the message round-trip times increase accordingly. The results are shown in the first bars of each diagram for the respective browsers in Fig. 5.

Client-Side Decision Making: In the second experiment, the proxy injects the whitelist from Listing 1.1, i.e. it matches exactly the URIs added by Rapportive. The resulting overhead is exactly the time required to come to a client-side decision. For a human user, this delay is not noticeable and the browsing experience is not affected at all. The results are shown in the second bar of each diagram for the respective browsers in Fig. 5.

Mixed Decision Making: The last experiment in essence combines both previous ones. However, the whitelist added by the proxy is not sufficient to come to a positive decision on the client side. As a result, an endorsement request is sent to the server subsequently. The time overhead is, similar to the first experiment, dominated by the communication with the endorsement server. Though in this last scenario the browsers also try to make a decision based on the received `csp-whitelist` header, the measured times are similar to the ones in the second experiment and the delays not noticeable for a human user. The results are shown in the third bars of each diagram for the respective browsers in Fig. 5.

Though the third scenario represents the "worst case", adding the time for the server communication to the time needed for browser internal decision making, the overhead for the client-side decision making is small enough and thus negligible compared to the networking overhead. Therefore, the mixed decision making scenario performs roughly the same as with server-side decision making only and comparably, an insufficient whitelist does not introduce an affecting disadvantage. However, the second experiment shows that the optimization through possible client-side decision making introduces a significant improvement and makes our approach practicable.

6   Related Work

Compared to the CSP standard 1.0 [36], the successor standard 2.0 [37] includes several new features and eliminates certain shortcomings. For example, the new `plugin-types` directive restricts the possible MIME-types of embedded media, the `child-src` replaces the `frame-src` directive to cover both, iframes and workers, or the `frame-ancestor` which attempts to supersede the X-Frame-Options HTTP request header. However, both standards note that they do not intent to influence the workflow of extensions. Our approach only detects policy modifications and is widely independent from the CSP specification. This makes the endorsement mechanism compatible with both CSP 1.0 and CSP 2.0.

Weissbacher et al. [39] measure a low deployment rate of CSP and conduct studies to analyze the practical challenges for deploying CSP policies. They point out that it is difficult to define a policy for a web page that utilizes the full potential of CSP. One of their studies is on inferring policies by running the server in the report-only mode for CSP, collecting the reports and helping developers to define and revise policies. Weissbacher et al. note the conflict of browser extension and web page functionality and suggest exempting extensions from the CSP policies altogether. Our mechanism offers flexibility on the server side, where exempting, denying or selectively granting are all possible alternatives.

Fazzini et al. propose AutoCSP [9], a PHP extension that automatically infers a CSP policy from web pages on HTML code generation. In our approach web pages are queried normally and a server is initially unaware of any installed extensions and possible CSP modifications. In fact, even after a modification, the server does not learn anything about installed extensions but only receives the modified CSP policy for endorsement. In this way, AutoCSP and our approach complement each other.

UserCSP [29] is a Firefox extension that allows a user to manually specify a CSP policy for web pages herself. Besides that this approach requires a certain level of expertise and a certain degree of insight into the web pages functionality, it cannot protect from non-compliant CSP policy modifications by other extensions. Other implementations infer a CSP policy based on the in the browser rendered page [16,33]. These approaches assume an untampered version of the web page, i.e. unmodified by browser extensions or untouched by web attackers. Therefore, they are helpful for finding a suitable CSP policy but the results give no guarantees and should be manually inspected by a web administrator.

The analysis of browser extensions has recently received more attention. The focus lies either on the detection of maliciously behaving browser extensions [1,18,32], infection and protection of extensions from dynamically loaded third party code [4] or the protection of web pages from malicious browser extensions [5,7]. Orthogonal to this, we do not analyze the extension behavior itself but rather observe how extensions affect a web page's security for the particular case of CSP policies.

In a line of work to secure JavaScript in browser extensions, Dhawan and Ganapathy [8] develop Sabre, a system for tracking the flow of JavaScript objects as they are passed through the browser subsystems. Bandhakavi, et al. [2] propose a static analysis tool, VEX, for analyzing Firefox extensions for security vulnerabilities. Heule et al. [15] discuss the risks associated with the trust that browsers provide to extensions and look beyond CSP for preventing privacy leaks by a confinement system.

Other works study the different development kits for extensions of common web browsers [3,7,19]. Though we have observed the effective behavior of content scripts in browsers, our interest has been only common practices of browser extensions on the market and the enforcement of CSP policies in case of content injections through content scripts into web pages.

7   Conclusion

We have investigated the empirical and conceptual aspects of the tension between the power of browser extensions and the CSP policy of web sites. We have shown that the state of the art in today's practice includes both invasive page modification and the modification of the CSP policy itself. This leads to three classes of vulnerabilities: third party code inclusion, enabling XSS, and user profiling. We have presented an empirical study with all free Chrome extension from Chrome web store identifying extensions with over a million of users in each category.

With the goal to facilitate a wider adoption of CSP, we have presented an endorsement mechanism that allows extensions and servers to amend the CSP policy on the fly. We have evaluated the mechanism on both the Firefox and Chrome versions of the popular Rapportive extension, indicating the practicality of the approach.

Following responsible disclosure, we have reported the results of our empirical study to Google. Since the time of the study, three extensions with invasive CSP modifications have been removed from the Chrome store, including the one with 1.2 million users that we discuss in the user profiling category.

Future work includes exploring the possibilities of user involvement in the CSP policy amendments. A GUI notification might be useful to allow ignoring the endorsement rejects from the server.

In this context, an empirical study along the lines of Maggi et al. [21] may reveal the real-world impact of restrictions imposed by CSP policies as described in this paper, together with their perception by human users.

Acknowledgments. Thanks are due to Federico Maggi, Adrienne Porter Felt, and the anonymous reviewers for the helpful comments and feedback. This work was funded by the European Community under the ProSecuToR and WebSand projects and the Swedish research agencies SSF and VR.

A Gmail CSP policy (12. January 2015)

```
script-src https://*.talkgadget.google.com 'self' 'unsafe-
    inline' 'unsafe-eval' https://talkgadget.google.com https:
    //www.googleapis.com https://www-gm-opensocial.
    googleusercontent.com https://docs.google.com https://www.
    google.com https://s.ytimg.com https://www.youtube.com
    https://ssl.google-analytics.com https://apis.google.com
    https://clients1.google.com https://ssl.gstatic.com https:
    //www.gstatic.com blob:;
frame-src https://*.talkgadget.google.com https://www.gstatic.
    com 'self' https://accounts.google.com https://apis.google
    .com https://clients6.google.com https://content.
    googleapis.com https://mail-attachment.googleusercontent.
    com https://www.google.com https://docs.google.com https:
    //drive.google.com https://*.googleusercontent.com https:
    //feedback.googleusercontent.com https://talkgadget.google
    .com https://isolated.mail.google.com https://www-gm-
    opensocial.googleusercontent.com https://plus.google.com
    https://wallet.google.com https://www.youtube.com https://
    clients5.google.com https://ci3.googleusercontent.com;
object-src https://mail-attachment.googleusercontent.com;
report-uri /mail/cspreport
```

References

1. Van Acker, S., Nikiforakis, N., Desmet, L., Piessens, F., Joosen, W.: Monkey-in-the-browser: malware and vulnerabilities in augmented browsing script markets. In: ASIA CCS 2014 (2014)
2. Bandhakavi, S., Tiku, N., Pittman, W., King, S.T., Madhusudan, P., Winslett, M.: Vetting browser extensions for security vulnerabilities with VEX. Commun. ACM **54**(9), 91–99 (2011). doi:10.1145/1995376.1995398
3. Barth, A., Porter Felt, A., Saxena, P., Boodman, A.: Protecting browsers from extension vulnerabilities. In: NDSS (2010)
4. Barua, A., Zulkernine, M., Weldemariam, K.: Protecting web browser extensions from javascript injection attacks. In: ICECCS (2013)
5. Bauer, L., Cai, S., Jia, L., Passaro, T., Tian, Y.: Analyzing the dangers posed by Chrome extensions. In: IEEE CNS (2014)
6. BuiltWith. Content security policy usage statistics. http://trends.builtwith.com/docinfo/Content-Security-Policy. (Accessed Februrary 2015)
7. Chang, W., Chen, S.: Defeat information leakage from browser extensions via data obfuscation. In: Qing, S., Zhou, J., Liu, D. (eds.) ICICS 2013. LNCS, vol. 8233, pp. 33–48. Springer, Heidelberg (2013)
8. Dhawan, M., Ganapathy, V.: Analyzing information flow in javascript-based browser extensions. In: ACSAC (2009)
9. Fazzini, M., Saxena, P., Orso, A.: AutoCSP: Automatically Retrofitting CSP to Web Applications (2015)

10. Google. Chrome web store. https://chrome.google.com/webstore/category/extensions. (Accessed February 2015)
11. Google. Chromium. http://dev.chromium.org/Home. (Accessed February 2015)
12. Google. Content security policy (csp) - google chrome. https://developer.chrome.com/extensions/contentSecurityPolicy. (Accessed February 2015)
13. Google. Gmail. https://www.gmail.com/. (Accessed February 2015)
14. Google. Reject the unexpected - content security policy in gmail. http://gmailblog.blogspot.se/2014/12/reject-unexpected-content-security.html. (Accessed February 2015)
15. Heule, S., Rifkin, D., Stefan, D., Russo, A.: The most dangerous code in the browser. In: HotOS (2015)
16. Javed, A.: CSP AiDer: An automated recommendation of content security policy for web applications. In: Poster at IEEE Symposium on Security & Privacy (2011)
17. Joyent. Node.js. http://www.nodejs.org/. (Accessed February 2015)
18. Kapravelos, A., Grier, C., Chachra, N., Kruegel, C., Vigna, G., Paxson, V.: Hulk: Eliciting Malicious Behavior in Browser Extensions. In: USENIX Sec. (2014)
19. Karim, R., Dhawan, M., Ganapathy, V., Shan, C.: An analysis of the mozilla jetpack extension framework. In: Noble, J. (ed.) ECOOP 2012. LNCS, vol. 7313, pp. 333–355. Springer, Heidelberg (2012)
20. LinkedIn. Rapportive. http://rapportive.com/. (Accessed February 2015)
21. Maggi, F., Frossi, A., Zanero, S., Stringhini, G., Stone-Gross, B., Kruegel, C., Vigna, G.: Two years of short urls internet measurement: security threats and countermeasures. In: WWW (2013)
22. mitmproxy. https://mitmproxy.org/. (Accessed February 2015)
23. Mozilla. Firefox nightly. https://nightly.mozilla.org/. (Accessed February 2015)
24. Nikiforakis, N., Invernizzi, L., Kapravelos, A., Van Acker, S., Joosen, W., Kruegel, C., Piessens, Vigna, G.: You are what you include: Large-scale evaluation of remote javascript inclusions. In: CCS (2012)
25. OWASP. Clickjacking. https://www.owasp.org/index.php/Clickjacking. (Accessed February 2015)
26. OWASP. Content security policy. https://www.owasp.org/index.php/Content_Security_Policy. (Accessed February 2015)
27. OWASP. Cross-site scripting (Accessed February 2015)
28. OWASP. Top 10 2013. https://www.owasp.org/index.php/Top_10_2013. (Accessed February 2015)
29. Patil, K., Vyas, T., Braun, F., Goodwin, M., Liang, Z.: Poster: UserCSP - User Specified Content Security Policies. In: SOUPS (2013)
30. Rapportive : Reviews : Add-ons for firefox. https://addons.mozilla.org/en-US/firefox/addon/rapportive/reviews/. (Accessed February 2015)
31. Syrian Electronic Army uses Taboola ad to hack Reuters (again). https://nakedsecurity.sophos.com/2014/06/23/syrian-electronic-army-uses-taboola-ad-to-hack-reuters-again/
32. Shahriar, H., Weldemariam, K., Zulkernine, M., Lutellier, T.: Effective detection of vulnerable and malicious browser extensions. Comput. Secur. **47**, 66–84 (2014). doi:10.1016/j.cose.2014.06.005
33. Sterne, B.: Content security policy recommendation bookmarklet. http://brandon.sternefamily.net/2010/10/content-security-policy-recommendation-bookmarklet/. (Accessed February 2015)
34. Taboola. Taboola — drive traffic and monetize your site. http://www.taboola.com/. (Accessed February 2015)

35. Can I Use. Content security policy 1.0. (Accessed February 2015)

36. W3C. Csp 1.0. http://www.w3.org/TR/CSP/. (Accessed February 2015)

37. W3C. Csp 2.0. http://www.w3.org/TR/CSP2/. (Accessed February 2015)

38. W3C. World wide web consortium. http://www.w3.org/. (Accessed February 2015)

39. Weissbacher, M., Lauinger, T., Robertson, W.: Why Is CSP failing? trends and challenges in CSP adoption. In: Stavrou, A., Bos, H., Portokalidis, G. (eds.) RAID 2014. LNCS, vol. 8688, pp. 212–233. Springer, Heidelberg (2014)

40. WhiteHat. Content security policy - whitehat security blog. https://blog. whitehatsec.com/content-security-policy/. (Accessed February 2015)

On the Security and Engineering Implications of Finer-Grained Access Controls for Android Developers and Users

Yanick Fratantonio[1]([✉]), Antonio Bianchi[1], William Robertson[2],
Manuel Egele[3], Christopher Kruegel[1], Engin Kirda[2], and Giovanni Vigna[1]

[1] University of California, Santa Barbara, USA
{yanick,antoniob,chris,vigna}@cs.ucsb.edu
[2] Northeastern University, Boston, USA
{wkr,ek}@ccs.neu.edu
[3] Boston University, Boston, USA
megele@bu.edu

Abstract. One of the main security mechanisms in Android is the permission system. Previous research has pointed out that this system is too *coarse-grained*. Hence, several mechanisms have been proposed to address this issue. However, to date, the impact of changes in the current permission system on both end users and software developers has not been studied, and no significant work has been done to determine whether adopting a *finer-grained* permission system would be feasible in practice.

In this work, we perform the first study to explore the practicality of the adoption of *finer-grained* system for the Internet permission. In particular, we have developed several analysis tools that we used to perform an empirical study on 1,227 real-world Android applications. The results of this study provide useful insights to answer the following three conceptual questions: (1) Is it practical to apply fine-grained access control mechanisms to real-world Android applications? (2) How can a system for fine-grained permission enforcement be integrated into the application development and distribution life-cycle with minimal additional required effort? (3) What are the incentives and practical benefits for both developers and end users to adopt a fine-grained permission model? Our preliminary results show that, in general, finer-grained permissions could be practical and desirable for Android applications. In addition, we show how the tools we have developed can be used to automatically generate and enforce security policies, and thus could be used to lower the burden of adoption of finer-grained permission systems.

1 Introduction

Smartphones and tablets have become an important part of our everyday lives. We use these devices to make phone calls, read emails, surf the web, make payments, and manage our schedules. As these devices have access to sensitive user information, they have become attractive targets for attackers, as is evident

© Springer International Publishing Switzerland 2015
M. Almgren et al. (Eds.): DIMVA 2015, LNCS 9148, pp. 282–303, 2015.
DOI: 10.1007/978-3-319-20550-2_15

from the continuous increase in the number and sophistication of the malware that targets these mobile devices [22,36].

The primary security mechanism on the Android platform is the permission system. The purpose of the permission system is to provide user-verifiable and OS-enforced constraints upon the runtime behavior of Android applications. All sensitive operations an application may perform (e.g., accessing the Internet, reading or sending text messages, using the NFC interface) are protected by specific permissions. An application must declare the set of permissions that it requires and these permissions must be approved by a user prior to its installation. At runtime, the Android OS acts as a reference monitor and ensures that the application cannot access resources that would require more permissions than those granted at installation time.

While the Android permission model is useful, it is affected by few weaknesses, one of the most important being that it is too *coarse-grained*. For example, Android's permission model for Internet access follows an all-or-nothing approach: Either an application can access the entire Internet (including any possible domain, IP, or port) or nothing at all. In many cases, however, Android applications only need to communicate with a much smaller set of endpoints. As an example, consider an online banking application that requires Internet access to connect to the bank server for checking the user's balance or making transactions. In this case, it would be sufficient for the application to be able to connect to a small set of domains that are under the control of the bank. Another example is constituted by applications that implement games or simple utilities (e.g., a flashlight): In this scenario, the applications would likely require internet access just to contact an online scoreboard, or for advertisement-related reasons. Hence, also in this scenario, they would need to access to only a small number of network endpoints.

In principle, a coarse-grained permission system does not support secure software development, as it prevents the developers from writing code that adheres to the principle of least privilege [28]: This makes an exploit against a vulnerable application more powerful, as it would have permission to access more resources. Moreover, a coarse-grained permission also makes malicious applications stealthier, as these applications would not need to reveal all the network endpoints at installation time. For these reasons, recent research works proposed a variety of approaches through which a finer-grained permission system can be implemented [9,10,18,21,27,31,33,34]. Even if all these works rely on technically-different solutions, they all share the same high-level goal: enabling developers and end users to specify and enforce fine-grained security policies.

While the technical aspects of finer-grained permission systems have been the focus of much research, the impact of such a modified permission system on users and developers has not been thoroughly studied: To the best of our knowledge, no significant work has been conducted to understand whether the adoption of a finer-grained permission model would be feasible in practice. Motivated by this observation, in this work we investigate on the security and engineering implications of finer-grained access control mechanisms and policies in Android.

To this end, we developed several analysis tools and we used them to perform an empirical study on how real-world applications make use of their permissions. In particular, we focus on the Internet permission, as it is the most widely used and studied permission, and it can be easily adapted to allow finer-grained permission specification.

Our study aims to shed light on the following three conceptual aspects:

- Is it practical to apply fine-grained access control mechanisms to real-world Android applications? (Sect. 4)
- Since specifying finer-grained permissions might be more laborious, how can a system for fine-grained permission enforcement be integrated into the application development and distribution life-cycle with minimal additional required effort? (Sect. 5)
- What are the incentives and practical benefits for both developers and end users to adopt a finer-grained permission model? (Sect. 6)

To perform this study, we first developed a *symbolic executor* (Sect. 3.1) to automatically analyze how applications access network resources. Our tool operates directly on Dalvik bytecode and determines, for each resource access (e.g., opening a network connection), the inputs that influence the resource identifier (e.g., domain names). Using the symbolic executor, we analyzed 1,227 Android applications to study how real-world applications access external resources. We find that a large fraction of the applications in our dataset use a limited set of resources, and that the identifiers of these resources are specified in the application code or in configuration files. This suggests that fine-grained permissions could be a practical mechanism, as application bundles contain the necessary information to extract tight security policies.

However, increasing the granularity of the permission system would require developers to invest more effort in permission selection and policy creation, as, currently, the developer is in charge of manually specifying the permissions needed by her application. Additionally, the task of manually generating a security policy is non-trivial, in the general case. For example, if an application contains a closed-source third-party component, it can be prohibitively difficult for a developer to manually specify an accurate, tight security policy. Thus, another aspect that we studied is if automatic tools (such as the one we developed) can be used to assist developers by automatically generating security policies. To this end, we developed a *policy extractor* component (Sect. 3.2), which processes the results from the symbolic executor into a set of fine-grained permissions required by the application. Our preliminary results are encouraging. In fact, we show that, for the applications in our dataset, the generated policies are small and accurate, and this suggests that the adoption of a finer-grained permission system might be practical for both developers and end users.

Finally, to lower the burden of adoption even more, we developed an *application rewriter* component (Sect. 3.3), which allows both developers and end users to rewrite an Android application (even when its source code is not available) to enforce a given security policy.

In summary, this paper makes the following contributions:

- We developed three different components (namely the symbolic executor, the policy extractor, and the application rewriter) to shed light on important security and engineering implications of finer-grained access controls for Android developers and users. Moreover, we make these tools available upon request. (Sect. 3)
- We performed an empirical study on how real-world Android applications make use of the Internet permission. We used our tool to statically analyze 1,227 applications, and, for 67.5% of them, it was possible to extract a nontrivial constraint (i.e., a constraint different from .*) for all their network accesses. We also performed several additional experiments that show how it is possible to automatically extract high-quality, initial security policies. In fact, we show that these policies are often precise (in 81.6% of the cases, no refinement is necessary), and small (for 87.8% of the applications, the respective policy is constituted by at most two domain names). (Sect. 4)
- We present how the three components we developed can be used in tandem to assist developers and end users, and to lower the burden of adoption of a finer-grained access control model. (Sect. 5)
- We provide a thorough discussion on the impact and the practical benefits that a finer-grained permission system would bring to all the actors in the Android ecosystem—developers and end users. (Sect. 6)

2 Overview

For this paper, we developed three different components, which we then used to gain insights related to the practicality of adopting a finer-grained permission system for the Internet permission. In this section, we provide an overview of these components and we describe their role within the context of this work. Figure 1 shows how the different components work together, and which insights are provided by each of them.

Symbolic Executor. The first component is a static analysis tool for Android applications that performs symbolic execution on Dalvik bytecode. This component computes, at each call site of an API method of interest (that we will refer

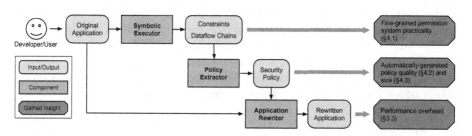

Fig. 1. Overview of the developed components, how they interact, and the insights they provide.

to as a *sink*), an over-approximation of the possible values for this method's arguments. In particular, we explore how Android applications access different sites on the Internet, and we study whether it is feasible to restrict their Internet access without breaking their functionality. We used this tool to perform an empirical study on how real-world applications use network resources. In particular, one of the goals of this experiment is to assess whether network endpoint identifiers are usually statically embedded in the application, or whether they are generated at runtime. This insight directly helps us understanding whether a fine-grained permission system would be practical for real-world deployment. In fact, if in most cases it would be possible to determine these resources only at runtime, it would not be feasible to meaningfully refine a given permission. The technical details of this component are discussed in Sect. 3.1.

Policy Extractor. The second component is a security policy extractor. Intuitively, this component takes as input the information extracted by the symbolic executor, and analyzes them to extract an initial security policy for a given Android application. For the Internet permission, a security policy consists of a set of possible network endpoints associated with their respective call sites. We then performed a series of analyses on these automatically-generated policies to first determine their quality (i.e., how well they "cover" the resources that are accessed at runtime) and their size (i.e., how many entries each policy contains). The technical details of this component are described in Sect. 3.2.

Application Rewriter. The third component we developed is a generic framework to rewrite Android applications. This tool modifies the application's Dalvik bytecode directly, and thus does not need access to source code of the application or any included third party libraries. This component is used to study the feasibility of automatically enforcing a security policy on an Android application by means of bytecode rewriting. In particular, this tool allowed us to understand whether it would be possible to retrofit off-the-shelf Android applications with finer-grained policies. Note how, ideally, the security policies should be enforced by the operating system itself, and hence this component would not be useful. However, in a practical sense, transitioning to finer-grained permissions might be performed incrementally, and hence our tool could be used to lower the burden of adoption. The details of this component are discussed in Sect. 3.3.

3   System Details

In this section, we discuss the technical implementation details of the main components we developed. First, we describe the implementation details of our symbolic executor, and the information it returns. Then, we present the details of the policy extractor component, which automatically extracts (initial) security policies. Finally, we discuss the application rewriter component, which is useful to enforce a security policy on a given Android application.

3.1   Symbolic Executor

Our symbolic execution engine takes an Android APK package as input, unpacks it, and extracts from it a number of artifacts. These include the DEX file with the application code, the application's resources (e.g., localized strings, image files, and UI layouts), and the manifest, which contains information such as the requested permissions as well as the entry points into the application (the main *Activity*, for example).

To disassemble application bytecode, we leverage `dexlib`, a library that is part of the open-source tool `apktool`. Then, the application's Dalvik bytecode is lifted to a custom intermediate representation, on top of which all the subsequent analysis passes operate. Our prototype is entirely written in the Scala language, and consists of a total of 10 K LOC. The next paragraphs describe the technical details of each of the main phase. Note that we do not consider the development of a symbolic execution engine for Dalvik bytecode as a research contribution. In fact, it is not novel (e.g., [20]), and, at least in principle, it would have been possible to re-use existing codebases. However, there are a number of aspects that are peculiar to our analysis. We describe these aspects in the remainder of this section.

Preliminary Steps. As the first step, the tool performs class hierarchy analysis to reconstruct the inheritance relations among the classes defined in the application and in the Android framework. Then, the tool computes the intra-procedural control flow graphs (CFG) of all methods comprising an application, and, finally, it reconstructs the application's super control flow graph (sCFG) by superimposing the inter-procedural call graph over the intra-procedural control flow graphs of each application method.

Forward Symbolic Execution. Our static analyzer performs forward symbolic execution as the basis for the discovery of constraints at privileged API invocations. This analysis step is performed directly on the Dalvik bytecode. Our symbolic execution engine models the semantics of all individual Dalvik virtual machine instructions over an abstract representation of program states, including the current program counter, abstract store, and local environment. Moreover, the invocation of the numerous entry points into the application that are exercised by the Android framework is modeled according to the rules of the various Android components' lifecycles.

Our tool performs a context-sensitive, inter-procedural data flow analysis. In particular, our analysis engine implements a generic framework for generating and merging program contexts. For this work, we opted to implement *2type+1H* type-sensitivity, an approach that has been shown to provide an excellent combination of precision and scalability, especially when analyzing object-oriented programming languages [30].

In addition to characterize which values can reach a specific API method, our static analyzer keeps track of the sources of values. That is, for each argument of an API method of interest, the analysis determines the source method (i.e., a method that reads values from other resources, such as files, network, intents) that "produced" the input value. This kind of information plays a key role when attempting to automatically generate precise security policies.

As an example, consider the snippet of code reported in Fig. 2. In this example, the method `foo` first uses the static string `url` to load a web page, and it stores the content of this web page in `res`. Then, the `extractUrl` method parses

```
public void foo() {
    String url = "http://my.example.com";
    Response res = loadFromUrl(url);
    String newUrl = extractUrl(res);
    Response newRes = loadFromUrl(newUrl);
}
```

Fig. 2. Example of a method that performs multiple "chained" network connections.

res to extract a new URL, which is stored in the newUrl variable. This new URL is subsequently used as a parameter to the second call to loadFromUrl, from which a second web page is downloaded. Intuitively, for the first network access, the application requires some initial information, taken from a string embedded in the program or read from a configuration file. After that, results read from the network are used to construct additional destinations (URLs, domains, etc.).

In this example, the static analysis will easily be able to infer the static value http://my.example.com as the input argument to the first Internet access. However, the analysis will not be able to determine the possible values for the second call to loadFromUrl. Nonetheless, the analysis will correctly identify that the result of the first call to loadFromUrl is the source that produces this input. In fact, even if the value of the second argument is statically unknown, it is ultimately derived from an access to the http://my.example.com URL. In other words, the information about the sources that are responsible for input values allows us to go back to the "root" of an access, thus providing useful information when characterizing even those sinks that cannot be statically constrained.

Symbolic Expressions. The result of the static analysis is a set of *symbolic expressions* that represent an over-approximation of all the possible concrete values that could be used by Android API sources (e.g., the path of a file read by the application) and sinks (e.g., the network domain names contacted by the application), as well as symbolic expressions that denote the origin and the destination of the corresponding values.

Symbolic expressions are essentially constraints (expressed as regular expressions) that represent sets of possible concrete values. One of the most critical objects to model with high fidelity are strings, as they are pervasively used to identify file system paths, network endpoints, or URLs. Our tool tracks not only concrete string values, but also symbolically models string expressions by recognizing string operations performed using well-known Java classes such as StringBuffer and StringBuilder. In case our analyzer cannot statically determine a constraint over the possible values that reach a given sink, then it conservatively returns the most generic constraint, i.e., .*.

Another object of key importance is the *Intent* object, which is extensively used by Android applications to perform inter-component communication, potentially across application boundaries. For example, the startActivity API method specifies an intent argument that contains information necessary for the system to determine which *Activity* should be launched in response to this service request. To correctly model this mechanism, the analysis takes into account how the intent resolution process operates. Moreover, it also models several other *complex* objects, such as the `Bundle` object, a key-value store used to pass auxiliary data along with intent-based service requests. Finally, our analysis models accessory objects such as the `Resource` object, which controls access to static values defined in XML-based resource files packaged with the application.

Android Framework Modeling. Since our tool analyzes applications in isolation from the Android framework codebase, proper models of important Android API methods are required. Mainly, these models allow the static analyzer to identify and track API methods corresponding to information *sources* and *sinks*, and to precisely associate origin and destination information. As a starting point to compile a list of API models, we consulted the resources provided by prior work [3,12,25], and we selected all those API that are relevant to our analysis. In total, our list is constituted by 174 API models.

Another key challenge is the proper modeling of implicit control flow transfers through the Android framework. Callbacks pertaining to the lifecycle of individual components (e.g., Activities) are well documented, and, therefore, it is possible to precisely model them through manual annotations (the authors of FlowDroid [2] followed a similar approach). For the remaining implicit control flow transfers, we used as a starting point the results obtained by EdgeMiner [7] – a system designed to extract a summary of all implicit control flows through the analysis of the Android framework itself.

3.2   Policy Extractor

The *policy extractor* generates an initial security policy based on the information generated by the symbolic execution engine. For the Internet permission, a security policy consists of a set of possible network endpoints, associated with their respective call sites. This section describes how this process works in detail.

The policy extractor first identifies the network endpoints that an application can contact, by analyzing, for all methods that connect to the Internet, the input parameters that specify the destinations of these connections. When the analysis finds that a parameter is one of a set of concrete string values, we extract the domain(s) from these strings, and add them to a set of permissible destinations. When the value is read from a file, we go back to the method that accesses the file, and we try to determine the file name. If a file name can be obtained statically, our component checks whether this file is bundled with the application (and statically exists on disk). If so, the file is parsed for domain names, which are then added to our set. When the destination value used in a network connection is read from the network (as in the example in Fig. 2), we go back to the method that performs the read and try to find the destination for that earlier read (`my.example.com` for the method `foo` in Fig. 2).

We then use this information to generate an initial security policy. In particular, the results from the symbolic execution engine allow us to generate a policy that not only indicates *which* resources are accessed (e.g., a set of network endpoints), but also *where* they are used (e.g., the call site of such sensitive methods). The precision of this information enables the specification of different permission sets for each component of the application. As we discuss in Sect. 6, this has several advantages with respect to the current permission system, which grants the same set of permissions to an application as a whole.

3.3 Application Rewriter

The last component we developed is a tool, called *application rewriter*, that modifies Android applications to enforce fine-grained security policies. The enforcing tool takes as input an APK file and a policy, and it returns as output a modified, self-contained APK where the given policy is enforced. In our context, a security policy specifies a constraint over argument values of a method *sink* at a given program location. Concretely, a policy is specified by a list of tuples in the format `<package_name>:<class_name>:<method_name>:<offset>:<param-idx>:<constraint>`, where the first four parameters uniquely identify a location within the application's code, `<param-idx>` defines the position of the argument for which the constraint is enforced, and `<constraint>` is the value (for example, a domain name) that should be allowed to be contacted by the method invocation at the specified location. Note that all parameters (except `<offset>` and `<param-idx>`) are regular expressions, and hence provide a high-degree of flexibility. Note also that our tool does not need to modify the permissions specified in the application's manifest. Hence, the permission set of the rewritten application is, by design, a strict subset of the original one.

The application rewriter is implemented on top of a generic, low-level API filtering engine. This engine works by disassembling a given application (by using `apktool`), and by modifying its bytecode so that a custom *enforcing method* is invoked just before every invoke instruction that could potentially reach a network sink. In particular, for APIs that accept values representing a URL, the enforcing method matches the actual argument value observed during runtime against any constraints that are specified for this call. If the observed value does not match the constraint, the enforcing method raises an exception, or, if possible, it modifies the values of the parameters that will be used by the subsequent call to the framework API. Moreover, since it is not always possible to precisely model the behavior of specific Android features (e.g., Java classloading, reflection, native code), we provide a choice to selectively disable these functionality at runtime, by placing enforcing code that throws proper Java exceptions when such features are used. We measured the overhead introduced by our instrumentation mechanism, and we determined it to be about $70\,\mu s$ per API invocation, which is negligible.

We note that the technique we used is similar to the ones proposed in concurrently-developed works [4,9,10]. For this reason, in the interest of space, we omit the technical details related to this component, and we prioritize the description of the truly novel aspects of our work. We invite the interested reader to consult these already-published works for more technical details.

4 Practicality Evaluation

In this section, we describe the results we obtained by running our tool over more than a thousand Android applications. We first evaluate the correctness

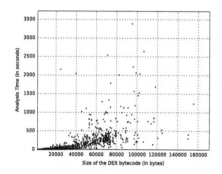

Fig. 3. Relation between DEX bytecode size (in bytes) and analysis time.

Table 1. Constraints for network-related API methods in the analyzed apps.

Category	Frequency
String	1,864
Prefix	209
Complex	620
Low	2,878
Total	5,571

of our approach and its usefulness in supporting the adoption of a finer-grained Internet permission system in Android. Then, we discuss the quality and the correctness of the static analysis results, we show that these results are useful as a starting point for automatically generating security policies, and, finally, we show how, in practice, these policies are often small, suggesting that the adoption of a finer-grained permission system would be practical for both developers and end users.

As a dataset, we selected a corpus of 1,983 applications from a previous random crawl of the official Google Play Store performed in 2012. As our study mainly focuses on the Internet permission, we only considered applications that required such permission. These applications belong to several different categories (e.g., games, entrainment, productivity, shopping, tools), and they are constituted, on average, by hundreds of methods. Their average APK size is about 830 KB, and their bytecode size varies from a few hundreds bytes to about 160 KB, representing small- and medium-sized applications on the market.

We analyzed all these applications with our symbolic execution engine. The experiment was performed on 15 virtual machines with 2 CPUs and 4 GB of memory each, and we set a one hour timeout for the analysis of each application. We successfully completed the analysis for 1,227 applications before the timeout was reached. The average static analysis time was 114.40 s. For these apps, Fig. 3 shows the relation between the size of the application and the analysis time required. As expected, analysis time and size are (loosely) correlated, although there are many outliers.

4.1 Results and Quality of Static Analysis

We first assess the quality of the symbolic expressions that our approach produces for the input arguments of network-related method calls. In the 1,227 apps of our dataset, we identified a total of 5,571 calls to sink methods. Table 1 shows a detailed breakdown of the results. The `String`, `Prefix`, `Complex`, and `Low` labels indicate the quality of the constraint associated to a given sink. In particular,

`String` denotes a set of constant string values; `Prefix` corresponds to a regular expression that represents a prefix (e.g., a URL without parameters); `Complex` refers to more complex regular expressions; and `Low` indicates the most generic (hence less precise) constraint, i.e., `.*`. Our static analyzer was able to determine a non-trivial constraint for 48.3% of the sinks (2,693 out of 5,571). Moreover, many of the extracted constraints provide useful insights into the application's behavior. For example, our analysis is able to extract complex constraints such as `"http://maps.google.com/?lat=\d+&lon=\d+"`.

As an additional experiment, we computed the number of sinks that are either constrained or whose *source* is meaningfully constrained (the *source* value is retrieved by following backward the data flow chains outputted by the symbolic execution engine, as described in Sect. 3.2). This condition is satisfied for 4,538 of the 5,571 Internet sinks. That is, in 81.4% of the cases, it was possible to characterize the *origin* of the value (either directly or indirectly) that reaches the security-sensitive API. This indicates that even if it is sometimes challenging to statically constrain a network sink, it is often possible to at least statically characterize the value of its *source* (as in the example provided in Fig. 2). This observation highlights an interesting pattern adopted by real-world applications: for the first network access, the application requires some initial information (taken from a string embedded in the program or read from a configuration file), and this information is then used as a starting point for determining the target of the other network sinks.

If we cluster these statistics in terms of number of applications (instead of number of sinks), we obtain similar results: our tool was able to completely constrain 483 applications (39.4%), while this number grows to 828 (67.5%) if the *source* information is taken into account. These results support the idea that it is often feasible to automatically refine the set of permissions requested by a given app, and that the automatic generation of policies is practical (as we will discuss in more detail in the next section).

Comparison with Dynamic Traces. To check the correctness of our static analysis, we first executed all the 1,227 applications in an instrumented emulator (we used the Google Monkey [15] to interact with the application under test, and we set a timeout of two minutes), and we extracted the dynamic traces, which consist in the list of methods that are invoked during the dynamic analysis, accompanied by detailed information about their arguments.

We first assessed the accuracy and the coverage of our static analysis tool by comparing the edges of the call graph generated by the static analysis with the call sequences contained in the dynamic traces. The rationale behind this experiment is that, since the static analysis is designed to produce an over-approximation of the actual program runs, we expect that all the code that is run dynamically was also analyzed statically. We found that ~97 % of the edges in the dynamic call graph are correctly covered by the static analysis. The sole reason for the missing edges is that some Dalvik instructions can implicitly throw an exception (for example, the `check-cast` instruction throws an exception at runtime in case of a type mismatch) for which our symbolic execution engine currently lacks support. However, since the static code coverage is high (as discussed in the *Code Coverage* paragraph below) and only very few edges are missing, we believe that these minor imprecisions do not undermine the validity of our analysis.

In a second step, we evaluated the correctness of the constraints that are statically extracted. To this end, we compared the statically-extracted Internet constraints with the actual argument values recorded in the dynamic traces. In total, we observed 6,259 dynamic invocations of 1,311 distinct sinks that are related to the Internet permission. The static analysis produced expressions for 1,307 of these sinks (4 sinks are not reached due to missing exception support). In all 1,307 instances the constraints returned by the static analysis covered all observed values, as expected.

Code Coverage. We estimated the static code coverage by counting the number of methods that are reached by the static analyzer. On average, our approach has a static code coverage of ~95 %. Similarly, we extracted the dynamic method coverage from the execution traces, and it resulted to be ~25 %.

Ideally, the dynamic code coverage would have been higher. As a future step, we could use more powerful GUI exploration techniques [26,35] to increase the dynamic code coverage. However, we do not expect significant differences in the results, as state-of-the art dynamic exploration techniques achieve only slightly-higher coverage (e.g., 27 %–33 %). Moreover, to the best of our knowledge, this is the first static analysis work targeting the Android platform that extensively evaluates the static analysis results with dynamically-generated execution traces.

4.2 Quality of the Security Policies

In the next step, we wanted to determine whether the static values extracted by our approach are useful to automatically generate security policies. To this end, we used the output from the static analysis to automatically build (initial) security policies for all of them. For this experiment, the policies are automatically built by our policy extractor component (described in Sect. 3.2), and by considering the set of second-level DNS names for each statically-determined network endpoint. We then used the previously-collected dynamic traces to check what would have happened if we had used our rewriting tool to enforce the policies.

We found that for 1,002 (81.6%) of the applications, our security policies would allow all network accesses that these applications attempt during runtime. In other words, in all these cases, it was possible to statically infer the set of domain names that the application would contact during runtime. In 972 cases, the domain names could be extracted from information contained in the application code base. This indicates that most developers hard-code all domain names into their programs. In 30 cases, it was necessary to get the domains from a configuration file, but the name of this configuration file was specified in the binary. Note that there are a handful of cases in which the dynamic trace shows that a piece of JavaScript is dynamically evaluated by the application. We assume that these scripts do not contact any domain outside our policies, and a quick manual investigation confirmed this assumption.

Table 2. Number of explicit authorizations required when enforcing the automatically-generated security policies.

Number of required explicit authorizations	Frequency	Percentage
No interaction required	1,002	81.66%
One explicit authorization	180	14.67%
Two explicit authorizations	42	3.43%
Three explicit authorizations	2	0.16%
Four explicit authorizations	1	0.08%
More than four explicit authorizations	0	0%
Total	1,227	100%

Note how this property holds not only for sinks contained in the main core application, but also for third-party libraries such as the popular AdMob advertisement library from Google. This might be surprising at a first glance, but we found that these Ad libraries actually only contact a few Google-related domain names (such as `admob.com` and `googleadservices.com`) to fetch their content. This makes sense because it allows Google to easily control the content that is displayed on millions of Android devices.

Policy Violations. We also investigated the 225 cases where our automatically-extracted policy was violated. We manually analyzed a random sample of 10% of these applications (23 in total) to have a better understanding of the reasons. We found that in 7 cases, the domains are actually present in the bytecode, but the analysis is not precise enough to extract the proper values. In 12 additional cases, the domains are in configuration files, but again, our approach is not precise enough to extract the values (and related file names) automatically. Only in 4 cases do applications load destination domains from the network, and these domains are not present anywhere in the program or resources. This confirms that, in most cases, the developer seems to have a clear understanding of the Internet resources that should be accessed, and our approach is a useful system to automatically infer initial policies. In the 19 cases above, a developer could easily add the missing domains to the policy manually.

Alternatively, an application could be modified to be paused if a policy violation is detected. During the pause, the user would be prompted whether she wants to permit the violating access. Existing research has established that frequent authorization prompts lead to warning fatigue [6]. That is, users tend to ignore and blindly grant authorization requests if such requests are too frequent.

To evaluate how often the user would be prompted for authorization due to a policy violation, we analyzed, once again, the dynamic execution traces from Sect. 4.1. Table 2 reports the breakdown of the results: user interaction would be required only for 18.4% of the applications; for 96.3% of the applications, the user would be prompted at most once; and no application would require more than four distinct authorizations. Because the user only makes these authorization decisions once per application lifetime, we believe that the number of authorization prompts is well within reasonable bounds.

Table 3. Size of the automatically-extracted security policies.

Policy size	Frequency	Percentage
At most one domain name	956	77.91 %
At most two domain names	1,077	87.78 %
At most three domain names	1,151	93.81 %
At most four domain names	1,175	95,76 %
More than four domain names	52	4.24 %
Total	1,227	100 %

As a final consideration, we note that even if automatically enforcing the security policies extracted by our approach works in a surprisingly-high number of cases, such an approach does not always makes sense. Consider, for example, a web browser application: in this case, the application would need to be able to access arbitrary domain names specified by the user, which means that it would be impossible to extract all the network endpoints through static analysis only.

4.3   Size of the Security Policies

As a final step, we investigated whether the adoption of the proposed fine-grained permission system would be practical. The intuition is that most of the applications access a limited set of resources (hence this approach would make sense), but what if, in practice, these policies are prohibitively large and cause too much overhead for developers to maintain or end users to review?

To answer this question, we analyzed the policies extracted for the 1,227 applications. Table 3, which reports the breakdown of the results, shows how the majority of the applications (87.8%) access at most two domain names. Frequently, one domain name is usually linked to a domain controlled by the owner of the application, while the other one is related to an advertisement framework. A prolific source for additional domains are widgets from popular social networks. This observation becomes apparent when we look at the most frequently accessed domain names. In fact, the domain name that is accessed the most is related to the AdMob advertisement framework, while the other most frequently-accessed domain names are related to well-known social platforms, such as Facebook, Google, and Twitter.

4.4   Discussion and Limitations

In the previous sections, we discussed the results we obtained by using our tools to analyze over a thousand Android applications. We believe that our preliminary results are encouraging, as they suggest that it would be possible to adopt a finer-grained permission system. In fact, the size of the extracted policies is often small, and the domain names that are accessed the most are easily linkable to known companies. As a possible additional step to lower the burden of adoption even further, it might make sense to integrate our system with an approach based on whitelisting, so that *trusted* domain names (such as the ones related to well-known advertisement frameworks and popular social platforms) could be automatically approved.

That being said, we acknowledge that our study suffers from few limitations. For example, while we believe that our dataset contains a sizeable number of applications, the current app store features many more applications (according to [32], more than a million). Thus, it is unknown whether our results generalize to the entire market. Another limitation relates to the fact that, for this study, we did not consider large and complex applications (e.g., the Facebook app) due to the fact that our analysis, at its core, uses symbolic execution, which is known to be affected by scalability issues. Finally, a drastic change in how developers implement Android applications (e.g., tunneling all network traffic through a single network endpoint) could affect the applicability of the fine-grained policies extracted by our analysis. Nonetheless, we believe that our preliminary results already offer useful insights related to an important security aspect of the Android framework. Moreover, the analysis primitives we developed can be used as building blocks to study further security aspects of Android applications that extend beyond fine-grained permissions.

5 Viable Workflows

In this section, we describe how the various actors participating in the Android ecosystem, namely developers and end users, would use a finer-grained permission system, and how they could take advantage of the components we developed. Even if the two categories of actors would use the system for different reasons, they would follow the generic, high-level workflow depicted in Fig. 1: the actor would use our components to statically analyze her application, generate initial security policies, and enforce them.

A developer would take advantage of a fine-grained permission system by writing a security policy to be enforced. Note that writing such a policy might not be a trivial task if external libraries are added, especially if their source code is not available. This is because it can be problematic to understand the full set of resources (e.g., contacted URLs) accessed by these libraries. Moreover, a developer might decide to enforce fine-grained permissions on a third-party component if it is not fully trusted (not only it could be malicious, but, more likely, it could open the main application to security vulnerabilities). In the case that the task of manually compiling a security policy is too burdensome, the developer could take advantage of our symbolic executor and the policy extractor components to automatically extract an initial security policy. Then, the developer could review it and adapt it to her own needs, if possible. At this point, the developer could use our application rewriting tool to rewrite the application so that the security policy is enforced.

The other actor of the system, the user, can then download the rewritten app and review the policy before deciding whether to install the application.

For instance, a user might be comfortable installing an app that only requires the ability to contact a single domain name managed by the application's developer, but she might prefer not to install an application that requires unconstrained Internet permissions. Even in this case, the user could take advantage of the symbolic executor and the policy extractor components to automatically determine an initial security policy, which can be then modified and used as input to the enforcing component.

Note how, in both scenarios, the usage of the enforcing component is superfluous on a modified version of Android that enforces fine-grained security policies. However, on standalone Android versions, our enforcing tool will benefit the community and lower the burden of adoption of fine-grained policies.

6   Security Implications and Benefits

A fine-grained permission system in Android would introduce a variety of significant security improvements that affect all the actors of the Android ecosystem. This section describes these aspects in detail.

Implications for Benign Applications. Several studies showed that Android applications often suffer from confused deputy vulnerabilities [8,11,14,16,23]. While a finer-grained permission system does not eradicate confused deputy vulnerabilities, it significantly reduces the negative impacts of their exploitation. Consider, for example, an application accompanied by a fine-grained policy that identifies all legitimate network endpoints. Even if this application suffers from a confused deputy vulnerability, an attacker could exploit it only to communicate with the endpoints explicitly listed in the policy – a vast improvement over the current unrestricted system.

Another security benefit of a fine-grained permission system is that it allows the specification of a different permission set for each component. This feature is useful whenever the application contains third-party libraries that often require different permissions than the core application. Consider, as an explanatory example, a gaming application that requires the Internet permission for connecting to a game-related scoreboard and to include advertisement. This application could be modified so that the game-specific component would be able to access only the game-related network endpoint, while the advertisement library would be able to access only the advertisement-related one. Note that this use case is currently not supported by the Android permission model. Instead, the current Android permission system grants the same set of permissions to an application as a whole, and all components within the application consequently enjoy the same privileges, thus violating the principle of least privilege.

Implications for Malicious Applications. A widely deployed finer-permission system would place additional constraints on malicious applications that declare excessive permissions. In fact, a malicious application would need to either explicitly specify the domain name of the server under their control, or ask for *unconstrained* network access: both options would make malicious applications less stealthy, as they would need to *reveal* part of their behavior. The security policy declared by an application could also be used as an additional feature to improve the accuracy of existing malware detection tools (e.g., [1,11,17,38]).

Moreover, this explicit mapping between applications and their network endpoints would make information related to the domain names more useful: for example, if a domain name is found to be part of malicious activities, it would then be trivial to identify and flag all those applications that are somehow related to that domain name.

Implications for End Users. A finer-grained permission system would allow a security-conscious user to make more informed decisions about whether it is safe to install a given Android application. These users would be more aware of the risks associated with installing an application that requests *unconstrained* network access, as such permission should be required only by very specific types of applications (e.g., web browsers). Moreover, in case the application would only require access to well-known domain names, the user would be able to install and use the app with greater confidence. We believe that a finer-grained permission system would benefit non-security-conscious users as well. In fact, even if they might not be able to take informed decisions on whether an application is suspicious or not, they would still (indirectly) benefit from the advantages described above. One last aspect to be considered when extending the permission system is that such extension might lead to confusion and, therefore, misuse. However, we note that the new extension would enforce, by design, a set of permissions that is stricter than the original one. Thus, in this context, confusion and misusage would not have negative security repercussions.

As a final consideration, it is worth noting that many of these benefits can be enjoyed only when the finer-grained policies are enforced by the end user or by the system. In fact, in the alternative scenario where the developer herself is in charge of enforcing a given security policy, one would need to assume a trust relationship, which, in most cases, is not realistic.

7   Related Work

Recent research efforts have focused on the analysis and improvement of the Android permission system. For example, Barrera et al. [5] observed that some Android permissions are overly broad (included the Internet permission). Other works aim to understand how Android applications use the current permission system. For example, Felt et al. presented Stowaway [12], and by using it, they found that many Android applications were over-privileged. Based on this observation, several research works [4,9,10,34] developed tools to rewrite applications to enforce finer-grained security policies. Other works proposed Apex [24], AppFence [19], and SEAndroid [29], which provide additional privacy controls for Android through user-defined security policies, data shadowing, and exfiltration blocking. More recently, researchers proposed ASM [18], a framework that provides a programmable interface for defining new reference monitors, Copper-Droid [31], which relies on syscall monitoring to enforce finer-grained policies, and DeepDroid [33], which aims to achieve the same goal by dynamic memory instrumentation. Our work is complementary to all these: in fact, the main goal of this work is to shed light on the security and practicality implications of finer-grained access control.

Several recent research works focus on discovering vulnerabilities within benign Android applications [16,23,37]. All these works discover a variety of serious vulnerabilities in real-world applications. These findings indicate that Android developers are often not aware of the many peculiarities of the Android framework, thus leading to severe vulnerabilities in real-world applications that, in most of the cases, lead to a confused deputy problem. As we discussed in Sect. 6, a finer-grained permission system would greatly minimize the threat posed by such confused deputy vulnerabilities.

Felt et al. [13] evaluate two different application permission systems: the Android permission system and the mechanism that is implemented for Chrome extensions. As opposed to the current Internet permission on Android, the permission system for Chrome allows the developer to narrowly define the resources (URLs specified as regular expressions) an extension can communicate with. An analysis of 714 popular Chrome extensions shows that for 60 % of the extensions, the developers explicitly list a narrow set of domains their extension can interact with. This study clearly shows that developers are willing to use a finer-grained permission system, if available.

A work that is close, in principle, to ours is by Jeon et al. [21]. In their work, the authors develop a simple analysis tool that aims to characterize how Android applications use the Internet permission: for their work, the authors developed a best-effort static analysis tool that first consults the application's string pool, it applies pattern matching on all the strings to extract those that *look like* URLs, and it then performs basic constant propagation. On the one hand, their overall goal is aligned with one of ours. In fact, as part of their experiments, the authors perform a study to characterize how many network resources are generally contacted by each application, with the goal of showing that this number is usually small and that, consequently, the adoption of finer-grained security policies is practical. On the other hand, the authors implemented an approach based on a best-effort, simple static analysis that is affected, by design, by false negatives. In particular, the authors specifically state that when their tool cannot statically constrain a network sink, such sink is ignored, instead of conservatively report a .* constraint, as our tool does.

This important limitation undermines the validity of their results, and leaves the "Is a finer-grained permission system practical?" question unanswered. In fact, consider, as an example, a browser application, which of course cannot be statically constrained (as the network endpoints to be contacted are chosen at runtime by the user). In this case, their tool would ignore all the unconstrained network sinks, and their results would suggest that it is possible to statically constrain the given application, which is incorrect. Instead, our approach would correctly return a .* constraint, the application under analysis would be correctly flagged as non-constrainable, and we would correctly conclude that a finer-grained permission system would not be practical in that case. In summary, while their results provide some interesting data, we believe they cannot be used to understand the practicality of a finer-grained permission system.

Moreover, the authors themselves point out that, to address the limitation of their work, one would need to perform inter-procedural analysis, modeling the heap, and modeling the Android Intent system. The static analysis tool implemented in our symbolic executor component precisely models all such aspects and it is designed to return an over-approximation of all the possible values that reach the *sink* methods.

8   Conclusion and Future Work

In this paper, we studied the security and engineering implications of a finer-grained permission system in Android. In particular, we focused on the Internet permission, and we developed several different analysis tools to shed light on the following three aspects: (1) Is it practical to adopt fine-grained access control mechanisms to real-world Android applications? (2) How can such a system be integrated into the application development and distribution life-cycle with minimal additional required effort? (3) What are the incentives and security benefits in adopting them?

Our preliminary results suggest that a finer-grained Internet permission would be practical. In fact, we found that applications in our sample typically require access to only a small set of resources, and these resources are explicitly referenced in the application's code or configuration files. Finally, our findings suggest that a finer-grained permission model for Android would entail a series of security benefits without overburdening developers or end users.

While our work mainly focuses on the Internet permission, it would be interesting to explore whether the adoption of a finer-grained permission system would be practical to protect other types of resources, such as file-system access, location information, or the user's contact list. We believe this constitutes a very interesting and important direction for future work.

Acknowledgements. We thank the anonymous reviewers and our shepherd Simin Nadjm-Tehrani for their valuable feedback. The work is supported by National Science Foundation (NSF) under grant CNS-1408632, and by Secure Business Austria. This work is also sponsored by DARPA under agreement number FA8750-12-2-0101. The U.S. Government is authorized to reproduce and distribute reprints for Governmental purposes notwithstanding any copyright notation thereon. The views and conclusions contained herein are those of the authors and should not be interpreted as necessarily representing the official policies or endorsements, either expressed or implied, of NSF, DARPA, or the U.S. Government.

References

1. Arp, D., Spreitzenbarth, M., Malte, H., Gascon, H., Rieck, K.: Drebin: effective and explainable detection of android malware in your pocket. In: Proceedings of the Symposium on Network and Distributed System Security (NDSS) (2014)
2. Arzt, S., Rasthofer, S., Fritz, C., Bodden, E., Bartel, A., Klein, J., Le Traon, Y., Octeau, D., McDaniel, P.: FlowDroid: precise context, flow, field, object-sensitive and lifecycle-aware taint analysis for android apps. In: Proceedings of the ACM SIGPLAN Conference on Programming Language Design and Implementation (PLDI) (2014)
3. Au, K.W.Y., Zhou, Y.F., Huang, Z., Lie, D.: PScout: analyzing the android permission specification. In: Proceedings of the ACM Conference on Computer and Communications Security (CCS) (2012)
4. Backes, M., Gerling, S., Hammer, C., Maffei, M., von Styp-Rekowsky, P.: AppGuard – enforcing user requirements on android apps. In: Piterman, N., Smolka, S.A. (eds.) TACAS 2013 (ETAPS 2013). LNCS, vol. 7795, pp. 543–548. Springer, Heidelberg (2013)
5. Barrera, D., Kayacik, H.G., Oorschot, P.V., Somayaji, A.: A methodology for empirical analysis of permission-based security models and its application to android. In: Proceedings of the ACM Conference on Computer and Communications Security (CCS) (2010)
6. Böhme, R., Grossklags, J.: The security cost of cheap user interaction. In: Proceedings of the Workshop on New Security Paradigms Workshop (NSPW) (2011)
7. Cao, Y., Fratantonio, Y., Bianchi, A., Egele, M., Kruegel, C., Vigna, G., Chen, Y.: EdgeMiner: automatically detecting implicit control flow transitions through the android framework. In: Proceedings of the Symposium on Network and Distributed System Security (NDSS) (2015)
8. Chin, E., Felt, A.P., Greenwood, K., Wagner, D.: Analyzing inter-application communication in android. In: Proceedings of the International Conference on Mobile Systems, Applications, and Services (MobiSys) (2011)
9. Davis, B., Chen, H.: RetroSkeleton: retrofitting android apps. In: Proceedings of the International Conference on Mobile Systems, Applications, and Services (MobiSys) (2013)
10. Davis, B., Sanders, B., Khodaverdian, A., Chen, H.: I-ARM-Droid: a rewriting framework for in-app reference monitors for android applications. In: IEEE Mobile Security Technologies (MoST) (2012)
11. Enck, W., Ongtang, M., McDaniel, P.: On lightweight mobile phone application certification. In: Proceedings of the ACM Conference on Computer and Communications Security (CCS) (2009)
12. Felt, A.P., Chin, E., Hanna, S., Song, D., Wagner, D.: Android permissions demystified. In: Proceedings of the ACM Conference on Computer and Communications Security (CCS) (2011)
13. Felt, A.P., Greenwood, K., Wagner, D.: The effectiveness of application permissions. In: Proceedings of the USENIX Conference on Web Application Development (WebApps) (2011)
14. Felt, A.P., Wang, H.J., Moshchuk, A., Hanna, S., Chin, E.: Permission re-delegation: attacks and defenses. In: Proceedings of the USENIX Security Symposium (USENIX Security) (2011)
15. Google: UI/Application Exerciser Monkey. http://developer.android.com/tools/help/monkey.html

16. Grace, M., Zhou, Y., Wang, Z., Jiang, X.: Systematic detection of capability leaks in stock android smartphones. In: Proceedings of the Symposium on Network and Distributed System Security (NDSS) (2012)
17. Grace, M., Zhou, Y., Zhang, Q., Zou, S., Jiang, X.: RiskRanker: scalable and accurate zero-day android malware detection. In: Proceedings of the International Conference on Mobile Systems, Applications, and Services (MobiSys) (2012)
18. Heuser, S., Nadkarni, A., Enck, W., Sadeghi, A.R.: ASM: a programmable interface for extending android security. In: Proceedings of the USENIX Security Symposium (USENIX Security) (2014)
19. Hornyack, P., Han, S., Jung, J., Schechter, S., Wetherall, D.: These aren't the droids you're looking for: retrofitting android to protect data from imperious applications. In: Proceedings of the ACM Conference on Computer and Communications Security (CCS) (2011)
20. Jeon, J., Micinski, K.K., Foster, J.S.: SymDroid: symbolic execution for dalvik bytecode. Technical report CS-TR-5022, University of Maryland, College Park (2012)
21. Jeon, J., Micinski, K.K., Vaughan, J.A., Fogel, A., Reddy, N., Foster, J.S., Millstein, T.: Dr. Android and Mr. Hide: fine-grained permissions in android applications. In: Proceedings of the ACM CCS Workshop on Security and Privacy in Smartphones and Mobile Devices (SPSM) (2012)
22. Lookout: 2014 Mobile Threat Report ((2014)). https://www.lookout.com/resources/reports/mobile-threat-report
23. Lu, L., Li, Z., Wu, Z., Lee, W., Jiang, G.: CHEX: statically vetting android apps for component hijacking vulnerabilities. In: Proceedings of the ACM Conference on Computer and Communications Security (CCS) (2012)
24. Nauman, M., Khan, S., Zhang, X.: Apex: extending android permission model and enforcement with user-defined runtime constraints. In: Proceedings of the ACM Symposium on Information, Computer and Communication Security (AsiaCCS) (2010)
25. Rasthofer, S., Arzt, S., Bodden, E.: A machine-learning approach for classifying and categorizing android sources and sinks. In: Proceedings of the Symposium on Network and Distributed System Security (NDSS) (2014)
26. Rastogi, V., Chen, Y., Enck, W.: AppsPlayground: automatic security analysis of smartphone applications. In: Proceedings of the ACM Conference on Data and Application Security and Privacy (CODASPY) (2013)
27. Russello, G., Jimenez, A.B., Naderi, H., van der Mark, W.: FireDroid: hardening security in almost-stock android. In: Proceedings of the Annual Computer Security Applications Conference (ACSAC) (2013)
28. Saltzer, J., Schroeder, M.: The protection of information in computer systems. Proc. IEEE **63**(9), 1278–1308 (1975)
29. Smalley, S., Craig, R.: Security enhanced (SE) android: bringing flexible MAC to android. In: Proceedings of the Symposium on Network and Distributed System Security (NDSS) (2013)
30. Smaragdakis, Y., Bravenboer, M., Lhoták, O.: Pick your contexts well: understanding object-sensitivity. In: Proceedings of the ACM Symposium on Principles of Programming Languages (POPL) (2011)
31. Tam, K., Khan, S.J., Fattori, A., Cavallaro, L.: CopperDroid: automatic reconstruction of android malware behaviors. In: Proceedings of the Symposium on Network and Distributed System Security (NDSS) (2015)

32. Viennot, N., Garcia, E., Nieh, J.: A measurement study of Google play. In: Proceedings of the ACM International Conference on Measurement and Modeling of Computer Systems (SIGMETRICS) (2014)
33. Wang, X., Sun, K., Wang, Y., Jing, J.: DeepDroid: dynamically enforcing enterprise policy on android devices. In: Proceedings of the Symposium on Network and Distributed System Security (NDSS) (2015)
34. Xu, R., Saidi, H., Anderson, R.: Aurasium: Practical policy enforcement for android applications. In: Proceedings of the USENIX Security Symposium (USENIX Security) (2012)
35. Zheng, C., Zhu, S., Dai, S., Gu, G., Gong, X.: SmartDroid: an automatic system for revealing UI-based trigger conditions in android applications. In: Proceedings of the ACM CCS Workshop on Security and Privacy in Smartphones and Mobile Devices (SPSM) (2012)
36. Zhou, Y., Jiang, X.: Dissecting android malware: characterization and evolution. In: Proceedings of IEEE Symposium on Security and Privacy (S&P) (2012)
37. Zhou, Y., Jiang, X.: Detecting passive content leaks and pollution in android applications. In: Proceedings of the Symposium on Network and Distributed System Security (NDSS) (2013)
38. Zhou, Y., Wang, Z., Zhou, W., Jiang, X.: Hey, you, get off of my market: detecting malicious apps in official and alternative android markets. In: Proceedings of the Symposium on Network and Distributed System Security (NDSS) (2012)

Provenance and Data Sharing

Identifying Intrusion Infections via Probabilistic Inference on Bayesian Network

Yuan Yang, Zhongmin Cai$^{(\boxtimes)}$, Weixuan Mao, and Zhihai Yang

Ministry of Education Key Lab for Intelligent Networks and Network Security,
Xi'an Jiaotong University, Xi'an, Shaanxi, China
{yuanyang,zmcai,wxmao,zhyang}@sei.xjtu.edu.cn

Abstract. Identifying whether system objects are infected or not on a compromised system is a complex and error-prone task. Most existing solutions follow a traditional causal analysis method which tries to precisely correlate potential infected objects with the entry point of an intrusion, also known as *intrusion root*, based on dependencies between objects. However, the entanglement of both legitimate, and malicious, actions makes it difficult to pinpoint the intrusion root and establish precise dependencies. In this paper, we propose a novel method to identify intrusion infections with a small number of observed intrusion symptoms and legitimate objects. This method does not require the identification of an accurate intrusion root and precise dependencies. In particular, we propose a new form of dependency network to encode dependencies of information flows and take temporal information into account. It captures potential propagation paths of an intrusion from a system-wide perspective. Then, based on the temporal dependency network, we develop a probabilistic Bayesian network model to characterize uncertainties of propagating infections along the dependency edges. Finally, we employ a probabilistic inference method to identify the intrusion infections with the help of only a few observed intrusion symptoms and legitimate objects. Extensive experimental results in synthetic and real-world scenarios demonstrate that our method is capable of identifying the infected objects even when the intrusion root is undetermined and dependencies are coarse-grained.

Keywords: Bayesian network · Probabilistic inference · Intrusion analysis

1 Introduction

Protecting computer systems from being compromised is very difficult if not impossible, due to the complexity of computer systems, the negligence of computer users, and the creativity of attackers. When faced with an intrusion, the most vital tasks for the computer users are recovering from the damage caused by an intrusion and fixing the vulnerability that allowed the break-in of an attacker. All these tasks require accurate post-intrusion analysis to identify system objects such as processes and files that have been infected by an intrusion.

© Springer International Publishing Switzerland 2015
M. Almgren et al. (Eds.): DIMVA 2015, LNCS 9148, pp. 307–326, 2015.
DOI: 10.1007/978-3-319-20550-2_16

However, identifying damages or infections of an intrusion has proven to be a challenging task due to the entanglement of both legitimate, and malicious, actions. Most of the entanglements are related to the infection of shared files. For example, legitimate actions may falsely depend on malicious activities by accessing infected files, and the situation will become more complicated if these files are heavily shared. Additionally, an object's time-varying security state can also cause entanglements. For example, a running process is temporarily hijacked as a "springboard" to infect other objects, then it is released and returns to normal running afterwards. As a result, this process's subsequent legitimate actions may appear to be dependent on its previous malicious actions.

To sort out these entanglements automatically and efficiently, many solutions have been proposed. Most of these solutions follow a traditional causal analysis method which tries to correlate all potential infected objects with the entry point of an intrusion, also known as *intrusion root*, based on the direct and indirect dependency relations between them. With a known intrusion root, which can be located by external methods like Backtracker [1], these solutions have focused primarily on exploiting various logging or tracking techniques [2–6] or devising feasible dependency rules [7–9] to establish precise dependencies.

While the previous work demonstrates its ability to identify the infected objects, it generally has following two limitations: First, it assumes the intrusion root is known or can be located with ease. However, exactly locating an intrusion root is difficult in many real-world situations due to *dependence explosion* problems [5]. Second, it is a non-trivial task to establish precise dependency relations between the intrusion root and all infected objects even with the help of byte-level information flow tracking techniques. For example, the dynamic taint tracking techniques could suffer from taint laundering problems [3], which may incur false negatives. Alternatively, these techniques could suffer from overtainting problems [10,11], which may incur false positives.

To address above limitations, in this paper, we propose a probabilistic inference method to identify intrusion infections based on a small subset of objects with known security state, which is effective even faced with an uncertain intrusion root and imprecise dependencies. The objects with a known security state, which are called *known objects* in this paper, include infected objects which are intrusion symptoms identified by security-tools, and legitimate objects labeled manually or by some automated techniques (e.g. white list). As our method aggregates evidence from multiple known objects, it is more robust than the traditional causal analysis method which relies solely on the limited evidence from an uncertain intrusion root.

More specifically, we first split an object into slices along the timeline to capture the time-varying security state of objects and construct a temporal dependency network to describe the complex information flows between object-slices from a system-wide perspective. The temporal dependency network is a directed graph where each node represents an object-slice and each directed edge represents the dependency relationship between object-slices. These dependency edges also reveal potential propagation paths of an intrusion. Then, to characterize uncertainties of propagating infections along the dependency edges, which are caused by an uncertain intrusion root and imprecise or coarse-grained dependencies, we develop a probabilistic Bayesian Network (BN) model based on the constructed temporal dependency network. The domain knowledge and observations are incorporated to estimate model parameters which represent these uncertainties quantitatively. Finally, we map the known objects to the observed variables in the Bayesian network, and leverage probabilistic inference to identify infected objects. The experimental results show our proposed method is effective to identify intrusion infections with both high precision and recall even when the intrusion root is undetermined and dependencies are coarse-grained.

The contributions of this paper is summarized as follows:

- Temporal dependency network on system object-slices. We propose a new form of temporal dependency network whose nodes represent object-slices and edges represent information flows between the object-slices. The temporal dependency network offers a system-wide view of the potential propagation paths of an intrusion.
- The probabilistic model to characterize the uncertainty. We develop a probabilistic Bayesian network (BN) model to characterize the uncertainties of propagating an intrusion in the constructed temporal dependency network and propose to utilize domain knowledge and observations to estimate model parameters which represent these uncertainties quantitatively.
- The probabilistic inference to identify the intrusion infections. We leverage probabilistic inference to discriminate the infected objects from the legitimate ones using evidence from all known objects.
- The experimental evaluation with four real-world scenarios and one synthetic scenario. Our method is capable of identifying the intrusion infections. On average, the experimental results, 95.88 % precision at 96.32 % recall (with 20 % objects as evidence) in four real-world scenarios, 92.32 % precision at 94.28 % recall (with 20 % objects as evidence) in the synthetic scenario.

The remainder of this paper is organized as follows. In Sect. 2, we briefly introduce the related work. Section 3 presents definitions relating to the temporal dependency network. Then we propose our Bayesian Network model for intrusion infections identification in Sects. 4 and 5 demonstrates the experimental results. Finally, Sect. 6 concludes our work.

2   Related Work

We relate our work to the dependency based forensic analysis, including backward tracking to locate the root cause of an intrusion [1,2,8], and forward tracking from the intrusion root to identify the infections of an intrusion [3,4,6,7,12]. Previous work demonstrates that an exactly located intrusion root is a prerequisite of identifying infections of an intrusion. With an intrusion root located by external methods such as Backtracker [1], it has tried to establish the precise causal dependency chains from the intrusion root to all infected objects. Taser [7] tracks OS-level information flows to establish dependency relations between system objects, however, with a conservative dependency rule, Taser may incur many false positives because it establishes undesirable dependencies between infected objects and legitimate objects.

Efforts have been made to improve over Taser by precluding unnecessary dependencies using simple heuristics [13,14]. In [13], optimistic dependency rules are devised to ignore dependencies established from low risk information flows. While the optimistic dependency rules can reduce false positives effectively, they may lead to false negatives (missing parts of the intrusion).

BEEP [5] partitions a long running process to multiple autonomous units, and combines OS-level dependencies with inter-unit dependencies to establish precise dependencies between a root cause and its symptoms. BEEP is not generally effective because a process cannot be refined to autonomous units unless its binary has been trained and instrumented. For processes of new installed applications, BEEP has to fallback to OS-level dependencies and loses precisions.

In [3,6], dynamic taint analysis (DTA) techniques are used to provide more precise and comprehensive dependencies. To reduce the performance impact of DTA techniques, they decouple the onerous analysis work from the production machine and perform fine-grained taint analysis during replaying on a dedicated server. Further, DiskDuster [3] takes a conservative propagation approach to minimize the false negatives caused by taint laundering problem, however, it eventually presents a user with a list of suspicious files which it cannot determine.

Being different from all previous work, we propose a probabilistic inference method, which is capable of identifying intrusion infections even without a determined intrusion root and precise dependencies.

3   Temporal Dependency Network

While information flows generated by access events can be exploited by attackers to propagate infections on a compromised system, they also provide evidence to analyze an intrusion by revealing potential propagation paths of infections. The traditional form of dependency network which treats system objects as nodes and information flows between them as edges is not suitable for accurate intrusion analysis because it only utilizes directions of information flows while neglecting temporal information [7,15,16]. The temporal information is critical for intrusion analysis because the security state of an object on a compromised system is time-varying and there exists temporal relationships between information flows. In this section, we define a new form of dependency network which takes temporal information into account to describe system-wide information flows.

3.1   Dependency Relationships

In this paper, we focus on OS-level information flow which is coarse-grained and the access events refer to system calls related to file operation and process operation like ReadFile, WriteFile, ProcessCreate, and so on.

To introduce temporal information into our dependency network, we first split each system object into slices along the timeline. We use a tuple (i, t) to denote an object-slice, where i is a unique number assigned each system object and t represents a discrete time point. An object-slice (i, t) can be regarded as an instance of object i at time t. Then we introduce two types of dependency relationships between object-slices. One is the inter-object dependency relationship between slices of different objects, and the other is the intra-object dependency relationship between slices of the same object.

Inter-object Dependency Relationship. The inter-object dependency relationship is established as there exists explicit inter-object information flows between slices of different objects. These explicit information flows are generated by observed access events. For example, when a process i read a file j at time t, then there is an information flow from the file j to the process i at time t. Then we have the following definition of the inter-object dependency relationship:

Definition 1. Inter-object Dependency Relationship: If there exists explicit information flow from an object i to an object j at time t, we say, slice $v = (j, t)$ depends on slice $u = (i, t - 1)$, denoted by $u \rightarrow v$. The arrow also indicates the direction of the explicit information flow between object-slices.

Intra-object Dependency Relationship. The intra-object dependency relationship is established as there exists implicit information flows between slices of the same object. These implicit information flows are generated because the slices of a process share the same memory space and the slices of the a file share the same disk space, and we assume that this implicit dependency relationship only exist between the adjacent slices of an object which is called *first-order* markov assumption. Then we have the following definition of the intra-object dependency relationship:

Definition 2. Intra-object Dependency Relationship: For each object i and each time point t, the slice $v = (i, t)$ is depends on the slice $u = (i, t - 1)$, denoted by $u \rightarrow v$. The arrow also indicates the direction of the implicit information flow between object-slices.

3.2   Temporal Dependency Network

We encode the object-slices into nodes of a graph, and dependency relationships defined in Sect. 3.1 between them into directed edges of the graph. We refer to this graph as temporal dependency network, which describes the system-wide temporal dependencies between system objects. We divide the dependency edges into two disjoint sets E_1 and E_2, according to the type of dependency relationships. Now, we give the formal definition of the dependency network.

Definition 3. Temporal Dependency Network.   A directed acyclic graph $G(V, E_1, E_2)$:

- $V = \{v = (i,t)\}$ is a set of object-slices.
- $E_1 = \{e(u,v) | u = (i,t_1) \in V, v = (j,t_2) \in V, t_1 = t_2 - 1, i \neq j\}$, $e(u,v)$ denotes an inter-object dependency relationship $u \rightarrow v$.
- $E_2 = \{e(u,v) | u = (i,t_1) \in V, v = (i,t_2) \in V, t_1 = t_2 - 1\}$, $e(u,v)$ denotes an intra-object dependency relationship $u \rightarrow v$.

Based on our definition of the dependency relationships, we can assert that the temporal dependency network $G(V, E_1, E_2)$ is acyclic because all edges in G are pointing from "past" nodes to "future" nodes. We illustrates the temporal dependency network for an example set of information flows in Fig. 1. In Fig. 1(b), each column represents the set of slices of all objects at specific time point, and each row represents the set of all slices of a specific object in a time interval. With splitting an object into slices along the timeline, the temporal dependency network is capable of describing the time-varying security state of system objects and the temporal relations between information flows.

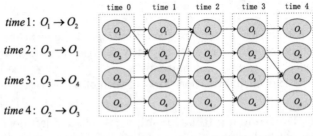

$time\,1: O_1 \rightarrow O_2$

$time\,2: O_3 \rightarrow O_1$

$time\,3: O_3 \rightarrow O_4$

$time\,4: O_2 \rightarrow O_3$

(a) information flows   (b) temporal dependency network

Fig. 1. Temporal dependency network for an example set of information flows

4   Proposed Method

4.1   Problem Description

We assume the time of the last *security checkpoint*[1] is the initial time, and at time T, some intrusion symptoms are detected which indicate our system has been compromised at an arbitrary time between 0 and T. We let $O = \{1, \ldots, N\}$ denotes the set of system objects (files and processes) that may be infected by the intrusion, and B denotes the collection of OS-level access events related to any object $i \in O$. Further, we assume that there exists observation on some objects provided by legitimate users or security-tools. We let $M = \{M_1, M_2\}$ denote the set of known object, where $M_1 \subseteq O$ denotes the set of known infected objects and $M_2 \subseteq O$ denotes the set of known legitimate objects. The task of intrusion infections identification is to generate a list of infected objects from $O \backslash M$.

---

[1] We assume periodic security checks are performed on computer systems, and a security checkpoint is generated if the computer system has never been compromised since last checkpoint.

4.2 Overview

In this paper, we focus on modeling and identifying the intrusion infections on objects even with an uncertain intrusion root and coarse-grained dependency relationships. Figure 2 illustrates the framework of our proposed method. We first construct a temporal dependency network $G(V, E_1, E_2)$ to capture all potential propagation paths of infections from all access events related to the intrusion. Representing each node as a random variable and defining conditional probabilities along each dependency edge in the temporal dependency network, we derive a Bayesian network $\mathcal{G}$ to characterize uncertainties of propagating infections along the dependency edges in G. We employ the Noisy-OR model to represent the uncertain infection relations between each node and its parents, which indicates the probability of a node being infected given whether its parents are infected or not. Finally, we leverage a method of probabilistic inference to identify infections under the Bayesian network given some objects with a known security state.

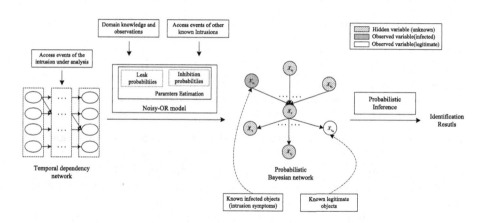

Fig. 2. The framework of our proposed method

4.3 Probabilistic Bayesian Network Model

To characterize the uncertainties caused by an uncertain intrusion root and coarse-grained dependency relationships, we develop a Bayesian network $\mathcal{G}$ based on the temporal dependency network $G(V, E_1, E_2)$. We assume each object-slice $v = (i, t) \in V$ as a binary random variable X_v, which represents whether object i is infected at time t or not, $X_v = 1$ if infected and $X_v = 0$ otherwise. Then, we resort to a Noisy-OR model to describe conditional probabilities, which model the uncertain relations between these random variables [17]. Considering a random variable X_v and its parent nodes $U = \{X_{u_1}, \ldots, X_{u_n}\}$, we divide the parent nodes U into two disjoints sets U_1 and U_2, where $U_1 = \{X_{u_k} : u_k \rightarrow v$ is an inter-object dependency relation$\}$

and $U_2 = \{X_{u_s} : u_s \to v$ is an intra-object dependency relation$\}$. The conditional probability $P(X_v = 1|\mathbf{u})$ represents object-slice v's likelihood of being infected given the security state (infected or legitimate) of its parent object-slices, where $\mathbf{u} = \{\mathbf{u}_1, \mathbf{u}_2\}$ is an assignment of parent nodes U.

We regard the variables U as the direct causes of X_v, and the multiple causes U are combined with a logical OR-gate to predict the the consequence X_v. Intuitively, it means an object-slice will be infected if any one of its parent object-slices is infected. Then, to model the situation that an infected parent object-slice fails to infect the child object-slice, we use inhibition probability $q_i^{(\cdot)}(v)$ to represent the possibility that this situation happens between u_i and v. Let $q_k^{(1)}(v)$ denotes the inhibition probability for $X_{u_k} \in U_1$, and $q_s^{(2)}(v)$ denotes the inhibition probability for $X_{u_s} \in U_2$. Further more, we introduce leak probability denoted by $l(v)$ to represent the object-slice v's likelihood of being infected even when all its parents are legitimate. Actually, it represents the probability of an object-slice is infected by an attacker from outside world. We describe the conditional probability $P(X_v = 1|\mathbf{u})$ as:

$$P(X_v = 0|\mathbf{u}) = (1 - l(v)) \prod_{x_k \in \mathbf{u}_1} \left[q_k^{(1)}(v)\right]^{x_k} \prod_{x_s \in \mathbf{u}_2} \left[q_s^{(2)}(v)\right]^{x_s} \qquad (1)$$

where $P(X_v = 1|\mathbf{u}) = 1 - P(X_v = 0|\mathbf{u})$.

Now, we explain how we estimate the parameters $l(v)$, $q^{(1)}(v)$, and $q^{(2)}(v)$ for each node X_v in $\mathcal{G}$ incorporating with domain knowledge and observations.

Leak Probability $l(v)$. We convert the domain knowledge about intrusion root into the leak probability $l(v)$. The intrusion root is defined as the entry point of an intrusion, and an object-slice $v = (i, t)$ is identified as the intrusion root implies that object i is infected by data from external resources (e.g. network) rather than data from internal resources (e.g. other object-slices) at time t. The leak probability which represents an object-slice's likelihood of being infected by data from external resources can equivalently represent the possibility that an object-slice is the intrusion root. The leak probability $l(v)$ is formulated as:

$$l(v) = \begin{cases} 1/|S|, & if\ v \in S \\ 0, & if\ v \notin S \end{cases} \qquad (2)$$

where S is the set of all suspicious intrusion root, and we assume a uniform distribution over all suspicious intrusion root. Any object-slice $v = (i, t)$ satisfy following two constraints can be a suspicious intrusion root:

- The object i is a process with remote network communications or a file located at removable devices;
- There exists directed paths from v to all known infected object-slices.

Inhibition Probability $q_k^{(1)}(v)$. We use inhibition probability $q_k^{(1)}(v)$ to model the uncertainty of propagating infection along the inter-object dependency relationship $u_k \to v$, which represents the possibility that an infected parent object-slice u_k fails to infect the child object-slice v. The inter-object dependency relationships are established by explicit inter-object information flows, and we observe that different inter-object information flow has different capability to propagate infections. For example, it is less likely for a tampered data file to infect the processes access it by *read* operation, while, it is more likely for a tampered executable file to infect the processes access it by *load* operation. Based on the observation, we divide the inter-object information flows into several categories (e.g. read file content, read file attribute, load executable file, write file content, create process) according to their related access events and assume the inhibition probability $q_k^{(1)}(v)$ is a function of the category of information flow (u_k, v). We compute inhibition probability $q_k^{(1)}(v)$ as follow:

$$q_k^{(1)}(v) = 1 - \frac{\sum_{(u,v) \in E_c} 1_{\{x_u=1 \wedge x_v=1\}}}{\sum_{(u,v) \in E_c} 1_{\{x_u=1\}}} \tag{3}$$

where c is the category of information flow (u_k, v), and the second term in Eq. (3) denotes the possibility that information flows in category c can propagate infections. E_c denotes the set of information flows in category c, which is established with access events of other known intrusions. (u, v) denotes the information flow from u to v, and $x(u) = 1$ denotes object-slice u is infected. $1_{\{A\}}$ is an indicator function that takes value 1 if predicate A is true and 0 otherwise.

Inhibition Probability $q_s^{(2)}(v)$. We use inhibition probability $q_s^{(2)}(v)$ to model the uncertainty of propagating infection along the intra-object dependency relationship, which essentially represents the possibility that an infected object recovers from infection. Many existing works assume that once an object is infected, it remains infected forever. In fact, an infected object can be recovered at arbitrary time in real-world situations, and the recovery will inhibit the propagation of infections between slices of the same object.

The recoveries of passive objects (e.g. files) can be indicated by OS-level access events explicitly. For example, the delete operation or restore(overwrite) operation on an infected file indicates its recovery from infection. We set the inhibition probability $q_s^{(2)}(v)$ for a passive object-slice $v = (i, t)$ as:

$$q_s^{(2)}(v) = \begin{cases} 1, & \text{if } i \text{ is deleted or restored at time } t \\ 0, & \text{else} \end{cases} \tag{4}$$

However, it is an non-trivial task to determine whether an infected active object (e.g. process) is recovered because we cannot observe explicit recovery operations on it. For example, a legitimate process is infected as the entry point of an intrusion, then the attacker migrates to another running process and release it. The release operation which recovers the infected process cannot be captured by OS-level access events. Although OS-level access events cannot explicitly indicate the recovery of an infected process, they still provide evidence about whether a process remains infected or not. Inspired by Mao's previous work on malware detection [15], we extend the principle they proposed from malware to all malicious processes (including the infected ones). The critical actions of malicious process are related to the writing of passive objects with high public level (e.g. files read by many legitimate processes) or reading of passive objects with high private level (e.g. files read by few processes) because the malicious intentions of an attacker are related to the infecting of more legitimate objects or stealing of valuable information. Based on the principle, we can estimate the inhibition probability $q_s^{(2)}(v)$ with behavior model--that is, if an active object behaves normally (e.g. without writing files with high public level and reading files with high privacy level) from time t, it is less likely for it to remain infected at time t, while, if the active object behaves abnormally (e.g. writing files with high public level or reading files with high privacy level) from time t, it is more likely for it to remain infected at time t. We reformulate $\mathcal{B}_{i,t} = \{b_{i,t}, b_{i,t+1}, \dots\}$ which denotes the access event fragment of an active object i from time t as:

$$\mathbf{F}_{i,t} = [r_1, r_2, \dots, r_{R_1}, w_1, w_2, \dots, w_{R_2}] \tag{5}$$

where r_j represents the number of different passive objects read at rank j respect to privacy level, and w_k represents the number of different passive objects written at rank k respect to public level. We select the top R_1 position rank for privacy and top R_2 rank position for public to reduce the dimension of the feature vector.

Then, we use the logistic regression model to map $\mathbf{F}_{i,t}$ to the inhibition probability $q_s^{(2)}(v)$ as:

$$q_s^{(2)}(v) = \frac{1}{1 + e^{-\theta^T \mathbf{F}_{i,t}}} \tag{6}$$

where the parameters θ are learned with access events of other known intrusions.

4.4   Probabilistic Inference

Under the Bayesian network $\mathcal{G}(\mathcal{V}, \mathcal{E}_1, \mathcal{E}_2)$, we perform probabilistic inference to identify intrusion infections by aggregating evidence from all known objects.

Before introducing the probabilistic inference, we first specify the observed and hidden random variables in $\mathcal{G}$. We divide the observed random variables into three disjoint sets $\mathcal{V}_0, \mathcal{V}_1$ and $\mathcal{V}_2$. Let $\mathcal{V}_0 = \{X_{v=(i,t)} : i \in O, t = 0\}$ be the set of observed random variables for the initial state of all objects. We consider all objects as legitimate at the initial time, i,e., $x = 0, \forall x \in \mathcal{V}_0$. We refer to the set of known infected objects as M_1, and their corresponding observed random variables as $\mathcal{V}_1$. For each infected object $i \in M_1$, although its initial infected time is unknown, it still remains infected at current time T. We set $x = 1, \forall x \in \mathcal{V}_1$ where $\mathcal{V}_1 = \{X_{v=(i,t)} : i \in M_1, t = T\}$. Finally, we refer to the set of observed random variables for known legitimate objects (M_2) as $\mathcal{V}_2$. For each legitimate object $i \in M_2$, we assume it has never been infected. We set $x = 0, \forall x \in \mathcal{V}_2$

where $\mathcal{V}_2 = \{X_{v=(i,t)} : i \in M_2, t \in [1,T]\}$. We treat the rest of the random variables as hidden variables whose values are unknown.

Then, we employ the Belief Propagation (BP) algorithm [17] which has been proved to be very successful in various domain to infer the probability distribution of $X_{v=(i,t)}$, denoted by $BEL(X_v)$, $\forall i \in O\backslash M$ and $t = T$. The inference of $BEL(x)$ is completed through iterative message passing along the dependency edges in $\mathcal{G}$. With the message passing in each iteration, a hidden random variable (unknown object-slice) can gather evidence from all observed random variables (known object-slices). For convenience, we present the algorithm under a typical fragment of a our Bayesian network as shown in Fig. 3, which consists of a node X_v, the set of all X_v's parents, $U = \{X_{u_1}, \ldots, X_{u_n}\}$, and the set of all X_v's children, $Z = \{X_{z_1}, \ldots, X_{z_m}\}$.

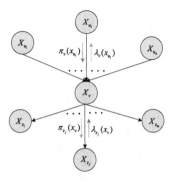

Fig. 3. Message passing in Bayesian network

For a typical node X_v, $\pi_v(x_{u_i})$ denotes the downstream message sent from X_{u_i} to X_v, and $\lambda_{z_j}(x_v)$ denotes the upstream message sent from X_{z_j} to X_v. Both $\pi_v(x_{u_i})$ and $\lambda_{z_j}(x_v)$ are incoming messages for node X_v. Intuitively, these incoming messages represent the neighbors' opinions about v's likelihood of being infected or legitimate. Meanwhile, $\lambda_v(x_{u_i})$ and $\pi_{z_j}(x_v)$ are outgoing messages for node X_v. These outgoing messages represent v's opinions about its neighbors' likelihood of being infected or legitimate. We illustrate these messages in Fig. 3. In each iteration, all messages are passed and each outgoing message from a node X_v to X_{u_i} is generated based on incoming message from the node X_v's other neighbors. Mathematically, the message-update equation for $\lambda_v(x_{u_i})$ is:

$$\lambda_v(x_{u_i}) = \beta \sum_{x_v} \prod_j \lambda_{z_j}(x_v)[\sum_{x_{u_k}:k\neq i} p(x_v|\mathbf{u}) \prod_{k\neq i} \pi_v(x_{u_k})] \qquad (7)$$

where β is a normalizing constant such that $\sum_{x_{u_i}} \lambda_v(x_{u_i}) = 1$. The message-update equation for downstream message $\pi_{z_j}(x_v)$ is computed similarly:

$$\pi_{z_j}(x_v) = \alpha \prod_{k\neq j} \lambda_{z_k}(x_v)[\sum_{\mathbf{u}} p(x_v|\mathbf{u}) \prod_i \pi_v(x_{u_i})] \qquad (8)$$

When the node X_v receives all incoming messages from its neighbors, we can compute $BEL(x_v)$ as follows:

$$BEL(x_v) = \alpha[\prod_j \lambda_{z_j}(x_v)][\sum_{\mathbf{u}} p(x_v|\mathbf{u}) \prod_i \pi_v(x_{u_i})] \tag{9}$$

where α is a normalizing constant such that $\sum_{x_v} BEL(x_v) = 1$.

The algorithm stops when the beliefs converge(with some threshold), or a maximum number of iterations has finished. At the end of the procedure, the belief of each object-slice is determined. The belief of an object i is set equal to the belief of its current slice $v = (i, T)$ as we are more concern about whether an object still remains infected at current time T. Then, we can classify them into one of the binary classes. For example, using a threshold of 0.5, if the object belief falls above 0.5, the object is consider infected.

5   Experimental Evaluation

5.1   Data Set

We use several different intrusion scenarios to evaluate our proposed method. For each scenario, there are eight sub intrusion cases as we run eight different malicious payloads[2]. The malicious payloads which embed the real malicious intention of attackers, are 32-bit portable executable (PE) samples obtained from VxHeaven [18] which is a well-known malware repository.

The data collection setup consists of two servers and one host. Server A is the attack platform which runs Metasploit. Server B mainly stores malware samples, and runs IIS server, ftp server, etc. The host machine is the attack target installed with Windows XP sp3 that contains vulnerable services and client programs. The attacker breaks into the host machine through various channels from the server A, then the shellcode in the compromised host machine downloads and executes malware samples from the server B. We employ Process Monitor [19] to collect access event data in the host machine. Data collections for each intrusion case lasted over a week as we assume that the last security checkpoint is generated three days before the break in of an attacker, and the intrusion can not be detected until four days later. Meanwhile, we emulate real-world usages to induce concurrent legitimate activities in the host machine. For example, we perform tasks including browsing a large number of webpages with IE 6.0 and downloading various types of files, reading and editing PDF documents with the Adobe PDF reader, receiving and sending emails with email client, managing files and directories with Windows Explorer and so on.

5.2   Methodology

We evaluate the performance of our proposed method under different intrusion scenarios and evidence settings.

---

[2] We randomly select 2 Backdoor, 2 Trojan, 2 Worm and 2 Virus that infect at least 10 system objects for each scenario from our malware data sets.

Intrusion Scenarios. We first introduce four real-world intrusion scenarios to describe how an attacker breaks into the target machine through various channels and propagates infection on the victim system. Then, considering the attacker may be aware of the dependency based intrusion analysis techniques, we also introduce a synthetic scenario to describe how an attacker tries to foil these techniques intentionally. Below, we describe each scenario in detail.

Scenario 1: Exploit Vulnerable Network Service
Description: The attacker exploits the vulnerability of the network service, and acquire the administrator privilege. Then the attack immediately migrates to another running process on the same machine. Next, the shell code in the second process downloads and installs malware on the victim machine. After that the attaker clears the log files to remove the footprints of the intrusion.

Scenario 2: Removable Device Autoplay
Description: The attacker infects the removable device, and modifies the autorun.inf file to make the removable device autoplay. When the legitimate user uses the infected removable device to download or backup files, the malware will be installed and executed.

Scenario 3: Drive-by-Download
Description: The legitimate user uses the IE 6.0 to surf the Internet and downloads various types of files. The IE 6.0 gets infected once the user visits a malicious website, then the attack immediately migrates to another running process on the same machine. Next, the shell code in the second process downloads and executes the malicious payload, as well as performs any other malicious actions.

Scenario 4: Social Engineering Attack by Phishing Email
Description: The legitimate user uses the email client to receive and send emails as usual, then he/she receives a well-designed phishing email attached with several malicious PDF documents. The unsuspecting user downloads these malicious PDF documents, and moves them to another directory which is usually used to store PDF documents. The Adobe PDF reader is infected once the user use it to load any malicious PDF documents, and the attack immediately migrates to another running process on the same machine. Next, the shell code in the second process downloads and executes the malicious payload.

Scenario 5: Synthetic Attack
Description: In this scenario, the attacker is aware of the dependency based intrusion analysis techniques and tries to foil these techniques by intermingle their actions with legitimate actions intentionally. More specifically, the attacker breaks into the target machine using the same intrusion channel as scenario 4, apart from the normal malicious activities described in scenario 4, he/she reads a large number of files which have been written by legitimate processes, and writes to the files which will be read by many legitimate processes.

Evidence Setting. A given evidence setting include whether the intrusion root is known, the ratio of known infected object and the ratio of known legitimate object. The ratio of known infected (legitimate) object is defined as the fraction of objects that have been marked as infected (legitimate) and need not be inferred. We set the ratio of known infected object equal to the ratio of known legitimate object in the following experiments, and we use *evidence ratio* to represent both ratio of known infected object and ratio of known legitimate object.

Experimental Settings. We design three groups of experiments to evaluate the performance of our proposed method.

In the first group of experiments, we examine the capability of our proposed method to identify infection region under the situation when the intrusion root is *known*. All experiments in the first group are running under scenario 1&2 respectively because the intrusion root can be easily located in scenario 1&2.

In the second group of experiments, we examine the effectiveness of our proposed method to identify infection region under the situation when the intrusion root is *unknown* (cannot be located exactly). This situation is more common in real-world. All experiments in the second group are running under scenario 3&4 respectively because the entanglement of legitimate actions and malicious actions in scenario 3&4 makes it difficult to locate the intrusion root exactly.

In the third group of experiments, we examine the impact of evidence ratio to the performance of our method. We evaluate the performance of our method using different evidence ratio under the situation when intrusion root is *known* and *unknown*. All experiments in the third group are running under scenario 5.

Training and Testing Sets. The experiment under each testing scenario consists of eight sub-experiments as we have eight sub-cases for each intrusion scenario. For all experiments under each testing scenario, we use the intrusion cases of remaining four scenarios as the training set. The model parameters are trained on the training set, then for each sub-case of the testing scenario, we construct the temporal dependency network and use our proposed probabilistic inference method to identify the intrusion infections. The ground truth of infections is determined with the help of AV scanning and manual inspection for each intrusion case.

Metrics. When reporting the results, the precision and recall are commonly used to represent performance. In our problem of identifying infections of an intrusion, precision is a measure of how many identified objects are truly infected objects, whereas recall a measure of how many truly infected objects have been identified. Since ideal method have both high recall and high precision, we use F_1 measure to combine both precision and recall into a single measure. The value of F_1 measure is high only when both precision and recall are high. Let the number of true positives, false positives, and false negatives be n_{tp}, n_{fp} and n_{fn}, precision is calculated as $n_{tp}/(n_{tp}+n_{fp})$ and recall is calculated as $n_{tp}/(n_{tp}+n_{fn})$. The F_1 measure which defined as the harmonic mean of precision and recall is calculated as $2n_{tp}/(2n_{tp} + n_{fp} + n_{fn})$.

Baseline. We conduct baseline experiments based on a traditional causal analysis method (Taser [7]) which traverses dependencies forward from the intrusion root to compute a causal dependency network that consists of the transitive closure of all infected objects. To establish dependencies, we introduce two representative dependency rules: one is conservative dependency rule which believes that all kinds of OS-level information flows can cause dependencies [7], and the other is optimistic dependency rule which assumes that only information flows with a high risk of propagating malwares can cause dependencies [13]. Furthermore, due to the original Taser method works only when the intrusion root is known, we adapt it for the situations when the intrusion root cannot be located exactly. When the intrusion root is unknown, we either randomly select an object from the set of *suspicious intrusion root* which is defined in Sect. 4.3 as the intrusion root or consider all objects in this set as intrusion roots, then the Taser method is performed with the given intrusion root. Table 1 lists the abbreviation and description of all baseline methods. We compare the baseline results to the proposed probabilistic Bayesian network inference (PBNI) method in following sections.

Table 1. Abbreviation and description of baseline methods

Abbreviation	Description
CTaser	Taser method with conservative dependency rule
OTaser	Taser method with optimistic dependency rule
CTaser-R	Conservative Taser method with random selected intrusion root
OTaser-R	Optimistic Taser method with random selected intrusion root
CTaser-A	Conservative Taser method with all suspicious intrusion roots
OTaser-A	Optimistic Taser method with all suspicious intrusion roots

5.3   Experiment Results

Experiment 1: Intrusion Root Is Known Under Scenario 1&2. We first examine the performance of our proposed PBNI method under the situation when the intrusion root is known with scenario 1&2 respectively. We set the evidence ratio as 0.2. For each case of a testing scenario, we randomly select 20% objects as known (evidence) to determine the security state for the remaining objects. To account for the effect of the randomness as we select the known objects randomly, we repeat the process for 50 times, and each time with independently selected known objects[3]. We can achieve a PR curve for each random sampling as illustrated in Fig. 4, and the performance of the testing case is summarized by averaging the best performance of each sampling. Table 2 and Table 3 present the average precisions, recalls, and F_1 measures for all 8 sub-cases of scenario 1 and scenario 2 respectively.

---

[3] We also use 10 times K-fold cross validation to repeat the process, where $K = 5(1/0.2)$, and both of the two methods achieve similar performance.

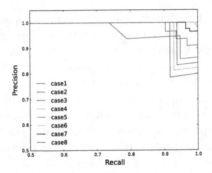

Fig. 4. PR curves of 8 sub-cases of scenario 1 for one random sampling

Table 2. Average Precisions, Recalls, and F_1s for all 8 sub-cases of scenario 1

Method	Precision	Recall	F_1
CTaser	0.2593	1.0	0.3703
OTaser	0.6961	1.0	0.8117
PBNI	0.9187	0.9814	0.9463

Table 3. Average Precisions, Recalls, and F_1s for all 8 sub-cases of scenario 2

Method	Precision	Recall	F_1
CTaser	0.2268	1.0	0.3289
OTaser	1.0	1.0	1.0
PBNI	1.0	1.0	1.0

The results in Tables 2 and 3 indicate that our PBNI method achieves better performance than the Taser methods when intrusion root is known. The CTaser method has the worst performance as it labels many legitimate objects as infected (the average precisions for scenario 1 and scenario 2 are 0.2593 and 0.2268) even though it can identify all infected objects (the average recalls for scenario 1 and scenario 2 are 1.0 and 1.0). The reason is that the CTaser method which uses the conservative dependency rule establishes many false dependencies between legitimate objects and infected objects. Meanwhile, the OTaser method outperforms the CTaser method in scenario 1&2. By exploring the data and results, we observe that the infections propagate through information flows generated by access events like *LoadImage*, *WriteFile* or *CreateProcess* in scenario 1&2, and this character can be captured by the optimistic dependency rule perfectly. Comparing the results of proposed PBNI method and OTaser method, our PBNI method exhibits same performance to OTaser method in scenario 2 and outperforms OTaser method in scenario 1. In scenario 1, the attacker breaks into the target machine by exploiting the vulnerable service *svchost.exe*, then he migrates to another process immediately to perform other malicious actions, finally, the released *svchost.exe* performs legitimate actions as usual in the following days. The OTaser method identify many legitimate objects as infected in scenario 1 (the average precision is 0.6961) because it believes that the infected *svchost.exe* process will remain infected forever. Our proposed method address this limitation by splitting *svchost.exe* process into slices along the timeline and inhibiting the propagation of infection from its "past" slice to its "future" slice as the *svchost.exe* process behaves normally from then on.

Experiment 2: Intrusion Root Is Unknown Under Scenario 3&4. We then examine the performance of our proposed PBNI method under the situation when the intrusion root is unknown with scenario 3&4 respectively. We also set the evidence ratio as 0.2. Tables 4 and 5 present the average precisions, recalls, and F_1-measures for all 8 sub-cases of scenario 3 and 4 respectively. The situations in scenario 3&4 are more complex because the entanglement of legitimate actions and malicious actions makes it difficult to locate the intrusion root exactly, and innocent legitimate user even helps to propagate the malicious data by moving the malicious pdf files to another legitimate directory (in scenario 4). While the Taser methods work poorly without a determined intrusion root, our proposed PBNI method is not affected by this and achieves significantly improvement to Taser methods. Furthermore, from Table 5, with the optimistic dependency rule, the OTaser-A method achieves a average recall 0.3561 for scenario 4, which indicates the optimistic dependency rule misses large parts of the attack in scenario 4. All these results indicate the limitations of Taser methods including other causal analysis methods – that is, they rely solely on the evidence from the intrusion root, while this evidence can be limited when faced with an uncertain intrusion root and imprecise dependencies. We address these limitations by aggregating evidence from all known objects to identify intrusion infections.

Table 4. Average Precisions, Recalls, and F_1s for all 8 sub-cases of scenario 3

	Precision	Recall	F_1
CTaser-R	0.2655	0.9756	0.3278
CTaser-A	0.1056	1.0	0.1881
OTaser-R	0.3794	0.6531	0.4273
OTaser-A	0.2406	1.0	0.2345
PBNI	0.9784	0.9638	0.9702

Experiment 3: Different Evidence Ratio Under Scenario 5. We further investigate the impact of evidence ratio on the performance of proposed PBNI method in scenario 5. Table 6 illustrates the performance of Taser methods and our PBNI method in scenario 5 under varying evidence ratio, and Table 7 illustrates the details of performance which are precision, recall and F_1 under varying evidence ratio. In Tables 6 and 7, KR denotes the intrusion root is known,

Table 5. Average Precisions, Recalls, and F_1s for all 8 sub-cases of scenario 4

Method	Precision	Recall	F_1
CTaser-R	0.2318	0.9631	0.3303
CTaser-A	0.1965	1.0	0.2957
OTaser-R	0.1037	0.1848	0.1185
OTaser-A	0.1303	0.3561	0.1716
PBNI	0.9382	0.9075	0.9136

Table 6. Average F_1s for all 8 sub-cases of scenario 5 with different evidence setting

	Method	Evidence ratio				
		0.05	0.1	0.2	0.3	0.4
KR	CTaser	0.5073	0.5081	0.5088	0.5074	0.5096
	OTaser	0.1263	0.1265	0.1257	0.1256	0.1247
	PBNI	0.9124	0.9283	0.9564	0.9688	0.9699
UR	CTaser-R	0.4505	0.4712	0.4788	0.4762	0.4778
	OTaser-R	0.1328	0.0973	0.0945	0.0945	0.0942
	PBNI	0.7309	0.8196	0.9051	0.9307	0.9412

Table 7. Performance of our method for scenario 5 with different evidence setting

Evidence ratio	Precision		Recall		F_1	
	KR	UR	KR	UR	KR	UR
0.05	0.8848	0.7288	0.9484	0.8356	0.9124	0.7309
0.1	0.9077	0.8515	0.9538	0.8255	0.9283	0.8196
0.2	0.9343	0.9120	0.9806	0.9050	0.9564	0.9051
0.3	0.9462	0.9299	0.9931	0.9360	0.9688	0.9307
0.4	0.9436	0.9457	0.9985	0.9399	0.9699	0.9412

while UR denotes the intrusion root is unknown. It can be seen that our PBNI method achieves better performance than Taser methods for all evidence ratio from 0.05 to 0.4, and the performance of our PBNI method improves steadily as more evidence is used. This is intuitive, since more evidence means more knowledge about the intrusion to be analyzed. We observe that when the number of evidence objects is limited (evidence ratio= 0.05, 0.1) in this synthetic intrusion scenario, a known intrusion root can help to improve the performance of our PBNI method significantly, while, with the increasing of evidence ratio, the performance improvement achieved by the known intrusion root decrease. It indicates whether the intrusion root is known or not has little effect on the performance of our PBNI method if we can acquire evidence from a fraction of objects with known security state (evidence ratio≥ 0.2).

We summarize the experimental results in various scenarios as follow:

- The encouraging experimental results, 91.97 % precision at 98.14 % recall in scenario 1, 100 % precision at 100 % recall in scenario 2, 97.84 % precision at 96.38 % recall in scenario 3 and 93.82 % precision at 90.75 % recall in scenario 4 demonstrate that our proposed method is capable of identifying infections of an intrusion even when faced with an uncertain intrusion root and coarse-grained dependencies.

- We also evaluate our proposed method in the synthetic scenario 5 where legitimate actions are heavily entangled with malicious actions. The experimental results, 72.88 % precision at 83.56 % recall under unknown intrusion root and 5 % evidence ratio[4], show that our proposed method is effective to identify intrusion infections based on a small set of known objects. Moreover, the performance our method improves steadily with more knowledge about the intrusion is acquired (91.20 % precision at 90.50 % recall under 20 % evidence ratio, 94.57 % precision at 93.99 % recall under 40 % evidence ratio).

6 Conclusion

In this paper, we propose a probabilistic inference method to identify the infected system objects from legitimate ones on a compromised system. Being different from the existing methods, which rely solely on evidence from the intrusion root, the proposed method further use evidence from all known objects (both legitimate and infected). We split an object into slices along the timeline to capture the time-varying security state of objects and propose a temporal dependency network to describe the temporal dependency relations between object-slices. Then, we transform the constructed dependency network to a Bayesian network and infer the probability for objects being infected by an intrusion. We employ Belief Propagation (BP) to perform inference efficiently. Experimental results on four real-world intrusion scenarios and one synthetic intrusion scenario demonstrate the effectiveness of our proposed method, and indicate our method is more robust than the traditional causal analysis methods to deal with more sophisticated intrusion scenarios.

Acknowledgments. The authors would like to thank the anonymous reviewers for their valuable comments and suggestions to improve the paper.

The research is supported by NFSC (61175039, 61221063, 61375040), Research Fund for Doctoral Program of Higher Education of China (20090201120032), International Research Collaboration Project of Shaanxi Province (2013KW11) and Fundamental Research Funds for Central Universities (2012jdhz08).

References

1. King, S.T., Chen, P.M.: Backtracking intrusions. ACM Trans. Comput. Syst. (TOCS) **23**(1), 51–76 (2005)

---

[4] We only have 2 intrusion symptoms in scenario 5 under 5 % evidence ratio.

2. Jiang, X., Buchholz, F., Walters, A., Xu, D., Wang, Y.-M., Spafford, E.H.: Tracing worm break-in and contaminations via process coloring: a provenance-preserving approach. IEEE Trans. Parallel Distrib. Syst. **19**(7), 890–902 (2008)

3. Bacs, A., Vermeulen, R., Slowinska, A., Bos, H.: System-level support for intrusion recovery. In: Flegel, U., Markatos, E., Robertson, W. (eds.) DIMVA 2012. LNCS, vol. 7591, pp. 144–163. Springer, Heidelberg (2013)

4. Kim, T., et al.: Intrusion recovery using selective re-execution. In: Proceedings of the 9th USENIX Symposium on Operating Systems Design and Implementation (OSDI 2010), pp. 89–104. USENIX Association, Vancouver (2010)

5. Lee, K.H., Zhang, X., Xu, D.: High accuracy attack provenance via binary-based execution partition. In: NDSS. Citeseer (2013)

6. Zhang, S., Jia, X., Liu, P., Jing, J.: Peda: comprehensive damage assessment for production environment server systems. IEEE Trans. Inf. Forensics Secur. **6**(4), 1323–1334 (2011)

7. Goel, A., Po, K., Farhadi, K., Li, Z., De Lara, E.: The taser intrusion recovery system. In: ACM SIGOPS Operating Systems Review, pp. 163–176. ACM (2005)

8. Goel, A., Farhadi, K., Po, K., Feng, W.: Reconstructing system state for intrusion analysis. ACM SIGOPS Operating Syst. Rev. **42**(3), 21–28 (2008)

9. Shan, Z., Wang, X.: Growing grapes in your computer to defend against malware. IEEE Trans. Inf. Forensics Secur. **9**(1–2), 196–207 (2014)

10. Cavallaro, L., Saxena, P., Sekar, R.: On the limits of information flow techniques for malware analysis and containment. In: Zamboni, D. (ed.) DIMVA 2008. LNCS, vol. 5137, pp. 143–163. Springer, Heidelberg (2008)

11. Slowinska, A., Bos, H.: Pointless tainting?: evaluating the practicality of pointer tainting. In: Proceedings of the 4th ACM European conference on Computer systems, pp. 61–74. ACM (2009)

12. Xiong, X., Jia, X., Liu, P.: Shelf: preserving business continuity and availability in an intrusion recovery system. In: Annual Computer Security Applications Conference, ACSAC 2009, pp. 484–493. IEEE (2009)

13. Shan, Z., Wang, X., Chiueh, T.: Malware clearance for secure commitment of os-level virtual machines. IEEE Trans. Dependable Secure Comput. **10**(2), 70–83 (2013)

14. Hsu, F., Chen, H., Ristenpart, T., Li, J., Su, Z.: Back to the future: a framework for automatic malware removal and system repair. In: 22nd Annual Computer Security Applications Conference, ACSAC 2006, pp. 257–268. IEEE (2006)

15. Mao, W., Cai, Z., Guan, X., Towsley, D.: Centrality metrics of importance in access behaviors and malware detections. In: Proceedings of the 30th Annual Computer Security Applications Conference, pp. 376–385. ACM (2014)

16. Zonouz, S.A., Berthier, R., Khurana, H., Sanders, W.H., Yardley, T.: Seclius: an information flow-based, consequence-centric security metric. IEEE Trans. Parallel Distrib. Syst. **26**(2), 562–573 (2013)

17. Pearl, J.: Probabilistic Reasoning in Intelligent Systems: Networks of Plausible Inference. Morgan Kaufmann, San Mateo (1988)

18. Vxheaven (2013). http://vx.netlux.org/

19. Cogswell, B., Russinovich, M.: Process Monitor (2014). http://technet.microsoft.com/en-us/sysinternals/bb896645.aspx

Controlled Data Sharing for Collaborative Predictive Blacklisting

Julien Freudiger[1][(✉)], Emiliano De Cristofaro[2], and Alejandro E. Brito[1]

[1] PARC (a Xerox Company), Palo Alto, USA
julien@frdgr.ch
[2] University College London, London, UK

Abstract. Although data sharing across organizations is often advocated as a promising way to enhance cybersecurity, collaborative initiatives are rarely put into practice owing to confidentiality, trust, and liability challenges. We investigate whether collaborative threat mitigation can be realized via *controlled* data sharing. With such an approach, organizations make informed decisions as to whether or not to share data, and how much. We propose using cryptographic tools for entities to estimate the benefits of collaboration and agree on what to share without having to disclose their datasets (i.e., in a *privacy-preserving* way). We focus on collaborative predictive blacklisting: Forecasting attack sources based on one's logs and those contributed by other organizations. We study the impact of different sharing strategies by experimenting on a real-world dataset of two billion suspicious IP addresses collected from Dshield over two months. We find that controlled data sharing yields up to 105 % accuracy improvement on average, while also reducing the false positive rate.

1 Introduction

Over the past few years, security practitioners and policy makers have called for sharing of data related to cyber threats and attacks. Prior work has shown that organizations are exposed to similar vulnerabilities, targeted by the same malevolent actors, and that collaboration could enhance timeliness and accuracy of threat mitigation [21,25,33]. The US government recently initiated efforts to encourage the private sector to share cybersecurity information to improve US cyber defenses [35]. At the same time, the private sector launched community-based initiatives such as the RedSky Alliance [30], ThreatExchange [1], DOMINO [39], and WOMBAT [36].

However, collaborative security initiatives have had little success due to the related confidentiality, privacy, trust, and liability challenges. Sharing security data may damage competitivity, reveal negligence, and expose sensitive and private information. In fact, data sharing initiatives are often opposed by the privacy community as potentially harmful to individuals [2], while organizations have little choice other than establishing "circles of trust," aiming to control potential loss of competitive advantage and data exposure. Alas, this creates the

© Springer International Publishing Switzerland 2015
M. Almgren et al. (Eds.): DIMVA 2015, LNCS 9148, pp. 327–349, 2015.
DOI: 10.1007/978-3-319-20550-2_17

need for lengthy out-of-band processes to establish trust, which hinders speediness and economic viability of such initiatives, as highlighted by a recent Federal Communications Commission (FCC) report [9].

1.1 Problem Statement

We investigate whether collaborative threat mitigation can be realized via a *controlled data sharing* approach, i.e., seeking an effective middle ground between sharing everything and sharing nothing, and helping organizations make informed decisions about *whether or not* to share data, and *how much*.

This raises a few compelling research challenges:

1. How can organizations *estimate benefits* of collaboration? What metrics can two organizations use to guide the decision as to whether or not they should share data?

2. Can we ensure that benefit estimation occurs in a *privacy-preserving way*, so that organizations do not need to disclose their entire datasets, but only the minimum required amount of information?

3. Once two organizations decide to collaborate, *how much* and *what* should they share?

We address these challenges in the context of *collaborative predictive blacklisting*, whereby different organizations aim to forecast attack sources, based on their firewall and Intrusion Detection Systems (IDS) logs, and also those generated by collaborating organizations. We model collaboration as a three-step process in which organizations first estimate the benefits of data sharing among each other, then establish partnerships with promising partners, and finally share data with them. We aim to investigate which collaboration strategies work best, in terms of the resulting improvement in prediction accuracy and false positive rate.

1.2 Roadmap

We experiment with different metrics for estimating the benefits of collaboration, using Jaccard, Pearson, and Cosine similarity of the logs, as well as the size of their intersection. We also test different degrees of data sharing, e.g., sharing everything or only information about attacks entities have in common. One crucial aspect of our work is to impose a fundamental constraint: Benefit estimation and data sharing should occur in a privacy-preserving way, which we attain via cryptographic tools for secure two-party computation (2PC) [38]. As research in 2PC has produced increasingly efficient and practical implementations, both for general-purpose garbled circuits [19] and special-purpose protocols (e.g., private set intersection [11,13,27]), the overhead introduced by the privacy protection layer is appreciably low (cf. Sect. 6.5).

Aiming to compare different strategies, we perform an empirical evaluation using a real-world dataset of 2 billion suspicious IP addresses collected from DShield.org [31] over two months. This dataset contains a large variety of contributors, which allows us to test the effectiveness of data sharing among diverse groups of victims. We perform a quantitative analysis of this dataset in order to identify victims' and attackers' profiles, among other features. This helps us clean the dataset and design a meaningful (controlled) data sharing experiment. We repeatedly select 100 victims at random and measure the accuracy improvement of the blacklisting algorithm, performing the prediction by means of a standard algorithm based on Exponentially Weighted Moving Average (EWMA) [33].

Our analysis yields several key findings. We observe that: (1) The more information is available about attackers, the better the prediction, as intuitively expected; (2) Different collaboration strategies yield a large spectrum of prediction accuracy, and in fact, with some strategies, sharing does not help much; (3) Collaborating with other organizations not only helps improve prediction, but also reduces the false positive rate; and (4) sharing information only about common attackers is almost as useful as sharing everything. As a results, we conclude that controlled data sharing can help organizations find the right balance between indiscriminate sharing and non-collaboration, i.e., sharing just enough data to improve prediction while protecting privacy.

2 Related Work

Previous work on collaborative intrusion detection has usually employed a centralized system where organizations contribute data to Trusted Third Parties (TTPs) in return for blacklisting recommendations. Zhang et al. [40] introduce the notion of highly predictive blacklisting for predicting future attacks based on centralized logs, while follow-up work by Soldo et al. [33] improve by using an implicit recommendation system and further increase accuracy. Although we re-use one of the prediction algorithms from [33], previous work [33,40] does not take into account privacy and relies on TTPs.

Prior research attempted to mitigate privacy challenges from security data sharing by relying on data anonymization and sanitization [3,24,28,32,37]. However, this makes data less useful [22,23] and prone to de-anonymization [8]. Other proposals require entities to send encrypted data to a central repository that aggregates contributions [4]. Locasto et al. [25] propose privacy-preserving data aggregation using Bloom filters, which, while constituting a one-way data structure, are vulnerable to simple guessing attacks. Secure distributed data aggregation is also discussed in [5,7]. While aggregation can help compute statistics, it only identifies most prolific attack sources and yields global models. As shown in [40], however, generic attack models miss a significant number of attacks, especially when sources choose targets strategically and focus on a few known vulnerable networks, thus yielding poor prediction performance.

Previous work has also looked at the possible value of building collaborative and distributed intrusion detection systems. Katti et al. [21] are among the first to study correlation among victims and demonstrated the prevalence of "correlated" attacks, i.e., attacks mounted by same sources against different victims. They find that: (1) Correlations among victims are persistent over time, and (2) Collaboration among victims from correlated attacks improves malicious

IP detection time. They also propose a collaboration mechanism in which victims learn from a centralized entity about other correlated victims, and can then query each other about ongoing attacks. Our work differs from [21] as we introduce a controlled data sharing approach and study distributed collaborator selection strategies based on similarity measures, model different data sharing strategies, measure true and false positives of blacklisting recommendations, and address privacy concerns using efficient secure computation techniques.

3   Preliminaries

This section introduces notations and relevant background information.

3.1   System Model

In the rest of the paper, we assume a group of entities $\mathcal{V} = \{V_i\}_{i=1}^n$, where each V_i holds a dataset L_i logging suspicious events, such as, suspicious IP addresses observed by a firewall along with corresponding (time, port). For each i, we denote with S_i the set of *unique* IP addresses in L_i.

Each entity V_i aims to predict and blacklist IP addresses that will generate future attacks. We consider a controlled data sharing model for collaborative predictive blacklisting, whereby entities estimate the benefits of collaboration in a privacy-preserving way, and then decide with whom, and what, to share. Each entity performs predictions based not only on its own dataset but also on an augmented dataset that comprises information shared by others, aiming to improve prediction and, at the same time, avoiding the wholesale disclosure of datasets. To this end, we turn to efficient cryptographic protocols for privacy-preserving information sharing, presented below.

3.2   Cryptographic Tools

Secure Two-Party Computation (2PC). can privately compute [38] allows two parties, on respective input x and y the output of any (public) function f over (x, y). In other words, neither party learns anything about the counterpart's input beyond what can be inferred from $f(x, y)$. Security of 2PC protocols is formalized by considering an ideal implementation where a Trusted Third Party (TTP) receives the inputs and outputs the result of the function: Then, in the real implementation of the protocol (without a TTP), each party does not learn, provably, more information than in the ideal implementation. The first 2PC instantiation, based on garbled circuits, was presented by Yao [38] – since then, more efficient constructions have been presented, such as [19].

Private Set Intersection (PSI). can [14] a server on input a set S, and a client on input a set C, interact so that the latter only learns $S \cap C$, and the former learns nothing (besides $|C|$). State-of-the-art instantiations include both garbled-circuit based techniques [18,27] and specialized protocols [12–14].

PSI with Data Transfer (PSI-DT). One possible extension of PSI [12] involves a server on input a set S where each item is associated to a data record, and a client on input a set C. PSI-DT allows C to learn the set intersection, along with the data records associated to the items in the intersection (and nothing else), while S learns nothing.

Private Set Intersection Cardinality (PSI-CA). more "stringent" variant of [11,14] PSI, only reveals the magnitude of the intersection, but not the actual contents.

Private Jaccard Similarity (PJS). can a server on input a set S, and a client on input a set C, can interact in such a way that the client only learns the Jaccard similarity [20] between their respective sets, i.e., $J(S,C) = \frac{|S \cap C|}{|S \cup C|} = \frac{|S \cap C|}{|S| + |C| - |S \cap C|}$. PJS can be instantiated using PSI-CA only, since secure computation techniques (including PSI-CA) always reveal the size of inputs (i.e., size of sets in PSI-CA).

In the rest of the paper, security of protocols discussed above is assumed in the honest-but-curious model, i.e., parties are assumed to follow protocol specifications and not to misrepresent their inputs, but, during or after protocol execution, they might attempt to infer additional information about other parties' inputs.

3.3 Predictive Blacklisting

Let t denote the day an attack was reported and T the current time, so $t = 1, 2, ..., T$. We define a training window, T_{train} and a testing window, T_{test}. Prediction algorithms usually rely on information in the training data, $t \in T_{train}$, to tune their model and validate the predictions for the testing data, $t \in T_{test}$.

The Global Worst Offender List (GWOL) is a basic prediction algorithm that selects top attack sources from T_{train}, i.e., highest number of globally reported attacks [40]. Local Worst Offender List (LWOL) is the local version of GWOL and operates on a local network based entirely on its own history [40]. LWOL fails to predict on attackers not previously seen, while GWOL tends to be irrelevant to small victims. Thus, machine learning algorithms were suggested to improve GWOL and LWOL [33,40].

We use the Exponentially Weighted Moving Average (EWMA) algorithm, as proposed by Soldo et al. [33], to perform blacklisting prediction. EWMA uses time series aggregation: It aggregates attack events from T_{train} to predict future attacks. Note that it is out of the scope of this paper to improve on existing prediction algorithms. Rather, we focus on evaluating the feasibility of controlled data sharing for collaborative threat mitigation and, specifically, on measuring how different collaboration strategies perform in comparison to each other.

Accuracy Metrics. As commonly done with prediction algorithms, we measure accuracy with **True Positives (TP)**, which is the number of predictions that correctly match future events. In practice, potentially malicious sources might not be blacklisted at once as blacklisting algorithms rely on several observations over time, such as the rate at which the source is attacking or the payload of suspicious packets. Therefore, it is important to distinguish between the *prediction* and the *blacklisting* algorithm: the former identifies potential malicious sources and/or creates a watch-list, which is fed to the latter in order to help decide whether or not to block sources. The prediction algorithm thus enables the identification of suspicious IP addresses that deserve further scrutiny and improve the effectiveness of blacklisting algorithms. Therefore, prior work [33,40] focused almost exclusively on measuring TP and ignored other accuracy measures such as false positives. By contrast, we decide to also study **False Positives (FP)**, i.e., the number of predictions that are incorrect. This measurement helps us better understand the possible negative overhead introduced by data sharing.

Upper Bounds. As in previous work [33], we use two upper bounds to evaluate the accuracy of the prediction, aiming to take into account the fact that a future attack can be predicted only if it already appeared in the logs of some victims. The Global Upper Bound GUB(V_i) measures, for every target V_i, the number of attackers that are both in the training window *of any victim* and in V_i's testing window. For every V_i, we also define the Local Upper Bound LUB(V_i), as the number of attackers that are both in V_i's training and testing windows.

4   Collaborative Predictive Blacklisting via Controlled Data Sharing

We outline our controlled data sharing approach for collaborative predictive blacklisting. It involves three steps:

1. Estimating the benefits of sharing security data between potential partners, in a privacy-preserving way (i.e., without disclosing the datasets);
2. Establishing partnerships;
3. Sharing data in a privacy-respecting way and guaranteeing that collaborating entities only share what is agreed upon.

4.1   Benefit Estimation

We consider several similarity metrics to estimate the benefits of collaboration: We report them in Table 1, along with the corresponding protocols for their privacy-preserving computation. We look at similarity metrics since previous work [21,40] has shown that collaborating with *correlated victims* works well, i.e., entities targeted by attacks mounted by the same source against different networks (around the same time). Intuitively, correlation arises from attack trends as correlated victim sites might be on a single hit list or natural targets of a particular exploit.

We consider two set-based metrics, i.e., *Intersection-Size* and *Jaccard*, which measure set similarity and operate on unordered sets, as well as *Pearson* and *Cosine* similarity, which provide a more refined measure of similarity as they also capture statistical relationships. The last two metrics operate on data structures representing attack events, such as a binary vector, e.g., $S_i = [s_{i_1} \ s_{i_2} \cdots s_{i_N}]$, of all possible IP addresses with 1-s if an IP attacked at least once and 0-s otherwise. This can make it difficult to privately compute correlation in practice, as both parties need to agree on the range of IP addresses under consideration to construct vector S_i. Considering the entire range of IP addresses is not reasonable (i.e., this would require a vector of size 3.7 billion, one entry for each routable IP address). Instead, parties could either agree on a range via secure computation or fetch predefined ranges from a public repository.

All the functions we consider are symmetric, i.e., both parties obtain the same value, however, some of the protocols used for secure computation of the benefit estimate, such as PSI-CA [11] and PJS [6], reveal the output of the protocol to only one party. Without loss of generality, we assume that this party always reports the output to its counterpart, which is a common assumption in the honest-but-curious model.

In practice, one could use any combination of metrics. Also, the list in Table 1 is non-exhaustive and other metrics could be considered, as long as it is possible to efficiently support their privacy-preserving computation.

4.2   Establishing Partnerships

After estimating the benefits of collaboration, in order to establish partnerships, entities could follow different strategies, acting in a distributed way or relying on a coordinating entity. For instance, an organization could request the collaboration of all entities for which estimated benefits are above a threshold (i.e., based on a *"local threshold"*), or enlist the k partners with maximum expected benefits (*"local maximization"*). Local approaches have the advantage of not involving any third parties, but may require complex negotiations in order to reach a partnership agreement, as collaboration incentives may be asymmetric, e.g., party A might be willing to collaborate with B, but B might prefer to do so with C. With centralized approaches, a semi-trusted server collects estimated benefits (but not datasets) and clusters entities so that those in the same cluster collaborate (*"clustering"*), or encourage sharing among the pairs with highest expected benefits seeking a global utility-vs-cost optimum (*"global maximization"*).

Naturally, an appropriate partner selection strategy heavily depends on the use-case scenario and the trade-offs that organizations are willing to pursue. Hence, some strategies might work well in different settings depending on economic, strategic, and operational factors. The evaluation of the different partnership strategies is an interesting research problem, particularly amenable to a game-theoretic analysis. In this work, we *do not experiment with different strategies to establish partnerships* and leave such an analysis for future work. As a result, in Sect. 6, we fix one partner selection strategy and focus on the evaluation of different benefit estimation and data sharing mechanisms.

Table 1. Metrics for estimating benefits of collaboration between V_i and V_j, along with corresponding protocols for their secure computation. μ_i, μ_j and σ_i, σ_j denote, resp., mean and standard deviation of S_i and S_j.

Benefit estimation metric	Operation	Private protocol
Intersection-Size	$|S_i \cap S_j|$	PSI-CA [11]
Jaccard	$\dfrac{|S_i \cap S_j|}{|S_i \cup S_j|}$	PJS [6]
Pearson	$\sum_{l=1}^{N} \dfrac{(s_{i_l} - \mu_i)(s_{j_l} - \mu_j)}{N\sigma_i\sigma_j}$	Garbled Circuits [19]
Cosine	$\dfrac{S_i S_j}{\|S_i\| \|S_j\|}$	Garbled Circuits [19]

Table 2. Strategies for data sharing among partners V_i and V_j, along with corresponding protocols for their secure computation.

Sharing strategy	Operation	Private protocol
Intersection	$S_i \cap S_j$	PSI [12]
Intersection with Associated Data	$\{(\text{IP,time,port})|\text{IP} \in S_i \cap S_j\}$	PSI-DT [12]
Union with Associated Data	$\{(\text{IP,time,port})|\text{IP} \in S_i \cup S_j\}$	No Privacy

4.3   Data Sharing

After two entities have established a partnership, they can proceed to share their data with each other. This process can occur in different ways, e.g., they can disclose their whole datasets or only share which IP addresses they have in common, with or without all attack events associated to common addresses.

Following our controlled data sharing approach, nothing is to be disclosed beyond what is agreed upon (and, ideally, what is beneficial). For instance, if partners agree to only share information about common attackers, they should not learn any other information. Possible sharing strategies we consider, along with corresponding privacy-preserving protocols, are reported in Table 2. Again, we assume that the output of the protocol is revealed to both parties.

Strategies denoted as *Intersection/Union with Associated Data* mean that parties not only compute and share the intersection (resp., union), but also all events related to items in the resulting set. Obviously, Union with Associated Data does not yield any privacy, as all events are mutually shared, but we include it to compare its efficacy to Intersection with Associated Data.

5   The DShield Dataset

As we aim to evaluate the viability of the controlled data sharing approach and compare how different sharing strategies impact prediction accuracy, we need to design an experiment involving real-world data pertaining to suspicious IP addresses and observed by different organizations. To this end, as done in prior work [21,33,40], we turn to Dshield.org [31]: this section introduces the data we collect from Dshield, and the methodology we use to clean it and to design a meaningful data sharing experiment.

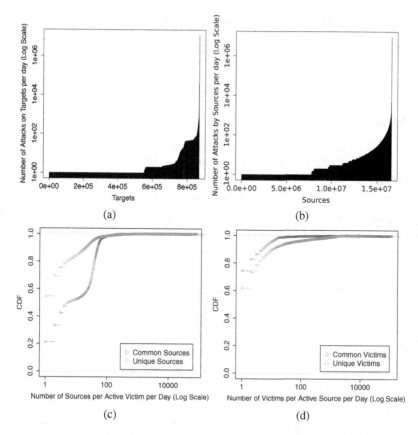

Fig. 1. Number of attacks per day: (a) on all targets, and (b) by all sources. CDF of the daily number of common and unique: (c) sources per active victims, and (d) victims per active sources.

5.1 Original Dataset

We obtained two months' worth of anonymized logs from Dshield.org [31], a community based repository of intrusion detection system logs that publishes blacklists of most prolific attack sources reported in these logs. Each entry in the logs includes an anonymized Contributor ID (the target), a source IP address (the suspected attacker), a target port number, and a timestamp, as illustrated in Table 3. Note that DShield anonymized the "Contributor ID" field by replacing it with a random yet *unique* string that maps to a single victim.

The data collected from DShield consists of about 2 billion entries, generated by 800 K unique contributors, including more than 16 M malicious IP sources, for a total of 170 GB worth of logs. We pre-processed the dataset in order to reduce noise and erroneous entries, following the same methodology adopted by previous work on DShield data [33,40]: We removed approximately 1 % of all entries, which belonged to invalid, non-routable, or unassigned IP addresses, or referred to non-existent port numbers.

Table 3. Example of an entry in the DShield logs.

Contributor ID	Source IP	Target port	Timestamp
44cc551a	211.144.119.042	1433	2013-01-01 11:48:36

5.2   Measurements and Observations

We performed a small measurement analysis of our DShield dataset, aiming to better understand characteristics of attackers and victims. Overall, our observations are in line with prior work [29,33] and demonstrate that attackers tend to hit victims in a coordinated fashion, confirming the potential for collaboration.

General Statistics. We observe that 75 % of targets contribute less than 10 % of the time, while 6 % of targets (50, 000 targets) contribute daily. We describe, at the end of this section how we filter out targets that seldom contribute. For more details and statistics, we refer to the Appendix.

Victims' Profile. Figure 1(a) shows the number of attacks per day on targets, with mean number of daily attacks on targets of 58.46 and median of 1. We observe three dist inct victims' profiles: (1) Rarely attacked victims: 87 % of targets get less than 10 attacks day, indicating many victims seldom attacked; (2) Lightly attacked victims: 11 % of victims get 10 to 100 attacks a day; (3) Heavily attacked victims: Only 2 % of targets are under high attack (peaking at 11 M a day). In other words, most attacks target few victims.

Attackers' Profile. Figure 1(b) shows the number of victims attacked by each source per day, with mean number of daily attacks of 45.85 and median of 2. We observe that 80 % of sources initiate less than 10 attacks a day. A small number of sources generates most attacks (up to 10 M daily). This indicates two main categories of attackers: Stealth and heavy hitters. In our data set, we observe that several of top heavy attackers (more than 20 M attacks) come from IP addresses owned by ISPs in the UK.

Attacks' Characteristics. Figure 1(c) shows the Cumulative Distribution Function (CDF) of the number of unique sources seen by each *active* target a day. We focus on active victims: Victims that did report an event on that particular day because, as previously discussed, many victims report attacks rarely thus creating a strong bias towards 0. The figure contains attackers shared with other targets (common attackers) and attackers unique to a specific victim. 90 % of victims are attacked by at most 40 unique sources and 60 shared sources. This shows that, from the victim's perspective, targets observe more shared sources than unique ones. Compared to previous work [21,33], this reinforces the observation that targets have many common attackers. Figure 1(d) shows that 90 % of sources attack 30 common victims and 60 unique victims. Although attackers share a large number of common victims, they also attack other victims. In Fig. 1(c) and 1(d), we observe again three types of victims and two types of attackers.

Observations. A significant proportion of victims ($\sim$70 %) contributes a single event overall. After thorough investigation, we find that these *one-time contributors* can be grouped into clusters all reporting the same IP address within close time intervals (often within one second). Many contributors share only one attack event, at the same time, about the same potentially malicious IP address. Similarly, many contributors only contribute one day out of the two months. These contributors correlate with the aforementioned one-time contributors.

5.3   Final Dataset

In order to select a meaningful dataset for our experiments, we remove contributors that do not report much information. Specifically, we remove victims that contribute either (1) only one event overall, or (2) only one day and less than 20 events over the two-month period. This reduces the number of considered victims from 800,000 to 188,522, resulting in the removal of about 2 million attacks. This filtering maintains a high diversity of contributors, and seeks to model real-world scenarios (as opposed to focusing on large contributors only).

In summary, our final dataset includes 2 billion attacks, contributed by almost 190 K entities over 60 days, each reporting an average of 200 suspicious (unique) IPs and 2,000 attack events.

6   Experimental Analysis

We compare different benefit estimation metrics and sharing strategies, by measuring improvements to prediction accuracy, using the final Dshield dataset. The dataset and the source code R used in our experiments are available upon request.

6.1   Experimental Setup

Our objective is to design an experiment that is easy to reproduce and enables a meaningful evaluation of controlled data sharing. We describe below our experimental setup and introduce our modeling assumptions.

Sampling of Potential Partners. Our final dataset includes 188,522 victims. In theory, we could evaluate the performance of controlled data sharing by considering all possible collaboration pairs. However, this would be impractical. As a result, we follow a *sampling* approach, i.e., we select 100 entities at random from all possible victims. We then evaluate different collaboration strategies considering the $100 \cdot 99/2 = 4{,}950$ possible pairs, and average results over 100 independent iterations. The random sampling model is *"conservative"* in the resulting improvement of the prediction accuracy, as it is likely to do worse than if entities considered non-random potential partners, e.g., organizations in the same sector.

Benefit Estimation and Partner Selection. We consider four privacy-preserving metrics for estimating the benefits of sharing (as discussed in

Sect. 4.1): *Jaccard*, *Pearson*, and *Cosine* similarity and *Intersection-Size*. Each metric is computed pairwise: For each metric, we obtain a 100×100 matrix estimating data sharing benefits among all possible pairs of organizations.

Recall from Sect. 4.2 that, while we mention a few possible strategies to select partners, we do not evaluate them in this paper, as such mechanisms are out of scope. For simplicity, we consider an approach similar to a *global maximization*: We partner entities with the highest values in the similarity matrix. Specifically, we select the top 1 % collaboration pairs (i.e., 50 pairs) with the maximum expected benefits. This is likely a conservative stance as we consider only a small number of partnerships (i.e., only few entities collaborate). This approach results in some entities sharing data with several partners, and others not collaborating with anyone. We define the *number of collaborators* as the number of distinct entities (out of 100) that are selected in the 50 collaboration pairs. We also define the *coalition size* as the number of other entities an organization collaborates with.

Sharing. As described in Sect. 4.3, we consider three types of data sharing strategies, (1) *Intersection*, (2) *Union with Associated Data*, and (3) *Intersection with Associated Data*. Since (1) is likely to yield poor results, we do not consider it in our experiments. With (2), partners share all data known by each party prior to current time t: It is a generous strategy that enriches others' datasets rapidly. Whereas, with (3), partners only share events from those IP addresses that attacked both partners (i.e., the intersection).

Prediction. We use a five day window to train our prediction algorithm ($T_{train} = 5$) and aim to predict attacks for the next day ($T_{test} = 1$). Although our dataset contains two month worth of data, in order to speed up our experiments, we focus our analysis over a one-week period, i.e., we predict attacks on days 6 to 12, using the previous five days as the training dataset.

Accuracy. As anticipated in Sect. 3.3, we measure the prediction success by computing the number of True Positives (TP), similar to prior work [33,40]. True positives correspond to successfully predicted attacks. We measure prediction improvement as:

$$I = (\text{TP}_c - \text{TP})/\text{TP},$$

where TP is the number of true positives before collaboration and TP_c is the number of true positives after collaboration. In the following, we give both improvement measures over all entities, and for collaborating entities only. Unlike previous work [33,40], we also measure False Positives (FP) aiming to measure the potential negative effects of controlled data sharing. This allows us to take precautions on the notion of data sharing and more effectively compare different benefit estimation and data sharing strategies.

6.2   Different Benefit Estimation Metrics

Determining the Value of α. Before testing the performance of different strategies, we need to identify appropriate α values for the EWMA prediction

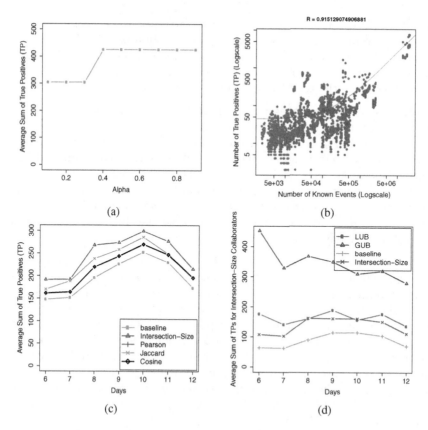

Fig. 2. (a) Number of true positives for different values of prediction algorithm parameter α. (b) Correlation between number of events known by targets, and their ability to predict attacks. The blue curve shows the linear regression (note the log-log scale). (c) Average sum of true positives over time for different benefit estimation methods. (d) Average sum of true positives over time among collaborators selected by *Intersection-Size* including upper bounds (LUB and GUB).

algorithm by evaluating the performance of the prediction. For small values of α, the prediction algorithm aggregates past information uniformly across the training window to craft predictions. In other words, events in the distant past have a similar weight to events in the recent past and the algorithm has a long memory. On the contrary, with a large α, the prediction algorithm focuses on events in the recent past. Figure 2(a) shows the evolution of the baseline prediction for different values of α, plotting the True Positives (TP) sum of all 100 victims averaged over 100 iterations. Values between $\alpha = 0.4$ and $\alpha = 0.9$ perform best. This can be explained by remembering the "bursty nature" of web attacks, as discussed in Sect. 5. As a result, we set $\alpha = 0.9$.

Baseline Prediction. We verify the effectiveness of the prediction algorithm by correlating the information known prior to collaboration with the ability to predict attacks. As expected, targets that know more about past attacks (large S_i), successfully predict more future attacks. We measure correlation $R > 0.9$ on average, which indicates strong correlation between knowledge and prediction. This suggests that collaboration helps prediction. We visualize the correlation between knowledge and prediction accuracy for all victims in our final dataset using the EWMA algorithm in Fig. 2(b).

Benefit Estimation Strategies. Figure 2(c) illustrates the accuracy of predictions for different benefit estimation strategies over the course of one week, *fixing the sharing strategy to Intersection with Associated Data*, as it is more conservative than sharing everything (i.e., the union). We sum the total number of TP for both "collaborators" (i.e., entities that do share data) and "non-collaborators" (entities that do not share data, thus performing as in the baseline). We observe that *Intersection-Size* performs best, followed by *Jaccard*, and *Cosine/Pearson*. The overall decrease in sum of true positives after day 10 is due to less attacks reported in those days (see Fig. 5(a)).

Improvement Over Baseline. In Fig. 2(d), we compare the prediction accuracy of the upper bounds, the baseline, and collaboration using *Intersection-Size* for benefit estimation (again, while sharing using *Intersection with Associated Data*). We sum the total number of TP for collaborators selected by the *Intersection-Size* metric. Remember that with the Global Upper Bound (GUB), every victim shares with every other victim and makes perfect predictions about known attackers, i.e., they have access to the ground truth. With the Local Upper Bound (LUB), organizations do not share anything but still make perfect predictions based on their local information. The accuracy of *Intersection-Size* predictions tends to match LUB, showing that collaboration helps perform as well as a local "perfect" predictor, even when considering only 50 collaboration pairs.

In Table 4, we summarize the prediction improvement given different benefit estimation metrics, reporting the mean, max, and min improvement, as well as the number of collaborators and coalition size. *Pearson* and *Cosine* provide a less significant prediction improvement than set-based metrics. Mean I for *Pearson* and *Cosine* is almost 0.4, i.e., a (40 % improvement over the baseline), while mean I for *Jaccard* is close to 0.6. Notably, *Intersection-Size* yields I equal to 1.05, resulting into a 105 % improvement over the baseline. Naturally, the improvement can also be measured for each entity: Maximum improvement with *Intersection-Size* is as high as 700 %.

False Positives. Figure 3 plots a Receiver Operating Characteristic (ROC) with the true positive rate (TPR) against the false positive rate (FPR) for different benefit estimation strategies (using *Intersection with Associated Data* to share data). Ideally, we would like to obtain values in the top-left corner (i.e., high TPR and low FPR). Interestingly, we observe that all sharing methods improve over the baseline (i.e., they are on upper-left of baseline), thus improving the TPR and reducing the FPR. This is a positive result indicating that controlled data sharing helps the prediction system perform better.

When using *Intersection-Size* to estimate benefits of sharing, TPR improves the most, but FPR does not decrease significantly, whereas *Jaccard* significantly reduces FPR at the cost of a lower TPR increase. We also measure the average

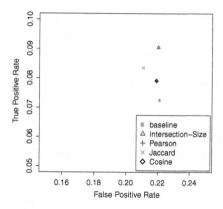

Fig. 3. ROC. The x-axis shows the FP rate defined as $FPR = FP/(FP+TN)$, where TN is the number of true negatives. The y-axis shows TP rate which is defined as $TPR = TP/(TP + FN)$, where FN is the number of false negatives.

Table 4. Prediction improvement I for collaborators, number of collaborators, and size of coalitions under different benefit estimation metrics. SD stands for Standard Deviation.

Benefit estimation metric	Improvement			# Collaborators		Coalition Size		
	Mean	Max	Min	Mean	SD	Mean	SD	Median
Intersection-Size	1.05	7	0	19.47	2.24	5.09	4.09	4
Jaccard	0.58	8	0	30.17	4.44	3.16	2.74	2
Pearson	0.37	8	0	18.08	1.40	5.20	3.15	5
Cosine	0.39	8	0	17.98	1.29	5.26	3.14	5

number of FP with *Intersection-Size* and obtain an average increase of 4 % over the baseline. In case data is shared using *Union with Associated Data*, FPR decreases even more, but at the cost of an average increase in FP of 55 % with *Intersection-Size*.

6.3   Analysis

First, we observe that metrics with a normalization factor (i.e., all but *Intersection-Size*) tend to favor partnerships with small collaborators. *Intersection-Size* leads to better performance because it promotes collaboration with larger victims. To confirm this hypothesis, we measure the set size of collaborators according to different metrics and confirm that metrics with a normalization factor tend to suggest partnerships with collaborators that know less. Second, *Pearson* and *Cosine* tend to select partners that are *too* similar: Maximum correlation values are close to 1, whereas maximum *Jaccard* values only reach 0.5. Although this implies that targets learn to better defend against specific adversaries, it also leads to little acquired knowledge. Third, depending on the metric, entities may partner with previous collaborators, or with new ones. We find that *Intersection-Size, Pearson,* and *Cosine* lead to stable groups of collaborators with about 90 % reuse over time, whereas *Jaccard* has larger diversity of collaborators over time. This is because about 20 % of victims have high *Jaccard* similarity compared to 4 % for *Pearson* and *Cosine*, thus providing a larger pool of potential collaborators. Hence, if *Intersection-Size* helps a few learn a lot, *Jaccard* helps many victims over time.

Statistical Analysis. A t-test analysis shows that the mean of the number of events known by collaborators differs significantly ($p < 0.0005$) across all pairs of benefit estimation metrics but *Cosine* and *Pearson*. If one categorizes collaborators as "large" if they have seen more than 500 events, and "small" otherwise, and consider *Cosine* and *Pearson* as one (given the t-test result), we obtain a 3x2 table of benefit estimation metrics and size categories. A χ^2-test shows that categorization differences are statistically significant: *Intersection-Size* tends to select larger collaborators, but also more collaborators than *Pearson/Cosine* (see Table 4). Other metrics tend to select small collaborators. We obtain $\chi^2(2, N = 448) = 191.99, p < 0.0005$, where 2 is the degrees of freedom of the χ^2 estimate, and N is the total number of observations.

Coalitions. Recall that, at each time step, different benefit estimation strategies lead to different partnerships in our analysis. Table 4 shows the mean, Standard Deviation (SD), and median number of collaborators per party for different collaboration metrics. We observe that with *Jaccard*, coalitions are smaller and thus entities tend to select less collaborators. Other metrics tend to have similar behavior and lead entities to collaborate with about 5 other entities out of 100. This is in line with previous work [21], which showed the existence of small groups of correlated entities. We also observe that, after a few days (usually 2), *Intersection-Size, Pearson,* and *Cosine* converge to a relatively stable group of collaborators. From one time-step to another, parties continue to collaborate with about 90 % of entities they previously collaborated. In other words, coalitions are relatively stable over time. Comparatively, *Jaccard* has a larger diversity of collaborators over time.

6.4   Different Sharing Strategies

The next step is to compare the average prediction improvement I resulting from different data sharing strategies. As showed in Fig. 4, *Intersection with Associated Data* performs almost as good as *Union with Associated Data* with all benefit estimation metrics. It performs even better when using *Jaccard*.

Sharing using the union entails sharing more information, thus, one would expect it to always perform better—however, organizations quickly converge to a stable set of collaborators, and obtain a potentially lower diversity of insights over time. With most metrics, the set of collaborators is stable over time in any case, and so union does perform better than intersection. As previously discussed, *Jaccard* tends to yield a larger diversity of collaborators over time and thus benefits more from *Intersection with Associated Data* as it re-enforces such diversity of insights.

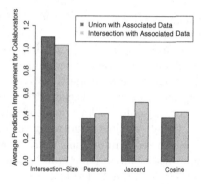

Fig. 4. Average prediction improvement for two different data sharing strategies: *Union/Intersection with Associated Data.*

6.5   Performance of Cryptographic Tools

We estimate the operational cost of using cryptographic techniques for the secure computation of the benefit estimation and the data sharing routines.

Excluding *Pearson* and *Cosine* metrics (due to lower accuracy improvement), the protocols for privately estimating benefits of collaboration (*Intersection-Size* and *Jaccard*) can all be realized based on Private Set Intersection Cardinality (PSI-CA). We chose the instantiation proposed in [11], which incurs computation and communication overhead linear in sets size. Privacy-preserving data sharing, i.e., *Intersection with Associated Data*, is instantiated using the PSI-DT protocol from [12]. We implemented protocols in C, using GMP and OpenSSL cryptographic libraries, and measured total running times using two Intel Xeon desktops with 3.10 GHz CPU connected by a 100 Mbps Ethernet link. Using sets of size 200, it takes approximately 400 ms to execute PSI from [12] and 550 ms for the PSI-CA from [11]. Assuming that 100 organizations are possible partners, there would be $100 \cdot 99/2$ pairwise executions of PSI-CA and PSI-DT in the worst case, yielding a total running time close to 54 s for PSI-CA and 40 s for PSI-DT. That is, it would take less than one minute for one entity to estimate benefits, using PSI-CA, with all other (99) parties, and also less than one minute to share data with all possible 99 partners. In summary, overhead is appreciably low and could accommodate real-world scenarios where interactions occur several times a day.

6.6   Take-Aways

Our experiments confirm that targets that know more tend to successfully predict more attacks. However, as indiscriminate sharing poses serious confidentiality, privacy, trust, and liability challenges, we have considered a controlled data sharing approach aiming to identify partners that help most. In our experiments, *Intersection-Size* proves to be the best metric to estimate the benefits of collaboration. Interestingly, we find that if victims' datasets are very similar, data sharing yields little gain, since there is little to learn. This is reinforced by the fact that similarity metrics with a normalization factor favor collaboration with victims with small datasets.

We find that sharing data with partners using *Intersection with Associated Data* performs almost as good as sharing everything (*Union*). Not only does intersection provide convenient privacy properties, it also indicates that there is more value in learning about current attackers than other potential attack sources. Intuitively, intersection reinforces knowledge about attackers known to a victim, whereas, union might help victims targeted by varying group of attackers. Thus, victims benefit as much from improving their knowledge about current attackers, as learning about other sources (that could possibly attack them next). In brief, good partners are related but not identical, and should share information about known past attackers.

Limitations. The DShield dataset used in our experiments might be biased toward small organizations that *voluntarily* report attack data. Thus, it might not be directly evident how to generalize our results. However, our findings indicate that controlled data sharing can remarkably improve prediction, and show statistical evidence that different collaboration strategies affect performance in interesting ways. We also make a few simplifying assumptions in our experimental setup, e.g., sampling 100 random organizations from the Dshield dataset, and establish partnerships by selecting the top 1 % pairs in the benefit estimation matrix. Although we leave the evaluation of the different partnership strategies as part of future work, our choices are conservative, thus yielding lower-bound estimates of the benefits of collaboration.

7   Conclusion

We investigated the viability of a controlled data sharing approach for collaborative threat mitigation. We focused on collaborative predictive blacklisting and explored how organizations could quantify expected benefits in a privacy-preserving way (i.e., without disclosing their datasets) before deciding whether or not to share data, and how much. We performed an empirical evaluation on a dataset of 2 billion suspicious IP addresses, contributed by 188,522 organizations to DShield.org over a period of two months. We observed a significant improvement in prediction accuracy (up to 105 %, even when only 1 % of all possible partners collaborate), along with a reduction in the false positive rate.

Our analysis showed that some collaboration strategies work better than others. The number of common attacks provides a good estimation of the benefits of sharing, as it drives entities to partner with more knowledgable collaborators. In fact, only sharing information about common attacks proves to be almost as useful as sharing everything. Our work is the first to show that collaborative threat mitigation does not have to be an "all-or-nothing" process: By relying on efficient cryptographic protocols, organizations can share only relevant data, and only when beneficial.

As part of future work, we intend to study other metrics for benefit estimation (e.g., dissimilarity, data quality [15]) and experiment with other prediction algorithms. We also plan to study and experiment with distributed partner selection strategies, possibly relying on the stable roommate matching problem [16]. Finally, we will explore how to adapt our approach to other collaborative security problems, e.g., spam filtering [10], malware detection [17], or DDoS mitigation [26].

Acknowledgments. We wish to thank DShield.org and Johannes Ullrich for providing the dataset used in our experiments, as well as Ersin Uzun, Marshall Bern, Craig Saunders, and Anton Chuvakin for their useful comments and feedback. Work done in part while Emiliano De Cristofaro was with PARC.

A. Additional Analysis of the DShield Dataset

General Statistics. We present in Fig. 5(a) the histogram of the number of attacks per day, indicating about 30 M daily attacks. We observe a significant increase around day 50 to 100 M attacks. Careful analysis reveals that a series of IP addresses starts to aggressively attack around day 50, indicating a possible DoS attack initiation.

Figure 5(b) shows the number of unique targets and sources over time. Detailed analysis shows a stable number of sources and targets. This stability confirms that it should be possible to predict attackers' tactics based on past observations. An analysis of attacked ports shows that top 10 attacked ports (with more than 10M hits) are Telnet, HTTP, SSH, DNS, FTP, BGP, Active Directory, and Netbios ports. This shows a clear trend towards misuse of popular web services.

In Fig. 6, we plot the CDF of the fraction of victims that contribute logs to DShield over two months, and observe that few victims contribute daily.

Predictability. Figure 7 shows the CDF of the Shannon entropy of the different log entry elements. Since entropy correlates with predictability (following Fano's

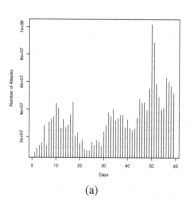

(a)

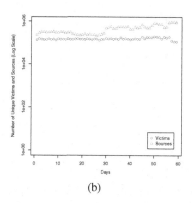

(b)

Fig. 5. General DShield characteristics: (a) histogram of number of attacks per day. (b) Number of unique targets and sources.

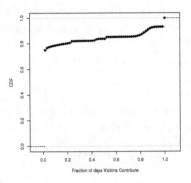

Fig. 6. Fraction of days each target contributes.

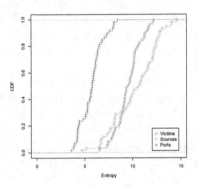

Fig. 7. CDF of entropy of different attack parameters.

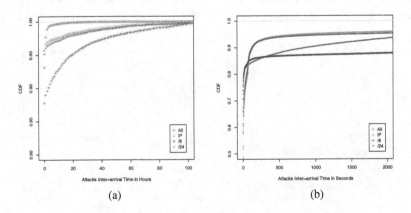

(a)   (b)

Fig. 8. CDF of inter-arrival time of attacks: (a) per hour, and (b) per second. All indicates the inter-arrival time of any attacks, /8 of common /8 subnetworks, /24 of common /24 subnetworks, and IP of the same IP.

inequality [34]), it helps estimate our ability to predict a given IP address, port number or target appearing in the logs. To obtain this figure, we estimate the probability of each victim, source or port being attacked each day. For example, for each port i, we compute:

$$\Pr(\text{Port } i \text{ on day } j) = \frac{\text{Attacks on Port } i \text{ on day } j}{\text{Attacks on day } j} \qquad (1)$$

We compute the entropy for each day and then aggregate it overall using the CDF. We observe that ports numbers have the lower entropy distribution, indicating a small set of targeted ports: 80% of attacks target a set of $2^7 = 128$ ports, indicating high predictability. We also observe that victims are more predictable than sources, as 90% of victims lie within a set of $2^{12} = 4096$ victims as compared to 90% of sources being in a list of $2^{14} = 16{,}384$ sources. Victims' set is thus significantly smaller and more predictable than attackers' set.

Intensity. Figure 8(a) shows the inter-arrival time of attacks in hours, and Fig. 8(b) shows the inter-arrival time of attacks in seconds. We observe that almost all attacks occur within 3-minute windows. IP addresses and /24 subnetworks have similar behavior. In particular, Fig. 8(b) shows that in short time intervals, 85% of /8 subnetworks have short attack inter-arrival time indicating the bursty attacks on such networks. Attackers target subnetworks for a short time and then disappear.

References

1. Facebook ThreatExchange. https://threatexchange.fb.com (2015)
2. Ackerman, S.: Privacy experts question Obama's plan for new agency to counter cyber threats - the Guardian. http://gu.com/p/45yvz (2015)
3. Adar, E.: User 49: anonymizing query logs. In: Query Log Analysis Workshop (2007)
4. Applebaum, B., Ringberg, H., Freedman, M.J., Caesar, M., Rexford, J.: Collaborative, privacy-preserving data aggregation at scale. In: Atallah, M.J., Hopper, N.J. (eds.) PETS 2010. LNCS, vol. 6205, pp. 56–74. Springer, Heidelberg (2010)
5. Bilogrevic, I., Freudiger, J., De Cristofaro, E., Uzun, E.: What's the gist? privacy-preserving aggregation of user profiles. In: Kutyłowski, M., Vaidya, J. (eds.) ICAIS 2014, Part II. LNCS, vol. 8713, pp. 128–145. Springer, Heidelberg (2014)
6. Blundo, C., De Cristofaro, E., Gasti, P.: EsPRESSo: Efficient privacy-preserving evaluation of sample set similarity. JCS **22**(3), 355–381 (2014)
7. Burkhart, M., Strasser, M., Many, D., Dimitropoulos, X.: SEPIA: Privacy-preserving aggregation of multi-domain network events and statistics. In: Usenix Security (2010)
8. Coull, S.E., Wright, C.V., Monrose, F., Collins, M.P., Reiter, M.K.: Playing devil's advocate: inferring sensitive information from anonymized network traces. In: NDSS (2007)
9. CSRIC Working Group 7.: U.S. anti-bot code of conduct for Internet service providers: barriers and metrics considerations (2013)
10. Damiani, E., De Capitani di Vimercati, S., Paraboschi, S., Samarati, P.: P2P-based collaborative spam detection and filtering. In: P2P (2004)

11. De Cristofaro, E., Gasti, P., Tsudik, G.: Fast and private computation of cardinality of set intersection and union. In: Pieprzyk, J., Sadeghi, A.-R., Manulis, M. (eds.) CANS 2012. LNCS, vol. 7712, pp. 218–231. Springer, Heidelberg (2012)

12. De Cristofaro, E., Tsudik, G.: Practical private set intersection protocols with linear complexity. In: Sion, R. (ed.) FC 2010. LNCS, vol. 6052, pp. 143–159. Springer, Heidelberg (2010)

13. De Cristofaro, E., Tsudik, G.: Experimenting with fast private set intersection. In: Katzenbeisser, S., Weippl, E., Camp, L.J., Volkamer, M., Reiter, M., Zhang, X. (eds.) Trust 2012. LNCS, vol. 7344, pp. 55–73. Springer, Heidelberg (2012)

14. Freedman, M.J., Nissim, K., Pinkas, B.: Efficient private matching and set intersection. In: Cachin, C., Camenisch, J.L. (eds.) EUROCRYPT 2004. LNCS, vol. 3027, pp. 1–19. Springer, Heidelberg (2004)

15. Freudiger, J., Rane, S., Brito, A.E., Uzun, E.: Privacy preserving data quality assessment for high-fidelity data sharing. In: WISCS (2014)

16. Gusfield, D., Irving, R.W.: The Stable Marriage Problem: Structure and Algorithms. MIT Press, Cambridge (1989)

17. Hailpern, B.T., Malkin, P.K., Schloss, R.: Collaborative server processing of content and meta-information with application to virus checking in a server network, US Patent 6,275,937 (2001)

18. Huang, Y., Evans, D., Katz, J.: Private set intersection: are garbled circuits better than custom protocols? In: NDSS (2012)

19. Huang, Y., Evans, D., Katz, J., Malka, L.: Faster secure two-party computation using garbled circuits. In: Usenix Security (2011)

20. Jaccard, P.: Etude comparative de la distribution florale dans une portion des Alpes et du Jura

21. Katti, S., Krishnamurthy, B. Katabi, D.: Collaborating against common enemies. In: IMC (2005)

22. Kenneally, E., Claffy, K.: Dialing privacy and utility: a proposed data-sharing framework to advance internet research. IEEE Secur. Priv. 8(4), 31–39 (2010)

23. Lakkaraju, K., Slagell, A.: Evaluating the utility of anonymized network traces for intrusion detection. In: Securecomm (2008)

24. Lincoln, P., Porras, P., Shmatikov, V.: Privacy-preserving sharing and correction of security alerts. In: Usenix Security (2004)

25. Locasto, M.E., Parekh, J.J., Keromytis, A.D., Stolfo, S.J.: Towards collaborative security and P2P intrusion detection. In: Information Assurance Workshop (2005)

26. Oikonomou, G., Mirkovic, J., Reiher, P., Robinson, M.: A framework for a collaborative DDoS defense. In: ACSAC (2006)

27. Pinkas, B., Schneider, T., Zohner, M.: Faster private set intersection based on OT extension. In: Usenix Security (2014)

28. Porras, P., Shmatikov, V.: Large-scale collection and sanitization of network security data: risks and challenges. In: New Security Paradigms Workshop (NSPW) (2006)

29. Pouget, F., Dacier, M., Pham, V.H.: Vh: Leurre. com: on the advantages of deploying a large scale distributed honeypot platform. In: E-Crime and Computer Conference (2005)

30. Red Sky Alliance. http://redskyalliance.org/

31. SANS Technology Institute.: DShield Data. https://www.dshield.org/

32. Slagell, A., Yurcik, W.: Sharing computer network logs for security and privacy: a motivation for new methodologies of anonymization. In: Securecomm (2005)

33. Soldo, F., Le, A., Markopoulou, A.: Predictive blacklisting as an implicit recommendation system. In: INFOCOM (2010)

34. Song, C., Qu, Z., Blumm, N., Barabási, A.-L.: Limits of predictability in human mobility. Sci. **327**, 1018–1021 (2010)
35. The White House.: Executive order promoting private sector cybersecurity information sharing (2015). http://1.usa.gov/1vISfBO
36. Worldwide observatory of malicious behaviors and attack threats (2013). http://www.wombat-project.eu/
37. Xu, J., Fan, J., Ammar, M.H., Moon, S.B.: Prefix-preserving IP address anonymization: measurement-based security evaluation and a new cryptography-based scheme. In: ICNP (2002)
38. Yao, A.: Protocols for secure computations. In: 23rd Annual Symposium on Foundations of Computer Science, FOCS, pp. 160–164 (1982)
39. Yegneswaran, V., Barford, P., Jha, S.: Global intrusion detection in the DOMINO overlay system. In: NDSS (2004)
40. Zhang, J., Porras, P.A., Ullrich, J.: Highly predictive blacklisting. In: Usenix Security (2008)

Author Index

Printed in the United States
By Bookmasters